Women & Po
in Ugand

Women & Politics in Uganda

AILI MARI TRIPP

The University of Wisconsin Press
Madison

James Currey Ltd
73 Botley Road
Oxford
OX2 0BS

The University of Wisconsin Press
2537 Daniels Street
Madison, WI 53718-6772, USA

Fountain Publishers
PO Box 488
Kampala

First published 2000

1 2 3 4 5 04 03 02 01 00

Library of Congress Cataloging-in-Publication Data
Tripp, Aili Mari
    Women and politics in Uganda
    Aili Mari Tripp.
320pp.   cm.
Includes bibliographical references and index.
ISBN 0-299-16480-2 (cloth: alk. paper).
ISBN 0-299-16484-5 pbk.: alk. paper)
1. Women in politics in Uganda. 2. Feminism in Uganda. 3. Women–
Uganda–Societies and clubs. I. Title
H01238. 5.U38175   1999
305:42′086761—dp21   99-28158

Typeset in 9.5/11 pt Palatino by Saxon Graphics Ltd, Derby
Printed in Great Britain by Villiers Publications, London N3

For Marja-Liisa and Lloyd Swantz

Contents

Contents

List of Tables

Maps

Photos

(source: *New Vision*)

Acronyms

31DWM	31st December Women's Movement (Ghana)
ACFODE	Action for Development
ADF	Allied Democratic Forces
CP	Conservative Party
DA	District Administrator
DMO	District Medical Officer
DP	Democratic Party
DSO	District Security Officer
EDF	European Development Fund
ESO	External Security Organization
FIDA	Association of Uganda Women Lawyers (international)
FOWODE	Forum for Women in Development
ISO	Internal Security Organization
JK	Juliet Kiguli (research assistant)
KCC	Kampala City Council
KY	Kabaka Yekka Party
LC	Local Council
LC1	Local Council 1 (village level)
LC2	Local Council 2 (parish level)
LC3	Local Council 3 (sub-county level)
LC4	Local Council 4 (county level)
LC5	Local Council 5 (district level)
NAWOU	National Association of Women's Organizations of Uganda
NCW	National Council of Women
NEC	National Enterprise Corporation
NEC	National Executive Committee of the NRM
NLA	National Liberation Army
NOCEM	National Organization for Civic Education and Election Monitoring
NRA	National Resistance Army
NRC	National Resistance Council (legislature)
NRM	National Resistance Movement
NGO	non-governmental organization
NWC	National Women's Council
PN	Primrose Naloka (research assistant)

RC	Resistance Council
RK	Ruth Kisubika (research assistant)
RM	Rebecca Mukyala (research assistant)
UAUW	Uganda Association of University Women
UAWO	Uganda Association of Women's Organizations
UCW	Uganda Council of Women
UNFRF	Uganda National Rescue Front
UNLA/F	Uganda National Liberation Army/Front
UPA	Uganda Peoples Army
UPC	Uganda People's Congress
UPDA	Uganda Democratic Peoples Army
UPE	Universal Primary Education
UPM	Uganda Patriotic Movement
UWCFT	Uganda Women's Credit and Finance Trust
UWESO	Uganda Women's Effort to Save Orphans
UWONET	Uganda Women's Network
YWCA	Young Women's Christian Association

Luganda Terms

abataka	residents
bibanja	plot of land
gombolola	subcounty
namasole	queen mother
kabaka	king
katikiro	prime minister
lubuga	queen sister
lukiiko	Buganda parliament
muluka	parish
saza	county

Preface

The women's movement in Uganda made an unexpectedly swift and visible entrance on to the political scene shortly after Yoweri Museveni's National Resistance Movement took over in 1986. Unlike women's movements in many African countries where significant sections had been captured by a ruling party or regime, Uganda's women's movement gained momentum from the fact that it remained relatively autonomous. This autonomy allowed it to expand its agenda, to become a political force in the country, and, perhaps most remarkably, to seriously challenge clientelistic (i.e., ethnic and religious) bases of mobilization that have plagued the country since independence.

This book incorporates, but also goes beyond, the concerns of several distinct but often overlapping bodies of scholarship. It argues that a key constraint on African politics is not too much state autonomy or the lack of state autonomy (both arguments have been advanced), but rather a deficit of *societal* autonomy. Societal autonomy implies the ability to make decisions relatively independently of external influences, be they state or even, in some instances, donor pressures. Without societal autonomy, there can be few challenges to existing bases of political mobilization in the state. Societal autonomy is ultimately the means whereby state legitimacy, which is in short supply, can be created or re-established. This book builds on the emphasis of the civil society literature on autonomy for the sake of "engaging the state". However, it takes us beyond this somewhat limited understanding of autonomy to look at other purposes of autonomy as defined by societal actors themselves, for example, being able to set a broader agenda, select their own leaders, and mobilize in ways of their own choosing.

The study, which is situated within a feminist institutional framework, explores some of the limits of new institutional approaches that frequently carry with them implicit assumptions that decentralization and the devolution of power will be of benefit to all. Yet even in the Ugandan case, where the state has been "relatively" accommodating to women's demands and women have been brought into political leadership at various levels, the rules, structures, and practices continue to promote an older, more exclusionary vision of politics, making it difficult for women to assert their interests. The problem for women is not just one of representation and voice; rather, it is a matter of whether they will have a say in making the rules that determine how politics is conducted.

The book also questions feminist notions of autonomy that equate it with marginalization. Women created and used pre-existing gender-based associations both at the local and national levels to assert their autonomy. They turned these older manifestations of isolation and marginalization to their advantage. Far from reinforcing women's subordination, they used their associations to resist a status quo in which women had few opportunities for real political influence and decision-making.

It explores the ways in which women's interests are articulated and expressed and how women often differ from men in the way in which they engage in politics. It also interrogates the notion of interests itself, showing the potentially transformative nature of struggles that appear superficially to be non-political and limited in scope. Case studies of local struggles of women's groups – over market space, starting a health clinic, redesigning an infrastructure improvement project, or ousting the corrupt leadership of a women's group – show how women were trying simultaneously to transform gender relations in their respective communities and to undermine structures that stood in the way of women's advancement and participation. Moreover, they were not just fighting for their share of the pie or for equal representation in the traditional sense of interest-group politics. These struggles were over the terms of women's involvement and the need to change the very rules of the institutions themselves to accommodate women's participation, leadership and interests.

I must make one important caveat before moving on: The study does not assume that all women share the same interests. A central claim of the book is that women's organizations have sought bases of unity cutting across various communal divisions. Nevertheless, the study also shows how class, education, ethnicity, religion, age, and other differences have shaped women's initiatives and aspirations. But since these varying interests can only be specified in particular contexts, I have left the analytical disaggregation of "interest" to the particular case studies described in the book. Similarly, I do not assume that all men oppose women's interests. Rather, I show how in many cases the women garnered support from men in their struggles. But the study does examine the gendered nature of many local-level conflicts and the way in which political interests came to be constructed along gendered lines.

Chapter 1 establishes why societal autonomy is so critical to political development. It situates the discussion of societal autonomy in relation to debates over state autonomy and disengagement as well as societal engagement and disengagement. It shows how the absence of societal autonomy has crippled many women's movements in Africa and, conversely, why women's movements have fought to remain independent of ruling parties and regimes.

Chapter 2 provides an historical background of women's political action and associational involvement from the pre-colonial period through independence in 1962 up to the National Resistance Movement (NRM) regime takeover in 1986. It demonstrates how the issue of associational autonomy has been an enduring concern of the women's movement. Chapter 3 shows how the constraints on the women's movement relate to the NRM's centralizing tendencies in relation to other sectors of civil society, including the media and non-governmental organizations (NGOs) more generally. Chapter 4 describes the gains Ugandan women have made in attaining political representation, pushing for legislative change and lobbying for their demands. It shows how the gains are in part a consequence of the rise of an autonomous women's movement. The second half of the chapter explores some of the efforts by the NRM to contain that autonomy and co-opt the movement, focusing on a number of struggles at the national level. Chapter 5 details the reasons for the growth of the movement after the mid-1980s. In Chapter 6, I describe one of the most important findings of the study. I show how one of the most significant consequences of women's associational autonomy has been the way in which women's organizations have mobilized along new lines, rejecting the politicization of ethnicity and religion. I also explain how and why the women's movement has begun to challenge clientelistic forms of state mobilization along communal lines.

The book then goes on to examine two urban and two rural case studies of gender-based community conflicts over control of resources involving women's associations and local authorities. I found that looking at the fault lines, fissures and conflicts gave me a better of sense of how women were challenging the existing institutional constraints on their participation. The case studies in Chapters 7, 8 and 9 explore conflicts between autonomous women's associations and local authorities over access to resources and influence. These conflicts bring into sharp focus several underlying issues, including (i) the limits of participation and representation for women within the local political structures and the particular ways in which women's experiences in the domestic sphere shape their political involvement; (ii) the way in which women use everyday local struggles to challenge their political exclusions and marginalization; and (iii) the importance of autonomous associations as a source of pressure for changes in local political norms, especially in resisting patronage politics.

I analyze the question of women's interests in a case study based in Kitumba (a fictitious name), Jinja District (Chapter 7). Here I look at how a women's group challenged local male authorities to let them establish and control a health clinic, fighting for the right of women to lead community activities. In this case, I show how women are not just another interest group. Their interests differ from those of men in the community in a way that makes simply giving them representation an insufficient solution to the problem of women's political expression. The problem is deeper and one that requires a more fundamental redesign of institutions and political practices to create the conditions within which women can more effectively give political expression to their particular concerns.

I continue the discussion of interests in Chapter 8 by examining events at Kampala's Kiyembe market, where a women's co-operative of 107 members fought to regain their market stalls after the town clerk had thrown half the women off their stalls and brought in male vendors to replace them. This chapter shows how a sex-segregated organization, which on the surface appeared to be formed along traditional cultural lines paralleling a gendered division of labor, was simultaneously working to challenge female subordination. It reveals how an organization formed around what Maxine Molyneux calls "practical gender interests" was in the same instance working to transform power imbalances between men and women, which Molyneux refers to as "strategic gender interests". The often cited dichotomy Molyneux sets up is challenged by this and other case studies presented in this book.

In a third case study (Chapter 9), I describe how women organizers in Kawaala, Kampala, were key actors in a community initiative that challenged the way in which the Kampala City Council was implementing an infrastructure rehabilitation project funded by the World Bank. The residents drew up an alternative plan, laying out new terms for community participation in the project that was to improve water supply, electricity, roads, sanitation and housing. This case study also took me to Washington, DC, where I interviewed the then World Bank representative responsible for the project. I was also able to speak to the then Vice President of the World Bank about this particular conflict. The chapter focuses on how women's exclusion from formal political channels forced them to rely on their own autonomous associations and networks to oppose the influence of patronage in their community. Marginalization meant that women had less at stake in perpetuating these patronage networks and everything to gain by opposing them.

While the first three case studies focus on dilemmas of establishing associational autonomy from the state, the final case study (Chapter 10) deals with the question of autonomy in relation to foreign and domestic donors. It shows how the availability of donor funding to women's organizations has created new struggles over accountability and donor dependence. I examine the internal learning processes within one rural umbrella women's organization in Kamuli to show how the association struggled with and changed an undemocratic leadership and organizational structure, while fighting for autonomy from donor dependence. The umbrella group, Kiribawa, involved a network of 5,600 women organized into 35 organizations in five counties. The women sought to create a genuine organization out of what had been intended by the leadership to be a "briefcase" or scam organization.

The concluding Chapter 11 explores the limitations of new institutional analysis and argues for adopting a gendered analysis of institutions. It draws comparisons between the four case studies and looks at problems of female participation and representation in national and local politics more generally, especially in the context of decentralization.

The study involved interviews and discussions with hundreds of leaders and members of national and local women's organizations, women entrepreneurs, politicians, policy-makers, opinion leaders, academics, journalists, NGO network representatives, Ugandan donors (for example, Uganda Women's Credit and Finance Trust), bankers, representatives of development agencies, bilateral and multilateral donors, religious leaders, and many others in Uganda. I also observed some of the proceedings of the Constituent Assembly in 1995 that culminated in the approval of a new Constitution. By talking to members of the Women's Caucus in the Assembly I was able to get a better handle on the impact women's organizations were having on the process.

I interviewed numerous women like Rebecca Muliira, Joyce Mpanga and Pumla Kisosonkole, who had been politically active in the pre-independence period. To capture the historical record I systematically surveyed the *Uganda Herald* (from the turn of the century), *Uganda Argus* and later, for the NRM period, the *New Vision, Monitor, Crusader, People* and relevant issues of *Ngabo*. I also drew on women's publications, including *African Women* (from the 1950s and 1960s) and the contemporary *Arise* magazine published by Action for Development. In addition, I went through all available copies of the *Uganda Church Review* up through the 1950s.

The project took me throughout southern Britain from Gloucestershire to Hertfordshire, Leicester, Cambridge, and London to interview British and Asian women who had led voluntary associations and been active in politics in Uganda in the

1950s and 1960s. While in Britain I looked up archival records at the Rhodes House Library in Oxford and the Royal Commonwealth Society Collection at Cambridge University Library. There I consulted diaries, speeches, documents of women's associations, and unpublished writings by women leaders of voluntary associations, colonial wives and other British nationals who lived in Uganda in the first half of the century.

To get a sense of the broader changes in associational and political life I carried out a cluster/stratified survey of 1,142 randomly selected citizens (80 percent women, 20 percent men) in the urban centers of Kampala, Mbale, Kabale and Luwero (see Appendix A for explanation of the survey methods).

The methodology and methods that evolved in the course of researching this book suggest some new ways of thinking about the power dimensions of research and how to go about theorizing at the grassroots. These particular insights are outlined in the second half of this preface.

Theorizing at the Grassroots

Out of an initial concern for accountability to the people I had interviewed, I returned to Uganda after writing most of my manuscript. With the help of a research assistant I translated the case-study chapters (Chapters 7–10) into Lusoga and Luganda and took them back to the women and men I had originally interviewed in these studies. We read the chapters to those women who were illiterate. It was without a doubt a very rewarding experience. Having seen what I had done with their stories, the women had more trust in me. But they were also able to take my analysis and push it even further than I could, especially along the lines of gender analysis. The first half of the book (Chapters 1–6) were reviewed by academics and women active in the national women's organizations in Uganda. Their suggestions were extremely helpful, although I discovered, not surprisingly, that many activists had vested interests in having the story told from their particular viewpoint. This meant that this book will undoubtedly not make everyone happy since it is impossible to satisfy every vantage point, especially approaches that contradict one another. Therefore, ultimately I must take responsibility for the way in which the issues are framed.

When I embarked on this research project, I had no idea that it would so thoroughly change my own perceptions, research methods, and research objectives. Like many feminist scholars, I was concerned about giving voice to grassroots women in the course of writing about the women's movement in Uganda. Even though current feminist scholarship has sought numerous and creative ways of giving these voices utterance through life histories, testimonies, multiple authorships, and oral histories, I was also aware that the success of these kinds of enterprises has been challenged. Critical thinking about feminist methods has questioned the naïvetés of scholars who overlook the inherent inequalities and power relations in conducting research, especially research that seeks to be more egalitarian, more collaborative, and concerned with hearing and giving voice to women at the grassroots.

Judith Stacey, for example, asks whether the appearance of greater respect for, and equality with, research subjects in the ethnographic approach, might not actually be masking a deeper and more dangerous form of exploitation. Personal lives, loves, tragedies that can be easily accessed through a more empathetic approach become "grist for the ethnographic mill, a mill that has a truly grinding power" (Stacey, 1991: 113). Daphne Patai argues that: "In the end, even 'feminist' research too easily tends to reproduce the very inequalities and hierarchies it seeks to reveal and to transform. The researcher departs with the data, and the researched stay behind, no better off than before" (1991: 149).

Such cautions are well taken. But they also can lead to paralysis and a cynical questioning of the utility and purpose of the whole research enterprise. Even given all the pitfalls and difficulties of representation that have been so thoughtfully raised in recent works on feminist methodology and methods (Marchand, 1995; Wolf, 1996), I found myself looking for ways to make cross-cultural dialogue and mutual learning useful both to myself as a researcher and to the women I interviewed. My real learning, in fact, began only after I had completed the bulk of the research and returned to Uganda, manuscript in hand.

I must admit I was most apprehensive and worried about taking the book back to the women involved in the case studies. I wondered: Do I have their stories right? Have I exaggerated my claims? Have I misinterpreted events, or worse still, committed cultural *faux pas*? Actually all these issues ended up being rather insignificant in our discussions, although the women did raise some minor points along these lines. What really interested the women in most of the case studies were two things. First, they were interested in the information that I had obtained from other players in the story, i.e., local government officials, World Bank officials, male vendors. But more surprisingly, they were fascinated by the analytical aspects of what I had described. They appreciated the opportunity to think through how their situation related to what was going on more generally in Uganda and to reflect on the gender dimensions of their struggles. This was the point at which I felt my learning began and our learning together and from each other started.

Now when I think back, I find it inconceivable that I would not have returned to the communities and benefited from the analyses of these women. It was not the raw data and their stories that ended up being most valuable, although they were crucial. Rather, it was their thoughtful analysis and reflection on the broader dynamics that ultimately were most important. These insights, where relevant, have been incorporated into the broader story I am telling with this book. In all four case studies, the women thanked me for my questions or, as one woman put it, for being able to "learn from my questions". They said they were glad I had made them think about things in new ways.

No longer did I feel that I was simply giving voice to grassroots women or sharing their experiences with other women through the written word, although this was one intended purpose of the study. In the end it was equally important that we engaged in discussions that were mutually beneficial. We were learning from one another and creating new knowledge together, going beyond our own limited perspectives.

Because the women in the case studies had been involved in intense conflicts, they had been forced to strategize, to think through the dynamics of the struggles, and consider the various players, their motives and tactics. Many tensions within the communities were brought to the fore. And so together we reflected on the limitations that local government put on women who wanted a voice. We talked about the particular problems faced by women because of the ambiguity of the situation where local government was "government" yet was also supposed to serve as the voice of the people. In Kitumba and Kawaala, the women linked the discrimination they faced to the fact that they were poor and illiterate women. The market women in Kiyembe linked their problems as market women to other forms of gender oppression, including being beaten by their husbands. They analyzed the power stratifications within their communities, and in the Kamuli case the women talked about how to deal with behind-the-scenes power brokers, of which I had not been aware.

In one case study I had overemphasized the split between the wealthy and the poor women that had pitted the women in opposing camps. In taking back the manuscript, I found that there was a secret alliance between the women behind the backs of the men. Even more interesting was the women's observation that it was the wealthier women's own lack of economic autonomy that kept them from asserting their common gender interests, while for the poor women their financial autonomy permitted greater freedom of action.

In another case study, market women explained why their co-operative was exclusively female. They explained how the gender-based organization was not simply a reflection of cultural norms, but that it was critical to defending their interests as women. In fact, this was a theme that ran throughout the case studies, but did not become evident to me until I discussed the manuscript with the market women.

Of course, our discussions were not drawing on academic feminist theoretical constructs, and, indeed, there was no reason for us to use this terminology. These were not their terms. But what was important to them related to the substance of various feminist debates.

I am not claiming that there are no power imbalances of the kind that feminist scholars like Stacey and Patai have warned us about. Sometimes I would delude myself into thinking that the inequalities were not there because the discussion flowed so easily. Surely, I thought, the women could see how much I had to learn from them and this would somehow put us on a more equal footing. I was younger than most of the women involved in the case studies, and I thought this also ought to have had an equalizing effect in a society where one gains respect with age. But then my research assistants would remind me of what I represented to the community women as a white, foreign, educated woman. Power differentials cannot be erased that easily, but neither are they zero sum, unidirectional or all-encompassing. Because they cannot be truly minimized, the most I felt I could do was to recognize them and try to be cognizant of the ways in which they might affect my research. Ultimately, it is my interpretation of the women's voices that endures through what I have chosen to give salience to in this book and I acknowledge that privilege. But I found, as one who is deeply interested in women's agency, that I needed to pay attention to how women analyzed their own circumstances. To be concerned about bringing in grassroots voices, I had to find ways of engaging in mutual learning and dialogue, and take people seriously at a conceptual level, not simply as a source of data.

I am left, then, with a question that goes beyond my original concern of how to give voice to grassroots women. I am more interested in learning how we educated outsiders, Africans and northerners alike, find the humility not just to listen and to give expression to grassroots voices, but also to enter into dialogue and theorize with women on our terms, on their terms and on mutual terms.

Acknowledgements

This book is a product of the intellectual input, generosity, kindness, and friendship of hundreds of people from Uganda to England, Denmark, the US and many other parts of this small world.

My first thanks go to my parents to whom this book is dedicated. They first took me to Uganda as a child in 1968 and introduced me to this fascinating country in its happier days. Uganda was never far from my consciousness when I grew up in Tanzania (1960–74), especially after Idi Amin's takeover in 1971. In the intervening years before the country's first president, Milton Obote, returned to power in 1980, he had fled to Tanzania and lived a few houses down the beach from my family outside of Dar es Salaam. Years later in 1987 in Dar es Salaam, I met international correspondent Cathy Watson, who had documented the National Resistance Movement takeover of Uganda in 1986 and renewed my interest in this country that had suffered beyond belief under Amin and Obote and was struggling to rebuild itself.

My deepest gratitude goes to my husband, Warren Tripp, and my children, Leila and Lloyd Max. Leila accompanied me to Uganda in 1993 and provided me with many useful insights into the country through the perceptive eyes of a four-year-old. She fell in love with the country and, as she left, remarked wistfully that she wished she could bring all the Ugandans home with us on the airplane! Warren persevered during the long stretches of time when I was away and could probably by now write his own book on "how to survive an intercontinental marriage". His patience, encouragement, and sacrifice throughout the writing process has been nothing short of remarkable.

I sincerely thank my team of research assistants in Uganda: Rebecca Mukyala, Juliet Kiguli, Primrose Naloka and Ruth Kisubika, who worked tirelessly, meticulously and with exceptional dedication, far beyond the call of duty. They patiently answered my ignorant questions, provided a terrific sounding board for my ideas, and eased the rough spots with humor. I value them as colleagues and research partners, but above all as friends.

I owe a debt of gratitude to many others in Uganda for their research assistance as enumerators, translators and transcribers: Gertrude Atakunda, the late Jollex Zawedde Semugoma, and the late Harriet Mudoola. Special thanks to my Kabale enumerators: Peace Kakira, Mary Betubiza, and 'Aunty' Nora Kagambirwe. They took such great interest in the survey that they decided to meet each evening, tired

xxvi   Acknowledgements

as they were, to analyze the day's interviews in discussions that were as illuminating as the surveys themselves.

I am equally grateful to Timothy Longman, Sharmila Rudrapa, Kathleen Mulligan Hansel, Lynn Khadiagala, Michele Claibourn, and Jessica Radder for their research assistance in transcribing tapes, coding and inputting the survey data, analyzing the data, proofreading, and commenting on chapters. Many thanks to my sister Eva Swantz-Rydberg for drawing the two maps.

Crawford Young, Michael Schatzberg, Sylvia Tamale, Joy Kwesiga, Barbara Saben, Deborah Kasente, Hilda Tadria, Olivia Mutibwa, Susan Dicklitch, Nelson Kasfir, Bonnie Keller, Ron Kassimir, Margaret Snyder, Holly Hanson, Lynn Khadiagala, Sita Ranchod, Mikael Karlstrom and my dissertator's group of Linda Beck, Gretchen Bauer, Bruce Magnusson, Kathleen Mulligan-Hansel, and Timothy Longman offered most valuable feedback by reading entire drafts or various chapters of the manuscript in its various iterations. Mikael Karlstrom deserves special mention not only because he, along with Holly Hanson, provided me with helpful suggestions on the section on Baganda women's history, but also because he has been my Uganda internet news lifeline over the past five years.

Many people sustained me during my visits to Uganda with their knowledge, assistance and friendship. These included the researchers at Makerere Institute for Social Research (MISR), among them Harriet Birungi, Rebecca Mukyala, Betty Kwagala, the late Emmanuel Nabuguzi, the late Dan Mudoola, James Katorobo, John Okidi, Abby Nalwanga Sebina, Mark Marquardt, Betsy Troutt, Janet Eisenhauer, and Patrick Mulindwa. I treasure Harriet Birungi's friendship, insights, and generosity with her time. I am especially grateful to her for introducing me to the Jinja case studies. John Okidi provided the Luo translations in Chapter 4. I also profited greatly from the kindness of the faculty in the Women's Studies Department at Makerere University, including Mary Mugenyi (who took my daughter and myself on a most interesting trip to Mbarara), Margaret Snyder, Deborah Kasente, and Victoria Mwaka. I am indebted to the MISR staff and also to MISR associates, including Dan Maxwell, Susan Dicklitch, Daniella Sacca, Paula Davis, Glen McKnight, Holger Hansen, Per Tideman, Renée Pittin, Susan and Michael Whyte, and many others who enriched my fieldwork experience. Susan Dicklitch and I enjoyed the best of times in Uganda, but also helped each other through some very painful experiences. Without a doubt, we got a glimpse of the ugly underbelly of the NRM regime. Sharing a house in Uganda with Dan and Joyce Maxwell was a bonus, given their extensive knowledge of the country. I gained immensely from their Uganda expertise, not the least of which included an in-depth education on rally car racing.

I was also an associate at the Centre for Basic Research and benefited greatly from my association with them and the use of their library.

Many scholars of Uganda provided most useful suggestions and insights into my project, including Teddy Brett, Cherry Gertzel, Anne Soerensen, Rita Laker-Ojok, Joe Oloka Onyango, Christine Obbo, Louise Pirouet and many others. My own graduate students who have worked in Uganda also provided me with invaluable perspectives and inspirations: Lynn Khadiagala, Jeremy Liebowitz, Ellen Hauser, Mustafa Mirzeler, Betsy Troutt and Janet Eisenhauer.

I shall never forget the hospitality and warmth I experienced when I visited Britain to interview women who had been active in Uganda as leaders of women's associations and involved in politics in the 1950s and 1960s. These women included

Olive Burkitt, Hemantini Bhatia, Peggy Parry, Sarla Markandya, Eileen West, Anne Tallantire, Sugra Namubiru Visram, and Nancy Kirwan. Frances Richardson provided me with invaluable documents from the Uganda Council of Women for which I am grateful.

I feel enormously privileged to have been able to meet the hundreds of women and men whose interviews provide the basis for this book. Their generous spirits and perseverance amidst enormous adversity are truly awe-inspiring. Enid Rwakatungu Kaggambirwa, Rebecca Mulira, and Miria Matembe are but a few of the most fascinating women I was fortunate enough to get to know. Unfortunately I cannot name them all but they should know I thank them from the bottom of my heart!

I gratefully acknowledge the use of photographs provided by *New Vision*.

Finally, this research was made possible by the generous assistance of the Social Science Research Council, the American Association of University Women, the John D. and Catherine T. MacArthur Foundation and the University of Wisconsin-Madison Graduate School Research Committee.

1 One of the hundreds of people protesting violence against women at a 17 January 1997 service in memory of three women murdered by their spouses in Kampala *(New Vision)*

2 Hajati Batte Sserunkuma demonstrates in Kampala, opposing violence against women, 23 December 1998 *(New Vision)*

3 Women and children demonstrating during the launch of a pressure group against rape and defilement 6 March 1994 *(New Vision)*

4 The Deputy Speaker of Parliament, Hon. Betty Okwir (Lira MP) is led by the Sergeant-at-Arms to the Parliamentary Hall on 12 March 1997 *(New Vision)*

5 Ethics & Integrity Minister Hon. Miria Matembe (right), State Minister for Regional Cooperation Amama Mbabazi (left), and Winnie Babihuga (Rukingiri Women MP) (center), in the Parliament lobby after debate, 19 February 1999 *(New Vision)*

6 Members of Parliament (left to right) Tezira Jamwa (West Budama), Winnie
Byanyima (Mbarara Municipality) and Beatrice Kiraso (Kabarole), 3 March 1998.
Byanyima was a leader of the Women's Caucus of the Constituent Assembly and a
founding member of Forum for Women in Development (FOWODE), which promotes
women's leadership skills. As a parliamentarian, Byanyima has been an outspoken
critic of corruption in top government circles *(New Vision)*

7 Hon. Joyce Mpanga, women's representative for Mubende district (center), greets
Hon. Geraldine Namirembe Bitamazire (left), women's representative for Mpigi
district, and the chairman of the National Youth Council, Herman Ssentongo (right) on
19 September 1996. Mpanga was the first Minister of Women in Development.
Bitamazire has been president of the National Association of Women's Organizations
of Uganda (NAWOU) and was appointed Minister of Primary Education in 1999
(New Vision)

8 The Vice President Dr. Wandira Kazibwe chats with the Minister of Public Service (later Prime Minister) Professor Apollo Nsibambi at the Parliament building in Kampala, September 1997 *(New Vision)*

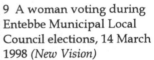
9 A woman voting during Entebbe Municipal Local Council elections, 14 March 1998 *(New Vision)*

10 Uganda People's Congress leader Cecilia Atim Ogwal voting in Lira, 27 June 1996, where she won the municipality seat *(New Vision)*

11 Ruth Owagage (the "Iron Lady of Jinja") voting in the elections in which she won the parliamentary seat for Jinja District, June 1996 *(New Vision)*

12 Esther Mpagi, member of Ntulume Village Women's Association, and secretary general of the National Association of Women's Organizations of Uganda (NAWOU), Florence Nekyon 13 October 1998 *(New Vision)*

13 Margaret Zziwa, Chairperson, Kampala District Women's Council, admires a hat at one of the craft stalls of Wandegeya Women's Club 18 October 1995 *(New Vision)*

14 Hon. Rhoda Kalema (Member of Parliament, Kiboga district) holds up a shield after being declared top woman achiever. A founding member of the Uganda Patriotic Movement, she was the party's secretary for its women's wing and later served as Deputy Minister of Culture & Community Development, and Deputy Minister of Public Service & Cabinet Affairs, 1989-91 *(New Vision)*

Uganda Districts *(Eva Swantz-Rydberg)*

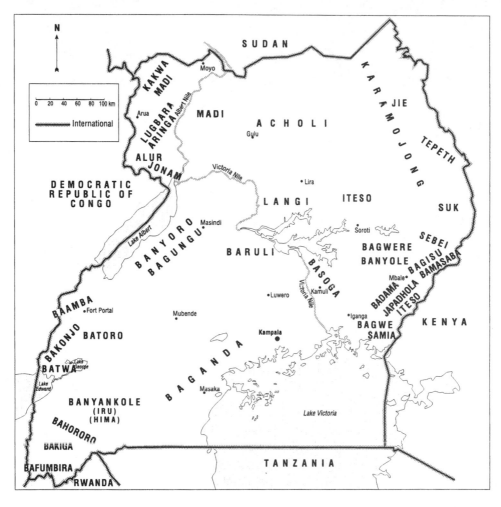

Uganda Ethnic Groups *(Eva Swantz-Rydberg)*

1

Women's Mobilization & Societal Autonomy

In Comparative African Perspective

I will not share "the political cake" with areas that voted against me, but will give them "some bits of the development cake".[1]

Ugandan President Yoweri Museveni, 1996

Sections of the press and some politicians have made "eating" acceptable and have placed it right at the centre of political debate. Struggling for the trappings of power is now at the centre stage, it has become acceptable and even fashionable. Values which we women care about such as caring, serving, building, reconciling, healing and sheer decency are becoming absent from our political culture. This eating is crude, self-centered, egoistic, shallow, narrow and ignorant. We should ban eating from our political language. Madam Chairman, . . . it is a culture which we must denounce and do away with if we are to start a new nation.[2]

Winnie Byanyima, Chair, Constituent Assembly Women's Caucus,
addressing Constituent Assembly, 3 August 1994

This book is a study of one of the central dilemmas in African politics: state limits on societal autonomy. It is a story of the Ugandan women's movement and why it has been as successful as it has in a relatively short period of time given significant constraints. Ugandan women have been able to make substantial inroads into political life through the local-level councils and in Parliament. Uganda leads most of Africa (with the exception of South Africa) in its efforts to promote women's initiatives and leadership. The women's movement differs from many other women's and social movements in Africa because it has been able to claim considerably greater autonomy from the state. Several additional factors also contribute to explaining why the Ugandan women's movement stands out in its political influence. These include changes in government policy, women's economic status, women's educational position and donor strategies, along with women's historical experiences with independent mobilization. And so this book takes a closer look at what accounts for this associational autonomy, given the state's concerted efforts to incorporate and co-opt the movement. It also explains why women's movements throughout Africa are particularly well situated to assert this independence from the state. Finally, the book explores the impact women's associations have had on Ugandan politics, both at national and local levels, showing at the same time how localized manifestations of autonomy translate into larger system effects. One of the most important consequences of this autonomy has been the ability of women's organizations to work against the grain of dominant trends that have politicized ethnicity and religion in a country that has suffered disproportionately from such tendencies.

Much of the literature on Third World and African states has argued that the basic constraint on politics is either too much or too little state autonomy. My study suggests that both these arguments overlook one of the most important elements of political development, that of *societal autonomy*. This deficit of societal autonomy emerged in the 1990s as one of the key obstacles to political liberalization, democratization and democratic consolidation. The absence of autonomy implies the curtailment of freedoms of expression and assembly and at times also limits on freedom of religion – key elements of what Fareed Zakaria and others have referred to as "constitutional liberalism". It also implies the inability of society to influence public policy and to demand state accountability and transparency in policy-making. Ultimately, the lack of societal autonomy weakens the state, preventing it from claiming legitimacy and legitimate authority.

The interest in whether the state could act independently of various social groups, classes, or society at large has generally been framed in terms of state autonomy and the 1980s discussion that "brought the state back in" (Evans, Rueschemeyer and Skocpol, 1985: 9). Scholars of African politics have examined problems relating to state autonomy in Africa and have adopted widely divergent explanations. At times the post-colonial African state has been characterized as highly autonomous, as a foreign and colonial import, sitting "suspended in 'mid-air' over society", as Goran Hyden once described it (1986: 194). This vision of the African state sees it as having been over-centralized, over-bloated, highly monopolistic, and directive (Wunsch and Olowu, 1991). Thomas Callaghy's earlier work sought to show how the African state adopted mercantilist policies in order to turn economic policy into the service of power itself, and to extend the capacity of the state to control economic activity (1984, 83). Callaghy (1984), Bayart (1993) and many others have portrayed African states as seeking a monopoly of control at the local level as well as in political and civil society as a whole. The state's authoritarian and expansionist project extended to curtailing the independence of the judiciary, strengthening the military, and concentrating power in the executive.

Crawford Young, drawing on the work of Christian Coulon and J. Copans, refers to this as the "integral state" that emerged in the 1970s. The integral state sought to transform society in a way that gave the state both complete autonomy from, and direct hegemony over, civil society through administrative, ideological and political control. Although the actual reach of the integral state was always incomplete, it served as a model and a normative vision of the relationship between state and society in the minds of state managers, elites and clients. Citizens were to be passive yet show their loyalty through participation in rallies, uncontested elections, and party mass organizations that were used by the state to control society (Young, 1994: 287–90).

Others have focused on a dilemma that seemingly contradicts the integral state image. They have been critical of the *lack* of state autonomy as manifested in clientelistic networks based on clan, lineage, ethnicity, religion and region (Boone, 1994; Forrest, 1988; Sandbrook, 1986). According to this second view, factionalism, personalized rule, and the appropriation and channeling of state resources along narrow lines undermined state autonomy and ultimately resulted in a loss of state legitimacy and capacity, giving rise to instability. On the economic front, for example, such manifestations of the lack of state autonomy have been used to explain everything from low producer prices in the rural areas to the subsidization of commodities for urban dwellers, expansion of parastatal companies and monopolistic marketing boards, and ultimately the dependence on imported food (Bates, 1981; Chazan and Rothchild, 1993; 184).

Neo-patrimonial rule has been said to prevail in Africa, with claims to authority based on personal relations of loyalty and dependence that stand above the law. Public office is sought for personal gain rather than to perform public service. Neo-patrimonial practices of patronage and clientelism have characterized bureaucracy rather than the purpose of administration (Bratton and van de Walle 1997; 62–3). In Africa clientelism, defined as patronage where a particular social group benefits, has often taken the form of what Richard Joseph calls "prebendalism", namely, the use of public office for personal gain and for the benefit of clients who share communal ties with the office-holder. In other words, state patronage networks commonly have coincided with ethnic or religious cleavages (Joseph, 1987; 1998, 54–8).

While the "too much" vs. "too little" state autonomy approaches cannot be entirely reconciled, it should be borne in mind that the integral state model was based on an elite vision of how states ought to govern, rather than an actual depiction of reality. Joel Migdal's work offers a way to bridge the two views by showing how all too often scholars have taken at face value the stated intentions of policy-makers, focusing excessively on the input side of the equation. Instead, Migdal suggests that scholars should examine real state capacity, i.e., "capacities to *penetrate* society, *regulate* social relationships, *extract* resources, and *appropriate* or use resources in determined ways." Weak states have failed most acutely in their ability to change social behavior and relationships and to use state resources to accomplish their goals through social planning and policy (Migdal, 1988: 5–6, 8–9). To understand the weakness of the integral state model, one has to look at the various ways in which societal actors have subverted state goals, often permeating the very institutions and leadership of the state with those subversions. This argument is implicit in the "too little" state autonomy approach.

The present study flips the emphasis on state autonomy and state capacity on its head. Instead of starting by asking how the state can extricate itself from these corrosive societal influences, it begins by looking at societal struggles to assert autonomy from a state that is both permeated by clientelistic networks *and* "integral" in its ambitions, albeit significantly less integral at the turn of the twenty-first century than it was in the 1970s. While relative state autonomy is important, relative societal autonomy is critical to removing personalistic forms of governance from the state. (The term "relative" underscores the necessary limitations on autonomy to ensure productive and co-operative state-society strategies.) There are few potential sources of pressure other than societal ones that could force the state to act in a legitimate fashion to address broader concerns independent of particularistic interests. For example, elite networks generally have had too much to gain from perpetuating the status quo. Elite networks in Africa have all too often been based on ethnic, religious, clan or regional interests, which means that those outside of power are seeking to build their power bases along those particularistic lines.

In contrast, organized cross-cutting societal interests of women, labor, students, professionals and other groups usually, although certainly not always, represent bases of mobilization that are fundamentally different from the personalized and clientelistic bases for neo-patrimonial rule. The project of state building, therefore, is seen as a bottom-up enterprise that comes from within society rather than detached from or even opposed to society. This approach could, for example, be contrasted with Migdal's view that strong states can emerge only after catastrophic conditions (such as war, revolution, mass migration, severe economic recession, famine) have undermined existing bases of social control (1988: 259–77).

The present study builds on Bratton's argument that political autonomy is the cornerstone of power, lying at the heart of struggles between state and society (Bratton, 1994a: 237). Bratton begins to disentangle the "too much" vs. "too little" state autonomy polarization in the literature and shows how both state and society engage in reciprocal political autonomy/disengagement that is deemed counterproductive. Neither state nor society in Africa is building capacity, nor are they working together to accomplish common goals (ibid.). Bratton argues that there are four basic patterns of state-society relations in Africa: (i) state-sponsored engagement occurs when the state seeks to regulate social behavior authoritatively through legal codes, central economic planning and other such means; (ii) state-sponsored disengagement can be seen when, for example, the state relinquishes authority to non-state actors, or in efforts to liberalize and privatize the economy; (iii) society-sponsored disengagement from the state includes popular non-compliance with laws, informal economic activities, and emigration (see also Chazan, 1982, 1994; Azarya, 1994); (iv) finally, society-sponsored engagement refers to efforts by citizens to influence how public resources are allocated by means of lobbying, voting, and collective action.

Bratton draws on some useful definitions of societal and state autonomy and societal and state capacity, which together constitute power. Autonomy implies the ability to make decisions independently of external forces. Capacity refers to the ability to implement those decisions, which depends on possession of "human, financial, material coercive, and symbolic" resources (Bratton, 1994: 235). For Bratton, states are more interested in political capacity and the ability to accomplish their goals, whereas societal organizations are more likely to focus on their ability to set the agenda. Even where societal capacity is weak, societal withdrawal or disengagement may influence the agenda, albeit indirectly.

One of the biggest constraints on African politics, according to Bratton, stems from the fact that both societal organizations and the state are too autonomous from one another and both have too little capacity. All too often states engage while societies disengage; societies engage while states disengage; or both disengage from one another (1994, 240–52).

Bratton's innovative schema for understanding state-society dynamics has some limitations that are reflected more generally in the literature. His equation of autonomy with disengagement is not entirely consistent with his definitions of autonomy and capacity. Further refinement of these definitions in the light of empirical African realities is necessary. Bratton's definition of state engagement, for example, comes closer to the integral state model of a highly autonomous state. Conversely, his definition of society-sponsored engagement as influencing public policy would require considerable societal autonomy.

In reworking Bratton's concepts I would suggest that *societal disengagement* is a defensive societal response to state repression and serious policy distortions. In contrast, *societal autonomy* is the ability of non-state collectivities to take decisions relatively independently of the state, communal groups, foreign donors or other outside pressures. One manifestation of societal autonomy is the ability of interest groups to influence state policy. State co-optation, repression and elimination of independent associations are examples of a lack of societal autonomy. These limitations, I would suggest, constitute the biggest constraint on politics in Africa today.

State disengagement is a consequence of the disintegration or implosion of the state, i.e., its inability to muster sufficient legitimacy, authority, resources and capacity to govern. It is hardly a result of conscious policy change, but it can have significant unintended policy consequences; for example, the existence of parallel markets eventually resulted in the liberalization of internal markets in many countries. Stateless societies are at one end of the spectrum of state disengagement, while state retreat by default (inability to provide social and public services, pay civil servants, etc.) sits at the other end. State retreat by design (for example, liberalization, privatization) falls somewhere between disengagement and autonomy. It arises as a consequence of economic decline and state disintegration, but it is an effort – albeit as a result of external and even internal pressures – to assert leadership and reclaim a measure of state autonomy.

State autonomy, then, is the ability of state actors to take decisions relatively independently of foreign, class, communal or other societal interests. Neo-patrimonial and clientelistic tendencies in African politics, along with extensive donor influences, pose the greatest challenges to state autonomy but for very different reasons and with different consequences.

Autonomy and disengagement on the part of both the state and society are distinguished by the extent to which the actions taken are active or defensive. Thus, the problem is not that most African states and societies are too autonomous from one another, as Bratton claims, but rather that they are not autonomous enough. When they do engage, the state's monopoly of coercion creates serious distortions in the context of the neo-patrimonial state. All things are not equal, and in the case of state and societal capacities, even an ineffective state generally has significant coercive powers at its disposal. The courts, the police and internal security forces can be mobilized to suppress societal actors in ways that make societal "engagement" of the state a non-issue, and disengagement becomes the only viable option. Moreover, even in democratizing and liberalizing contexts, states seek to "engage" society by incorporating, co-opting, eliminating and harassing independent organizations, leaving societies with little choice but to disengage. Even the most benign of African states such as Tanzania reveal their capacity for dirty tricks and outright repression when associations start asserting themselves in ways that challenge state hegemony.

The question is how to break these politically dysfunctional state-society relationships. It is difficult to imagine where the impetus for change would come from, if not from those sectors of society that have not benefited from the status quo and are challenging state coercion and co-optation. As Gyimah-Boadi puts it:

> Clearly, Africa's civil societies are among the chief engines driving the continent's political development. With their increased sophistication and mounting capabilities, they are helping to drive the shift from unalloyed state hegemony to nascent pluralism. Their growing self-awareness and determination to defend their autonomy against all efforts at suppression or cooptation (especially those originating from the state) are signs that they are here to stay (1998: 22).

The remainder of this chapter explains why associational autonomy is so crucial in the current African context, followed by a discussion of why women's associations are particularly important to this debate, more so in many cases than other societal actors. The chapter describes the varied ways in which states and ruling parties have attempted to delimit women's mobilization, even in the context of multi-party politics. This is followed by a discussion of the various reasons why women's associations have sought autonomy beyond the civil society notion of "engaging the state". It returns to an earlier theme in the chapter to explore the utility and limitations of the civil society notions of "exit, disengagement and withdrawal" in the context of the discussion of autonomy. The chapter concludes by looking at the Ugandan case and why it is particularly well suited to a study of associational autonomy and women's movements.

Why Associational Autonomy Matters

The literature on civil society focuses on associational autonomy as necessary in order to enable societal actors to gain leverage with which to demand policy changes. While this is critical, associational autonomy is also important for many other reasons. Most significantly, autonomy has allowed organizations to operate outside of state-based patronage networks. They have often created new norms of association that are distinct from the patterns of participation associated with state-led institutions. In the case of many women's associations, these norms have included challenges to dominant patterns of clientelistic politics built along ethnic, religious, regional, clan and other such particularistic lines. Associational autonomy from the state has in many cases become a basis for associational legitimacy.

In Senegal, for example, 200,000 peasants participate in the Federation of Senegalese Non-Government Organisations (FONGS) founded in 1978. FONGS is an umbrella national organization of 23 farmers' associations and one urban association that has attempted a strategy of autonomization as a means of establishing legitimacy. The strategy emerged out of a concern that peasant resources and structures might be claimed by the state, which continues to reduce services and inputs. The new leaders do not belong to long-established patronage networks and as a result they have been able to make negotiations with the state over producer prices more transparent. Negotiations with rural extension centers, for example, have succeeded in becoming more open regarding services and other matters. Moreover, the peasants no longer pay illegal unofficial fees, which in the past had resulted from arbitrary interactions with the state and a lack of trust (Lachenmann, 1993).

Autonomy also enables non-governmental actors to determine and broaden their own goals, regardless of whether or not they conform to the goals of central or local government, political parties, donors or other powerful actors. In the case of Tanzania, autonomy from state institutions permitted organizations to take up issues like violence against women, land reform, children's rights, environmental concerns, constitutional reform, and many other politically sensitive demands that to this day are rarely initiated by associations affiliated with the dominant party.

Autonomy has permitted organizations to select their own leadership rather than have their officeholders selected by government or party officials based on political loyalties, as was the case with so many African associations after independence until the early 1990s. It also allows associations to organize in ways of their own choosing.

Autonomy has meant that organizations can directly pursue collective action aimed at improving the welfare of the community by building a neighborhood well, road, clinic or school. Urban youth associations in Dakar, Senegal, and Kampala, Uganda, became frustrated with the lack of government public services and began to take matters into their own hands. Young people in Dakar who were part of a "Clean, Make Clean" movement formed groups to collect garbage, and clean and paint buildings, shaming community leaders and public officials into making their own improvements in the city (Landell-Mills, 1992,558). A similar voluntary association in Kampala started cleaning public toilets and marketplaces and painting pedestrian crossings near schools, similarly challenging the city authorities to do more in the provision of basic services.

Hometown voluntary organizations are another form of association directly tackling local developmental issues. They became increasingly popular throughout much of Africa in the period of economic decline after the 1980s, filling in gaps left by the retreat of the state. Sometimes they involved a resuscitation of older forms of organization, while in other instances they were new formations. Studies in eastern Yorubaland and Western Nigeria describe hometown voluntary associations which have existed since the colonial era but gained in importance in the 1980s. They build schools and medical facilities, install electricity, water pipelines and telephone facilities, and have even provided infrastructure for postal services (Barkan et al., 1991; Trager, forthcoming). Membership is open to individuals in the community who participate in meetings and planning. The associations tax their members to finance projects, ensuring compliance through social pressure. In some areas they have become the apex organization for the associational activities of all the communities. They often mediate between local and national interests and enjoy a high level of legitimacy within their respective communities.

For organizations at both the national and local level, autonomy has allowed marginalized sectors of society like women to challenge the existing distribution of resources and power that has discriminated against them. Throughout East Africa, for example, women's organizations in the 1990s began to devise strategies and mobilize to increase the number of women running for political office, to find ways of gaining access to business credit, and to improve women's legal standing (Tripp, 1996).

Women and Associational Autonomy

Given that the problem of associational autonomy is a fundamental one for most social movements in Africa, one might wonder why this book focuses on women's associations. Because women have been more marginalized politically than virtually any other sector of society, they have had more to gain and less to lose by altering the status quo. Many women's organizations are exceptionally well situated to challenge neo-patrimonial practices. Although cultural norms have often structured participation along gendered lines, exclusion from the benefits of state incorporation and patronage politics has also restricted women to their own organizations. This culturally and politically prescribed marginalization may have turned out to be fortuitous. While at times reinforcing women's isolation, these organizations ironically have provided an autonomous base from which to challenge women's exclusion from public life, demand accountability from the authorities, and seek critical institutional changes that affect society more broadly. Even at the local level, these challenges take the form of small conflicts over access to resources, which when viewed as isolated incidents do not appear to be very significant. But when seen in aggregate and as part of a social movement, they add up to a slow but nevertheless incremental chipping away at institutions that block women's political, economic and social empowerment. At the local level, women's "roll up your sleeves and get on with it" self-help strategies are a refreshing break from past notions of relying on a state that today has little to offer.

The issue of autonomy has been so central to women's mobilization in Africa that Ifi Amadiume has argued that the struggle of women's movements to defend their autonomy and self-governance has been *the* "central characteristic of indigenous women's movements in Africa" (1995: 63). In a book on the Kenyan women's movement, Wanjiku Kabira and Elizabeth Nzioki similarly conclude that ". . . the first and most important issue to resolve is the question of autonomy" of the women's movement from the state (1995: 72–3).

The efforts of women's organizations in Africa to protect their autonomy are indicative of a very different impulse from that of neo-patrimonial politics, which has sought to restrict women's mobilization to non-political concerns. Moreover, state clientelistic practices and patronage politics stand directly in the way of the efforts of women's movements to expand an agenda independently of a particular government or ruling party. To mount pressure on the state, Ugandan women's organizations have worked to include a broad cross-section of women irrespective of their ethnic, clan, religious and other backgrounds. They have found that they need the breadth to build their movement. Thus, any political limits on autonomous association will remain one of the biggest constraints on the growth of the very societal forces that could push for greater accountability, limit neo-patrimonial practices, and create conditions for greater democratization in Africa more generally.

Women's organizations have been fighting to preserve their autonomy since colonialism, as this book demonstrates in the Ugandan context. Similar historical struggles have been found in other parts of Africa. For example, in the case of the Nnobi Women's Council in Nigeria, Amadiume shows how its authority was undermined by the state from the time of the colonial presence and throughout the post-colonial period. A dual sex governance system was replaced by kingship and chieftaincy, eliminating the authority of the most senior *Ekwe* woman, who had veto rights in Nnobi public assemblies (1995: 57). The colonial administration encouraged the formation of ethnically based self-help associations and in 1951 the Nnobi Welfare Organization (NWO), run by a small number of male executives, was formed. Gradually this organization began to challenge the decisions of the Women's Council. It divided it, took over its leadership, limited its powers, and placed it under its own tutelage. The final blow came long after independence, in 1982, when the NWO took over the Council's historic mandate of controlling the marketplace. The town Union launched a market improvement project that required an increase in market taxes which was bitterly resisted by the women, who had not been consulted. They saw that the efforts to improve the market were being made at the cost of undermining their traditional power base (1995, 35–68). Thus, the struggle for autonomy is not a new one, but in the context of the post-colonial state it has taken on new dimensions, which are examined below.

Strategies of State Hegemony and Women's Mobilization

Banning Old Organizations, Creating New Mass Organizations

Women's associations, like other societal groups, have faced a whole range of state strategies to control and limit their autonomy. In the most extreme situations, as in Uganda under Idi Amin, independent women's organizations were simply banned and replaced by government-sponsored organizations. Even Kwame Nkrumah disbanded the Federation of Ghana Women and launched the National Council of Ghana Women under the control of his Convention People's Party (Staudt, 1986: 208).

More common, however, were attempts to create new mass organizations that were tied to the clientelist networks found in the state (Widner, 1997: 69). Frequently the leading women's organization was an affiliate of the single ruling party, created by the party itself (for example, the 31st December Women's Movement in Ghana which is tied to the National Democratic Congress; Umoja wa Wanawake wa Tanzania, which is affiliated with Chama Cha Mapinduzi; or the Women's League of the United National Independence Party in Zambia). The National Congress of Sierra Leone Women that was tied to the All People's Congress was charged with building the party membership and serving party needs, although studies showed that women members received little more than promises of benefits in return (Steady, 1976). Through such controlling mechanisms, the women's wings were unable to cater to women with other political allegiances. Moreover, they were unable to fight forcefully for women's interests that might be at odds with the priorities and goals of the ruling party. For example, in the early post-independence period in Mali, the National Union of Malian Women could not take up any women's issue that diverged from the interests of the ruling party (McNeil, 1979). These women's wings were so crippled by party control that in Zambia one woman parliamentarian remarked that the women's wings should be abolished since "they are the biggest single obstacle to women's political participation" (Ferguson et al., 1995: 22).

The organizational structures of the women's wings paralleled those of the party and mimicked their rigid undemocratic structures and leadership. As women's rights activist Dr Maria Nzomo explained in reference to Kenya:

> The structures in the organizations are sometimes no different from government structures. They are authoritarian. You see a lot of authoritarian women leaders who started in 1963 and don't want to give up. It is a tragedy they have not moved in 20 years.[3]

The lure of patronage was ever present, especially for the elite women who made up the leadership of these organizations. The Better Life Program (BLP), founded by Nigerian President Babangida in 1988, was a case in point. Large sums of money were pumped into the organization so that by 1991 the BLP had established over 7,000 co-operatives, 1,000 cottage industries, 200 farms and gardens, 500 shops, 200 welfare schemes, and 500 women's centers that held classes for handicrafts, cooking, literacy and gardening. However, in practice, only national and local elite women benefited from the BLP. Moreover, the BLP was primarily an urban-based organization that paid little attention to rural women. Local elites organized fund-raising drives in which the wealthy would pledge large sums of money, while the poor would hand over their *naira* directly. After the ceremonies, the fund-raisers found that few of the pledged funds were collectible. Meanwhile the poor had lost their hard-earned funds (Vereecke, 1993: 86).

Co-opting Independent Organizations

In other instances, independent organizations were simply co-opted or heavily influenced by the ruling party, as in the case of Maendeleo ya Wanawake in Kenya (MYW). Although MYW, which was founded in 1956, had received government assistance since independence, the ruling party, the Kenya African National Union (KANU), increasingly tightened its grip on the organization and eventually took it over, making it a virtual party wing. In 1981 the hand of KANU was seen in the MYW's withdrawal from the women's umbrella organization, the National Council of Women of Kenya. After the pull-out, President Moi effectively elevated the MYW to be the sole representative of all Kenyan women. It was deliberately kept apolitical and any attempts to assert itself politically were swiftly squelched. Gradually nods of approval and presidential assurances turned into directives and harsh reprimands. In 1985 the organization found itself in a financial quagmire and the government stepped in, taking charge. By 1989 the government/KANU was managing the MYW's national elections.

KANU continued to control the organization as Kenya became a multi-party state, even after the MYW formally separated from KANU in 1992 through a constitutional change. KANU instructed the MYW to postpone its national elections at least four times after 1992 to suit KANU interests. When the elections were eventually held in March 1996, the party's heavy hand was evident from the way in which the elections were run and the electoral outcome was by no means coincidentally weighted toward pro-KANU candidates (Nzomo, 1996; Onsando, 1996; 26). None of the new leadership belonged to any of the opposition groups, nor was there representation of the country's largest ethnic group, the Kikuyu. Moreover, the MYW's new leader, Zipporah Kittony, was a KANU stalwart and a member of the same Kalenjin ethnic group as the president.[4]

Legal Restrictions

Another strategy for controlling women's and other non-governmental organizations involved efforts to restrict the registration of NGOs. Governments have also tried to co-ordinate NGO activities by setting up umbrella and apex organizations and attempting to co-opt existing umbrella organizations. For example, since Tanzania embarked on the multiparty path, the government has systematically sought to create "quasi-independent" umbrella or apex organizations of NGOs, women, business, labor, and the media in order to monitor and control these groups and to pre-empt any possible challenges that might emanate from these sectors. In each instance, they have met with resistance from the various interest groups.

African governments have sought to pass legislation regarding NGO policy that would allow them to monitor and control NGOs (Bratton, 1989: 577; Ndegwa, 1996). Part of the impetus for government initiatives to co-ordinate NGOs has come from a desire to collect better data on their activities, which in some countries are quite extensive and exceed government capacity and initiatives in key sectors. The impetus also comes from a stated desire to prevent the duplication of NGO activities in particular localities, to promote the accountability of NGOs to government, to co-ordinate government-NGO initiatives, to ensure more efficient utilization of scarce resources, and to prevent the formation of "briefcase" NGOs. There is often the desire to eliminate the confusion over which agencies are in charge of monitoring various NGOs. Frequently the responsibility has been shared between ministries of foreign affairs, finance, women, community development, and labor.

However, legislation pertaining to NGOs has generally been laced with provisions that gave the government undue advantage in controlling and curtailing NGO activity. Legislation and proposed legislation frequently gave government the potential to abuse the power to register and deregister organizations, and to control their financing processes. Moreover, motivations behind the legislation appeared to be excessively weighted toward security concerns and controlling NGOs that were deemed to be too "political" or confrontational.

The Kenyan Parliament passed a NGO Co-ordination Act in 1990 to get a grip on the activities of NGOs in the country. It was modified substantially as a result of two years of pressure from NGOs, insisting on their ability to operate free of state interference (Ndegwa, 1996: 31). Similar efforts were initiated by the Tanzanian government in the 1990s to co-ordinate and control NGOs. These met with immediate resistance from the NGO community, 80 percent of which is made up of women's organizations. In particular, NGOs have raised objections to the government's policy statement that "NGOs as legal entities are restricted from engaging in any activity that will be construed to be political in nature" but were allowed to "engage in debate on development issues". Thus, even in a multi-party context, the threats to associational autonomy persist and new types of threats have emerged, as detailed below.

State Strategies in the Context of Political Liberalization

Political liberalization and the opening up of political space in the 1980s and 1990s gave rise to new independent women's associations that challenged the hegemony of the women's wings and associations tied to the ruling party. In a few countries the party-affiliated women's organizations tried unsuccessfully to detach themselves from the ruling party. With party funds drying up, this was initially seen as a strategy to attract funds from donors, who were more inclined to support NGOs than party-affiliated organizations. The Organization of Mozambican Women, Organização da Mulher Moçambicana (OMM), for example, separated from the ruling party, FRELIMO, along with its other mass organizations when the country adopted a multi-party system in 1990. Then six years later it opted to rejoin FRELIMO, having remained a de facto FRELIMO mass association unable and unwilling to shake off its party affiliation. FRELIMO, for its part, needed the OMM to build its own voter base even though the latter's popularity was declining in the rural areas (Scott Kloeck-Jenson, personal communication 1998; Sheldon, 1992; personal communication 1998)[5]. In Tanzania a somewhat similar scenario unfolded involving the Women's Union, Umoja wa Wanawake (UWT). With the adoption of a multi-party system, leaders of the Women's Union attempted to break from the ruling party, Chama Cha Mapinduzi (CCM), in the early 1990s, but met with fierce resistance within the top echelons of the party. The attempted separation failed, in part because the CCM wanted to be assured of the women's vote in the country's first multi-party elections in 1995. Women constituted over half the electorate and the UWT had historically been important in mobilizing the women's vote.

The main source of autonomous women's mobilization has therefore come from the emergence of new independent women's organizations. However, the multi-party context within which many of these organizations emerged led to suppression, intimidation and outright efforts to ban the most autonomous of the women's organizations. In Zimbabwe, the leaders of the independent Association of Women's Clubs (AWC) were suspended in 1995 from their functions. The matter was taken to court and in 1997 the courts struck out a key part of the Private Voluntary Organizations Act on the grounds that it violated the Constitution. The court order also provided for the executive committee of the National Council of the AWC to resume its activities.[6]

In Tanzania, the independent Tanzanian Women's Council (BAWATA) faced similar government repression. In 1996 it was suspended under pressure from the Tanzanian ruling party's women's organization, the UWT, and the Ministry of

Community Development, Women's Affairs and Children. BAWATA had been formed by the UWT as a semi-independent organization, but when the BAWATA leadership unexpectedly steered it toward complete independence, the ruling party and the UWT turned against the organization. President Mkapa, who had the possibility of running for a second term, succumbed to UWT pressure to ban BAWATA, no doubt having calculated that the UWT delivers a large proportion of the CCM vote. Other women's organizations have also faced difficulties in getting registered under various pretexts and since June 1996 there has been a ban on the registration of NGOs. Part of these tactics are efforts to suppress existing independent organizations or to prevent the emergence of organizations that might pose a challenge to the government and the ruling party. BAWATA took the matter to the High Court and challenged the country's Societies Ordinance on the ground that the government's action was unconstitutional and in violation of international human rights conventions to which Tanzania is a signatory. BAWATA eventually won its case against the government, but was undermined as an organization in the process.

Women's organizations faced other kinds of intimidation and threats as a consequence of their autonomous actions. The Greenbelt Movement (GBM) in Kenya, formed in 1977, was supported by the government in its early years because it appeared to be a benign women's tree-planting organization. However, as the association began to make linkages between planting trees, human rights, women's rights and democracy, it ran into hostility from the Moi regime. When the 50,000-member organization began to assert its independence and challenge the authorities on policy matters, it faced severe repression. It opposed the government's plans to build a skyscraper in downtown Nairobi's Uhuru Park to house the KANU headquarters. It also protested against the damming of rivers as well as efforts to convert public parks into parking lots, office complexes and private plots. Women marched in support of Mothers of Political Prisoners in 1992. Greenbelt Movement leaders openly challenged the politicization of ethnicity by the Moi government and opposition parties in the context of elections (Ndegwa, 1996: 81–107).

As the Movement adopted a more confrontational stance vis-à-vis the Moi regime around 1986, the government began actively to harass the organization. It evicted the GBM from its premises, arrested its world renowned leader Wangari Maathai for rumor-mongering, and physically attacked a demonstration by a group of women hunger strikers calling for the release of 52 political prisoners. In 1993, death threats forced Maathai into hiding. Civic education seminars and other meetings were similarly subject to harassment and intimidation by the authorities (Michaelson, 1994; Ndegwa, 1996: 102).

Consequences of State Strategies

In Africa as elsewhere, women have been able to make limited gains at times through ruling party-sponsored women's organizations, ministries of women, and other state-related institutions. However, the co-optation of women's organizations has overwhelmingly had the net effect of keeping women's mobilization apolitical and of narrowing the agenda to issues that do little to change gender imbalances fundamentally. More importantly, women in state-sponsored institutions have frequently been incapacitated when it comes to mounting a significant challenge to the state on key policies affecting women. Where there have been exceptions, as in Brazil in the early 1980s, it is because there was a visible feminist presence in the state institutions themselves (Alvarez, 1990).

Beyond Civil Society

Much of the literature on civil society in Africa has been useful in opening up the discussion of autonomy, but has ended up focusing on ways in which civil society has used its autonomy to "engage" the state. Notions of civil society that became especially important in the 1990s saw it as that part of society that both engaged the state and also possessed partially autonomous economic, religious, intellectual and political institutions distinct from those of the state and the family or clan. In the African context, civil society has been described as an important part of the movement for political liberalization and democratization (Bratton, 1994a; Fatton, 1995: 75). It has also been seen as a broker, buffer, and representative between state and society (Harbeson, 1994: 294). Some have even argued that the state is the guarantor of the autonomy of civil society (Mamdani, 1996).

To the extent that autonomy is valued, it is seen mainly as a position from which to engage the state rather than as an end in itself. The civil society literature tends to treat autonomy as important only in so far as it gives societal actors leverage with which to lobby and to influence the state. Chazan, for example, argues that the problem in Africa is how to identify and cultivate civil society from the many existing forms of associational life (1992: 279). Her definition narrows the notion of civil society to the section of society that "interacts with the state, influences the state, and yet is distinct from the state" (ibid. 281). Formal, registered, middle-class and urban-based organizations, such as churches, human rights organizations, professional associations, and other such NGOs, are seen as capable of engaging the state in appropriate ways to bring about policy changes (Chazan, 1992: 287; Woods, 1992, 78).

The present study starts with, but goes beyond, the civil society case for autonomy in which autonomy is seen as the key to gaining *leverage with which to demand policy changes from the state.* Clearly, autonomy has granted Ugandan women's organizations the necessary distance from the National Resistance Movement to demand changes in legislation pertaining to land, domestic relations, rape, and many other concerns. Women have also used this leverage to seek greater political representation and leadership. This study, however, goes further than the civil society argument in some basic ways. It looks at why autonomy is so critical to society itself (Amadiume, 1995: 57).

Challenges to Patronage Politics and Sectarianism

Women in Africa have sought autonomy not only to demand policy changes but, perhaps most importantly, to situate themselves, in the process of fighting for greater equality, at the forefront of struggles against patronage politics and corruption. Patronage has rarely benefited women as a group. Moreover, it has usually disadvantaged them by ensuring that their political representation is limited. These exclusions are evident from the small number of women who have won parliamentary seats or been appointed to ministerial and cabinet positions. Women's absence from the formal political arena is frequently a reflection of their absence from informal clientelistic networks.

To the extent that patronage infused women's organizations tied to the ruling party or regime, it kept the leadership of the organizations in many cases focused on personal advantage rather than on a commitment to the broader goals of a women's movement. It all too often served the purpose of intensifying divisions along religious, ethnic, racial, and regional lines. In other instances, women's wings and organizations tied to the state catered to one group of women at the expense of other groups, generally focusing on urban women at the expense of rural women, married women rather than single women, older women rather than younger women, and sometimes less educated women as opposed to better educated women.

Perhaps ironically, then, in the process of fighting for greater political representation, women have transformed their exclusions into bases for challenging the status quo, patronage politics, and corruption. It is because women were outside the existing power structures and patronage networks that they so often found themselves strategically positioned to resist these same networks. Whether it is Women in Nigeria (WIN), the Greenbelt Movement in Kenya or the Women's National Coalition in South Africa, women have used their autonomy to minimize differences among them in order to build broad movements and coalitions united around common gender concerns.

Uganda is a prime example of this phenomenon. Large numbers of women's organizations have consciously rejected what is called the politics of "sectarianism", based on the religious and ethnic identities that have so seriously divided the Ugandan polity and contributed to years of conflict. Increasing numbers of women have sought new bases for mobilization across ethnic and religious lines, especially around economic and community welfare activities. Chapter 6 explores this phenomenon in greater detail, so suffice it to say here that not only are women mobilizing themselves in ways that seek to include broad sections of the female population irrespective of background, they are also voting in accordance with their non-sectarian identification, and they are also articulating these concerns in public fora.

These concerns have become part of the program of regional women's organizations and conferences as well. For example, 1995 meetings between women from Rwanda, Kenya, Tanzania, and Uganda in preparation for the UN Women's Conference in Beijing highlighted the issue of sectarianism in one of their key resolutions, which stated that "women can transcend religious traditions and doctrines, racial and national barriers, to join together with men in facilitating global peace, starting from the individual, to the family, society, nation and continent".

Women have often been depicted as the embodiment of national, ethnic, racial or religious identities. Their bodies and morality have often become a battleground over the preservation of particularistic identities because of their critical role in sustaining the future of a particular group through their procreative abilities, as socializing agents for children, and as transmitters of group values, traditions and identity (Moghadam, 1994). The experience of African women's movements from South Africa to Kenya, Nigeria and Uganda points to numerous examples where women have challenged such narrow and divisive impulses. They have sought to build linkages around common gender concerns in spite of sharp societal divisions. Associational autonomy has made it possible for women's organizations to disconnect from political parties and institutions that have frequently been built along more particularistic lines.

Broadening Goals

Autonomy in the context of this study has to do with the *capacity of women's organizations to determine and broaden their own goals,* regardless of whether or not they conform to the goals of central government, local government, political parties, donors and other powerful actors. Women's associations, for example, have needed autonomy in order to be able to press for an agenda for women that does not simply serve the interests of patronage networks. To the extent that patronage has tied women's organizations to ruling parties and governments in Africa, it has also constrained their agendas and tied their objectives to those of the authorities. It has forced them into building up the voter base and cheering section of those in power, without allowing them to demand power for themselves or to make demands of their own.

Women's organizations were generally kept apolitical, focused on narrowly defined "development" activities such as family planning, nutrition, health, women's morality, childcare and homemaking skills (Hirschmann, 1991; Geisler, 1987; Nzomo, 1996). This served to marginalize their leadership and channeled women into mobilizing around a narrow set of issues, which in a country like Zambia under UNIP resulted in a focus on women's morality (Geisler, 1987). Women's wings were often reduced to serving at celebratory functions, i.e., dancing, singing, and cooking at state functions (Nzomo, 1996). Former President Banda, for example, required women from the League of Malawi Women (the women's wing of the Malawi Congress Party) to be present at all official functions, dressed in party uniforms, singing and dancing in his praise (Hirschmann, 1991: 1683).

Women's organizations thus became an important vehicle through which to control votes, women's contributions to politicians and their allegiances. Given the large number of women voters, this support was vital. For example, Kenya's Maendeleo ya Wanawake (controlled by the ruling party, KANU) helped the umbrella organization National Council of Women of Kenya (NCWK) and the national machinery for women, the Women's Bureau, to register about 23,000 women's groups by 1990 representing millions of women. Registering the groups helped the ruling party and government keep track of the organizations and exploit them to support the electoral campaigns of male politicians. For years they saw women's groups as easy sources of support, which they could manipulate and patronize without the fear that the women would challenge them (Nzomo, 1996). Governments also used women's associations to suppress other independent women's organizations. Kenya's rulers, for example, tried with uneven success to use the MYW to muzzle women in other women's organizations and keep them in line (Onsando, 1996).

The contrast between Ghana and Uganda highlights the difference autonomy makes to the women's agenda. The Jerry Rawlings regime in Ghana shares many characteristics with Uganda under Yoweri Museveni, but the women's movement does not have the same autonomy from the regime as that enjoyed by women's organizations in Uganda. Ghana's Provisional National Defence Council (PNDC) is similar to Uganda's NRM in that both are populist governments that came to power through a military takeover. Moreover, like the NRM, the PNDC has sought legitimacy through the creation of popular grassroots councils at the local level. It resembles the NRM in encouraging the mobilization of women. It has reformed laws affecting women, including inheritance laws and the banning of degrading widowhood rites. The national machinery charged with co-ordinating women's activities, the National Council for Women and Development (NCWD), has been active in promoting such legislation. Women in both countries share a similar profile: they have equivalent rates of adult literacy,[7] enrolment in primary schools,[8] and involvement in economic activity.[9]

The critical difference between the two countries with regard to women lies in the area of autonomy. The women's movement in Ghana has been constrained by the government in terms of growth, vitality, breadth of its agenda and capacity to afford major changes in the status of women. By trying to subsume the entire women's movement within the PNDC via the creation of the 31st December Women's Movement (31DWM) in 1981 as one of its "revolutionary organizations", the regime has crippled the women's movement and limited it to publicizing and promoting government policies. As Tsikata put it: the relationship between women's groups and the regime "has been maintained at the expense of the women's struggle . . . . In so doing women's issues have been shelved; or at best, they have received very casual attention" (1989: 89). The close ties between the 31DWM and the government/ruling party have basically kept the organization from exerting pressure on the government to adopt policies that would promote the welfare and interests of women (Dei, 1994: 140; Mikell, 1984). As 31DWM has absorbed many independent women's organizations at the grassroots level, women have been left with muted representation.

Conversely, as the Ugandan example shows, the proliferation of independent associations has allowed women's organizations to expand their agendas to take on women's rights issues more forcefully, to fight for greater female political representation, and to challenge patronage politics itself and the narrow bases along which it is often built. The women's movement has been able to broach publicly many different issues, ranging from women's representation in office to domestic violence, rape, reproductive rights, sex education in the school curriculum, female genital mutilation, women's rights as human rights, sexual harassment, disparaging representation of women in the media, and other concerns that have rarely been addressed by women's movements in countries where the single party has dominated the movement. Where, in Africa, autonomous movements emerged in the 1990s, non-partisan women's organizations were formed to promote women's leadership and involvement in politics and to unite women from different locations on the political spectrum around common gender-based interests. These include organizations like the Society for the Advancement of Women (Malawi), the Women's National Coalition (South Africa), the National Women's Lobby Group in Zambia, and the National Committee on the Status of Women in Kenya. These organizations have focused on improving women's leadership skills, promoting civic education, assisting women running for office, and pressuring political parties to endorse more women candidates. As the leader of one such non-partisan organization in Tanzania put it: non-partisan organizations can create an "independent voice for women which political parties find very difficult to ignore in a democracy" She added, her non-partisan group, "should be able to unite women with different ideological beliefs around a common cause of women's emancipation."[10] This, then, gives women greater leverage with which to lobby for women's rights inside their own political parties because they can point to a potential constituency of women voters who are committed to particular goals.

Concretizing the Agenda

While, at the national level, the capacity to set a broad agenda has been a key benefit of autonomy, at the local level autonomy has also allowed women's organizations to address immediate and concrete needs of the community in a tangible way. Women in Uganda, perhaps more often than men, tend to define and engage in politics in a distinct way characterized by the pursuit of tangible results. They do this through concrete action aimed, for example, at changing a household income level, building a neighborhood well or improving the provision of education in the community. They mobilize to resolve the problem at hand, by plunging in and doing the necessary work themselves. Women's hands-on approach to political action of this kind is closely related to the high demands placed on them in the household to provide and care for all household members. Women tend to be on the frontline when it comes to taking care of the health and educational needs of the family, in addition to feeding, providing water, and clothing household members. These responsibilities increased exponentially with the economic crises that devastated so many African economies in the 1980s.

There is an immediacy to women's mobilization that does not wait for a magic moment to bring about sweeping changes that would alter the course of history. Certainly women have been at the forefront of movements for democratic reform in Mali, Kenya, Sierra Leone and elsewhere. But they have also had a broader sense of political change that does not limit itself to demonstrations, electoral politics, national conferences, and other more dramatic assertions of public voice. One Congolese scholar, Musifiky Mwanasali, who carried out research on the informal economy in Kisangani in the early 1990s, found that, in the midst of a climate of uncertainty about the country's economic and political future, women not only participated in public protest actions but were more concerned than men with concretely making an immediate and perceptible difference in improving the quality of life by increasing their involvement in various "micro-organizations" and survival strategies.[11] The political impact of such activities does not draw the headlines that riots or demonstrations attract, but it does dramatically change the political dynamics of society.

Selecting Leadership

The capacity to select their own leadership and organize themselves in ways of their own choosing, free of party/government manipulation, is another critical benefit of autonomy. State-initiated women's organizations may be built by drawing on a wide base of support from grassroots women, but they have often ended up benefiting only a few elite women who have personal ties with the national leadership. It is not uncommon to find male party or government authorities exercising indirect control of the women's organizations through their wives, sisters and daughters who are in the leadership of the organization. Leaders are therefore not generally selected on the basis of merit, nor are they usually women who have built up their own leadership base or had their own mass following. Amina Mama calls this the "First Lady Syndrome". She shows how it has been used as an anti-democratic female power structure which claims to advance the interests of ordinary women "but is unable to do so because it is dominated by a small clique of women whose authority derives from their being married to powerful men, rather than from any actions or ideas of their own". In the long term their organizations undermine women's interests by "upholding the patriarchal status quo" (1995: 41).

Maryam Babangida, the wife of one of Nigeria's military leaders, Ibrahim Babangida, is often associated with this First Lady Syndrome. A secretary by profession, she became president of the Nigerian Army Officers' Wives Association when her husband became Chief of Army Staff in 1983. She had not been active in the women's movement, but when her husband seized power in Nigeria in 1985, she decided to make her mark by launching a Better Life for Rural Women Programme (BLP) in 1987 to promote literacy, vocational training, social welfare and health programs, and income-generating projects throughout the country.

She was assisted by the wives of civil service chiefs and professional academic women at the national level. At the regional level, wives of state governors and of local government chairmen were selected to head local branches of the organization that was popularly referred to as the "bitter life programme for rural women".

Such nepotism contributed to poor organizational leadership, but it also ensured that what resources were made available to the organization remained at the top. "The endless parades of the over-dressed wives of the military across the pages of the newspapers and the nation's television screens soon began to provoke criticism from several quarters," writes Amina Mama. She describes how, even though Maryam Babangida declared that the BLP was self-financed, the organization was in fact unaccountable to its membership. BLP leaders used the organization's resources to stay in five-star hotels, to pay for expensive air travel, and to take out costly full-page newspaper advertisements to congratulate Maryam Babangida on being chosen as Woman of the Year in 1989.

Meanwhile rural women's goods were sold at a 1988 Better Life Fair with no compensation. What loans women obtained from the BLP were at exorbitantly high interest rates (Mama, 1995: 49–51). Between 1987 and 1992 the BLP received $18 million, little of which remained for rural women's groups after the office buildings, vehicles, staff salaries, and overseas travel had been covered. In 1989 a lawyer, Gani Fawehinmi, sought a court injunction to restrain the military government from authorizing additional public funds for Maryam Babangida since she had no duties assigned to her in the organization. Later a government-appointed National Commission for Women also sought greater accountability from the BLP, but was dissolved by a 1992 military decree before any of its recommendations could be implemented (Abdullah, 1995: 214–17; Okonjo, 1994: 521). For many women, the biggest frustration was not just the loss of resources, but the way in which women like Maryam Babangida promoted an extremely conservative politics that emphasized women's traditional roles as wives and mothers, with no mention of their rights (Mama, 1995: 52).

Challenging Existing Resource and Power Distributions

For organizations at both the national and local levels, *autonomy has allowed women to challenge existing resource and power distributions that have discriminated against them.* Other disempowered groups (young people, the landless, the urban poor, the self-employed) have used autonomy for similar purposes, but of these groups women in Africa tend to have longer histories and more experience in mobilization. Women have demanded not just greater political representation, but also to be listened to in local councils or legislative bodies. In other words, they have also used their autonomy *to demand changes in the way politics is conducted.* For example, the fact that the electorate in Uganda has almost come to expect money, beer or some token of appreciation from politicians running for office, has the effect of excluding large numbers of women from aspiring for office. Generally women cannot afford these payments, but more importantly they often find such practices reprehensible. Similarly, women candidates are subject to culturally biased public statements, media coverage, and sentiments opposed to their participation because they are women. They find themselves caught between a rock and a hard place: Some are penalized for being single women, others for being married women and neglecting their household duties. Some are told not to run in their parents' district, but then are also told not to run in their husband's district, etc. Non-partisan women's organizations have challenged these practices that have become impediments to women's full political participation.

Isolated in women's wings of ruling parties or in their own organizations, women were actively discouraged from seeking political office. Even by the late 1990s, the average proportion of female parliamentarians in Africa stood at 12 percent (compared with 38 percent in the Nordic countries, 12 percent in the European countries (excluding the Nordic countries), 14 percent in Asia, 15 percent in the Americas, and 3 percent in the Arab states (see Table 1.1). Women who were appointed to ministerial positions rarely found themselves in the key ministries of finance, industry, agriculture, defense, or foreign affairs. Instead they were relegated to the ministries of culture, community development, social welfare and other ministries considered secondary in the government pecking order. Not only were women excluded from formal party politics, but more importantly they also confronted exclusions in the informal clientelistic networks, which had powerful political influence.

Often rulers made a few token appointments of women to silence those pushing for greater female representation. In Kenya, the few women rewarded with key decision-making appointments were often given the positions in order to help clean up a government parastatal or ministry that had been destroyed by mismanagement and corruption. As soon as the job was done, the woman would be replaced by a male manager (Nzomo, 1996).

When women attempted to struggle for power, male politicians were often quick to advise them to stay out of politics, which was defined as a male domain in which women had no business being involved, according to Wanjiku Kabira and Elizabeth Nzioki. Any attempt by women's groups to become involved in politics was seen as going beyond acceptable bounds (1995: 72–3).

Defenses Against State Repression

Autonomy has been critical to *resisting the state* through strikes, demonstrations, petitions, media exposés of corrupt leaders, and the other manifestations of opposition that became increasingly common in the 1990s, as movements against authoritarian and military rule mounted.

Women openly resisted corrupt and repressive regimes through public demonstrations. In Mali, one of the most dramatic and bloody clashes between President Moussa Traoré and demonstrators occurred when 2,000 women marched in front of the Ministry of Defense in 1991. The killing of women and children so incensed the public that Traoré was forced to make major concessions to the opposition before his overthrow in a military coup, which set in motion the process of political transition. In Sierra Leone, women were the only section of society that openly defied soldiers in 1996 by staging mass demonstrations at a critical period when the military were considering postponing the elections, scheduled for 26 February 1996 (Bangura, 1996: 29).

Similarly, in 1992 in Uhuru Park at the center of Nairobi, Kenya, women found themselves in a violent confrontation with police when they went on a hunger strike in support of political prisoners. Women stripped themselves naked to heap the most vehement curses on the military police who were trying to break the strike. This powerful statement of condemnation of the government authorities left an indelible impression on the minds of the populace.

The Challenge of Associational Autonomy

In sum, autonomy allows women's movements not only to engage the state as the civil society approach emphasizes, but also to fulfill independent goals of the movements and organizations themselves. It allows women's organizations to establish and expand their own goals and, in particular, to challenge society-wide norms and practices that harm women, for example, domestic violence, sexual harassment, female genital surgery, the disparaging representation of women in the media, and hostility towards female political candidates. Autonomy allows organizations to take up causes and pursue legislation on issues that are not always popular with the authorities. Women are encouraged to seek political office and politicize their activities. Autonomy allows women's organizations to address immediate and concrete localized concerns as well; to select their own leadership without government or party interference; to challenge patronage practices and exclusions based on ethnicity, race, religion and other lines; to challenge discriminatory distributions of resources and power; and to defend organizations against state predation and repression.

Beyond Disengagement

In spite of these many activities that go beyond lobbying the state, the civil society literature treats anything short of directly engaging the state as exit, withdrawal or disengagement, which is often seen as not only peripheral but even counterproductive to the project of civil society. Some argue that, in contrast to civil society, many local organizations, "by ignoring the government," are undermining the government's authority and thus cannot be considered part of civil society (Chazan, 1992: 287). According to the civil society perspective, disengagement, by definition, places these strategies outside "civil society" and consequently outside the realm of meaningful political action. From the perspective of many civil society approaches, disengagement or exit is seen as a shirking of responsibility in the public arena, while autonomous civil society is characterized by voice, engagement, and a willingness to participate and risk retaliation (Azarya, 1994: 97–8).

The notion that local associations that do not "engage" the state are necessarily undermining it is, for the most part, implausible. It is difficult to imagine how the hundreds of women's organizations in Uganda encountered in this study would in any way, directly or even indirectly, have undermined the state. Organizations have often created resources that have made it possible for people to sustain themselves where the state has failed to provide the most basic social and public services or to guarantee a living wage. These strategies, rather than eroding state capacity, have diverted pressures that might have otherwise been placed on the state. Moreover, the state would have been unable to respond to these pressures. Women's organizations in Uganda at the local level found themselves digging the wells, building the roads and maternity clinics, and taking other self-help measures in the community. It is difficult to see how such concrete collective action could in any way be interpreted as undermining the state.

Moreover, when the state has resorted to violence against its citizens, it makes little sense to speak of engagement as a strategy. As Stephen Bunker explained in the case of rural producers:

When the state begins to use violence against local organizations, the peasants no longer attempt to bargain with it. Instead, they withdraw from controlled crop markets as much as possible to avoid forced appropriation because any contact with the state is dangerous (Bunker, 1987: 19).

Although the idea of autonomy in this study goes beyond exit, withdrawal and disengagement, these concepts are understood in several different ways in the literature. One approach is to focus on disengagement as a survival strategy. For example, during periods of economic shortage, Victor Azarya and Naomi Chazan argue that finding ways to cope became a form of disengagement. These were usually strategies that included internal migration, emigration to neighboring countries or the West, political exile, shifts from export to food crop production, participation in the informal economy, smuggling, and the creation of parallel markets like black currency markets to evade government-controlled markets (Azarya and Chazan, 1987; Bayart, 1986).

Still others have described disengagement in the context of political culture, with an emphasis on witchcraft, fundamentalist revival movements, independent churches, and millenarian movements that represent "counter-symbolic systems of authority," as René Lemarchand refers to them. Other forms of exit include the distribution of information outside the official media, satire, gossip, and ridicule of those in power (Bayart, 1986: 113; Lemarchand, 1992). Célestin Monga, for example, shows how official slogans, speeches, bywords and verbal tics of leaders are mimicked and mocked. He argues that people have crafted and perfected forms of indiscipline as resistance to the state. Their inventiveness has been channeled into defying "everything that symbolizes public authority" (1996: 117, 148). In this same vein, Michael Schatzberg characterizes the citizenry's desire for autonomous political space as "unquenchable" in the face of a repressive state that only allows "political participation on its own terms". People in Zaire/Congo resisted the state by refusing to participate in political cheerleading, dancing, singing and marches under Mobutu. They exited to the forest and islands, joined religious sects, gossiped about the leadership, retained firearms illegally, participated in wildcat strikes and in the informal economy (Schatzberg, 1988: 138–9). I draw similar parallels in the case of urban Tanzania, where the informal economy also became a site of resistance against the government's rules that violated the norms of justice for the poor (Tripp, 1997).

Others have used the idea of "withdrawal" to describe forms of evasion of the state and the market through the peasant household. Allen Isaacman (1989) shows how peasants derive their autonomy from their access to land and their ability to mobilize labor power via the household. Goran Hyden (1980), similarly, has described the exit of the uncaptured peasantry who withdraw from the control of the state and the market. As Chazan (1992) argues, the peasants are "pointedly detached from the market and the state".

These understandings of exit are useful up to a point, but they need to be refined and integrated into a broader understanding of societal autonomy. What this study shows is that neither engagement, disengagement nor even assertions of autonomy are an absolute state of existence, but rather they are part of a repertoire of strategies which individuals, kin, and associations employ to cope with economic and political crises, to resist government repression or unpopular policies and to bring about political and economic change.

For example, the notion that the peasantry can detach themselves from the state or the market is especially problematic because rarely has the state, much less the market, permitted individuals or communities to do so completely. Even under circumstances of severe repression, as was the case in Uganda under Amin and Obote's second regime, it made little sense to talk about withdrawal from the state (Kasfir, 1994: 120). Under the more benign current regime the state makes its presence felt through local government structures (Local Councils) that compel widespread participation. Even the most isolated "disengaged" organizations find that to carry out their activities they frequently have to apply for government funding, become registered, consult with the various district offices and ministries, and use government facilities.

Moreover, as Bunker has shown, "exit" can even be used as a lever to strengthen engagement of the state (Bunker, 1987; Hirschmann, 1970). In Bunker's study of co-operatives in Bugisu, Uganda, he shows how peasants used the threat of exit to expand the local political arena through their own associations and their autonomy within that arena. Through these associations they were able to use the threat to reduce the production of cash crops or withdraw from the market to communicate their needs and demands to the state (Bunker, 1987: 13–14). This he sees as an explicit challenge to the conventional notions of engagement and political collective action that focus on interest groups, elections, and party involvement.

Similarly, in my own study of the informal economy in Tanzania, I show how exit or massive non-compliance resulted in policy changes. I explain how unlicensed, unregistered, economic strategies involved the creation of new institutional resources. Widespread non-compliance through informal economic activities forced the government to ease restrictions on micro-entrepreneurial activities and to legalize various economic pursuits to make it easier for people to make a living under extremely difficult circumstances. At the same time, people's involvement in informal sector activities served as a cushion, albeit a thin one, against the hardships brought on first by economic crisis and later by austerity measures that were part of structural adjustment in Tanzania (Tripp, 1997).

In the same vein, Janet MacGaffey employs a notion of exit to show how the second economy in Zaire/Congo was a form of resistance to the state. She describes exit in terms of evading taxes, trading without licenses, refusing to comply with market or transport regulations, and obtaining scarce goods that were officially unavailable. She argues that both urban and rural dwellers were able to evade control largely through the second economy. In Zaire, unlicensed traders were commonly called *lutteurs* or strugglers, and smuggling was generally perceived as an act of rebellion against an unjust political and economic system and against dominant groups. Bodo peasants in Wamba Zone, Haut Zaire, described their flight into smuggling and artisanal gold mining in the 1980s as a reaction to abuse by local administrators who imposed excessive taxes and engaged in false weighing practices and other forms of exploitation (MacGaffey, 1986: 174–5).

Thus, "exit" can be seen as resistance, as a strategy of survival, as evasion of a repressive state, or an attempt to create political space outside of the state. Associations may vary their strategies, at times disengaging and evading the state, and at other times seeking autonomy in order to press their demands with the state. Organizations generally are not trying to decide whether to "engage" or "not to engage", but rather they respond to political opportunity structures with a variety of strategies ranging from disengagement to autonomous engagement. The Ugandan context is a particularly useful one in which to examine many of these issues for reasons that follow.

The Ugandan Context

Since the National Resistance Movement's takeover of government in 1986 the women's movement has become one of the strongest mobilized societal forces in Uganda. The movement had its antecedents during the colonial period and continued to grow after independence under the first Milton Obote regime (1962–71) until the military takeover by Idi Amin, who suppressed women's organizations. These openly re-emerged under Obote's second regime (1980–85), although they did not flourish until the NRM came to power, bringing with it relative stability.

The women's movement pressured the NRM regime to elevate women to key positions in the government as ministers, cabinet members, permanent secretaries, members of special commissions, and other key posts. Uganda led the way with the first woman vice-president in Africa.[12] With roughly 18 percent female representation in parliament since 1989, and a minimum of one-third female representation in local government ensured by the 1995 Constitution, Uganda has exceeded most African countries in terms of female political representation; only South Africa, Namibia, Mozambique and the Seychelles have comparable or higher rates of representation in Africa (see Table 1.1). Women's organizations were active in the process of revising the 1995 Constitution, which adopted extensive provisions to enhance the position of women. They have also pursued other key legislation affecting women. These are but a few of the important changes that occurred in a relatively short time after the NRM takeover.

This study explains how the women's movement was able to assert itself so forcefully. Although there are many factors that are critical in explaining this change, the most important one, which sets the Ugandan women's movement apart from many other women's movements in Africa, has to do with the autonomy of women's organizations, an autonomy that did not come easily and remains a struggle to maintain. Women's organizations have had to fight to hold on to their own independent forms of mobilization, while the NRM regime, like its predecessors, has sought ways to incorporate and control women's activities.

After the 15 years of institutional decay that followed Idi Amin's takeover in 1971 and continued under Milton Obote's second regime (referred to as Obote II), Uganda began to experience a revival of local and national governance structures after Yoweri Museveni's NRM regime took over in 1986. One of the most important changes, which will be explored at length in this study, involved the creation of a multi-tiered system of Resistance Councils (RCs), which in 1995 became known as Local Councils (LCs), to promote grassroots participation in local government, starting at the village level. (I will refer to the councils both prior to and after 1995 as Local Councils to avoid confusion.)[13]

Other institutional reforms included the implementation of an economic recovery program (begun in 1987), along with the extensive liberalization of crop authorities, the privatization of parastatals, and strengthening of incentives for the private sector (for example, implementation of a new investment code) in order to reduce the role of the state in the economy. As a result, the economy showed a remarkable turnaround in less than a decade, becoming the thirteenth fastest growing economy in the world by the mid-1990s.

Constitutional reform, which resulted in the adoption of a new Constitution in 1995, was aimed at strengthening democracy, leaving the future of multi-partyism to be decided by a referendum in 2000. In 1990, Uganda embarked on a major civil service reform effort that aimed to revive the civil service from being inefficient,

Table 1.1 Women's Political Representation in Africa, 1999 (% women)

| | Legislature | | Executive |
	Lower or Single House	Upper House or Senate	Ministerial level
Angola	16	6	
Benin			10
Botswana	9		6
Burkina Faso	8	12	17
Burundi	6		7
Cameroon	6		3
Cape Verde	11		13
Central African Republic	4		5
Chad	2		5
Comoros	0		0
Congo	12		6
Côte d'Ivoire	8		8
Djibouti	0	0	0
Eritrea	15		
Ethiopia	2		10
Gabon	8		7
Gambia	2		0
Ghana	9		11
Guinea	9		9
Guinea Bissau	10		4
Kenya	4		0
Lesotho	4		6
Liberia			5
Madagascar	8		0
Malawi	6	6	9
Mali	12		10
Mauritania	4	0	0
Mauritius	8		3
Mozambique	25		0
Namibia	22	4	10
Niger	1		
Nigeria			3
Rwanda	17		9
São Tomé and Principe	4	0	
Senegal	12	18	7
Seychelles	23	31	
South Africa	30	12	20
Sudan	5		0
Swaziland	3	13	0
Tanzania	16		13
Togo	–		–
Uganda	18		10
Zambia	10		6
Zimbabwe	14		3

Source: UNDP, 1995: 60-2, 84-5: InterParliamentary Union. http://www.ipu.org/wmn-e/world.htm

dysfunctional, demoralized and unresponsive to its one-time reputation of having been one of the best in Africa. Yet another institution-strengthening measure involved a major army demobilization endeavor, which was surprisingly carried out with minimal disruptions, considering the enormous challenges of finding new occupations for the demobilized soldiers.

After coming to power, the NRM regime launched a decentralization program that claimed to be a dramatic break with the centralizing tendencies of previous governments. By 1996, the efforts, which had taken place within the context of Uganda's decentralization program, were being heralded as "impressive" by World Bank observers (Langseth, 1996: 1, 19). In 1993 and again in 1997, decentralization efforts were expanded with the shift of substantial control from central government to local authorities. The local councils were the key vehicles through which political power was to be devolved to the grassroots and local democracy strengthened (Ottemoeller, 1995: Tideman, 1994). Administrative decentralization was introduced with the 1993 Local Government Statute, and financial decentralization, starting in 1997–8, involved large unconditional block grants going to district and sub-county councils. District Councils are responsible for improving feeder roads, rehabilitating health care centers, promoting small-scale export agribusiness and improving primary education. In addition, they manage local markets, maintain water sources and oversee sanitation. According to observers, these efforts to enhance local participation have made Uganda's process more comprehensive than any other such initiative taken elsewhere in Africa to date (Villadsen, 1996: 60–61).

The government has encouraged women's mobilization and has demonstrated relatively greater responsiveness than most African authorities to women's concerns, mainly as a way of currying political favor with this large constituency. National and local women's organizations began taking advantage of these new political spaces and started bringing new concerns to bear in the institution-building process in Uganda. Large numbers of women seized on Museveni's call to mobilize to justify organizing themselves with a vigor and in ways the government perhaps did not anticipate. But most important, they did so in a way that gave them a critical distance from government.

Thus, Uganda is an excellent country in which to examine the impact of the women's movement for several reasons: (i) the government has been relatively successful in institution-building as compared with its African neighbors; (ii) the NRM has been more responsive than most African governments to pressures from the women's movement to enhance women's equality in political, economic, educational and other spheres; (iii) Uganda has one of the strongest women's movements in Africa; and (iv) central to the argument of the book, the women's movement is, for the most part, autonomous. Its autonomy, in large measure, explains its unique vitality. This is not to say that Ugandan women's organizations do not face continuing pressures for incorporation/co-optation. Affirmative action policies, giving women top leadership positions, and creating government-sponsored Women's Councils, are measures with two sides to them: they can invigorate women's participation but they can also be used as mechanisms of silencing, co-optation, and creating new dependencies and patronage networks. In this sense, many Ugandan women leaders face the dual challenge of engagement in political life while maintaining loyalty to women's causes, which may be at odds with government goals. The challenges of maintaining autonomy in Uganda are not dissimilar to the experiences of women's movements throughout Africa. Because Uganda has moved so far in such a short time, it is useful not only to examine why these changes have occurred, but also the persistence of institutional constraints on women's participation and leadership.

At the same time, the developments in Uganda parallel the growth of autonomous women's associations in other parts of Africa in the 1990s. These developments have coincided with the relative decline in influence of the older women's associations that were tied to the ruling party or regime. In Uganda as in other parts of Africa, new organizations have emerged to cope with declines in state provision of social services and in response to economic crisis. They are taking advantage of emerging political spaces that have allowed greater room for NGOs and are benefiting from donor strategies that favor non-state initiatives. In Uganda, as elsewhere in Africa, much of the diversity of women's organizations can also be explained by the increase in the education of women, especially in higher education. In the 1990s there have been growing numbers of women's associations – of lawyers, doctors, engineers, scientists and other professionals. These simply would not have been possible in the 1960s and 1970s when the pool of women trained in these professions was much smaller.

Frequently, women's organizational autonomy is regarded with suspicion because it can end up highlighting women's institutional isolation and ineffectiveness. Kathleen Staudt, for example, argues that women's autonomy reinforces their marginality in conventional politics (Staudt, 1986: 207). The present study is indeed alert to these potential pitfalls of autonomy, but nevertheless concludes that on balance autonomy is critical to the advancement of women. Through a series of case studies of local conflicts over access to resources as well as an analysis of the national women's movement, it will show how women in Uganda seized on their autonomy which was initially a result of marginalization, and surprisingly turned it around and used it to their advantage.

Autonomy born of marginalization does not automatically translate into leverage with which to challenge the status quo, and perhaps more often than not results in immobilization. What additional factors, then, need to be taken into account in explaining an apparent increase in women's efforts to defend their rights in Uganda? The four case studies of conflicts described in this book provide some clues, which are also representative of women's struggles more generally in Uganda. (i) One of the main factors was an ideological sense of entitlement to equality of opportunity and rights that emerged within women's organizations and was also fostered by the NRM itself. Moreover, the NRM delivered on many of its promises to women by supporting constitutional changes, allowing for greater female political representation, and other measures to advance the position of women. (ii) State inability to provide social and welfare services shifted the burden to communities and individuals, often resulting in a variety of women's self-help strategies. These kinds of changes in opportunity structures encouraged women to push for even greater gains. (iii) Women had increasing access to economic resources which could benefit the women's movement because of their heightened involvement in business. (iv) Shifting donor strategies away from state support helped bolster the women in the non-governmental sector, especially at the national level. (v) Women had greater access to educational opportunities, which became an especially critical factor at the national level. (vi) And finally, the fact that women also had pre-existing associational experiences which they could draw on gave them invaluable organizational resources.

While all these factors were critical to enhancing women's collective bargaining power, none was as critical as associational autonomy. I demonstrate this by making three kinds of comparisons in the chapters that follow. First, as argued earlier in this chapter, the Ugandan women's movement differs from many other women's movements in Africa, for example, the movement in Ghana, in that it is more autonomous and hence has had greater impact. Ugandan women, like women in many other African countries, have benefited from changes in economic resources, educational opportunities, populist governments that encouraged women's participation, and organizational capacity, yet they have not enjoyed the same level of strength and vibrancy as the women's movement. Thus, autonomy is especially important in a region which has a history of one-party rule that has tended to eliminate independent associational activity through harassment, banning and co-optation of organizations and other forms of control.

Second, I show how the women's movement has been strengthened and has had a broader agenda as a result of associational autonomy, especially when contrasted with earlier periods in its history when dependence on government and the ruling party was more pervasive (Chapter 2). Third, I explain how women's associations have been more autonomous than other sectors of Ugandan society, and this has consequently given them greater leverage (Chapter 3).

This book, then, is a story of how Ugandan women sought to redefine the meaning and the terms of their own participation in public and private arenas. Their incursions into the public realm suggest new ways of thinking about citizenship, politics and political participation that represent a dramatic break from the neo-patrimonial tendencies that are so prevalent in Africa today. Far from passively watching from the sidelines, Ugandan women are actively writing their own scripts which envision alternative ways of ordering political, public and private life. Many are auditioning for the parts as they seek public office, lead their own organizations and push for new ways of engaging in politics. But whose play gets produced, who produces and directs it, and how it is produced remain to be seen.

Notes

1 Pan African News Agency, 27 May 1996.
2 *Proceedings of the Constituent Assembly, Official Report*, Wednesday, 3 August 1994, p.1490.
3 In a presentation to the USAID Gender and Democracy in Africa Workshop, Washington, DC, 28 July 1995.
4 *Africa Confidential* 3,(11) (24 May 1996): 6–7.
5 "OMM returns to Frelimo," *Mozambiquefile* 241 (August 1996): 4–5.
6 High Court of Zimbabwe, SC 15/97.
7 Adult female literacy as a percentage of male literacy in Ghana stood at 67 percent and in Uganda at 65 percent (1992) (UNDP, 1995: 53)
8 Female enrolment in primary school as a percentage of male enrolment in Ghana stood at 87 percent and in Uganda at 89 percent (1990) (UNDP, 1995: 53).
9 Female involvement in economic activity as a percentage of male involvement in Ghana stood at 63 percent and in Uganda at 65 percent (1994) (UNDP, 1995: 59).
10 Mnzavas, Asha, "Women Firm on their Right to Organize Themselves," *Sunday Observer*, 26 January 1997, p.7.
11 Personal communication, Musifiky Mwanasali, October 1993. See also Mwanasali (1994).
12 There have been other top African women leaders. The first head of an African state in this century was Zauditu, Empress of Ethiopia, who ruled between 1917 and 1930. Other female heads of state have included Dzeliwe Shongwe, Queen-regent of Swaziland, who ruled in

1982–3, followed by Ntombi Thwala, Queen-regent, 1983–6. In more recent years, Ruth Perry has been on the six-member collective presidency of Liberia, serving as Chairman of the Council of State since 3 September 1996; she is the first non-monarchical head of an African state. Elizabeth Domitien was Africa's first female Prime Minister, serving in the Central African Republic between 1975 and 1976. Other women Prime Ministers have included Sylvie Kinigi, Prime Minister of Burundi, 1993–4, and Agathe Uwilingiyimana, Prime Minister of Rwanda, 1993–4, who was assassinated in office.

13 The Local Council system is a hierarchical one. All adult residents belong to their village LC and elect 9 members to the executive committee at the first level, LC1. All LC1 executive committees in a parish form LC2. LC3 is formed similarly out of the LC2s at the sub-county level, and the LC3s form LC5 at the district level, skipping the county level.

2

A Foot
in the Door

Historical Dimensions
of the Women's Movement
in Uganda

You know, when a door has been opened for one person, that person should put her foot down there and let the door remain open until all the others are in . . . . to bring the others forward.

Pumla Kisosonkole, on becoming the first African
woman in the Legislative Council in 1956[1]

Women's involvement in politics under the National Resistance Movement (NRM) has its roots in an earlier period of activism beginning around the 1940s, when they began to form national organizations to seek the advancement of women. Women's efforts under the NRM to bridge differences, to seek associational autonomy, to get more women into office, and to change laws that affected the status of women are not new. In fact, these have been enduring struggles since the 1940s, although the forms, the players and the political context have changed. It is useful to look at the earlier periods in the history of the women's movement in order to appreciate the profound changes that occurred since the mid-1980s.

This chapter first examines the role of women in political life during the pre-colonial period, looking in particular at Buganda in south-central Uganda, Ankole in the west, Teso in the east, and Acholi in the north. The historical record on women's roles is thin, and the selection of these few groups is based on the availability of secondary documentation. The chapter then looks at the rise of the women's movement and the struggles women underwent to give voice to their concerns.

Women in Pre-Colonial Buganda Politics

Buganda had been the most powerful kingdom in the interlacustrine area, and was used by the British to extend their rule outside of Uganda at the turn of the century. As the administrative and commercial center of the country, it has always played a key role in the politics of Uganda, with the Baganda making up almost one-fifth of the population. It was also the area where Protestant and Catholic missionaries first established themselves and from which they launched many of their evangelizing initiatives in the rest of Uganda. The Church Missionary Society arrived in 1877 and the Catholic White Fathers in 1879 (Brown, 1981: 107).

Women's political position in Buganda appears to have undergone substantial changes with the beginning of state formation between the fourteenth and nineteenth centuries. Prior to the thirteenth century, Kintu, the first king, is credited with bringing together a loose alliance of clans, who lived in their own territories with a clan head as chief (Gray, 1934: 266), although his historical origins have been the source of considerable debate (Ray, 1991: 99). State formation, which intensified from the seventeenth through the nineteenth centuries, involved the gradual destruction of the authority of the clans and the rise of the power of the king (kabaka), which was exercised through county (saza) chiefs. A Baganda state brought together under the Kabaka people of different clans, languages and customs in a common territory and sharing a common language and culture.

In the thirteenth, fourteenth and even fifteenth centuries women are said to have ruled as kabaka; Sir John Gray claims that there is abundant evidence of this, although much of this early history is semi-mythological. One such ruler was Naku, the daughter of Mukibi, the founder of the Lugave clan. She married Kimera, who is credited with having established Buganda as a kingdom during the thirteenth or fourteenth centuries (Kaggwa, 1971 [1901]; Ray, 1991: 98). However, Gray argues that she was de facto ruler since Kimera's only claim to authority was the fact that he had married the daughter of a king. In fact, she eventually had her husband killed, suspecting that he was to blame for her son's death. Naku was so powerful that every king that followed Kimera took a wife from her clan and called her Naku (Gray, 1934: 267; Kaggwa, 1971 [1901]: 16–17). The Baganda queen Nanono, wife of Kabaka Nakibinge (1494–1524), gained her fame from a battle with the Banyoro at Mpigi, which the Baganda lost. On learning that the king had died in battle, she rallied the Baganda warriors and prevented further losses. Thereafter she ruled the country for eighteen months and would have been chosen kabaka had she had a male child (Gray, 1934: 267; Kaggwa, 1971 [1901]: 28). Princess Nassolo also made her mark in Buganda history when she led her brothers in a rebellion against the brutal king Kagulu (1674–1704). She killed Kagulu and was responsible for choosing his successor (Kaggwa, 1971 [1901]: 62–6).

To gain access to land through labor and taxes, peasants had to develop clientelistic relations with the kabaka. Clientelism was also the means by which clans or lineages within them gained access to political office. Because only men could become clients, women could obtain land only through their husbands or fathers. It was not until the early twentieth century that women were allowed to inherit or own land. Women's capacity to negotiate claims on land from men in this earlier period depended on their ability to fulfill various obligations including childbearing and cultivating. Women thus became the basis on which patron-client relations were built. At the same time, women's exclusion from clientelism and their status as dependants of their husbands also kept them out of direct involvement in political life (Musisi, 1991: 757–62; Sacks, 1979: 208–10). There is no doubt that this had an impact on post-independence patterns of clientelism and the marginalization women faced not only in formal political representation but also in informal clientelistic relations.

The practice of elite polygyny, which expanded significantly in the nineteenth century, became an integral part of the process of state formation, resulting in women's loss of claims to political leadership. The expansion of polygyny heightened the stratification of society because the control of large numbers of women through marriage was a sign of wealth, prestige and political control (Musisi, 1991). Women were appropriated through raids and the conquest of new territory as well as through marriage. They could be inherited from a predecessor king; they could be married women abducted from their husbands; they could be given as gifts by individuals; or they could be female relatives brought in by existing elite wives. Claims on women thus became signs of prestige for the king and his generals and officials (Kaggwa, 1971, [1901]: 187). Clans seeking political power or favors would supply the king with their women for marriage. The kings, in their turn, sought wives from most of the Baganda clans to ensure their loyalty. In addition, in order to consolidate clan support, the sons of the king adopted the totems of their mothers and not of their fathers, a practice which continued long after its real purpose was forgotten (Gray, 1934: 261). Similarly, chiefs exchanged women between themselves and the king for political, economic or other benefits such as exemption from paying taxes or for cattle.

Both women and men were ranked in society by titles. Wives of chiefs, of the *kabaka* and of royals were superior in status to peasants and to males inferior to their guardians (Schiller, 1990: 457). In some ways, however, peasant women had greater personal freedom than royal women because their husbands could generally afford only one wife and therefore relied solely on them. Moreover, unlike royal women, peasant women did not need escorts to travel and could run away to their relatives if their husbands mistreated them (ibid.: 458).

Like ordinary women, however, women of the ruling class were also excluded from clientelistic relations and could not inherit any chiefship property. Princesses, nevertheless, retained many privileges, including the right to own land. They were shown great respect by chiefs and were exempted from many restrictions faced by ordinary women, although they were not officially permitted to marry or bear children until the 1800s. This effectively kept their offspring from gaining access to the kingship. Indeed, succession to the Buganda throne was granted only to royalty from the father's side; however, succession was decided by the king's mother's clan (Musisi, 1991: 773–6; Roscoe, 1911: 232). Kingship began to decline as the chiefs gained in power in the 1800s, around the time that princesses started to marry and have legitimate children. Under Mutesa I (1824–84) princesses were given to chiefs to consolidate their patron-client relations (Musisi, 1991: 776).

While the expansion of polygyny in the nineteenth century undercut some of the authority women had held when clans were the dominant form of political organization, elite women remained politically influential. Most of the Buganda chiefs and the prime minister were under the control of the elite titled wives of the king. The majority of the king's wives were non-titled women, the lowest ranking ones being captives or daughters of unimportant chiefs or peasants who were responsible for the bulk of the household chores. The titled wives, however, were privy to state secrets and their offspring had the potential to become future kings. They also participated in military campaigns; Princess Nakuyita, for example, was second in command of Sunna II's army in the early 1800s (Kaggwa, 1971, [1901]: 121; Musisi, 1991: 782–6). The titled wives were heavily involved in court politics and in vying for power through their sons and clans. One princess, the favorite wife of the king, and another titled woman in Mukaabya Mutesa's court were instrumental in deposing the prime minister, Kayira, because they felt he had claimed too much power (Kaggwa, 1971, [1901]: 149–52).

Of the three individuals who could be addressed as *kabaka* or king, two were women – the queen mother (*namasole*) and the queen sister (*lubuga*); along with the princesses, they wielded considerable informal political power through their lineage positions (Schiller, 1990: 462, 472). The *namasole* had her own court and estates and exercised powers that resembled those of the king (Gray, 1934); she was the most important woman in Buganda. The *lubuga* was one of the king's half-sisters with the same father as the king, and was also the daughter of a woman with no sons. She became the official "wife", although the king was forbidden to have sexual relations with her, nor could she have any children. She effectively shared the throne with him and had the same powers he had, for example, she controlled land throughout the country with estates in each district, and she had her own courts and her own chiefs with the same titles as those of the king's chiefs (Musisi, 1991: 782–6, Roscoe, 1911: 84, 237).

The position of the *namasole* and *lubuga* were undermined when Uganda became a British protectorate in 1894. The Uganda Agreement of 1900 between the British and the *kabaka* recognized the *kabaka* as the ruler of Buganda. He was to administer the territory through indirect rule via the *Lukiiko*, which was considered to be the native council. The Kingdom of Buganda was divided into 20 counties (*saza*), subdivided into sub-counties (*gombolola*) and parishes (*muluka*), with a chief and council at each level. Buganda became a province of Uganda but the Buganda government retained its king, prime minister (*katikiro*), and five other ministers including the ministers of finance, justice, health, education and natural resources. All of these positions were subject to the British monarch's approval. The *lubuga* was not mentioned in the 1900 Agreement and the *namasole* receive only scant mention, indicating that the *namasole* of the Kabaka Daudi Chwa was to be paid an allowance during her lifetime but this allowance was to be discontinued for future queen mothers. Thus, the two political positions of consequence for Baganda women were effectively denuded of their significance by British rule.

While the position of elite women was undermined, other positions gained in importance. The prime minister became more powerful. The *Lukiiko*, which was made up of an irregular conglomeration of notables and chiefs and had met sporadically in the past, now became a formal body with regular meetings of chiefs and deputies. Senior chiefs were given stable tenure in government positions, while junior chiefs lost land and power; these highest ranking chiefs then gained authority under British rule. However, it was not only royal women whose roles were diminished in this period. The influence of the *kabaka* and the clan leaders was also weakened. Where once the peasants had been the political clients of chiefs – a relationship that implied mutual obligations – they now found themselves relegated to being simply their tenants or serfs as the chiefs gained land. The new freehold land system meant that clans lost their power to allocate property, while their control over clan burial grounds was also diminished (Apter, 1961: 109–13).

Women in Ankole, Teso, and Acholi Politics

In one of the other three Ugandan kingdoms, Ankole, female chiefs were common at the turn of the century (Maddox, 1946 [1901]. In fact, the only female *gombolola* chief appointed by the British administration, Julia Kibubura, was from Ankole (Morris, 1957; 3). Women leaders were sometimes credited with extraordinary powers. Ankole was renowned for its female diviners who included well-known women like Murogo, Nyatuzana, Kyishokye and Kibubwa. For example, the king (*mugabe*) Rwebishengye appointed the famous diviner Murogo to work for him as a spy on the Banyoro north of Katonga. Murogo and her female descendants were allegedly able to turn themselves into cows and mingle with the cattle herds of the enemy, and they worked for the kings for several generations in the Ibanda area (ibid.: 3–4).

In the eighteenth and nineteenth centuries in Teso, prior to the Baganda conquest, almost all social institutions had political functions. The basic social unit of this Eastern Nilotic group was the *ekek* or extended family, headed by the eldest family member elected by the adult male members of the *ekek*. The *ateker* or clan was another institution of importance, headed by someone chosen by consensus by the elders. Both women and men attended and participated in clan meetings, but women were not permitted to attend interclan meetings if it was feared that they would involve conflict. If the meetings were deemed safe, women could attend them (Webster et al., 1973: 130). The Iteso clans differed from the other Bantu or Nilotic clans. They did not claim to be descendants of a particular ancestor nor did they have a common totem. Clans did not own land or cattle, which were instead owned by individuals. Law and order was administered through a council of male elders, *etem*, which was a territorial rather than a clan institution. The men of one *etem* hunted and fought together, and they were also initiated into age-sets together (Lawrence, 1957: 66, 68).

The main female position of importance was the *apolon ka etale*, the woman in charge of rituals that governed the taboos of the clan. She was the most senior woman in the clan with the most experience of taboo functions. Her task was to ensure that newly married women were initiated into the clan taboos; this in effect gave her control of the women and children in the clan. Women also featured as foretellers in Iteso society, with some like Amongin becoming widely known and revered (Webster et al., 1973: 107–8, 169). Before and after going to war, the Iteso warriors would consult with a foreteller, who would advise them on what rituals to perform. Foretellers not only predicted the outcomes of wars, fishing and hunting expeditions, and other future events, they also had spiritual powers to heal the sick and to prevent witchcraft directed at an individual. With this ability to predict the future, they were able virtually to control the military leaders of the nineteenth century.

In contrast to the Iteso, women were never entirely absent from political leadership among the Acholi or the other Nilotic groups in northern Uganda. Even among the groups that came to form the Acholi, where descent was carried through male lineage, women were able to claim kingship. Up until the late seventeenth century, Acholi societies had been primarily small-scale acephalous groupings of people living in village and often in multiple village groupings (Atkinson, 1978: 138–55). In the late seventeenth and early eighteenth centuries, Acholiland was transformed into a series of over 70 polities or kingdoms. They borrowed from Bunyoro-Kitara in the south concepts and structures of political leadership like kingship or chiefship, organized tribute and royal drums (ibid.: 156). The Luo-speaking Palwo, who had been among the earliest Luo migrants to Bunyoro, had women leaders. This is evidenced in the story of the woman Nyawir, to whom the Bacwezi rulers of northern Bunyoro gave royal regalia as symbols of her authority in the Bacwezi system and taught her how to organize her territory and collect tribute (ibid.: 160). By and large, however, after the formation of kingdoms, kingship was passed down from the king (*rwot*) to his eldest son. In a few areas like Puranga, women were permitted to assume the position of *rwot*, notably Ica Auru and Aroko in the mid-1800s, and Akongo, when the son was too young to rule at the time of the king's death (ibid.: 447, 580–1; Onyango-ku-Odongo and Webster, 1976, 150).

Women's Associations under Colonial Rule

The earliest women's voluntary associations were started by Christian missionaries and the wives of colonial administrators and businessmen soon after Uganda became a British Protectorate in 1894. The education of girls went hand in hand with the growth of these associations, giving women the necessary skills to lead voluntary organizations that were affiliated with national and international bodies. The first girls' school, Namirembe Girls School, was started in 1898 by a British woman missionary. Gayaza Girls Boarding school was started on 18 January 1905, by the Women Missionaries Conference of the Church Missionary Society. By 1930 there were boarding schools for girls in Gayaza, Toro, Ankole, Busoga and Kigezi, in addition to two large central schools (Bird, 1930, 113). The education of women meant that they could also become active in the leadership of the Anglican church and by the 1930s women were sitting with men on Church Councils and were being elected to Diocesan Educational Boards, and to the Church Synod and various other bodies (Allen, 1930: 115).

The earliest national women's association was the Protestant Mothers' Union, founded in 1906 in Budo by British missionary wives. In 1908 it was opened up to Ugandan women, who were mainly wives of male students at King's College, Budo. Eventually the Mothers' Union came to have chapters in dioceses throughout the country and relied mostly on Africans for leadership (Bell, 1960: 339). Its initial objectives included promoting Christian principles of marriage, upbringing of children and Christian living.[2] The Catholic counterpart of the Mothers' Union, the Catholic Women's Clubs of Uganda, was established as a national organization in 1959 to co-ordinate the many individual women's clubs which had come into existence since 1952.

Other secular organizations were formed in this period as well. The Girl Guides were started in 1921 by Foster Smith of the Church Missionary Society. By 1945 there were 800 Brownies, Guides, Rangers and Cadets of all races in Uganda (Jenkins, 1945: 55). In the 1930s and 1940s the Uganda Women's League was active in establishing nursery schools, educating nursery school teachers and building maternity wings in hospitals. It was later absorbed into the Red Cross, but in 1946 it became the basis for the formation of the Uganda Council of Women.[3] The Uganda Women's Emergency Organization was formed in response to the outbreak of war in September 1939. It provided food for soldiers, ambulance drivers, first aid, secretarial services, clothing and supplies that were sent to armies serving in Africa.[4]

The big growth in voluntary women's associations came in the late 1940s and the early 1950s. In 1946 the Ministry for Social Development started working with women to help establish community clubs. These began in Buganda and Busoga and gradually spread throughout the country. The initiators worked first with co-operative county (saza) chiefs before launching the clubs. They were influenced by the rural Women's Institutes started in Britain in 1919 but their structure was actually taken from the American 4-H clubs, with a committee made up of a President, Treasurer and Secretary, who were elected annually. This model for organizing local women's groups has remained intact to this day. Each member would pay a subscription fee on a regular basis. The main resistance to the clubs came from husbands who were reluctant to let their wives participate. In the clubs, women learned sewing, knitting, repairing clothes, child welfare, nutrition, housekeeping, and cooking. They also sang, danced and played games.

The women took all the initiative in starting and maintaining the clubs, electing their own officials, keeping their own books, and fixing the subscription (Senkatuka, 1948). The clubs were started only where women asked for help in getting them off the ground.[5] However, even those clubs that sought help from the Community Development Officer were independent. They primarily sought help to purchase supplies and equipment, to obtain assistance in running the club, and to gain access to lectures and demonstrations on various subjects through the Welfare and Community Development Department (Senkatuka, 1955: 45). The clubs had as their motto: "Women's Clubs for Good Homes, We Learn to be Good Wives, Good Mothers and Good Citizens" (Hastie, 1962). Behind this motto was the idea that women would have to be prepared as citizens and learn new skills to respond to the challenges of this new period in Uganda's history just as men's roles were also changing (Akello, 1982: 10).

Women's organizations sprang up to meet other new challenges. The Young Women's Christian Association came into existence in 1952. It was started as an attempt to deal with a new problem of primary school-leavers that cropped up in the 1940s after the introduction of a new education system. Girls aged 13–15 began moving into urban centers looking for jobs. Various women's organizations responded to the situation and helped start the YWCA and launched a hostel in Kampala to accommodate working girls at a reasonable cost.[6] Member of the Legislative Council Barbara Saben successfully lobbied the Council for funds for the hostel. The YWCA was also active in promoting leadership courses, pressing for reforms in marriage and divorce laws, lobbying for the rights of women, carrying out citizenship education, and conducting projects in health, education, agriculture, and cookery.

The goals of the women members were often very different from the stated goals of the association in which they participated. For example, even though religious organizations put a lot of emphasis on care of the family and on becoming better wives and mothers, women themselves often saw their involvement in the clubs as a way of connecting to broader developments in the country. This sentiment persisted into the post-colonial period. For example, in the 1970s in Kigezi, an area where women's clubs were almost entirely religious (Catholic or Protestant), the main reason given in a survey for joining a club was to get involved in the country's development (32 percent) and to get rid of ignorance (32 percent), while only 5 percent mentioned learning ways of caring for the family (Bagyendera, 1977: 56).

Similarly, these early organizations served the purpose of giving women leadership skills, which became critical in expanding their participation in the public sphere. For example, Yemina Kabogozza Musoke, one of the pioneer members of the Mothers' Union, the Uganda Council of Women and the YWCA, explained in an interview that her involvement in these organizations benefited her personally by giving her an awareness of the broader concerns of women in society and the relationship between women's problems in the home and in society. She recalled how women in Gulu used to come to her and tell her their experiences:

> They were oppressed . . . they had a lot of work . . . digging with babies on their backs, going to the well, doing all the jobs without the help of a man. They told us they had to grind millet on stones. So when they reported this to us, we made a report to the Agricultural Department. Then they started thinking of importing grinding mills into the country to grind maize and millet and to alleviate the burden of women. Later on other labor-saving devices were brought in.[7]

Musoke also learned how to speak in public through her involvement in these organizations. She gained confidence by travelling to conferences internationally and within Uganda and found that she had learned to defend herself when challenged. Nakanyike Musisi has argued that the missionary education of women had a dual and contradictory function. It was aimed at helping women better fulfill their functions as wives, mothers and guardians of the household; at the same time it introduced women to new careers and earning power. In the process, many women developed a consciousness of themselves that went far beyond the expectations created by the educational system (1992: 186). Much the same argument could be made about these early women's clubs and organizations, which had both limiting and empowering dimensions. These organizations, even the religious ones, played a critical role in giving women the necessary skills for political action on issues that were of concern to women. It is probably no exaggeration to state that all women politicians today gained experience that was critical to their involvement in politics through organizations like the Mothers' Union, the Uganda Council of Women, the YWCA, and the Forward Society. In fact, one of the first major political actions by Ugandan women involved a group that formed out of the Mothers' Union to mount an anti-colonial protest surrounding the deportation of the *kabaka* in 1953.

Protesting at the Deportation of the Kabaka

One of the characteristics of the current movement is the embeddedness and at the same time the fluidity of associations, i.e., the capacity to transform an organization with one set of goals into a very different kind of organization, sometimes with a political purpose in mind. A dramatic case in point was the way in which women mobilized to protest the British Governor's deportation of Kabaka Mutesa II in 1953. The *kabaka's* popularity was waning and he was widely perceived as a frivolous playboy. When the British Government announced that it might form an East African Federation, the *kabaka* seized on this issue, demanding assurances that such a federation would not be created and insisting on a timetable for Buganda's independence. The British rejected these demands but the *kabaka* persisted. When the British failed to get him to sign a document stipulating that Buganda would remain a province of Uganda, he was deposed and deported to Britain. The deportation was opposed not only by the Baganda, but also by the western kingdoms, Busoga, Lango, Acholi and other parts of the protectorate (Mutibwa, 1992: 14).

The governor, Sir Andrew Cohen, saw himself as initiating a process of independence and regarded the kingdom of Buganda as an obstacle in the way of creating a unified nation-state. He erroneously believed that by eliminating the *kabaka* he was undermining conservative monarchism and paving the way for a more progressive nationalism. He seriously misread the situation and was unaware of how deeply not only the Baganda but also the non-monarchist nationalists and people in other parts of the country would resent the deportation. Their belief was that Cohen was turning the country over to white settler rule (Wrigley, 1988, 30).

After the deportation of the *kabaka*, women leaders worked within the Mothers' Union to form an alliance of subgroups called *Banakazadde Begwanga* (Mothers of the Nation) within various Mothers' Union chapters. One of the leaders of the protest, Sara Mukasa, was the President of the national Mothers' Union and also the wife of the well-known Muganda chief, Ham Mukasa. The women leaders had travelled to different parts of Buganda and Uganda to rally support for the *kabaka*. They organized three busloads of women who went to the Governor's mansion to air their grievances.[8] Most were Baganda but many belonged to other Ugandan groups. The governor had indicated that he wanted to speak with only five women (Deborah Kiwanuka, Mrs. Kayizi, Mrs. Nabigari, Rebecca Mulira and her mother, Sara Mukasa), but they refused to leave the three busloads behind and brought all the women with them.[9] The women wore sad faces and long sashed clothes of fig bark and left their hair uncombed as though they were in mourning. They were quiet and refused to sit on chairs, covered their faces with their hands, and refused to accept the tea that was offered them. In protest, they spoke only in Luganda, refusing to speak English, although many knew it very well.

They handed the Governor a memorandum reprimanding him for not consulting the mothers of the nation before deporting the *kabaka*. They argued that only the Baganda had the right to dethrone their king, and since Mutesa I had invited the British into Uganda, the Governor had no right to deport the *kabaka*. Moreover, Uganda was a British protectorate not a colony, they argued. "Therefore, Sir Andrew Cohen, you are wrong," Rebecca Mulira told the Governor. According to the Governor's secretary, the women made a "most effective plea" with which "Cohen could only express sympathy" (Griffith, 1952–4). Years later when Rebecca Mulira visited the former governor in England in 1967, he admitted that she had been right. Cohen reportedly told her that "From that day I respected you all the more because I saw that you behaved boldly as I never expected other leaders would."

Anglican Bishop Leslie Brown, who had been asked by the women to arrange the meeting with the governor and accompany them as an intermediary, later wrote that the Governor was for the first time made aware of the depth of feeling that the deportation had aroused among the Baganda. As a consequence of this protest and the enormous outpouring of opposition throughout Buganda, the Governor met with the *Lukiiko*, where he conceded that Uganda should become an African state and committed himself to revising the 1900 Agreement. A Commission led by Sir Keith Hancock made recommendations to revise the Agreement which were accepted by the *Lukiiko* and the *kabaka* returned from exile two years later on 17 October 1955 (Brown, 1981: 104–6).

The protest at the Governor's mansion was not an isolated event in women's resistance to colonial rule in this period. In another episode, Governor Cohen had gone to a party given by a nationalist, Ignatius K. Musazi, at which a troupe of dancing women chanted in Luganda, "Governor Hall [Cohen's predecessor] stole our cotton". Not understanding the song, the Governor and his wife joined in the applause much to the amusement of the Baganda attending the function (Griffith, 1952–4). The story was spread widely as part of the anti-colonial culture that had emerged.

These actions represented the beginning of women's involvement in modern-day Buganda politics. After 1955 when the king was returned, women were brought into all councils (*muluka, gombolola, saza*) up to the parliament level (*Lukiiko*).[10] Sala Ndagire of Kalisizo was the first woman to run for the *Lukiiko* in 1957 for Buddu, Masaka District.[11]

The Uganda Council of Women and Interest-Group Politics

The movement to promote women's rights began in earnest when the Uganda Council of Women (UCW) was started in 1946, emerging out of the Uganda Women's League.[12] It was formed by European and African women who wanted to

Table 2.1 Representation in Parliament

Year	Female	%	Male	%	Total
1962	2	2.2	88	97.8	90
1967	0	0.0	82	100.0	82
1980	1	0.7	142	99.3	143
1989	42	17.6	196	82.3	238
1996	52	19.0	224	81.0	276

Source: Cabinet Library

create an organization made up of women of all races, religious backgrounds, and political affiliations to take up issues of mutual concern (Brown, 1988: 20; White, 1973: 47). A decade later, in 1957 it had a membership of 2,000 with nine chapters throughout the country.[13] Africans, Asians and Europeans were all represented in its membership, along with women of many different religions and denominations, including Anglicans, Catholics, Sunni Muslims, Ismailis and Hindus. Its membership, however, tended to attract those who could speak English, giving it a reputation of being an elite organization because only educated women could participate. Most of its African membership was made up of women educated in schools in Buganda who were married and employed as teachers, community development workers, or in other social service agencies (White, 1973: 47). This, however, changed in 1965 when the UCW opened its membership to non-English-speaking women.[14] Already in 1962 the association had sought to reach illiterate, non-Christian rural women by forming links with the Community Development Women's Clubs, which were organized throughout the country under the Ministry for Community Development (ibid.: 63).

As independence neared, the UCW sought to prepare women to influence public opinion and government policies which affected women, the family and home.[15] Toward this end it promoted literacy, education, leadership skills and civic education for women, launching a Citizenship Education Committee in 1961 to encourage women to take part in community affairs. It spearheaded a voter education drive with the Uganda Association of University Women in 1961 and 1962 in preparation for the parliamentary elections. The Citizenship Education Committee ran leadership training courses for officers of the UCW throughout Uganda, and held workshops on the responsibilities of office-holders and on how to organize committees and membership and fund-raising drives, in addition to program organization and operation (White, 1973).

The UCW took on a variety of activities. It started a Women's Centre to house women travelling and attending conferences and professional meetings;[16] it trained nursery school teachers; it lobbied for the training of girls and women; it worked with women prisoners in Luzira and Mengo prisons and it held needlework and language classes (English for African and Asian women and Luganda for European women). The organization had successfully appealed to the government to build cheap houses at Naguru for low-income people. It initiated a School for the Deaf at Namirembe and helped start other women's organizations like the YWCA.[17] It also initiated a small women's magazine, *Nyabo,* got a women's page started in the *Uganda Argus* newspaper, and in 1956 ran a page in the Luganda-language weekly

Uganda Empya. It also initiated numerous legislative changes affecting the status of women.

The organization involved itself from time to time in local disputes. For example, Maliko Lwanga, *gombolola* chief of Omukulu we Kibuga, aroused the anger of women in Kibuga when he began arresting hundreds of women and charging them as prostitutes. To add insult to injury they were jailed and fined. The women appealed to the UCW to do something about Lwanga. A meeting of 150 women passed a resolution denouncing the chief and urging his removal from his post. A new organization, the Uganda Voice of Women, was formed out of the struggle, and a delegation of six women went to the prime minister (*katikiro*) of Buganda to present the resolution to him.[18]

Women were poorly represented in the Legislative Council, even though they showed a keen interest in voting. For example, in the Legislative Council elections in October 1958, there were more women than men at many polling stations in the northern, eastern and western provinces of Uganda and a heavy turnout of women at all stations.[19] The interest women showed in electoral politics spurred the UCW to promote female political representation. Indeed, many of the first women in the Legislative Council had been leaders in the UCW. Barbara Saben and Alice Boase were nominated as the first women representatives in the Legislative Council (Legco) in 1954 out of a total of 60 members; Saben was a founder member of UCW and Boase its president from 1953 to 1955. In 1956 Pulma Kisosonkole was nominated to the Legco as the first African woman representative, followed by Sarah Nyendwoha (Ntiro) in 1958. By independence, Florence Lubega, Frances Akello, Joyce Masembe (Mpanga), Miriam Mitha and W. H. L. Gordon had also served on the Legco. The appointments of these first African women representatives were the result of pressure from the UCW. Specifically it was the Uganda African Women's League that had written to the Governor asking that he appoint African women to the Legco.[20]

Pumla Kisosonkole, who was UCW President from 1957 to 1960, described the difficulties she faced in getting accustomed to this new role as a woman:

> When I was nominated in 1956, I accepted to sit in the Legislative Council, even if I did not have much to contribute. Later on I became strong and started pushing on issues for women. . . . At the very first sitting, I put up my hand quickly to respond to a discussion, lest I get frightened to talk after all the others had contributed (Kisubika, 1993: 72).

Sugra Visram, Florence Lubega and Eseza Makumbi (who had starred in an American movie *A Man of Two Worlds*) were elected to the *Lukiiko* in February 1962 in the pre-independence Buganda elections. After the general elections of April 1962, Visram and Lubega were nominated to the National Assembly as representatives of Buganda and Makumbi served on the East African Legislative Assembly until 1977. Once in parliament, the women focused on social issues like education, health, housing and women in business.

No women held seats in parliament from 1962 until the NRM came to power in 1986, apart from Visram and Lubega whom the Buganda *Lukiiko* delegation sent to the National Assembly in 1962, the brief presence of Rhoda Kalema and Geraldine Bitamazire in 1979–80 and Theresa Odongo-Oduka in 1980–85. Women fared no better in local and urban councils, in which women made up only 2 percent of all delegates (White 1973: 223). Uganda, however, did have the first African woman mayor on the continent: Janet Wesonga became mayor of Mbale in 1967.[21] The British Barbara Saben was the first woman mayor of Kampala in 1961/62.

Women entering politics in the 1960s confronted many of the same obstacles as they face today. In 1962 Democratic Party candidate Ansuya Pandya was attacked by her Uganda People's Congress-Kabaka Yekka opponent in the race for the Kampala Municipal Council. Her male opponent, Kara Teja, announced that "the lady should be entered in beauty competitions – and forget about elections". Pandya responded:

> This makes me angry. Mr. Teja has worked with me for two years on the Parent-Teacher Association of Arya Samaj Girls School. He knows my record of social service and that I am not just a fashion queen. . . . I have never appeared in any fashion parades or beauty competitions, and I don't want to be put on exhibition . . . . Mr. Teja is afraid that I might beat him and hurt his dignity.[22]

Women's organizations like the UCW challenged the parties for their lack of commitment to promoting women leaders. In 1962 they asked Prime Minister Milton Obote to include a woman in Uganda's United Nations delegation and in response he appointed Pumla Kisosonkole to the 1963 delegation. But, although Obote pledged to do more in the way of promoting women leaders, he did little to make good his promises. In 1964 he rejected the women's organizations' request for seats reserved for women in the National Assembly (White, 1973: 226) and instead told them to educate themselves so that they could become able politicians. Some women leaders asked Obote's Uganda People's Congress for support in speech writing, transportation and campaign tactics, because they felt women needed a boost in some of these areas. They were told by the UPC secretary-general that this aid would be discriminatory and would undermine their political competence as UPC candidates. Under the auspices of the Uganda Association of Women's Organizations, various women's organizations then decided to help 10 women candidates run their campaigns. However, the elections were not held because Obote's government was overthrown by Idi Amin in 1971.

Minimizing Difference

In interviewing women leaders of all races (Africans, Asians, and Europeans) about women's political activity and associations in the 1950s and 1960s, I was struck by how all of them mentioned that one of the biggest contributions of the women's movement at that time was to bring all the races together to work co-operatively. The organizations prided themselves on their attempts to minimize the importance of religion, race, ethnicity and political affiliation so that these would not stand in the way of their efforts to form a pressure group (White, 1973: 42). The process of integration was a gradual one. For example, the Red Cross, as far back as 1918, organized racially integrated activities between the Asian and British communities of women, but not with African women.[23] By the late 1930s the Red Cross involved all races. By the 1950s this kind of integration had become institutionalized and organizations made a point of including women of all races. The idea of inclusiveness is an enduring feature of the women's movement today (see Chapter 5), although it is being built along different lines because race is less salient, while ethnicity, religion and region have become more important differences.

The Uganda Council of Women was particularly active in these early years in providing leadership to facilitate dialogue, co-ordinate opinions, and express the common concerns of women's organizations (White, 1973: 43). It saw itself as a leader not only in Uganda but in Africa in its ability to build a multiracial organization.[24] From its inception, its goal had been to "bring women of all the different races in Uganda closer together so that they could get to know each other".[25] As Hemantini Bhatia, a UCW leader of Indian descent, explained to me:

> I remember I read a paper at a conference of the Uganda Association of Women's Organizations on behalf of the Uganda Council of Women. And I was very openly frank and happy to say that here we felt like one. We were like sisters – the Africans, the Asians, and the Europeans ... Pumla [Kisosonkole] was so happy. When I got down from the podium, she came up and embraced me, and she kissed me and said she was so happy to hear an Indian woman say that. I'm giving you this background just to show you that we were all so friendly. It was not only a political movement, we were very good friends. And that is why I think we lasted so long.

Other organizations also exhibited this same kind of bridging role. The Indian Women's Association, at its inception in 1939, was formed to bring together Indian women of all castes, creeds and religions. Modelled on the Mandali organizations in India at the time, its aim was to further the education of Indian women in Uganda. At the Association's foundation, some women spoke in Urdu, others in Gujarati, and others in English. One of the members explained that

> The purpose of their Mandali was to awaken sympathy and fellow-feeling amongst the women of all castes, creeds and races. They must learn to feel that there was no difference between poor and rich, between educated and uneducated, between Indian, European and African. That feeling of equality could not be developed unless they mixed freely and open-heartedly among the sisters of all their own communities. [26]

This emphasis on unity was extended to the organizations' posture toward political parties, which in this period were being built along religious lines. Although individual members could participate freely in party politics, the UCW itself veered away from aligning itself with a particular political ideology and party, fearing that this would cause unnecessary divisions within the organization, divert its members' attention from their goals, and compromise their autonomy. Instead, they focused on particular issues of mutual concern. Mary Tiberondwa told a meeting of the Ankole branch of UCW in Mbarara in 1964 that women in Ankole must stop working on the basis of political parties, and religious or tribal differences, arguing that they would not advance unless they put their differences aside and worked in a unified manner. In the same speech she condemned the way in which both the UPC and Democratic Party (DP) men had excluded women from running in elections in Ankole.[27]

Sugra Visram was a woman who in many ways embodied these attempts to build linkages between the various communities. Her involvement in women's associations was central to these efforts. She was a founding member of the UCW, the YWCA and the Family Planning Association, which were all multiracial organizations. She was also a member of the Uganda Muslim Women's Society and several other voluntary organizations. Born in Uganda in 1923 to an Ithnasheri family, in 1941 she married the grandson of a well-known East African businessman and Ismaili, Allidina Visram. Sugra was greatly influenced by Allidina, who was known as a philanthropist and a great believer in building a multiracial society, funding multiracial schools and taking other initiatives to further this goal throughout East Africa.

Sugra Visram was adopted by the Ganda Mamba clan and given the name Namubiru, which she accepted proudly in the knowledge that the Mamba clan is known to have strong willpower. She was a businesswoman when she entered politics in 1962 as a member of the Buganda nationalist party, Kabaka Yekka (KY).[28] She had a considerable Baganda following and was especially appreciated because she spoke Luganda fluently and often wore Kiganda clothes.[29] As she recollected thirty-five years later:

> I'll give credit to Ugandan people for one thing . . . when I was campaigning with Ugandan women, nobody ever said that I was an Asian. Everyone said "she is our Muganda woman. She is Ugandan and she is part and parcel of us." I was very proud of that.

Visram was elected to the *Lukiiko* of Buganda and, as already mentioned, was later nominated to represent Buganda in the Ugandan parliament.

When Visram helped found the YWCA she discovered that she could not sit on the Executive Committee because the organization had a policy of only allowing Christian members. Because she and other non-Christians had been such active leaders in the organization, the YWCA branch was given special permission from head office to allow Muslims and members of other religions to join the YWCA, which by then had a growing Hindu and Muslim membership. This was in part due to the efforts of an American leader of the Uganda YWCA, Susan Stille, who after some heated arguments amongst chapter members, convinced them that the "C" in YWCA embraced everyone.[30]

Visram socialized with YWCA and UCW members who were both African and European. "We used to go for Christmas dances," she explained. "And our family used to go with an African family. So I was the first Asian woman to dance with African men. And my husband would dance with African women. And that was scandalous because nobody did that. But we broke the ice."

All these gains in building multi-racial communities of women were reversed with Amin's expulsion of the Asian community in 1972. The European community had also diminished since independence in 1962, and dwindled further with the instability and insecurity that came with the Amin regime. Amin's expulsion of the Asians met with opposition from Asian women like Visram. Amin had summoned all Asians to be counted at Kololo airport in Kampala. Visram and her family were among them. Amin addressed the Asians who had assembled, accusing them of being thieves and of milking the country. Visram explained how she had boldly confronted Amin, whom she knew personally:

> I don't know what happened to me, I still can't believe it. I burst out and said, "Your Excellency, please can you go back to the radio and say that we are not exploiters. We are indigenous people . . . . This is our home." And I told him our forefathers had put sweat and blood into this country. And he looked at me. And everybody was so shocked that I had told him off.[31]

Reforming Marriage, Divorce, and Inheritance Laws

In the 1950s and 1960s, the women's organizations, often led by the UCW, launched numerous campaigns to press for the rights of women. They were particularly active in trying to reform the laws pertaining to marriage, divorce and inheritance. Prior to independence, two systems of law, customary and protectorate, operated simultaneously in Uganda, diverging significantly in the area of family law. Most Ugandans in practice abided by customary law, especially as it related to family matters. Customary law tended to condone polygamy and the use of bride price, and in many parts of the country widowed women were subject to losing their children and property to the husband's family; the husband's brother might even claim the widow as his wife.

In contrast, protectorate law was established in 1902, in part to bring uniformity to the legal system in Uganda, since each ethnic group had its own set of customary practices. The Marriage of Africans Ordinance of 1904 was a replica of British marriage law. It provided for the marriage and registration in a civil or Christian ceremony of a monogamous couple, both of whom were at least 21 years of age and had agreed by mutual consent to the contract, thus allowing African Christians to marry in a church ceremony without all the formalities required of British subjects. Another ordinance provided for the legalization of marriage between Muslims.

During the colonial period the Church was eager to see all Africans adopt monogamy, since it considered polygamy immoral (White, 1973: 163). Colonial administrators, while sharing the sentiments of the missionaries, were more reluctant to abolish customary law entirely. In the mid-1950s, Ugandan women began to raise concerns about their marriage, divorce and inheritance rights. A Namirembe Young Wives group within the Mothers' Union launched a grassroots movement in 1956 to reform family law. The group included such well-known figures as Pumla Kisosonkole, Rebecca Mulira, Rhoda Kalema and Eseza Makumbi in addition to Europeans like Barbara Saben, Catherine Hastie (who worked with Community Development), and Winifred Brown (the wife of the Anglican Bishop). The movement was sparked off by a situation in which a young Muganda woman had been widowed and left to care for her young children, deprived of her land, property and cows.[32] She came to Rebecca Mulira for assistance, and Mulira, who was chairing the Young Wives association, got her group to start studying the marriage laws and taking action. Another group, that came out of the Mothers' Union and was led by Sara Mukasa, formed a Widows' League in 1958 to protest against the treatment of widows by the clan heads who were depriving widows of their homes and property and subjecting them to insults, contempt and ridicule after their husbands had died (Brown, 1988: 18). The women involved in the struggle sent a memorandum to the *Lukiiko* attacking the inheritance laws.

The Baganda women were not the only ones protesting against marriage and inheritance customs. In 1956 a group of Acholi UCW women also sent the Governor a strongly worded memorandum attacking the practice of polygamy.

> We do not want to be treated like a goat whose master treats it as he likes . . . A man cannot support his family properly if he has many wives . . . Women in Acholi are treated like slaves who cannot complain even if they are being treated unkindly or cruelly (Brown, 1988: 7–9)

The grassroots movement to reform these family laws was led by African women, but European women provided sympathetic channels of communication and sources of encouragement. They helped to interpret the British marriage laws through various publications and helped translate the laws into local languages, according to Winifred Brown (1988; 2).

In 1953, the UCW resolved to pressure the government to make the registration of marriages obligatory, putting all types of marriages on an equal footing. It believed that registration would protect the rights of a woman as a monogamous wife. It was also hoped that this would end the view that customary marriages were inferior and would limit polygamy. The UCW urged district councils to pass bylaws requiring the registration of all customary marriages. As a result, in 1955 the District Administration Ordinance gave the district councils the right to pass by-laws regulating matters of marriage and divorce.

Having made some gains, the UCW set out to educate the public about the status of women in relation to marriage laws, publishing booklets and holding conferences to draw attention to these laws, in addition to questions of bride price, property and inheritance. In 1960 a national UCW conference decided that the issue of abolishing bride price was premature and required further public awareness. However, the conference passed a resolution on inheritance stipulating that the eldest son of the first wife should be the principal heir and that the widow and children should receive the main shares of a deceased man's property. A further resolution on marriage recommended that all marriages should be registered and that there should be one law for marriage, divorce and inheritance to replace all existing laws. It was resolved that a woman should be able to divorce her husband on grounds of cruelty and that a widow should not be compelled to marry a member of her deceased husband's clan (Brown, 1988: 30–31; White, 1973).

These resolutions were passed on to the Attorney General's office, which ignored them in spite of pressure from Barbara Saben and Sarah Ntiro in the Legislative Council. The Attorney General indicated that the time was not right for such legal revisions. Nevertheless, the UCW Committee on the Status of Women continued to put pressure on church leaders, district administrators, and other key policy-makers and opinion leaders.

In 1963 the newly independent government set up a Commission on Marriage, Divorce and the Status of Women led by Hon. W. W. Kalema, in direct response to pressure from the UCW (Kalema, 1965). The Commission traveled throughout the country soliciting views from individuals and organizations on the subject. The issue of marriage was raised in parliament soon after the Commission was appointed and provoked roars of laughter and heated debate, giving the impression that the legislators did not consider the matter a serious one. The main outcome of the Commission was a Succession Act, which was introduced to the National Assembly for debate in 1967 but was never passed. However, in 1972 Idi Amin issued Decree No. 22 as an amendment to the statutory Succession Act, which allowed for the wife and children to receive a large enough portion of the deceased husband's estate to be able to maintain themselves.

Hindu Women's Rights

Although little progress was made in the general area of family law, some gains were made in changing laws pertaining to Hindu marriage and divorce. In 1960 the UCW took up the issue of the legal status of Hindu women, having found that there was no legal recognition of customary Hindu marriage under protectorate law; this meant that the Ugandan courts could not hear cases affecting most Hindu marriage and divorce disputes. It was estimated that about 90 percent of Hindu marriages were not legally recognized under protectorate law. Yet there were numerous incidents of Hindu women being burned alive, being poisoned by their mothers-in-law, and suffering indignities that stemmed from their lack of legal rights. Hindu wives could not claim maintenance for themselves or their children if they were deserted by their husbands. Moreover, they could not claim any inheritance of property nor could they sue for divorce or claim custody of their children in the event of a divorce (White, 1973: 145–6).[33] As Hemantini Bhatia, one of the leaders of the UCW, put it:

> I was imported into this country [Uganda] when I got married in 1952. And when I came here, to my great shock the Asian women here, especially the Indian women, were not as free as they are in India. . . . There was no legal document to protect them. And the courts here said they had

no jurisdiction over the marriages. They were married in India and when they came here they had no protection whatsoever. So the men very conveniently could just drop them off like a piece of furniture and get someone else from another village in India. And these women were left with nothing and no help and the court could do nothing to help.[34]

The UCW Status of Asian Women Committee was chaired by Sarla Markandya, along with Hemantini Bhatia, Neela Korde, a lawyer, and Nalini Patel, who served as secretary to the Speaker of the Parliament. The Committee was set up to look into the legal status of women. It held meetings in the Hindu community, and sought to influence its key members, lobbied Legislative Council members, especially the women members, wrote letters to the newspapers and publicized the plight of Hindu women. In spite of initial resistance from some members of the Hindu community, including the Indian Women's Association, the Committee went ahead and drafted a Bill, which eventually received the unanimous support of all the Hindu communities representing the various Hindu sects. By March 1960, even the Indian Women's Association was trying to exert pressure on the community to support the new legislation.[35] The Hindu Marriage and Divorce Bill was brought before the Legislative Council in 1961 and was passed.

Even though the initiative was led by Hindu women, women of all races and religions in the UCW worked together to support this Bill. As Bhatia explained: "The best part of this was that it was not just us: the African ladies and the European ladies all backed us. It was such co-operation. There was no discrimination."[36]

Struggles over the Employment of Married Women

While for most rural women the dilemma of combining work and motherhood was not an issue because they had no choice, middle-class educated women felt that social attitudes barred them from seeking employment. Similarly, prior to independence, married women in the civil service could only be hired on a temporary basis, which meant they could not qualify for pensions, hospital benefits, insurance, terms of notice or housing benefits (White, 1973: 203). In Jinja, for example, in 1950 when women were first employed in large numbers, the local African District Council debated the matter for four days and finally voted 65 to 12 to abolish female employment, stating that "To employ women for such work is contrary to our customs. Women's work is to maintain land, housewifery and motherhood" (Elkan, 1956).

At a conference in 1960 the UCW agreed that women should be given the opportunity to combine a career with being a mother and therefore sought equal work contracts for both men and women. It submitted a memorandum to the Legislative Council demanding that women be given maternity leave and permanent contracts and that married women civil servants not be transferred to other parts of the country if this meant separating them from their husbands and family (White, 1973: 204). The matter was taken up by the Commission on Africanization and later by the Kalema Commission in 1964, which was also petitioned by many women's organizations on the matter.

Finally in March 1968 Obote announced new terms of service for female civil servants. The new law provided for qualified women, married or unmarried, to be able to apply for full-time permanent employment. Women would receive equal pay with men and were subject to the same conditions of service.[37] In addition, they were entitled to 120 days maternity leave and could extend the leave for a further 90 days on half pay.

Further agitation by the Uganda Association of Women's Organizations after the 1968 decree resulted in the Ministry of Public Service and Local Administration's

Establishment Notice No. 24, of 16 October 1972 (under Amin) allowing women civil servants to take maternity leave by the 38th week of pregnancy or before if their condition was such that they could not work. They could resume work 21 days after the birth. This meant that women would not have to take more than one month's maternity leave. Obote's compulsory 120 days maternity leave was especially hard on lower ranking civil servants who had only 14 days annual paid leave to cover their maternity leave (White, 1973: 210–11).

Women and The Right to Vote

Although women Legislative Council members like Barbara Saben argued strongly that women should have the right to vote and stand for election in all of Uganda's districts, in the first Legislative Council elections in 1956, women were denied this right. In 1961 the UCW and women in other voluntary associations met with Milton Obote and Benedicto Kiwanuka, who at the time were leaders of the majority and opposition parties, and urged them to extend the franchise to women. All parties agreed and the first Ugandan Constitution of 1962 granted women aged 21 the right to vote (White, 1973: 218).

Women's Mobilization Around Taxation

The issue of taxation of women was especially important in mobilizing women's interest groups nationwide in the 1960s. For example, when the Toro legislature (*Rukarato*) voted in 1961 to levy a Ush. 5 educational tax on men and wage-earning women, a Batoro women's organization issued a memorandum to the Batoro Prime Minister condemning the action. In their memorandum, they argued that the action was an insult to women and that if women were to pay taxes, "they should be treated equal to men as far as appointments go".[38] The women ended up having to pay the tax, but continued to threaten to refuse payment unless women were considered for positions in the district administration and given a voice in local politics (White, 1973: 138–9).

The issue was also raised in the Bunyoro legislature in 1960 and the Teso legislature in 1962, where the tax on women was rejected. Similarly, the Buganda legislature (*Lukiiko*) passed an amendment to the Buganda Graduated Tax Law in 1962 requiring all working women to pay income tax. One hundred Baganda women appealed to the *kabaka* to rescind the amendment and it was revised to require only unmarried women over 18 to pay a graduated income tax.[39] Still dissatisfied with the outcome, 300 women held a demonstration at the Clock Tower in Kampala, declaring that they would withdraw their support for the Buganda government on the grounds that making women pay tax was degrading to them and a violation of Baganda custom.

Women were by no means of the same mind on the issue of taxation, however, and the differences largely cut across class lines. Elite and educated women tended to favor the taxation of women on the grounds that if women were to be accepted as equal to men, they would need to act as full-fledged citizens and pay taxes like men. The UCW, for example, passed a resolution indicating that women should pay taxes as "a contribution to the development to full citizenship of their country by giving them the right to vote and stand for elections".[40] Women who did not pay taxes were not allowed to vote in legislative elections, sharply limiting the number of women eligible to vote.

However, those opposing the taxation of women were also arguing for equity along a different dimension. They maintained that waiving the women's tax would be a way of recognizing women's enormous contributions to social welfare. Care of children and the household was already a form of taxation women were paying, they argued. They pointed out that large numbers of women were responsible for paying for the education of their children with little if any assistance. At one point in 1967 when the Minister of Regional Administration suggested that the West Mengo District Council assess married women's earnings together with those of their husbands, the majority of council members felt that married women would not want their husbands to interfere with their money and that such a motion would lead to domestic disturbances.[41] This suggests that non-pooled household arrangements were commonplace in Buganda and that women were not eager to reveal their true earnings to their husbands for fear that the husbands could lay claim to their resources which were vital to the survival of the household.

In 1962 the central government had forbidden all but the Buganda *Lukiiko* to levy taxes on women, but by 1968 almost every district council in Uganda had successfully passed resolutions levying a graduated tax on all women over 18 years of age. The Regional Administrations had issued instructions to the local authorities requiring employers to assess a graduated tax payable by both men and women staff on their salaries and wages and to deduct it as payment to Local Authorities starting in 1969.[42]

The Struggle for Associational Autonomy

Although the UCW had received subventions from the Ministry of Community Development prior to independence, it began to show signs of concern after independence that the money coming from the Ministry meant that the government would have leverage over the organization. To assert its autonomy it refused to accept government funds for a literacy campaign that was sponsored by UNESCO.

The issue of associational autonomy, however, became increasingly important as the UCW and the newly independent government became polarized. Government officials attacked the organization for being too elitist and too dependent on foreign experts and funds as a way of discrediting it. In 1964 the UCW discussed whether all the national women's organizations should federate and create one body with the aim of co-ordinating their different goals throughout the country.[43] Most affiliated organizations thought that the UCW should restructure itself and take on the new role of co-ordinating women's organizations, but none thought it worth reconstituting the UCW as a new National Council of Women (White, 1973: 87). Nevertheless, quiet negotiations led to the decision to form a new organization called the Uganda Association of Women's Organizations (UAWO), which came into existence in February 1966 with the president's wife, Miria Obote, as its Honorary President.[45] As it turned out, the UAWO was to be the *de facto* mass women's organization of the UPC, which meant that its commitment to the UPC superseded its own goals. Its main aim, according to the Prime Minister, was to co-ordinate programs, exchange information, engage in joint action among member organizations and "most impor-tantly with Government".[45] All the key national organizations came to be affiliated with the UAWO.[46]

It is no accident that the UAWO was formed as Uganda became a one-party state in 1966, at a time when the UPC was attempting to bring all interest groups (stu-dents, trade unions, youth) under its influence. The UAWO became a quasi-wing of the UPC with its secretary, Mr E. Mambule Kigundu, serving as the executive of the National Council of Social Services, which is part of the Ministry of Community Affairs. The first UAWO officers were all UPC supporters or wives of UPC ministers and senior civil servants. For example, Mrs Kalule-Settala, the chair of the UAWO, was the wife of the Minister of Finance.[47] At this same time, the Ministry of Planning and Community Development began to make plans to federate all community development women's clubs in the country.[48]

Predictably, the UAWO's lack of autonomy meant that it dropped many of the lobbying efforts that had characterized the UCW's program. Women still visited cabinet ministers and wrote letters to public officials, but their requests were put on the back burner in favor of other issues that were considered more pressing. More-over, women had to demonstrate their allegiance to the UPC government in order to gain any recognition at all. Without its own popular backing, the UPC increas-ingly used organizations like the UAWO to draw on as a power base and held at bay any organizations that might challenge its dominance (White, 1973: 91–8).

This was markedly different from the UPC's relations with women's organiza-tions prior to independence. In fact, none of the political parties were particularly interested in the women's organizations at the time of independence. The leaders of the political parties had been invited to speak at the UCW's key 1961 Women Look Ahead Conference prior to the elections that had been organized to plan post-independence political strategies for women. However, neither the UPC nor the DP sent representatives nor did the women's wings of the parties participate, leaving the UCW with the distinct impression that the parties were not interested in women's participation or leadership. When the UCW later called on the three par-ties to negotiate with it, the UPC neglected to hand over its manifesto and seemed uninterested. Kabaka Yekka told the women it would work with them but not on an equal basis and that the women would have to operate behind the scenes. The Democratic Party, however, said that women could be involved in politics but that it would depend on their character. If a woman was fit to be in parliament she could run for election, but if she was only fit to lead at the *muluka* level, then this is where she would remain. After independence the DP issued a statement commending the UCW and other women's organizations for encouraging women to play an active role in politics (Brown, 1988: 36).[49]

The UPC's relations with women's organizations changed considerably after 1966, however, when Uganda became a one-party state. Women's organizations were not banned, but the instability, the suppression of party activists, and the ban-ning of large meetings created fears that made it difficult for organizations to thrive. It became harder for women's organizations to press their demands, especially under the UAWO rubric. They increasingly had to support the UPC to receive favors and their members had to perform the role of "social hostesses" at UPC func-tions (White, 1973: 239). By 1972 the UCW had disintegrated mostly because of the disruptive political situation at the time. The problems of autonomous association were to be compounded even further under Amin's regime.

Amin's National Council of Women

Obote's army chief of staff, Idi Amin Dada, staged a military coup on 25 January 1971, and overthrew Obote. The notorious Amin regime was marked by state-initiated violence against civilians, the massacres of Acholi and Langi soldiers, the expulsion of all Asians from the country in 1972, and economic disarray. Women experienced Amin's rule as particularly oppressive. One of his first measures in 1973 was to ban miniskirts, wigs, and trousers on the basis that they presented a threat to public morality and on grounds of anti-colonialism and anti-Westernism. The ban on trousers was later lifted when Amin realized that they were a style of clothing worn by women in Muslim countries. He also banned the use of creams, perfumes and deodorants. Amin's militia attacked women who allegedly violated these bans, on the pretext of maintaining law and order (Akello, 1982).

As part of his crusade to impose morality, Amin ordered the city streets to be cleared of unmarried women, all of whom were alleged to be prostitutes. As a result the streets became deserted and at times the only people around were policemen.[50] His military officers also mounted a crusade to force single Ugandan women to marry. As part of his morality campaign, Amin appointed Elizabeth Bagaya, Princess of Toro, as Foreign Minister, and later dismissed her, trying to humiliate her as an immoral woman. Bagaya was Uganda's first woman advocate, and was admitted to the bar in 1966.[51]

Amin encouraged his Muslim officers to rape Christian girls with the intention of impregnating them. Moreover, it was not uncommon for military personnel to organize collections of girls from the university, high schools, training centers and hospitals for the "entertainment" of Amin's men.

Amin declared that all independent women's organizations would gradually be abolished and, in a move reminiscent of UPC manipulations of the UAWO, announced the planned formation of one national body that would unite all women in Uganda. The United Nations, in preparing for the UN Decade of Women, had called on countries to set up national organizations to promote the development of women. Amin seized on this as a pretext for launching a national women's organization, which he said would have a department of religious affairs to take over the functions of the Mothers' Union and the Catholic Women's Guild.[52] In view of this threat, women from various groups, led by the Uganda Association of Women's Organizations, called on the government to leave the organizations alone. They asked for women to be placed in key government positions, and made numerous other demands to enhance women's political, economic and social status. The UAWO also protested at the harassment of women wearing mini dresses and the kidnappings.[53]

Women's organizations came together again in 1976 and under pressure from Amin decided, in a split vote, to start a parastatal organization that would have contacts with independent associations. Even though they had issued a statement resisting the abolition of these associations, Amin passed a decree in 1978 establishing the National Council of Women (NCW), at the same time banning all other women's organizations like the Mothers' Union and the YWCA. Article No. 4 of the decree states: "For avoidance of doubt, it is declared that with effect from the commencement of this decree, no women's organisation shall continue to exist, or be formed except in accordance with this decree." Thus some organizations became dormant in this period, while others like the Traditional Birth Attendants and the YWCA operated quietly underground. When Amin directly threatened YWCA leader Joyce Mungherera with execution if she did not close down her organization, she went into hiding and continued working underground. As a result of these kinds of efforts, the organization survived and by the 1990s had 1.5 million paid-up members and a staff of 1,000, making it one of the largest NGOs in Africa and the largest YWCA affiliate in the world.

Amin's 1978 ban was in direct contradiction of the NCW's constitution, which stipulated that women's associations should be affiliated to it. Yet when the chairperson of the NCW, Molly Okalebo, asked the Ministry of Justice for clarification on the decree, she was told not to register any member in the names of the former organizations since the Council was to advocate national unity and national consciousness.

Upon the formation of the NCW in September 1978, a 26-strong executive committee was elected that was accountable not to the constituency of the organization, but to the Ministry of Community Affairs, which controlled its staff and budget. The NCW knew it could not exist without the independent women's organizations, but their leaders were afraid to join it. Caught between a rock and a hard place, some organizations sent delegates to NCW meetings to avoid being labelled as "saboteurs" and "imperialist stooges" (Tadria, 1987; NCW, n.d.: 2). Nevertheless, most women's organizations "deeply resented" the creation of the NCW and saw it as "having the potential to infringe on the freedom of association which had been enjoyed by women during the pre and post independence eras", according to a history of the organization written by the NCW during the NRM period (NCW, n.d.).

Amin used the constitution of the UCW as a guide for the NCW. He gave it a meager Ush. 15 million to get started, which gave rise to suspicions that it was nothing more than an organization established to spy on women's activities. Not surprisingly, women's organizations saw the NCW as a vehicle of suppression. In the rural areas community development workers and NCW supporters were commonly seen as coercive agents (Ankrah, 1987).

After the Tanzanian army ousted Amin in 1979, women leaders were quick to denounce the 1978 decree. Most of the NCW projects started under Amin were abandoned (NCW, n.d.: 5). The NCW chairperson, Molly Okalebo, announced in November 1979 that parts of the decree would be repealed; she condemned Amin's move to abolish independent organizations and ban external grants to voluntary organizations. The same call was made by the NCW executive committee in 1981.[54]

After the overthrow of Amin, members of the NCW were not sure whether the new government would recognize the council and feared that they might be victimized because of their association with the organization. Some of the NCW leaders were forced to flee the country and others had to keep a low profile (NCW, n.d.: 5). As Florence Nekyon, long-time NCW secretary general, put it:

> In any given regime there are always a group of women who come to represent Ugandan women: Those who are close to the government . . . If you want anything to be done you have to pass through this group of women – women who are close to power.[55]

After 1979, the NCW attempted to reconstitute itself to help women of the formerly banned organizations and provide a forum where representatives of women's organizations could make contacts and exchange information.[56] Foreign funds began to come in as the UN Voluntary Fund for Women (later renamed UNIFEM) donated money in 1981 for a poultry farm and France sent funds for a day care center.[57]

But the NCW's independence was shortlived. Under Obote's second government, the UPC soon attempted to turn the NCW into a party organ, although it never entirely succeeded. Nevertheless, this interference created problems for the women who were still trying to work with the organization and wanted it to have a measure of autonomy (Guwatudde, 1987: 11). Meanwhile, the women's wing of the UPC was trying to dominate all women's organizations through the NCW. Not surprisingly, this meddling resulted in splits within the organization; its president belonged to the UPC and the secretary general's husband was a Democratic Party (DP) leader, which affected the functioning of the organization. The UPC controlled the new NCW delegation to both the 1980 UN Conference for women in Copenhagen and the 1985 Nairobi Conference. Rhoda Kalema, the deputy minister of Culture and Community Development, was supposed to lead the delegation to Copenhagen but she had a falling out with Vice-President Paulo Mwanga, who canceled her trip at the last minute. Similarly, women had started to raise funds to attend the Nairobi conference and the government stopped them and instead handpicked its own delegation. In fact, the UPC manipulations concerning the Nairobi conference became the catalyst that spurred the move for an independent women's movement at the time (see Chapter 4).[58] The realization was growing that it was not only the women's movement that was at stake, but the future of the country itself.

Despite such outside control, the NCW sought to establish a ministry for women during the Obote II regime. In part, this arose because it was felt that women did not have sufficient avenues to express their interests in government. The NCW felt hampered by bureaucratic stumbling-blocks. At the time there was only one woman in parliament and women leaders believed that having a women's ministry was critical in giving voice to women's demands in government.[59] But these plans did not materialize with the Obote II government and the NCW remained a semi-parastatal under the Ministry of Community Development.

The relationship between the NCW and the UPC was an uneasy one because many women within the organization were displeased with the UPC's interference. These tensions became evident at the first International Women's Day celebration to be held in Uganda on 8 March 1984. President Obote was under pressure from various other ministers not to attend the function. On learning this, some UPC women tried to persuade him to address the celebrations, which he did. In his speech he blasted the women as mothers of the rebels in the bush, i.e., Museveni's National Resistance Army, which at the time was mounting a guerrilla war against the Obote government. Nevertheless, the women asked Obote to establish 8 March as a national holiday. Rose Mbowa had composed a national women's anthem for the occasion which the women sang. Miria Obote, the president's wife, gave her own speech encouraging the women and the president was forced to make this small concession of establishing the national holiday.[60]

With Tito Okello's seizure of power in a coup in September 1985, the NCW organized over 2,000 women to demonstrate in the streets of Kampala for peace and against the mistreatment of women by the military (Ankrah, 1987: 15). During the Okello regime, insecurity was at its height in Kampala. Schoolgirls were being kidnapped in Luwero and taken to the military barracks; rape by the military was widespread. Kampala was divided into sections, with different areas under the control of different armies involved in factional fighting. The women's demonstration was significant because it was the only peace march organized in this period. But it was also important because NCW women were openly stating that they would no longer be the wing of a ruling party or regime. They had made a bid for autonomy by asserting their opposition to the regime. Their action laid the basis for the emergence of a truly autonomous women's movement after 1986, a movement which will be described in the following two chapters.

The committee of women's NGOs that had planned the peace march wrote to the Minister of Internal Affairs and the Minister of Defense in October 1985, complaining of the treatment of women at the road-blocks. They condemned the fact that many women were being forced into marriages in Luwero District and were being raped. The memorandum called for the elimination of road-blocks, medical treatment and compensation for the women who had been brutalized, punishment of the soldiers guilty of these crimes, and the issuing of identity cards for all (Ankrah, 1987: 14).[61]

The women's organizations held a peace seminar and invited the Minister of Foreign Affairs, Olara Otunu, and the commander of the army, General Basilio Okello, to address them. The General told the women that they deserved to be raped. He blamed the army thefts of handbags, watches, perfumes, shoes, and dresses on the women themselves, asking the women how the soldiers would get these commodities for their women if they did not steal them.[62]

A second memorandum was sent in December 1985 by the same NGO co-ordinating committee, which had also drafted the NCW country statement for the UN Decade for Women Conference in 1985 (Ankrah, 1987: 16). This memorandum was much more hard-hitting than the first and set out the political, social and economic causes that lay behind the conflict. It demanded that women be consulted on major national issues and be given key ministerial posts and positions, arguing that the inability of women to penetrate power structures and have a say on matters of war and peace stood in the way of peace. The Okello regime was toppled by the NRM before it was able to respond, but the memorandum was significant in that it was the precursor of efforts to launch independent women's rights organizations in the months that followed.

Conclusion

In order to appreciate the changes that occurred in the women's movement under the NRM, it has been necessary to retrace the evolution of women's mobilization in the pre- and post-independence periods. Although the changes will become apparent in the subsequent chapters, several continuities emerge from this brief history which persist under the NRM. The scope of the agendas and the level of activity by women's organizations were most extensive during periods of greater autonomy from the government. The movement was most constrained during the Amin period, when government meddling and co-optation were at their height. This persisted throughout the Obote II period. Although the indifference to women's concerns during Obote's first regime dampened possibilities for activism, the overt suppression under Amin was far more destructive. The other persistent theme that emerges from the pre-independence period is the way in which autonomy also afforded women the capacity to work along multi-racial, multi-ethnic and multi-religious lines. The political manipulations of the women's movement under Amin and Obote II lessened the possibilities for these kinds of alliances and fomented tensions among women where they had not previously existed. Those women leaders closest to the regime through personal ties with the country's leaders benefited the most from the patronage links. These developments clearly fit patterns that emerged in other African one-party states and dictatorships, as detailed in Chapter 1. The following chapters show how the expansion of autonomous activity by women's organizations challenged these constraining patterns of clientelistic politics and created a more inclusionary political culture within the organizations themselves.

Notes

1 Interview RK, Pumla Kisosonkole, 14 October 1992.
2 *UAWO Newsletter* July 1968.
3 Report on Women's Conference held on 11 October, 1946, Uganda Women's League.
4 "History of Uganda Women's Emergency Organisation", *Uganda Herald*, 26 March 1941, 6.
5 "African Women's Clubs", *Uganda Herald*, 8 April 1948.
6 By 1968 the YWCA had a membership of 5,000 throughout the country.
7 Interview RK, Yemina Kabogozza Musoke, Mbale, November 1992.
8 Interview RK, Deborah Kiwanuka, Bunamwaya, Mpigi, 5 November 1992.
9 Interviews with Rebecca Mulira, Kampala, 2, 5, 9, 11 July 1995.
10 Interview RK, Deborah Kiwanuka, 5 November 1992; Kisubika, 1993: 57–8.
11 "Woman Stands in Lukiko Election," *Uganda Argus*, 2 February 1957, p.2.
12 Report on Women's Conference held on 11 October, 1946, Uganda Women's League.
13 "Uganda Council of Women Looks Back on Ten Years," *Uganda Argus*, 14 November 1957, p.4.
14 "U.C.W. Talks Open Today: 150 Delegates are Expected," *Uganda Argus*, 23 November 1965.
15 Jane Bell "Education for Leadership," 1961 speech.
16 Report on Women's Conference held on 11 October, 1946, Uganda Women's League.
17 "Bringing Women of Uganda Together," *Uganda Argus*, 6 June 1956.
18 "Women of Kibuga Denounce Chief," *Uganda Argus*, 2 March 1957, p.5.
19 "Women Outnumber Men at Polls," *Uganda Argus*, 23 October 1958, p.3.
20 Interviews with Rebecca Mulira, Kampala, 2, 5, 9, 11 July 1995.
21 "Mbale Gets Woman Mayor," *Uganda Argus*, 19 October 1967, p.3.
22 "Mrs. Pandya 'she should stick to fashion' is Angry with Mr. Teja," *Uganda Argus*, 11 September 1962, p.3.
23 "Mrs. Coryndon Red Cross Fair at Jinja," *Uganda Herald*, 25 October 1918.
24 "Uganda Council of Women Meeting," *Uganda Herald*, 5 May 1949.
25 "Uganda Council of Women Looks Back on Ten Years," *Uganda Argus*, 14 November 1957, p.4.
26 "Indian Women's Association Enthusiastic Kampala Meeting: Ladies of All Castes Unite," *Uganda Herald*, 22 March 1939.
27 "Call for Unity: Don't Work on Basis of Political Parties . . . " *Uganda Argus*, 6 May 1964, p.3
28 Interview with Sugra Visram, London, January 1996.
29 Interviews with Rebecca Mulira, Kampala, 2, 5, 9, 11 July 1995.
30 Personal communication, Barbara Saben, 30 June 1999.
31 Interview with Sugra Visram, London, January 1996.
32 Interviews with Rebecca Mulira, Kampala, 2, 5, 9, 11 July 1995.
33 "Move to Improve the Status of Asian Women," *Uganda Argus*, 8 June 1960, p. 3.
34 Interview with Hemantini Bhatia, 5 July 1995.
35 "Meetings Support Welcomed by I.W.A.," *Uganda Argus*, 8 November 1960, p. 5.
36 Interview with Hemantini Bhatia, 5 July 1995.
37 "President to Stamp Out 'Corruption by Tribe': Equality for Women in Civil Service," *Uganda Argus*, 16 March 1968, p.1.
38 *Uganda Argus*, 1 March 1961, p. 5.
39 "Women Tax Row in Lukiko: Working Wives Must Pay, Too, Say Members," *Uganda Argus*, 12 November, 1962, p. 3.
40 Report of the UCW Conference on The Status of Women in Relation to Marriage Laws. Kampala, 1960.
41 "Tax Women -'and Drive Children to Theft' ", *Uganda Argus*, 30 December 1967, p. 6.
42 "Married Women and Graduated Tax," *Uganda Argus*, 9 December 1968, p. 6.
43 "Women Determined to Face Challenge: Association Inaugurated," *Uganda Argus*, 26 February 1966, p. 13.
44 "Stronger Voice for Women," *Uganda Argus* 26 February 1966, p.4.
45 "Women's Group is One Year Old," *Uganda Argus*, 31 March 1967, p. 13.

46 These organizations included the Uganda Catholic Women's Clubs, the Family Planning Association, the Mothers' Union, the Muslim Women's Society, the Uganda Association of University
   Women, the YWCA, the Women's Corona Society, the Uganda Council of Women and the
   Uganda Women's Muslim Organisation. "Women's Groups Decide to Co-ordinate their Work,"
   Uganda Argus, 26 April 1965, p. 5.
47 "Pioneering Women's Group Opens Eyes of People – Mrs. Obote," *Uganda Argus,* 20 January
   1968, p.3.
48 "Federation Plan," *Uganda Argus,* 9 February 1966, p.3.
49 Interview RK, Yemina Kabogozza Musoke, Mbale, November 1992.
50 "Varying Views on Girls of the Night," *Uganda Argus,* 29 April 1972, p.13.
51 "Uganda's First Woman Advocate Received at the Bar," *Uganda Argus,* 18 October 1966, p. 5.
52 Rebecca Katumba, "Uganda's Women Resolve to Unite," *Uganda Argus,* 30 November 1972, p. 1.
53 "Play an Effective Role, Women Told," *Uganda Argus,* 23 November 1972.
54 Eva Lubwama, "Women's Call," *Uganda Times,* 23 January 1981, p.3.
55 Interview RK, Florence Nekyon, Kampala, December 1992.
56 Rebecca Katumba, "Woman Leader Answers Critics," *Uganda Times,* 2 August 1979.
57 Rebecca Katumba, "Let us Attempt to Integrate the Women in our Development Efforts," *Uganda
   Times,* 11 April 1981, p.15.
58 Interview Florence Nekyon, Kampala, 21 May 1993 and RK December 1992.
59 Interview RK, Florence Nekyon, Kampala, December 1992.
60 ibid.
61 ibid.
62 ibid.

3

The National
Resistance
Movement

Closing Political Space

The use of the colonial and archaic law of sedition to promote the views and opinions of the ruling class, groups or cliques and to suppress alternative or opposing views . . . must be opposed by all reasonable democratic and freedom-loving Ugandans.

The Free Movement's (civic organisation) response
to the 1998 arrest of leading journalists[1]

Consolidating Power at the Center

Yoweri Museveni has been hailed by the foreign press, diplomats and even by some academics as a new style African leader to be emulated in his almost single-minded pursuit of economic development, fiscal discipline and the free market (Berkeley, 1994; Caplan, 1997; McKinley, 1998). Donors were pleased with the success of restructuring the civil service, the retrenchment of large sections of the armed forces, the privatization of parastatal companies, the return of confiscated properties to Asians who had been ousted under Idi Amin in 1972, the country's decentralization policies, and many other economic reforms introduced by Museveni.

There is no question that Museveni has initiated many positive institution-building endeavors and in this regard he stands apart from the majority of Africa's contemporary leaders. But on balance, the pattern of personalized rule and ethnically based clientelistic politics is clear and has become increasingly the norm under the National Resistance Movement (NRM) since it took power in January 1986. Museveni's policies have tended to fit the neo-patrimonial mold that has been so characteristic of authoritarian, semi-authoritarian and more recently even of democratic regimes in Africa.

Right from the outset, Museveni's takeover was strikingly different from that of previous governments. When the National Resistance Army (NRA) marched into Kampala, the foreign press noted that residents were surprised to discover that there was none of the looting which they had always remembered from past takeovers (Gargan, 1986). Museveni had built a disciplined army operating under a harsh Code of Conduct that permitted summary trials and executions of soldiers who violated it. In spite of criticism from international human rights organizations, the NRM argued that such measures were necessary to limit human rights violations against civilians (Mutibwa, 1992: 188).

Two months after taking power, the NRA, which consisted of about 20,000 fighters, had succeeded in bringing most of the country under its control. Originally known as Ugandan Freedom Fighters, the NRA had been formed in 1980, taking to the bush after the Uganda People's Congress party won the elections, which were widely perceived as having been rigged. It then launched a guerrilla war against the government of Milton Obote. In this period it was largely made up of Baganda, Banyankole, Bakiga and Banyoro troops. Initially in 1981 the fighting had been confined to the Luwero triangle north of Kampala, but by 1983 it had spread north and northwest of the capital, covering roughly 4,000 square miles of territory mainly situated in Buganda's Luwero, Mpigi, Mubende, and Mukono districts. By 1984 the NRA numbered over 6,000 soldiers and was active as far as the Ruwenzori Mountains.

When Yoweri Museveni and his political movement, the NRM, came to power, Uganda was in disarray. Museveni faced two major challenges: one was to try to rebuild the institutions of governance and the second was to build unity in a country that was severely divided. Uganda's institutions and infrastructure were badly damaged after years of conflict and instability. Under Idi Amin, according to Brett, the "regime became little more than a criminal conspiracy against the public, and the institutional apparatus was turned from a mechanism for delivering services into one for extracting surpluses from an almost helpless population" (Brett, 1994: 57).

Political spaces opened up after the NRM takeover, in part due to the fact that the NRM had yet to consolidate its hold over the country. But as it created and solidified its control over various institutions, it also began to tighten its grip on those political spaces. What was billed as a "no-party system" increasingly began to resemble the classic one-party African state, although with some important differences. Uganda's brief and disastrous experience with multi-party rule under Milton Obote remained fresh in people's minds. This experience contrasted sharply with the relative stability in most of the country since the NRM came to power. The new peace, combined with Uganda's rapid economic growth, initially won Museveni and his movement considerable popular support and many were willing to overlook the persistent constraints on democratization. The NRM's political platform was expressed in a Ten-Point Program, which was to form the basis of a nationwide coalition of political and social forces. It called for the restoration of democracy, security and social services; the elimination of all forms of sectarianism along ethnic and religious lines; the consolidation of national independence; the creation of a self-sustaining mixed economy; the elimination of corruption; redressing the errors that resulted in population dislocations; and co-operation with other African countries (Museveni, 1992: 278–82).

At the outset, the NRM was able to gain support by posing as a nationwide movement that encompassed a wide array of interests, all of which had their own reasons for opposing the second regime of Milton Obote. Museveni's base had initially been in Buganda and the western parts of the country, but he badly needed to claim legitimacy throughout the country. Thus, while the NRM had the backing of the southerners and westerners, northerners were apprehensive about the takeover and feared that the NRM would exact revenge on them.

Rebel Insurgency in the North

It was not long after the NRM came to power that the country was faced with rebel insurgency in the North and East. The NRM also confronted opposition from the well-established Democratic Party (DP) and Uganda People's Congress (UPC). To pacify the opposition, the movement incorporated leaders of various political interests, including guerrilla factions that Museveni had been fighting only a few months earlier. An amnesty was extended to all combatants, police, and personnel in prison and state security agencies who might be liable to prosecution. Former rebel groups were incorporated into the NRA, including the Uganda National Rescue Front (UNFRF), whose leaders had been associated with the government of Idi Amin. The Cabinet included leaders of the Democratic Party, the small Conservative Party, and the Uganda Patriotic Movement (UPM), which Museveni had led in 1980.

The NRM sought to appease a wide range of groups by giving them representation within the movement. Museveni courted the Baganda and, in particular, the pro-monarchy Ganda, the Protestant clergy, large sections of the Catholic establishment who were frustrated with the Democratic Party, members of the UPM, his own supporters who had backed him along ethnic lines, former Amin supporters from the West Nile, and some leftists from the eastern part of the country (Onyango-Obbo, 1997). Excluded from this initial coalition were members of the Okello government, the Uganda National Liberation Army (UNLA), and the UPC, although eventually the UPC came to be represented in the government.

Guerrilla activity persisted in Gulu and Kitgum and more generally in the North and East of the country. Initially the fighting was between the government's National Resistance Army and rebels of the Uganda People's Army (UPA), the United Democratic Christian Movement and the UNLA (Ofkansky, 1996: 64). In this early period, Alice Lakwena led the armed Holy Spirit millenarian movement, which was crushed in 1987 after which she fled to Kenya. The NRM signed a peace accord with a major faction of the Uganda Democratic Peoples Army (UDPA, previously UNLA) in 1988 and another 3,000 UPA fighters also accepted an amnesty the same year. Many UPA and UDPA personnel were integrated into the NRA ranks (ibid.: 63). In February 1990 the NRA placed 200,000 civilians in guarded camps in eastern and western Uganda to isolate them from the remaining guerrillas; this resulted in a high number of deaths due to lack of food, water, shelter and medical care. Thus, the NRM strategy was to offer peace agreements and unconditional amnesties on the one hand, while, in other instances, the NRA stepped up military operations. In this period, Betty Bigombe, who was Minister of State for the Pacification of the North, was instrumental in getting the rebels to participate in peace talks and lay down their arms. The NRM also launched a multi-sectoral Northern Uganda Reconstruction Program to build up the infrastructure and economy of the region.

Armed resistance, persisted, however, as new rebel groups emerged. Although the Museveni regime has talked about suppressing the remnants of rebel armies, it has continued to fight fierce battles in the late 1990s with the Sudanese-backed Lord's Resistance Army led by Joseph Kony (Alice Lakwena's cousin) which has inflicted systematic violence on people in the North since 1989. The situation has become a humanitarian crisis with hundreds of thousands of civilians internally displaced, while famine, illness and insecurity have plagued the northern population. In the North-west, the NRA has had to contend with the West Nile Bank Front, which, funded by Sudan, has for many years had bases in Congo, and was led by a former member of Idi Amin's cabinet. In addition, the NRA has been battling against several bands of fighters called the Allied Democratic Forces (ADF) located in the Ruwenzori Mountains. The ADF is an odd mixture of ex-soldiers of the

Mobutu regime and the defeated Rwandan regime, the National Army for the Liberation of Uganda, and Muslim fundamentalists known as the Salaaf Tabliqs.

No-Party Politics

Instead of constructing alliances based on political and programmatic interests, Museveni built up support through patronage (Mamdani, 1994). All interests were artificially subsumed under the no-party NRM "movement". The NRM tried to distinguish itself from other political parties on the grounds that it represented "non-sectarian" interests and eschewed the politicization of ethnicity, religion and region along party lines. The major communal cleavages in Uganda have historically fallen along several lines, many of which were sources of the civil strife in the country until the NRM takeover (see Chapter 6).

However, each successive government – from Obote I through Amin, Obote II, Okello up to Museveni – manipulated ethnicity and religion in its bid to remain in power. Despite its non-sectarian rhetoric, even the NRM has played the ethnic card. Clientelistically based appointments began to go increasingly to a narrower group of loyalists. By 1995 it was clear that the NRM had tightened its grip in a way that left little room for meaningful power-sharing. The crucial debate over the future of multi-partyism in the Constituent Assembly was resolved in July 1995 after four days of deliberations and a walk-out by the multi-party forces. The NRM prevailed with 199 votes in favor of continued no-party rule, with 68 opposed and 2 abstentions.

As power became more concentrated within the NRM, many of its old allies fell out of favor or became highly disillusioned with the movement. The Catholics' allegiances were divided during the 1996 presidential race between Museveni and his Democratic Party opponent, Paul Ssemogerere. By the mid-1990s, the Buganda-NRM relationship had fallen into disarray as the government sought to play sections of the royalty off against one another, while keeping King Ronald Mutebi's role circumscribed to an apolitical one. Should he venture too far beyond his role as a cultural symbol of Buganda, he risks losing various privileges and sources of funds made available by the government. The debate over the Land Bill in 1998 revealed the depth of Baganda disillusionment with the regime. By the late 1990s, however, there was the growing perception on the part of non-westerners (i.e., those citizens who do not come from the west of Uganda) that Museveni favored his own people from the west when it came to government appointments (Onyango-Obbo 1997).

The "no-party system" not only circumscribed the activity of the opposition parties, it also gave the NRM a rationale not to institutionalize itself as a political party since it was to be a movement representing the entire population. This left key elements of political control highly centralized in the NRM. Moreover, these centralizing tendencies became stronger with the 1995 debate over the Constitution, which marked a watershed in the consolidation of power within the NRM. As a result, there has been little impetus to democratize the NRM internally and power has remained concentrated at the top. The NRM has never held elections for any of its leaders, nor has it convened any popularly elected body to vote on policies (Kasfir, 1998: 61).

By the end of 1998, the lack of democracy within the NRM had clearly taken its toll. A number of serious corruption scandals had been uncovered, many of which involved the president's close associates and relatives, including a brother and brother-in-law. Even the NRM caucus in the parliament was now openly critical of the President, following the lead of the government newspaper, *New Vision,* and the independent *Monitor,* which broke several of the corruption stories and carried critical coverage and editorials.

As one member of parliament, Winnie Byanyima, put it in a 15 December 1998 interview with *New Vision:*

> The fact that the people implicated are members of his family is dangerous for him because, however much he denies, if he does not take action, it is seen that it is because he has something to do with it . . . . The President receives this report and says, "I don't act on allegations, I am investigating, my brother was stupid but he was well intentioned." How can he expect us to continue believing his cleanliness. He had better take an action for the sake of this Movement. I will continue to vouch for the President as an honest and transparent leader if he will distance himself and take action on the corrupt. I would like him to side with Parliament.[2]

Byanyima has been at the forefront of exposing several key corruption scandals involving top government representatives. However, these particular remarks were echoed a week later by many NRM members of parliament after a stormy meeting between Museveni and the caucus. Byanyima's outspoken anti-corruption stance won her two national honors in 1997: Parliamentarian and Woman of the Year (Tamale, 1999: 180).

In 1999 the NRM brought the Referendum Bill to parliament at the eleventh hour with little time for debate on a decision that paved the way for the 2000 referendum on whether Uganda would have a movement, multi-party or some other kind of democratic system. The Bill was steamrolled through parliament and Museveni signed it even though the required 90 member quorum was not reached (only 50 members of parliament voted on the bill). The overwhelming lack of support for the referendum, which the NRM is expected to win, is indicative of major divisions within the NRM itself and growing disillusionment with the country's top leadership.

NGOs, the media, and other sectors of society have operated relatively freely, but always under the shadow of efforts to control their activities through legislative mechanisms. Not unlike other semi-authoritarian and authoritarian regimes in Africa, the government systematically sought to create laws that would circumscribe civil society and ensure NRM control of its activities. It claimed for itself extensive powers with which to regulate NGOs, women's organizations, youth organizations, political parties and the media. When taken together, the policies begin to reveal a pattern of control typical of post-independence one-party states. It is worth examining in some detail how the efforts to dominate women's mobilization (see Chapter 4) fit a broader pattern of tightening NRM control. The creation of Women's Councils in 1993 had the intended goal of bringing all women's associations under the watchful eye of the Movement and undercutting the autonomy of grassroots women's organizations. These same patterns of incorporation are also evident in other sectors.

The NRM and the Media

Some of the fiercest resistance to NRM domination has come from the media. In January 1986, Museveni assured journalists of press freedom. Overnight, the streets were inundated with competing newspapers eager to feed a population starved of alternative points of view and genuine news coverage. Certainly there has been considerable liberalization of the press since the time of Amin, when "the price for fearless investigative reporting was a trip to the Nile in the boot of a car," according to *Africa Now* magazine (Mutono, 1994). The situation was not much better under Obote II, when, in 1984, eight journalists were arrested and spent 19 days in Makindye Barracks where they were tortured and forced to watch mass murders.

Museveni's policy of tolerating a relatively free press was a break with such practices. But it was not long before the government became concerned about the Pandora's box that it had opened and questioned the utility of such unmitigated freedom. Editors were soon imprisoned on treason charges and some publications were banned. Individual journalists came under repression. One incident that gained international attention was the arrest of two journalists who the government thought had overstepped their bounds in questioning Zambia's President Kaunda at a news conference in 1990. In the 1990s, editors of the *Monitor, Citizen, Uganda Confidential, The Shariat,* and *Weekend Digest, Sunday Review, Patriot,* and *Crusader* faced detentions, harassment, censorship and were taken to court by the government for various stories they published (Bakunzi, 1995a; Kiggundu, 1994; Kiragga, 1993; Gureme, 1994; Mutono, 1994; Mutumba, 1995; Oguttu, 1992; Wasike, 1994a, 1995a). The editor of *The Crusader* newspaper, George Lugalambi, was arrested in November 1998 along with his reporter and *New Vision's* Mbarara bureau chief, James Mujuni. They were charged with sedition for publishing articles criticizing Museveni and the NRM.

At one point, a ban was placed on government advertising in the most widely read non-government newspaper, *The Monitor* (Asedri, 1993). One consequence of this kind of harassment was the closing down of newspapers: in the late 1980s there were roughly thirty English language papers and magazines; by the late 1990s there were only two major English daily newspapers.

The fact that the government's own paper has published some of the most critical articles pertaining to press freedom speaks volumes about the intensity of resistance to government control of the media. The government introduced a Media and Press Bill in 1991 and again in 1993 to try to control the media, but the bill was shelved when journalists mobilized against it (Kawamara, 1993). It was rejected by both the Uganda Newspaper Editors and Proprietors Association and the Uganda Journalists Association (UJA), which submitted 36 amendments which were not considered, much to their disappointment (Wasike, 1994b). They objected to a number of provisions, including one that would have led to the suspension of a journalist in the event of a complaint simply being filed against him/her with a Media Council that the government would appoint.

The Press and Journalists Statute of 1995 likewise met with fierce opposition from journalists and parliamentarians alike. This Bill, which was eventually passed, gave the Ministry of Information powers to license journalists on an annual basis and to appoint members of a Media Council that would be formed to regulate and enforce the conduct of journalists through disciplinary measures. Opposition to this Bill came from all quarters, including the Law Reform Commission and the Uganda Human Rights Commission, on the grounds that it was unconstitutional. Even the deputy editor-in-chief of *New Vision* argued against it, saying that "At this point in our history we need less laws and more freedom for development" (Wasike, 1995b). Journalists continued to oppose the statute and the UJA president, Tamale Mirundi, was quoted in 1998 as saying that journalists should not give it wholesale support because it contained "draconian provisions which infringe on media freedom". He warned journalists not to apply for the practising licence as required by the statute because future dictatorial regimes might be able deny them such certificates or use such provisions to force them to toe the government line.[3]

NGOs under Scrutiny

Non-governmental organizations also faced similar efforts to monitor their activities. In 1989, a Non-Governmental Organizations Registration Statute was passed, requiring all NGOs to register with a National Board for Non-Governmental Organizations based in the Ministry of Internal Affairs. In addition to approving applications, the Board was to guide and monitor organizations in carrying out their activities and could revoke a certificate of registration if the organization failed to operate in accordance with its constitution and if such revocation was considered in the public interest. Many of the regulations were so excessive that they were impractical to enforce. For example, organizations were to apply in writing to the local councils and the District Administrator seven days in advance of their visit if they were to have contact with people in a rural area. Similarly, members of the organization were not officially allowed to benefit economically from its activities, even though most local-level self-help groups commonly include income generation as one component of their activities.

Needless to say, these regulations were not generally implemented but their existence has been indicative of the suspicion with which the government regards this sector. Moreover, the National Board for Non-Governmental Organizations is made up of members from nine Ministries and one member from the Office of the Prime Minister, the Internal Security Organisation (ISO) and the External Security Organisation (ESO). The ISO and ESO presence suggests a preoccupation with security, especially in view of the lack of threat generally posed by NGOs.

In practice, however, the NRM has been relatively accommodating to NGOs, with some important exceptions. The regime's practice stands in stark contrast to the experiences under previous regimes, which carried out repression against any real or imagined sources of organized opposition. However, much of the state's relaxed position suggests accommodation by default, i.e., state weakness and inability to enforce measures regulating NGOs. Government officials make numerous declarations about the need to co-ordinate and oversee NGO activities and their donor funding, but little such co-ordination has actually taken place. When national NGOs have complained about the government, it has been to suggest that government officials treat them as competitors attempting to supplant government functions, as agents of foreign domination, and as organizations with endless sources of donor funds and little to show for it (Kwesiga and Ratter, 1993: 23–4). Some of the major attempts to control NGO activities have involved Members of Parliament and District or Local Council leaders who sought to interfere primarily for reasons of personal or political gain, sometimes under the guise of government regulation.

Apart from problems of capacity, organizational problems also act as a hindrance to greater government supervision of NGO activities. The External Aid Co-ordination Department of the Ministry of Finance and Economic Planning is supposed to oversee NGOs which obtain external aid, but in practice it mainly supervises funds coming from the World Bank and UN agencies. Other bodies that register and/or have jurisdiction over NGOs include: District Administrations, the Registrar of Companies, and the Ministries of Lands and Surveys, Foreign Affairs, Justice, Relief and Social Rehabilitation, and Local Government. There is little co-ordination among them regarding NGOs, although some efforts were made by Sarah Ntiro when she was Director of the Aid Co-ordination Secretariat in the Prime Minister's Office (1986–92). During her tenure she met with NGOs monthly, but since she left this post the meetings have dwindled in number. Her main concern in trying to co-ordinate the activities was that, owing to weak internal co-ordination and planning, NGO agendas tended to be donor-driven and Ugandans consequently had little negotiating power.

By 1992 only 703 organizations had applied for registration (Kwesiga and Ratter, 1993: 10). Many smaller organizations register with the church body to which they are affiliated or the umbrella organizations with which they are associated, such as the National Association of Women's Organizations of Uganda, and the Uganda Community-Based Associations for Child Welfare, National Union of Disabled Persons of Uganda, Uganda Community-Based Health Care Association, Uganda National Theatrical Association. Only a few organizations have been denied permission to register or have had their registration revoked. Most of these have been religious organizations carrying out questionable activities. But the main problem is that there are no real guidelines indicating which organizations should register and which do not need to, though by law all are supposed to be registered.

Although there is little regulation of NGO activity, the fact that regulatory laws are in existence means that they can be enforced if the regime feels sufficiently threatened by various activities. The National Organisation for Civic Education and Election Monitoring (NOCEM) is a case in point. NOCEM was made up of a number of human rights, religious, media and legal rights associations, in addition to several women's organizations, including Action for Development (ACFODE), the Uganda Federation of Business and Professional Women and the Association of Uganda Women Lawyers (FIDA). Its aim was to carry out civic education and conduct election monitoring during the Constituent Assembly elections. Despite the fact that it was non-partisan and included members with past and present affiliations with the NRM, UPC, DP and the Conservative Party, the Commission of the Constituent Assembly banned the organization. Prior to this, the President had attacked NOCEM on 26 January 1994, accusing it of being a partisan organization. The announcement of the withdrawal of its accreditation gave no reason for its disqualification (Ofwono-Opondo, 1994). NOCEM faced harassment by the NRC representative in Mukono and was banned by the District Executive Secretary in Bushenyi and the District Administrator in Mpigi.

In an interview at the time the chairperson of NOCEM and president of the Uganda Law Society, Salome Bosa, pointed out that NOCEM was a new organization and faced both internal and external problems.[4] Internally, it had made a few innocent mistakes with some individuals who had not been properly screened. Those who were found to be adopting partisan positions were expelled immediately (Nzinjah, 1994). One such member, Amos Muhindo, had been working in Kasese and was identified as a former UPC Youth Winger who had a bad political record in the early 1980s. NOCEM argued that the problem was in part one of NRM inexperience with such an independent body and its functions. It also argued that, in some cases, the complaints against NOCEM had been launched by government officials who were attempting to rig elections in favor of movement politics by delegitimizing NOCEM's non-partisan activities.

Eventually NOCEM was allowed to operate and it worked with ACFODE, the Uganda Joint Council of Churches, the Uganda Media Women's Association, the National Association of Women's Organizations in Uganda, the Organization of University Moslem Women of Uganda and several other NGOs to form a collaborative Civic Education Joint Co-ordination Unit (CEJOCU) that was involved in voter and civic education in addition to monitoring elections. CEJOCU was supported not only by donors but was also recognized by the state.

The experience of NOCEM shows that, even though NGOs are tolerated, the NRM is ready and willing to limit their autonomy if there is the slightest possibility that they might prove to be too much of a challenge. But most importantly, this example demonstrates how important it has been for women's organizations to defend their autonomy.

Parent Teacher Associations Under Fire

The case of Parent Teacher Associations (PTA) is another especially clear example of how the NRM has sought to limit associational independence. The negative consequences of these limitations have been acutely felt by broad sections of the population. Uganda has a large public school system (90 percent of schools are public). From the 1980s up until 1996, 90 percent of school funding came from PTAs, which paid for school maintenance, salaries, educational materials, and furniture. In the 1960s these organizations were intended to build lines of communication between teachers and parents. As the country fell into civil war in the 1970s and government sponsorship of the educational system unraveled, the responsibility fell to parents to raise the funds and run the schools, which they did through the head teacher and a board of governors or a management committee. This parental responsibility continued throughout the years of conflict and persisted after Museveni took over in 1986. Parents not only raised the tuition fees, but they also provided school transport, midday meals, school supplies, textbooks, buildings, dormitories, teachers' houses, equipment, animals and school farms that supplemented the teachers' salaries (Senteza-Kajubi, 1991: 324). In the process, imbalances arose because poorer parents could not afford the fees and hence were unable to educate their children.

In a bid to gain votes in the 1996 presidential elections, Museveni announced the abolition of the PTAs and introduced Universal Primary Education (UPE). This was popular when it was initially announced because it promised to allow poorer households to send their children to school. However, it quickly lost support after its implementation in 1997, since the government did not have the resources to deliver quality education to the majority of schoolchildren. Teachers were not paid for months at a stretch, and large numbers of schools did not have adequate numbers of teachers or school supplies. Classes increased in size from 40 students to 110 on average.

The difficulties the UPE program faces today point to many of the harsh realities facing developing countries with a weak tax base. The trade-off Uganda faces is between allowing the voluntary sector to run the educational system, resulting in inevitable inequalities, and promoting a state-sponsored educational system that provides less than adequate education to all, while at the same time pushing Uganda into deeper dependence on external donors. Superimposed on this situation are the political calculations of a benign authoritarian regime that wants to stay in power at all costs and therefore has little tolerance for the kind of unrestrained societal autonomy that the PTAs represented.

Political Parties and the NRM

Although some observers argue that the NRM accepts the inevitability of party competition in the long run (Brett, 1995: 209–28), its actions suggest a different orientation. Uganda had been a multi-party system from 1962 to 1966 under Obote II and then a one-party system under Obote II from 1980 to 1985, with the last multi-party elections taking place in 1980. It became a "no-party" system with the NRM takeover in 1986, after which an agreement was reached between the NRM and the opposition parties stipulating that the parties would not engage in political activities. Parties were allowed to exist but they were not able to field candidates in elections. The National Resistance Council (NRC) was to be in power for five years, after which the NRM promised that the population would be free to elect a new government.

As the 1990 deadline approached, a Bill was speedily rammed through parliament on 11 October 1989, with no time for debate or consultation. Moreover, it was brought to the floor after a long debate over the budget. The vote gave the NRC another five years to remain in power without seeking election, although the local councils had to seek election in 1992. Museveni reminded the opposition parties that their political activities were suspended and a closed session of the NRC passed a resolution to this effect. Few ordinary citizens were even aware that the NRC had extended NRM rule until much later. Museveni insisted at the time that a multi-party political system was unnecessary in Uganda. By the mid-1990s, the NRM leadership was arguing that no-party democracy had produced regular and relatively clean elections since 1986, especially when compared with the irregularities associated with the 1961, 1962 and 1980 general elections. Moreover, it was evident that Museveni had little interest in moving towards multi-partyism (Ofkansky, 1996: 61).

This no-party system was reinforced by the 1995 Constitution, which stipulated that a referendum should be held in 2000 to decide whether the country should adopt a multi-party system when it went to the polls in 2001. Article 72 of the Constitution forbids parties under the movement system from holding conferences or public rallies or campaigning for candidates in any election. They cannot open branch offices, hold delegates' conferences, or offer a party platform. They can, however, operate headquarter offices, own newspapers and other publications, and hold authorized national meetings.

Multi-partyists feared that the playing field was greatly distorted not only by the 1995 Constitution, but also by the subsequent passage of the Movement Bill and by bringing the local council system firmly under NRM control. Several pieces of legislation undermined the institutionalization of political parties. The NRM Bill, which was renamed the "Movement Bill 1997" after wide criticism by multi-partyists and movement supporters alike, contains provisions that require all adult Ugandans to belong to the Movement system. The highest organ of the Movement, the National Conference, is made up of the chairperson, vice-chairperson, all the MPs, all the resident district commissioners, members of the district executive committees, the national political commissar and the mayors of municipalities. It also includes one delegate elected by an electoral college for each sub-county.[5]

The Bill, which passed with 71 votes – less than the required two-thirds quorum – was opposed by multi-partyists and many pro-democracy advocates on the grounds that it was unconstitutional. They feared that it would destroy freedom of association by making membership of the Movement mandatory. It was seen as enhancing the authority of the executive, while reducing the powers of a legislature that already had limited powers. It was also seen as a ploy by the NRM to entrench a *de facto* one-party system in Uganda, ensure the abolition of the opposition political parties, and turn the local councils into NRM branches.[6]

Certainly the Bill appears to have all the features of a competitive one-party regime if one regards the NRM as a political party. Such a regime allows for competition within the framework of the single party (in this case, the NRM), but public institutions are built upon one-party domination under the control of a strong executive president. Uganda thus could be said to resemble Ghana under Kwame Nkrumah, Guinea under Sekou Touré, Tanzania under Julius Nyerere, and Zimbabwe under Robert Mugabe. These types of regimes were/are concerned with mobilizing ordinary people into politics, but at the same time they exclude certain groups and factions from the party's central organs. Non-party social groups are often undermined and co-opted. Requiring all Ugandans to be a part of the Movement suggests another parallel with competitive one-party regimes in which there is a strong identification between the nation, the party and the leader. The viability of the regime is tied to the skills of a particular leader, who in the Ugandan case is clearly Yoweri Museveni (Chazan et al., 1988: 138–40).

The consequence of such centralizing tendencies has been to erode all political parties, the NRM included. The UPC and DP are weaker today than they were in 1994. Moreover, no new parties of consequence have emerged. The NRM itself is losing popularity, as seen in the 1998 Local Council district level (LC5) elections in which incumbents lost their seats in Mbarara, Kabarole, Kasese, Iganga, Mubende, Kampala, Mpigi, Gulu, Masaka, Soroti, and many other places. In Kampala NRM candidates lost to multi-partyists in all four divisions of the city (Mwenda, 1998). The NRM evidently lost a considerable share of the vote when its 30 percent showing in the LC5 elections in Kampala is compared with the 70 percent support it received in the 1996 parliamentary elections, and the 60 percent in the 1996 presidential elections (Ssemogerere, 1998).

The NRM is attempting to further consolidate its position by drafting a Political Organizations Act which would regulate political parties in the event that the referendum in 2000 favors multi-partyism. The Bill provides for the control of the registration of party members and the funding of political parties in Uganda.[7]

Local Council Innovations

Perhaps the NRM's most successful effort to incorporate societal interests into the Movement framework came with the institutionalization of local government. In part, this success is due to the fact that the local councils were given a measure of autonomy and increasingly greater resources. The councils frequently reflected pre-existing power configurations at the local level.

When Museveni came to power, Uganda had little experience with state sponsored local-level governance. The NRM set up Resistance Councils (RCs) throughout the country modelled on the lines of the village Resistance Councils that had been established during the guerrilla war in Luwero to facilitate communication between the NRA and the population (Tideman, 1994: 26, 29). Many of these original RCs had been destroyed in Obote's genocidal offensive against civilians in 1983 and 1984 in the context of the regime's military sweeps against the guerrillas (Burkey, 1991: 4). By 1987-8 the government issued statutes governing the RCs, thus establishing a new system of local government involving local Resistance Councils and Committees. The Resistance Councils were renamed Local Councils in the 1995 Constitution. To avoid confusion, the councils are referred to as local councils throughout this book, even for the years prior to 1995.

Local Council 1, which was made up of the entire adult population of the village, elected nine members to a LC1 committee. Each committee elected two members to form the LC2 council, which in turn elected a committee of nine. The pattern repeated itself at the LC3 (sub-county), the LC4 (county) and LC5 (district) levels. The LC4 level was generally inactive, but it formed the electoral college for the NRC elections. Each committee consisted of a chairman, vice chairman, secretary, and secretaries for youth, women, information, mass mobilization and education, security, and finance (Brett, 1992: 40).

This council system was an advance on previous forms of local government under both colonial and post-colonial rule, in that it gave local communities greater control of their own affairs with relatively little interference from central government. The local councils could make and enforce local bylaws, settle civil cases and customary law land disputes, and decide to embark on local self-help projects (Burkey, 1991: 11). Although in the early years after the NRM takeover, the LCs were highly popular and their meetings were well attended, this level of involvement tapered off with time, so that by 1991, Burkey reported that LC meetings at the 1 and 2 levels had a relatively low turn-out. She attributed this to the onerous duties that were demanded of the LCs without commensurate powers, authority and autonomy in decision-making (1991: 12). No doubt their lack of resources and compensation contributed equally to the lack of enthusiasm for the LCs.

The 1993 Local Governments (Resistance Councils) Statute was an important step in devolving power and financial autonomy to local authorities, replacing the centrally appointed District Administrator with the elected Chairman of the District Council. With the 1993 Statute, the Local Councils became even more important as participatory vehicles to promote local involvement in maintaining security; carrying out self-help projects; planning and implementing development plans; collecting government revenue (LC3 could now keep 50 percent of the graduated tax collected within their jurisdiction); mediating local domestic and land disputes as well as minor misdemeanors; carrying out judicial functions; and overseeing the provision of educational, medical, water and road services outside the jurisdiction of central government. These functions were further consolidated with the 1997 Local Government Bill that brought the 1993 Statute in line with the 1995 Constitution and furthered the decentralization of powers and services to the local level.

While the decentralization of power and the institutionalization of local councils became vital measures in enhancing local control and decision-making, the extent to which they were intended to subsume all local participation blurred the lines of accountability and narrowed the fora for popular participation. The focus on the councils as the main vehicles for popular participation also limited possibilities for interest-group formation and coalition-building. As Mamdani (1988, 1993, 1994) and Ddungu (1989) have pointed out, it delayed the development and emergence of political parties that could coalesce various societal interests. The councils limited the possibilities for making politics issue-oriented by keeping the basis of electoral contestation personality- rather than platform-based. This often ended up being translated into clan, ethnic and religious identification, as evident in the 1998 local elections. Moreover, the councils limited the freedom of assembly and expression by making residence the main basis for political participation. Although independent associations in Uganda generally operate freely, the impulse to contain all participation within the local councils acted as a constraint on associations asserting their interests, and effectively depoliticized their activities.

Local councils were originally designed to be organs of the people, of the state and of the NRM – all in the same instance. This created a certain ambiguity in their purpose and function that is borne out in the case studies. As organs of the people, they were intended to be the key arena for popular participation and were expected to hold civil servants and the state accountable to the people. At the same time they were under the jurisdiction of the Ministry of Local Government, acting as extensions of the government. And finally, they served as the political organ of the NRM, which was supposed to be a substitute for political parties by containing members of all parties and political leanings within the Movement. Political party activity and campaigning, however, remained suspended, as previously indicated (Burkey, 1991: 5; Ddungu, 1989; Mamdani, 1988).

By attempting to amalgamate popular interests within the state and the no-party movement, the NRM was seeking to create a basis for legitimizing itself at the grass-roots level by encouraging a form of local-level democracy (albeit initiated from the top down). It was attempting to institutionalize itself as a permanent fixture within the government, much the same way as the Chama Cha Mapinduzi party tried to do by entrenching itself within the Tanzanian government by blurring the lines between government and party. However, in the Tanzanian case, with the transition to multi-party democracy in 1992, the party was forced to disentangle itself from the government. The NRM, on the other hand, has not even represented itself as a party, even though it has behaved increasingly like one and less like the all-inclusive movement it aimed to be initially.

All these elements of NRM policy outlined above – its stance toward the women's organizations, the media, NGOs, political parties and local government - when viewed in conjunction, begin to form a pattern that is not unlike those seen in other neo-patrimonial one-party states in Africa. It is within this context that the women's movement emerged to resist incorporation.

Notes

1   James Tumusiime,"Government Under Fire for Arresting Scribes, Chapaa", *Monitor*, 25 December 1998.
2   "Byanyima Clarifies Capital Radio Talk," *New Vision*, 15 December 1998.
3   "UJA Rejects Act," *New Vision*, 30 October 1998.
4   Interview with Salome Bosa, Kampala, 4 July 1995. Bosa is currently a High Court judge.
5   "V.P. Can't be Deputy Chair of NRM – Bill," *Africa Online News Bulletin*, 25 January 1997.
6   "Critics Tear up NRM Bill," *The Monitor*, 15 February 1997; "Prof Mujaju Slams Museveni's Praise Singers," *The Monitor*, 8 February 1997; "Fireworks Expected as NRM Bill Moves to House," *The Monitor*, 13 February 1997.
7   "NRM Says No Compromise Over Political Parties," *Africa Online News Bulletin*, 15 September 1997.

4

The Political Impact
of the Women's Movement
under the NRM

"Is the NRM Over-Liberating the Woman?" was the question posed for debate at a 1995 Kampala Think Tank Foundation seminar.[1] The speaker, Mary Maitum, who had been a member of the Constitutional Commission that drafted the 1995 Constitution, answered the question with a resounding "No". She argued that "the greatest hurdle in liberating the Ugandan woman is not only in policy and laws or the Constitution – important as these are – but in the realization of society . . . . that women are as important as men and must work together, side by side in the development of our country". She continued, "Women and not the Government hold the key to their liberty and that of society."

The topic of the seminar arose out of a popular view that, without the National Resistance Movement (NRM) takeover, the current women's movement in Uganda would not have been as strong as it is today. Some go so far as to argue that the women's movement is an NRM-initiated movement.[2] Others claim that the advances made by women "are due to the bureaucratic or paternalistic concessions by the NRM administration rather than victories attained from the struggle" (Kiggundu, 1992). Perhaps the preponderance of women's groups organized by Local Council 1 Women's Secretaries and women's strong voting patterns in most parts of the country in support of the NRM might appear to suggest that the NRM initiated the women's movement. Certainly NRM openness has been critical in encouraging the growth of the women's movement and has provided the necessary opportunity structures for the movement to thrive. However, the ability of the women's movement to maintain its autonomy and to claim new resources (see Chapter 5) have proved to be of even greater consequence. This chapter explores the gains women have made in the political arena and attributes them to the growth of the women's movement since the mid-1980s. It shows how the autonomy of the movement was critical to its success, and explores in depth a major struggle between independent women's organizations and the NRM over the fate of the National Council of Women. The chapter then looks at the various ways in which women's autonomous forms of mobilization are maintained through gender-specific organizations, multipurpose organizations, and small and informal groups.

Throughout the Amin and Obote II period, the national women's movement had been closely tied to the respective regimes and had become highly insulated. At the time of the 1986 NRM takeover, a small independent women's movement began to establish linkages with international women's organizations and sought to adopt radically new goals. Fortuitously, many of the leading women's rights organizations, like Action for Development (ACFODE), had begun mobilizing at a critical juncture immediately before the NRM takeover. This meant that when the NRM came to power, they had already developed a strategy to push an agenda that would catapult women into key political positions and allow them to lobby for other important demands. The NRM clearly had not developed a policy on NGOs when the women's associations began to assert themselves. Thus, women's organizations were well positioned at this critical juncture to help shape the regime's policy regarding voluntary associations. Moreover, there was a growing pool of visionary, strong and capable women leaders ready to help open up political space at this key moment.

Leaders of national women's organizations point to the 1985 UN Decade of Women conference in Nairobi[3] as a turning point in the history of Ugandan women's associations. Women activists in non-governmental organizations, many of whom had attended the conference on their own independently of the official delegation, returned from Nairobi with a new sense of urgency to begin revitalizing and creating autonomous women's associations. At the Nairobi conference of 15,000 women from 140 countries, the Ugandan participants got a sense of how far women in other countries had come. They felt that the women's movement in their own country had been stalled by tyrannical regimes and was badly in need of a jump-start. They left Nairobi inspired and committed to changing the status of women. Upon their return they immediately started to mobilize women, and stepped up their efforts after the NRM takeover in January 1986.

At the outset, the NRM did not have any particular program addressing women's concerns. In fact, Museveni's Ten Point Program, which is the NRM Manifesto, makes no mention of women (see Chapter 3). Human rights activist and NRM supporter Joan Kakwenzire recalls that one of Museveni's first speeches to women in 1986 was a "disheartening speech", in which he spoke of transforming women's status by bringing about changes in society more broadly and asked women to "pull up their socks" and not make too many pleas for help.[4] In the early years of the NRM, the regime also harbored suspicions of women's NGOs, suspicions which diminished but nevertheless persisted into the 1990s. This was evident when Museveni's wife, Janet Museveni, and Sister Rose of the Daughters of Charity first approached Museveni about starting the Uganda Women's Effort to Save Orphans (UWESO), one of the first women's NGOs to be formed after 1986. Even Museveni's own wife and the nun had to argue vigorously to persuade him to give them the go-ahead.[5] After being warned by the NRM Directorate of Women's Affairs about UWESO, Museveni called in Joyce Mpanga, an NRM veteran who was involved in UWESO's leadership, to tell him what "all this nonsense about UWESO is".[6] He wanted to be certain that his wife was not going to run against NRM policies.

But gradually, as a result of women's lobbying efforts, Museveni changed his tune regarding NGOs. He also began to see the possibilities of tapping into women's organizational capacity in order to promote his own goals. Under pressure from women leaders, he came to consider women as a political asset in building his no-party movement. Women had earned considerable respect through their participation in the 1980–85 guerrilla struggle against Obote's forces, which had helped them establish themselves as a force to be reckoned with. Prominent leaders like Joyce Mpanga, who had watched Museveni become increasingly aware of women's issues, insisted that "the NRM has been very genuine in supporting the emancipation of women and Museveni as a person is very supportive".[7] Seeing the women's endorsement as critical to the regime's success, the NRM encouraged them to form clubs at the LC1 level and supported their leadership at all levels of the LC system, reserving one seat for a women's secretary at all council levels. This had already been the practice during the guerrilla war in areas which the NRM controlled, such as Luwero. However, with the NRM takeover, some people were concerned that women would be marginalized in this one seat. For this reason, new organizations like Action for Women in Development (ACFODE) vigorously pushed for a provision that would allow women to contest all positions on the LCs (Ankrah, 1996: 21).

Women and Political Representation

Shortly after the 1986 NRM takeover, 20 leaders of the National Council of Women (NCW), ACFODE and other NGOs paid a courtesy call on President Museveni with a memo in hand, requesting that women be represented in the government leadership. As one of the women put it: "fortunately we had enough contacts within the NRM and so we began to remind them that we were there lobbying for women before the NRM came to official power and therefore we deserved to talk to the leadership."[8] Museveni asked the delegation to identify such women leaders, and subsequently they circulated curricula vitae and made recommendations on how to fill various leadership positions. Many of these recommendations were adopted immediately, including the appointments of nine women ministers, among them Gertrude Njuba as Deputy Minister of Industry, Victoria Sekitoleko as Minister of Agriculture, and Betty Bigombe as Deputy Minister, Prime Minister's Office. Eight out of 75 ministers were women in 1989. Connie Byamugisha was appointed a Judge of the High Court in 1988 after being promoted two years earlier to the position of Acting Chief Magistrate.

By 1995, women constituted 17 percent of all ministers, 21 percent (7 out of 32) of all Permanent Secretaries, 35 percent (12) of all Under Secretaries, and 16 percent of all District Administrators. Women were also represented on National Commissions and parastatal boards. For example, there were two women among the 21 representatives on the Constitutional Commission that drafted the new Constitution (Miria Matembe and Mary Maitum). There was a woman on the six member Human Rights Commission; three women on a 27-member Education Review Commission; and two women on the nine-member Public Service Reorganization Commission. By 1994 there were also four women judges (17 percent) and five chief magistrates (23 percent) (Busharizi and Emasu, 1995; Kakwenzire, 1990; Matembe, 1991).

A cabinet reshuffle at the end of 1994 resulted in the promotion of Specioza Wandira Kazibwe, former Minister of Gender and Community Development, to be Vice President. But much to the disappointment of many women's groups, Museveni appointed only six women to the 51 ministerial posts after the 1996 elections. Specioza Kazibwe resumed her position as Vice-President and took on the additional portfolio of Minister of Agriculture, Animal Industry and Fisheries.[9]

Debates over the Reservation of Seats for Women
Women also made considerable headway in parliament, largely due to the fact that the NRM reserved special seats for women. At independence there was a 2: 88 female: male ratio in parliament, in 1967 there were no women members of parliament; and by 1980 there was still only one female (Teddy Oduka) out of 143 members of parliament. In the 1989 National Resistance Council (parliamentary) elections, however, 34 of the seats were reserved for women; two women (Rhoda

Kalema and Victoria Sekitoleko) won their seats in open contests against male candidates, three women were nominated by the President and two were "historical members," appointed because of their participation in the guerrilla war led by the National Resistance Army. Thus, in the 1989 elections women claimed 41 (17 percent) of all parliamentary seats. By 1996, 52 women (19 per cent) held parliamentary seats, 39 of them reserved seats.

Although the reservation of special seats for women has been a contentious issue in Uganda, as in other countries in Africa where such measures have been taken, Uganda's brief experience with reserved seats has generally been positive. Opponents of this policy tend to focus on the political motivations of the measure, arguing that it is simply a political maneuver by the NRM to win women's votes and ensure a solid block of female NRM supporters in parliament. However, supporters of reserved seats believe it is a necessary but temporary measure to encourage women to enter political life and to make them politically visible so that the electorate eventually becomes accustomed to voting for women as leaders. Christine Oryema Lalobo, who ran in the 1994 Constituent Assembly elections in Gulu, expressed this sentiment succinctly:

> People here have not been used to women leading and being in positions of authority. This is true for both men and women. Even most women prefer quiet fellow women. Some women started through affirmative action. It was good and is still good. But I feel that the women, starting with myself, should go it straight with men. We vote for men, they should also vote for us. I see it that way . . . In Acholi, traditionally people think they cannot send women. But there is an Acholi saying, "*Gwok ma dako bene mako lee*" (Even a female dog also catches an animal in a hunt.)[10]

One of the most important consequences of the reserved seats was to give women the exposure, political experience and confidence to run on their own in open electoral contests. This was clearly evident in the 1994 Constituent Assembly elections in which 36 women ran in direct contests against male candidates and one quarter of them (9) won seats (3 in Mukono district alone and 3 in Busoga).[11] A woman trade union leader beat five male candidates in elections for the two seats reserved for the National Organisation of Trade Unions (NOTU) in the Constituent Assembly. Altogether there were 52 women in the Constituent Assembly, making up 18 percent of the assembly members. The vice-chairperson of the Constituent Assembly was also a woman, Victoria Mwaka.

In the 1996 parliamentary elections the number of women contesting open seats dropped to 26, while one-third (8) won.[12] Meanwhile 109 women sought the 39 district women's seats in parliament, representing an overall increase in the numbers of women candidates. The women who won in open contests with men ran on anti-corruption tickets (Winnie Byanyima) and on appeals to the interests of women and youth (Proscovia Salaamu Musumba).

These developments in the political arena were reflected in the remarks of women surveyed for this study in 1993. When asked about the changes in women's status after the NRM takeover in 1986, they overwhelmingly responded that the biggest changes related to women's participation in politics, standing for office, becoming public and government leaders, and being able to express themselves publicly to a greater degree than in the past. Similarly, three-quarters of them regarded female leaders as equal or more effective than male leaders. However, men tended to disagree. In Kampala, for example, women were almost 4 times more likely than men to see women more effective as leaders than men (see Table 4.1). When asked which female leaders they viewed as most effective, of the national leaders mentioned the most common responses in all four towns were Miria Matembe (NRC representative from Mbarara and former president of ACFODE), Janet Museveni (wife of President Yoweri Museveni and patron of UWESO), Speciosa Wandira Kazibwe (Vice-President and Minister of Women in Development, Youth and Culture), Victoria Sekitoleko (former Minister of Agriculture) and Betty Bigombe (former Minister of State in the Prime Minister's Office for the Pacification of the North). The only deviation from these top choices was in Luwero, where Dr Germina Ssemogerere ranked highest and Miria Matembe and Janet Museveni had less support. During the 1996 presidential election, Janet Museveni accompanied her husband on the campaign trail and her appearance usually drew what one observer called "a magical response from the crowd" when she made a speech (Lupa-Lasaga, 1996). At the time of the survey, Winnie Byanyima had not returned to Uganda from her studies abroad but she would no doubt have figured prominently in such a survey in the late 1990s.

Strategies Promoting Women's Political Representation

In the 1990s, many of the new organizations showed an interest in politics for the first time. For example, the Uganda Women Entrepreneurs Association Limited (UWEAL) was actively involved in discussions on the constitution-making process and had four of its members standing in the 1994 Constituent Assembly elections (Birungi, 1994). Another organization, Forum for Women in Development (FOWODE), was formed in 1995 to promote women's political leadership. It lobbied the Electoral Commission to hold women's elections for parliament before the general elections, because in previous elections some of the male candidates who won had campaigned for certain women candidates. During the 1996 presidential and parliamentary elections, a newly formed women's network, Uganda Women's Network (UWONET), issued a "women's manifesto," raising key issues of concern to women in Uganda that could be used as a basis for evaluating candidates running for office. The manifesto included issues like "peace, stability and unity in diversity; gender balance, equality and affirmative action; poverty and economic empowerment of women; violence against women; protection of the rights of the family, orphans, children with special needs and the aged; people with disabilities; and women and health".[13]

The 1997 Local Government Bill raised issues relating to women's access to political leadership. Although parliament had passed the Local Government Bill in

Table 4.1 Effectiveness of Women Leaders: Views of General Population Surveyed (%)

| | KAMPALA | | KABALE | | MBALE | | LUWERO | |
| | Men | Women | Men | Women | Men | Women | Men | Women |
	(n = 133)		(n = 140)		(n = 50)		(n = 50)	
Women leaders more effective than men	6	22	12	30	6	9	17	21
As effective as men	64	54	43	41	49	63	44	57
Less effective than men	23	14	39	26	27	8	17	9
Other	1	1	0	0	0	2	0	1
Don't know	5	9	6	2	18	18	22	12

December 1996 by 152 votes to 16, Museveni vetoed it, rejecting an article (108e), which set minimum academic qualifications for local council (LC) chairpersons at the LC3 and LC5 levels (O Level for LC3 chairpersons and A level for LC5 chairpersons). Women's groups had opposed the O level requirement on the grounds that it would disqualify many suitable women because of their lower educational levels.[14] Even though there had been strong opposition from MPs to revising the qualifications, Parliament succumbed to pressure from women's organizations, women MPs and the President and threw out the leadership requirements.[15]

Women's increased mobilization has meant that they have raised their political activity at the local level. In all four towns surveyed, increasing numbers of women voted in each LC election from 1987 to 1989 and 1992. By 1992 an average of three-quarters of the women voted in the four towns surveyed with only slightly more men voting than women. In contrast, during the early years of the NRM regime, there were cases where the LC1 chairperson (a man) was elected to the women's post because no woman ran or was allowed to run, for example, Arua, Bushenyi (ACFODE, 1988: 62; Ddungu and Wabwire, 1991: 40). By 1992 the situation had changed considerably and women were paying more attention to the women who ran for LC positions. One-third of the survey respondents reported having as many as two women in the LC1 committee in Luwero, Mbale and Kampala and close to one-half in Kabale. Less than 10 percent had 3 or more women LCs with the exception of Luwero, where over 20 percent of the LCs had 3 or more women members. Burkey also found more female LC officials in Luwero and Rakai relative to Mbale or Nebbi in her 1991 study (1991: 23). It is likely that the longer experience with the LC system in Luwero accounts for the greater number of women active as local council leaders. It is also possible that it is a consequence of the greater freedom enjoyed by Baganda women relative to other groups in terms of economic opportunities, inheritance rights and control of financial resources.

Women's Associations and Political Participation

Women's increased involvement in associations has also spurred greater involvement in local-level politics. In fact, women involved in organizations were more likely to be active in LC politics. In all four towns surveyed roughly two-thirds of the women involved in associations had actively supported and campaigned for particular candidates in the most recent 1992 LC election. Sarah Kabukaire's study in Kamuli also found that many of the leaders of the women's organizations were LC leaders at various levels. No doubt their involvement in women's organizations catapulted them into LC leadership (Kabukaire, 1992: 60, 70).

The connection between women's associations and running for office was evident even at the parliamentary level. For example, the former women's representative to the NRC from Mukono, Victoria Ssebagereka, attributed her involvement in politics to her beginnings in grassroots women's organizations. As she explained:

> It was the women who saw some leadership qualities in me, when I started a little self-help group, so they kept sending me up. And when these LCs started, I am one of the people (being in the National Association of Women) who mobilized the grassroots. I was then elected from my little village . . . and taken up to the district to represent the women. (Simwogerere, 1994)

Those women MPs who were active in mobilizing women, generally did so via independent women's associations, either through national women's associations or through groups in their districts. Loi Kageni Kiryapawo, NRC representative from Tororo, started an umbrella body, North Tororo Women's Association (NOTOWA), to co-ordinate women's groups in the district. Miria Matembe was an outspoken leader of ACFODE, while Irene Wekiya, MP for Jinja, was involved in several associations in her district. This connection between women's political activity and women's organizations is by no means a new phenomenon. Erina Muherya, who was a leader in the Mothers' Union and was elected in 1954 president of all the women's organizations in Bunyoro, was also in the Bunyoro *Luki-iko* (legislature) at the time.[16] Similarly Pumla Kisosonkole, who was the first African woman to be nominated to the Legislative Council in 1958, felt that her experiences in the YWCA and Mothers' Union were critical to her political career.[17] Joyce Mpanga, another early woman member of the Legislative Council in 1960, belonged to the YWCA, NCW, Mothers' Union, Forward Society and the Association of Women Teachers.[18]

Although a focus of the women's movement has been on increasing women's representation in political leadership, women have also pushed successfully for greater acceptance of female leadership and participation in many other arenas that were traditionally closed to women. Non-governmental associations are selecting female leaders in greater numbers. For example, Salome Bosa (who later became a High Court judge) was elected head of the Uganda Law Society in 1993, and Harriet Diana Musoke was elected to the same post in 1998.[19] Deepa Verma was elected president of the Makerere University Law Society in 1995, followed by Sheila Braka in 1997. Mary Musoke, national women's table tennis champion, was unanimously voted "Sportsman [sic] of the Year 1993" by the Uganda Sports Press Association (USPA), chosen by 10 media agencies that took part in the exercise (Wamanga, 1994). Women are even entering traditionally male sports associations like the Uganda Motor Association, which sponsors rallies. Already in a short time two sisters, Eve and Betty Ntege, have made their mark on the rallying scene (Ndawula, 1996).

In other arenas like religious institutions, new pressures are mounting to bring women into the higher circles of leadership. Dr Therese Tinkasimire, a Catholic sister and head of the Department of Religious Studies at Makerere University, has raised these issues publicly, demanding that the African Catholic Bishops be taken at their word when they state that men and women are equal before God:

> At the Parish level, the priest or pastor and his curate and all the immediate subordinates are men. The Parish council, where all the decisions are made, is comprised of ninety percent men. Ironically, the implementors of these decisions are women. Going up the ladder to the Diocesan level, the situation becomes even worse. There are no women representatives on the Diocesan Council. In some Dioceses, the Bishop dictates to women what they are supposed to do . . . Catholic women would like to be admitted into the inner circles of church ministry . . . As it is now, the gifts and talents of women are not being fully utilised by the church (Tinkasimire, 1996: 12–13).

Similarly, in the Anglican Church of Uganda women are pressing for larger leadership roles. At a meeting of the first national convention for Uganda's Anglican women clergy, 30 clergywomen from dioceses throughout the country accused the church of discriminating against them, vowing to resist the oppression of women in the church. Arguing that women are the backbone of the church membership, Grace Ndyabahika, Chairwoman of the National Clergywomen's Fellowship, told the convention: "Most women clergy are school chaplains and assistant tutors, but none are bishops. They have been left out of the mainstream leadership."[20]

Establishing a Women's Ministry

In addition to greater political representation and participation, pressure from women's organizations has forced the Museveni government to consider women's issues at a national level in ways not addressed by previous governments. Action for Development (ACFODE), which was formed in November 1985 by 30 women, held a major conference of women's organizations and NRM representatives in Mukono, 8–13 December 1986 (funded by UNIFEM). They met to call national attention to the developments at the UN Women's Decade conference in Nairobi and what they felt were the implications for women in Uganda.[21] It was here that ACFODE publicly pressed for a ministry for women, for every ministry to have a women's desk, and for women's representation in local government at all levels. It also called for the repeal of the 1978 Decree which had created the National Council of Women (NCW) under Amin, and for an umbrella organization independent of government funding that was not housed in the Ministry of Local Government as had been the case with the NCW.

Most of these demands were met. In 1988 a Ministry of Women in Development was established in the Office of the President as a Ministry of State. Later it became a full ministry when it merged with Youth and Culture in 1991.[22] Three years later, after a protracted struggle with the Civil Service Reform Commission, it was reconstituted as the Ministry of Gender and Community Development. The ministry saw itself as responsible for the overall formulation and co-ordination of policies on women and as a catalyst for sensitizing government organs to gender issues. As the first minister of women, Joyce Mpanga, explained, "Policy makers and programme planners tend to ignore women as production agents who contribute to national development. They merely treat women's concerns as welfare issues."[23] Specifically, the ministry's objectives included seeking equal rights for women through changes in the law and in institutional arrangements; integrating women's concerns in the national and district development programs; fostering women's income-generating activities and enterprises; and engendering full participation in decision-making within the political and development process.[24] Mpanga relied heavily on women's organizations in this early period of establishing the ministry. As she explained:

> I had the backing of many many women . . . . I attribute most of my success to their being able to help me. I worked with leaders of ACFODE and other organizations and met with them on a weekly basis to get their input in shaping the ministry.[25]

Other ministries also began to address concerns of the women's movement. For example, the Ministry of Health developed programs targeting women's participation, including immunization, maternal and child health, family planning, nutrition, AIDS, and clean water programs. Mpanga also worked closely with Victoria Sekitoleko, who was then Minister of Agriculture, to develop a joint strategy concerned with food security (Kakwenzire, 1989).

Pressures for Legislative Change

Along with the political gains mentioned in the previous section, one of the main accomplishments of the women's movement after the mid-1980s was the broadening of its agenda to press for key legislative changes. This was possible mainly because, unlike under previous regimes, the movement remained autonomous, even in the face of pressures of co-optation. In a very short period after the NRM takeover, many different kinds of organizations began to lobby on a variety of issues that extended far beyond the concerns of women's organizations of the past. Some examples of the kinds of new broader issues national women's organizations have pressed for with varying degrees of success are given below. They give some sense of the contours of the women's movement in Uganda and the extent to which it has been able to campaign for changes in women's status.

Women's groups and women MPs were active in debates over the proposed 1998 Land Bill right from the start. Women MPs and organizations like the Uganda Association of Women Lawyers (FIDA), the Forum for Women in Democracy (FOWODE), and the Uganda Women's Network (UWONET) clashed with President Museveni over the Bill. Museveni told a workshop organized by FOWODE in April 1998 that a woman should not have an automatic right to her husband's property at marriage. "Museveni is a (male) chauvinist," one workshop participant remarked after hearing his views. "I thought he was enlightened but he has not yet shed off his mentality. It was an unfortunate statement from a leader of [sic] the beacon of hope of Africa" (Kagambirwe et al., 1998). Even some of Museveni's staunchest parliamentary supporters like Miria Matembe openly challenged his stand on the Bill.

In the course of the parliamentary debate on the Land Bill, UWONET raised issues pertaining to the Land Committees and Land Tribunals to ensure that women had adequate representation on these bodies in accordance with the Constitution, and that in settling disputes the District Land Tribunals explicitly took into consideration the rights of women and their children to land security. FIDA also presented its views to the Parliamentary Committee charged with revising the Land Bill, arguing, among other things, that the certificates of occupancy and of customary ownership should be issued in the names of husbands and their wives (Katunzi, 1998). These provisions were incorporated into the Bill. The provision for spousal co-ownership of land was moved by Matembe and was adopted by Parliament, but when the debate was written up in the legislative record, the changes were nowhere to be seen. By dropping the clause in Article 40, the law would permit unscrupulous men to sell family property without the consent of their wives. The Uganda Land Alliance, a consortium made up of various local and international NGOs and women's organizations (FIDA, UWONET, and Akina Mama wa Afrika, etc.), protested at the omission as did key MPs. The MP for Mbarara Municipality, Winnie Byanyima, warned the Movement that it would lose women's support if it did not amend the Land Act.

FIDA has also worked closely with the Ministry of Women in Development, Youth and Culture (later known as the Ministry of Gender and Community Development and after 1998 as the Ministry of Gender, Labour and Social Development) to draw up a Domestic Law Bill. This Bill would give women more rights in divorce, marriage and other personal relations in which they face discrimination due to customary practices concerning inheritance and property rights. For example, there is no provision for the dissolution of marriage other than for adultery, cruelty or desertion. The 1964 Divorce Act makes it easier for a man to divorce a woman than for a woman to divorce a man. While a man only has to prove that the woman has committed adultery, adultery alone is insufficient grounds for a woman seeking divorce. Moreover, the legal meaning of adultery is biased in favor of men: a man commits adultery only if he has sexual intercourse with a married woman, but intercourse with an unmarried woman is not considered adultery. Yet if a woman has an affair with an unmarried man it is legally considered adultery.[26] The Domestic Law Bill would ensure equal rights for both men and women with respect to these issues.

Constitutional Reform

Women's organizations were also active in the entire process leading up to the adoption of the 1995 Constitution. As a result of these efforts, key provisions affecting women were adopted in the Constitution. Although there is a long road ahead in actualizing these provisions, it is significant that the Constitution lays the basis for such struggles.

The Ministry of Women in Development worked with women's organizations in 1991 to co-ordinate a nationwide discussion of the Constitution as it was being drawn up. From these discussions, a memorandum was drafted and sent to the Constitutional Commission, which had issued an open invitation to any group or section of the population to submit memoranda. The Ministry's memorandum addressed questions of national concern, such as national language, but also issues of particular concern to women, including the elimination of discrimination on the basis of sex, which would involve the repeal of marriage, divorce, inheritance and property laws that discriminate against women.

Women were active in writing the Constitution, in the race for the Constituent Assembly (CA) and in the Assembly itself. Out of a total of 286 delegates to the Assembly, 52 (18 percent) were women. Most of these participated in a Women's Caucus, a non-partisan organization aimed at building consensus among women delegates on issues related particularly to women's concerns. It lobbied the CA; worked with sympathetic male CA members; held seminars and other functions to improve the lobbying, campaigning and presentation skills of its members; collaborated with women's NGOs; and ran a CA Gender Information Center (GIC) that provided support to women delegates in debating the Constitution. The Center ran a weekly radio program that allowed women delegates to share their views with the public. It published educational materials, monitored debates, offered legal consultancy services to women delegates, and provided facilities for meetings (Friedrich Ebert Foundation, 1995: 16, 19, 22).

Some of the most important provisions for women include the following:

- The Constitution provides for equal protection for all people under the law, regardless of sex, race, color, ethnic origin, tribe, religion, social or economic position, political opinion or disability.
- The Constitution ensures women's right to equal opportunities in political, economic and social activities. It guarantees reserved seats for groups marginalized on the basis of gender or other reasons for "the purpose of redressing the imbalance which has existed against them". Moreover, it calls for the creation of an Equal Opportunities Commission that would ensure that this principle is applied. This preferential treatment provision can be applied to education, politics, economics, and other areas. It allows for one woman to run for parliament as a women's representative in each district. Women may also run for openly contested seats. Women can claim one third of the local government council seats. This last provision was one fought for vigorously by the CA women delegates.

- The Constitution allows for women to be eligible for the same jobs as men, and they should be paid the same as men for the same work. Women are given job protection before and after pregnancy.
- The Constitution recognizes the "significant role women play in society". This permits recognition of the heavy responsibilities women shoulder in contributing to the income and welfare of the family and to society. It allows for the protection of the family, thereby paving the way for the enactment of a law that addresses domestic violence. There is recognition of women's unique contributions to society and for these to be recognized through laws that facilitate women in bearing children through maternity leave.
- The Constitution supports customary values in so far as they promote human rights, freedom, human dignity and democracy, but prohibits "laws, cultures, customs and traditions which are against the dignity, welfare or interest of women or which undermine their status . . ."
- The Constitution requires the state to register all births, marriages and deaths, thus giving protection to women who have customarily not registered their marriages, and are therefore especially vulnerable in terms of their rights in the event of their husband's death. It protects widows, allowing them to keep their deceased husband's property; to decide on a burial place for their husband; to choose where they themselves want to be buried; and it gives them the right to reject being married to their husband's brother. Widows have the right to act as guardians of their children on the death of their husbands.
- The Constitution sets a minimum age of marriage at 18. It also provides for equal rights in marriage and equal rights to acquire and use property, and to share family property on the dissolution of the marriage. Married women have the freedom to attend and participate in meetings. Women have the right to choose whom to marry since forced marriages are forbidden.
- The Constitution allows foreign men who marry Ugandan wives to claim Ugandan citizenship. In previous constitutions, citizenship was granted only to foreign women who married Ugandan husbands.
- Finally, the Constitution protects children and vulnerable persons against abuse, harassment and ill-treatment. This refers to women in specific occupations, including domestic service, barmaids, secretaries, and women who travel at night, e.g., nurses and midwives (Friedrich Ebert Foundation, 1995: 27–43; Waliggo, 1996b).

Lobbying on New Fronts

Rape and Child Molestation

Women's organizations first became vocal on issues of rape and child molestation in the early 1990s, with the growing incidences of rape and child abuse in both rural and urban areas that were seen as linked to the high rates of HIV infection. Uganda had the highest number of HIV positive people in Africa according to the World Health Organization, and women were the fastest growing group affected. Some men were preying on young girls in the belief that they were less likely to be infected with the disease, while other men infected with HIV were found to be raping women.

Uganda's women parliamentarians were instrumental in passing amendments to the penal code (Sections 117, 118, 122 of Chapter 156) in 1990 that made rape a capital offense and punished hotel owners for allowing prostitution on their premises. While the amendments drew attention to the fact that women took the issue of rape and sexual harassment very seriously, in practice they did little to deter rape. In fact, there was a continued increase in the number of reported cases of rape in the years that followed. Moreover, no cases were brought to trial and no action was taken by the Ministries of Education, Internal Affairs and Justice in spite of protests by women lawyers, parliamentarians and activists. This raised questions in some circles about the seriousness with which the law was regarded. Others felt that the punishment for rape was too severe in a society where many men, even those in the legal profession, did not take rape seriously. Moreover, they felt the punishment conflicted with the goals of human rights activists.

Several hundred women and some men belonging to various organizations took to the streets on 17 December 1991, to press the government to take stronger action on defilement, which according to Ugandan law is defined as sexual intercourse with a girl below the age of 18.[27] They protested the Ministry of Justice's foot dragging on implementing Chapter XV of the Penal Code that would provide for a family division in the Uganda courts to facilitate privacy and speedy prosecution of sexual offenses and for a system of counseling for victims of sexual abuse. They also demonstrated in front of the Ministry of Education and Sports, calling on the ministry to investigate all forms of sexual abuse in educational institutions and punish teachers who defiled their female students. At the demonstration, an eight-year-old girl who had been defiled by her teacher presented the Minister with a petition (Bonnie Keller, personal communication, 1997). They protested in front of the Ministry of Internal Affairs, where they petitioned for the observance of the international conventions on the treatment and custody of persons in correctional facilities, arguing that cases under Chapter XV of the Penal Code be handled expeditiously and with greater seriousness. They called for the establishment of a family desk at every police station to process cases of abuse (Weebe and Ogola, 1992).[28] Likewise they petitioned the Ministry of Local Government to educate members of the Local Councils and committees not to settle these cases out of court, but to bring them to justice.

The demonstrations were aimed not only at getting ministries to act on existing legislation, but to draw public attention to the intense disgust and anger women felt about rape and especially defilement. At Makerere University male law students and lecturers commonly treated rape as a laughing matter, and LC courts were known to fine rapists a chicken for defiling young girls. Attempting to draw attention to the seriousness of these crimes, Miria Matembe, then president of ACFODE, addressed the demonstration and made her famous statement that: "Men are in possession of a potentially dangerous instrument which should be cut off unless it is properly used." This provocative comment drew the attention of the media and the public and became one of the most widely publicized quotations in women's movements around the continent (Muhangi, 1991).

At the same time, many male fellow parliamentarians attacked her viciously, entirely missing the point of her comment and accusing her of being deranged. Letters to the editor vilified her. A typical letter written two years after Matembe made her remark criticized her but did not condemn rape, arguing instead: "I would similarly urge my fellow men to wake up and show these rebellious women that we were created by God to rule over them and that they were created out of our rib and they will never be equal to men."[29] One MP, Rebecca Kadaga, wrote a letter to *New Vision* in Matembe's defense, explaining:

The comment made by Mrs. Matembe on castration was a reflection of the outrage that parents felt in cases like the recent one, reported at Central Police Station, Kampala, where a baby of six months was defiled and died soon after. There are several more including children aged two or three.[30]

Several NGOs, including FIDA, petitioned the Ministries of Women in Development, Youth and Culture, Education and Sports, Health, Justice, and Local Government in 1993, criticizing them for being indifferent to escalating rates of defilement and sexual abuse of children. In particular, they targeted the Ministry of Justice for permitting LCs to deal with defilement cases, which ought to be handled by law enforcement agencies and treated as a capital offense. This meant that they could only be tried by the High Court (Bitangaro, 1993; Mugisa, 1993).[31]

As a result of government inaction on the issue of rape, an anti-rape coalition was formed 5 March 1994, to create greater awareness of rape, defilement and incest; to publicize and follow up on cases of rape and other forms of sexual abuse; and to conduct research on the causes of rape, its effects and ways to reduce it. The coalition aimed to provide counseling to victims and their families and to remove impediments to legal reform on sexual offenses. The Pressure Group on Rape and Defilement, which is based in Rukungiri, Kampala, Mbale, Kabale and Kapchorwa, was made up of FIDA, ACFODE, NAWOU, the Uganda Muslim Women's Association (UMWA), the Medical Foundation, Butabika Hospital and other groups (Nviri, 1994a).

Education for Women

For the women's movement, changes in education policy have been viewed strategically as the key to getting women into leadership positions. Already the larger pool of educated women has made it easier to appoint more women to high-ranking civil service positions or as judges. In the 1960s women in such positions were almost unheard of.

In spite of such gains, girls'/women's educational opportunities lag behind those of boys/men. Secondary schools for girls have consistently produced higher O and A level scores than boys' schools. For example, in the 1998 O-level examinations seven out of the top ten scores went to girls even though considerably fewer girls sat the exams (Mugagga, 1998). Nevertheless, the ratio of girls to boys in secondary school was 63: 100 in 1990. There are many reasons for this, including lack of money for school fees, domestic obligations, family income-generating necessities, pregnancy, and early marriage (Kigozi, 1993). Thus the pool of female applicants to the university is small relative to that of males.

For women's associations, expanding the pool of university-educated women is especially critical in helping push women through "the glass ceiling" of top positions, particularly in politics.[32] This is why the Uganda Association of University Women (UAUW), ACFODE, and other groups quietly lobbied the Faculty Senate at Makerere University and got the admissions standards changed for women entering university.[33] At a special meeting of the University Senate on 14 June 1990, it was decided that qualified women would be admitted, but the cut-off for women was set at 1.5 points below that for men (hence the reference to this as the "1.5 struggle"). As a result, the percentage of females enrolled at Makerere rose from 30 percent in 1991 to 40 percent in 1996 (Kamya, 1996). In 1994 this 1.5 policy was extended to agricultural colleges. The UAUW has also continued to support a scholarship fund for women at university level.

The creation of a Women's Studies Department at Makerere in 1987 was another important success of the women's movement. The UAUW, along with ACFODE, pressured international donors and university authorities to help establish the department. The MA program enrolled its first students in 1990. To date, it is the only Women's Studies department in an African university, and the fact that it offers an MA degree makes it unique by most international standards. The department offers seminars that are attended by the public, and has proved to be an important resource for women's associations and international organizations. One-third of its students are male (Margaret Snyder, personal communication, 1997).

At the primary and secondary school levels, the Women Engineers, Technicians and Scientists in Uganda (WETSU) conducted career guidance in schools and initiated a women's Science Award to encourage science education among girls. One of the main goals of the organization was to increase the number of girls studying science and technology (Gipwola, 1995).

Finally, ACFODE, which has been leading women's activism in the area of education, helped the Ministry of Education introduce sex education into the curriculum for teenagers attending upper primary school (junior high) to address issues like the AIDS epidemic, which is greatly affected by the position of women.

Rights of Particular Interest Groups

Women's organizations lobbied on other fronts as well:

- The Kapchorwa Council of Women petitioned the government to take measures to bring an end to female genital surgery, which, unlike the rest of Uganda, is prevalent in Kapchorwa District. In response, the government sponsored a study carried out by women leaders and academics in 1990 to investigate the impact of the custom. The issue has also been taken up by the Association of Uganda Women Doctors and ACFODE, along with the Women's Global Network on Reproductive Rights and other such women's organizations.
- Numerous organizations lobbied actively in support of the rights of disabled women. For example, the West Nile Association of the Handicapped (WENAH) in Arua publicly raised the issue of able-bodied men raping disabled women, which according to the group, increased women's problems if they became pregnant.[34] The National Union of Disabled Persons of Uganda (NUDIPU) protested the fact that disabled women had been excluded from most women's programs directed by the Ministry of Women (Bongyereirwe, 1993: Serwanga, 1993).
- FIDA lobbied to get the Police Bill suspended and amended so that searches and arrests carried out by police would be consistently done with a court warrant by officers in uniform and accompanied by a civil leader of the area. Their aim was to avoid impostors claiming to be police (Mutazindwa, 1993: 11).
- FIDA also worked to protect children's rights in a variety of ways. It opposed boarding schools for the very young, sought to make primary education free, pressed to abolish child labor, encouraged censorship of films to protect children, and fought to protect the rights of the unborn (Lubwama, 1990).
- ACFODE led the way in drawing public attention to the plight of domestic servants, condemning their abuse and mistreatment, including severe beating, emotional torture, deprivation of food and non-payment.
- Women like Baker Kazibwe and the Uganda Women's Football Association worked successfully to introduce women's soccer throughout the country. They sought corporate and government sponsorship for games, equipment, training and uniforms, all of which have been difficult to come by (Zziwa, 1996: 15).

- The United Help for Widows and Orphans Association (UHWOA) sought an audience with President Museveni in 1993 to obtain legal aid to administer the estates of their deceased husbands. The organization was formed in 1991 and within two years had a membership of over 5,000 active members and 20,000 orphans, who felt that the government had long neglected them and had reneged on promises to provide pensions and subsistence money. They wanted to draw public attention to the fact that the facilities the government had established to help widows and orphans were being misused or underutilized. In particular, the Jinja and Masindi Army Boarding Schools, which were set up with priority for orphans, ended up catering primarily to non-orphans who were admitted fraudulently.[35]

Expanded Use of the Media

Women's organizations also began to use the media vigorously to promote their causes. ACFODE started a women's page in the government-run *New Vision* almost with the newspaper's inception in 1988 and then in 1994 began to publish a four-page *Women's Vision* supplement. In 1994, groups like ACFODE and NAWOU, along with the Foundation for Human Rights Initiative, the Human Rights and Peace Centre, the Department of Political Science at Makerere, Radio Uganda and Uganda Television launched a program called "Link" that involved seminars, discussions and radio and television programs, a news bulletin, and newspaper articles aimed at providing information and civic education to interest the public in the constitution-making process. ACFODE itself published a regular bulletin as part of this program called *The Link Bulletin*, that included articles about the Constituent Assembly proceedings, debates among influential figures with varying viewpoints, and in-depth articles on the issues being discussed in the Assembly. Part of the impetus for this program was to broaden its work to include men as well.

Several magazines covering women's concerns emerged, including *Arise* (launched in March 1993) published by ACFODE, *The Voices*, published by Forum for Women in Development (FOWODE), which is a non-partisan women's organization, *The Plida* published by the Association of Uganda Women Lawyers (FIDA), and a publication by the Ministry of Gender and Community Development. NAWOU intermittently put out a magazine called *Newsletter*. ACFODE also had a legal counseling column in *The Weekly Topic* newspaper and other papers started similar columns. The *New Vision* also carried pieces by a columnist, Mary Okurut, who regularly covered women's issues, in particular women and politics.

International Visibility

Thus, an important consequence of autonomy has been an increase in the capacity of women's organizations to assert themselves on new fronts to push for the advancement of women and the betterment of society in general. It has allowed for agendas that go beyond older associational strategies that simply sought to improve women's capabilities as wives and mothers. The fact that many women have begun to take up these battles not only with the government but in their day-to-day lives and communities makes the changes all the more significant.

As a result of such activities, the Ugandan women's movement slowly began to attract international attention, hosting numerous regional conferences relating to women's concerns for East Africa and Africa more generally. Ugandan women gradually became visible in numerous international fora and in the leadership of key international bodies and organizations. For example, an international women's organization, Isis-International Cross Cultural Exchange (ISIS-WICCE), which was formerly based in Switzerland, moved to Kampala in 1993 to strengthen its regional and international connections. Uganda was selected over Namibia and Zambia explicitly because of the gains of its women's movement.

What follows is a key example of how women have sought to maintain autonomy at the national level in the struggle over the formation of the National Association of Women's Organizations of Uganda under the NRM regime. Such assertions of autonomy at the national level are replicated in many ways at the local level, as the remainder of the book will demonstrate.

The National Council of Women and the Struggles to Protect Autonomy

As noted in Chapter 2, Idi Amin established the National Council of Women (NCW) by presidential decree in 1978 to serve as an umbrella organization for NGOs. It was established as a national machinery in accordance with the World Plan of Action of the UN Decade for Women that was promoting national machineries to speed up the integration of women into public life. Nevertheless, there was little doubt that Amin had his own political objectives in creating the NCW to control women's associations. Many women's organizations were coerced into joining the NCW and independent organizations were largely curtailed during Amin's regime. Nevertheless, even during these difficult years, many women's associations continued their activities, keeping a low profile (ACFODE, 1988: 25; Guwatudde, 1987: 12; National Council of Women, 1991: 2).

Initially, the NCW was placed under the Ministry of Youth, Culture and Community Development. Later with the reorganization of ministries it came under the Ministry of Local Government and then was placed under the Ministry of Women in Development in 1988. Under Obote's second regime (1980–85), it was subject to the manipulations of the women's wing of the Uganda People's Congress, which treated it like a party organ (Tadria, 1987: 88). However, many of its members are adamant to this day that they were not UPC members, nor did they appreciate UPC interference in their organization. They often risked being labelled "anti-governmental" because of their independent attitudes.

The NCW was not the only organization subject to such manipulations. The Uganda Media Women's Association, which was revived in 1990, had been monopolized by the wives of high-ranking officials and politicians under Obote II, leading to its collapse in 1985.[36] Similarly, branches of the Mothers Union were commonly linked to the UPC at this time. However, as a semi-parastatal, the NCW had less autonomy than most of these organizations and found itself constrained by the ministerial bureaucracy.[37]

The NCW grew with several hundred organizations affiliated to it, including religious, youth, income-generating, savings, trade union, social welfare and government organized associations. It had representatives in 33 districts whose activities included maintaining national Safe Motherhood, legal education, and day care programs along with a Masulita Housing Project. The NCW supported revolving loan projects, provided training to member groups, organized seminars and published a newsletter to facilitate exchanges between groups. It also provided material, financial and technical assistance to various affiliate groups.

It was at the tail-end of the Obote II regime that women activists began to consider reviving an independent women's movement in Uganda. A large number of women leaders wanted to attend the UN Decade for Women meeting in Nairobi in 1985 but could not because they were not part of the handpicked delegation, which consisted mostly of wives of government officials and NCW members who supported the government. This infuriated many women like Hilda Tadria, ACFODE's first president, who said a decade later:

> In my mind I kept saying to myself, when this is over I would like to start a women's organization which no government would control . . . The government wanted specific people to go to Nairobi and the National Council of Women made sure it selected women who supported the government and UPC to go to participate. For me that was the major, the real, reason for thinking about an autonomous women's organization, so that you don't let the government dictate who your members are. If you are a women's organization, the women are your members, not the women who support the government.[38]

Several women, however, did attend the meeting in Nairobi as individuals and not as part of the official delegation led by President Obote's wife, Miria Obote, and Margaret Luwuliza Kirunda. They returned to Uganda inspired to revitalize the women's movement. The Nairobi conference, however, coincided with the coup that overthrew Obote in July 1985, leaving the nation in disarray. One of the first steps the NCW took following the coup was to organize a peace march in Kampala in September 1985 to assert its independence from the UPC and to try to convince women's organizations that it was indeed an organization representing all women in Uganda, not simply UPC supporters (Tadria, 1987: 88).

A further effort to push for associational autonomy was taken through the formation of ACFODE in November 1985 by 30 individuals led by Hilda Mary Tadria, Joy Constance-Kwesiga, Ruth Mukama and Maxine Ankrah. Tadria, who convened the first planning meeting, explained her vision at the time:

> First of all, for me, I had three main objectives. One was to make sure that no one owns the organization, so that we have an organization whose leadership changes regularly. Secondly, I wanted to make sure that it was an organization that would address the issues of women at the grassroots, not an organization for Kampala or anything like that. And thirdly, I remember saying to people that we have to have a constitution to enable us to operate.[39]

ACFODE quickly became one of the most vocal groups in this period, as it was formed largely as an assertion of women's organizational autonomy. One of the first initiatives it adopted was to demand the repeal of the Decree that created the NCW and to advocate the formation of a genuinely independent umbrella organization. The ACFODE leadership argued that, because the NCW had been a political organization in the past and had a history of being manipulated by the UPC, it needed to be disbanded and replaced by another co-ordinating body.[40] Although there were hints at the time that ACFODE might replace NCW as an umbrella organization, ACFODE itself never officially claimed that it intended to do so. ACFODE leaders argued that the UPC influence on the NCW in the past had shaped the organization in a "conservative" mold, preventing it from overhauling its leadership and from taking the lead in addressing some of the fundamental bases of women's subordination in Uganda. Some ACFODE members depicted NCW's focus on income-generation as a diversion from activism surrounding women's rights (ACFODE, 1988: 29, 40). This necessitated autonomy from political parties, allowing women's associations the liberty to act. ACFODE, in contrast, saw its own organization as free from such manipulations and unconstrained in setting its agenda. As one ACFODE member put it: "We could strategize, we had the connections so that if I came here and said that we needed a women's studies program, nobody was going to stand in the way."[41]

Although it may be true that the NCW did not lead the way in many of the movements for legal and educational reform, it did become involved in many of the same initiatives as ACFODE in the 1980s and 1990s and included among its affiliates organizations which played a leading role in fighting for women's rights.[42] Nevertheless, at the time, ACFODE and many other women's organizations sought to do away with the NCW's parastatal status, which in many ways symbolized the lingering potential for government control of this important organization. They objected to the fact that the NCW's leadership was appointed by the regime in power and not by the women themselves.

Efforts to repeal the 1978 decree and recast the NCW as an independent organization were complicated by the involvement of the NRM Secretariat, which had a different agenda with respect to the NCW. It wanted to see the NCW abolished, but at the same time to replace it with an organizational framework that would serve the NRM politically in much the same way as the NCW had served the UPC, especially in its later years.

As women's associations continued to flourish under the NRM, the government made continued efforts to control the mobilization of women at the national and local levels, primarily through the Directorate of Women's Affairs in the NRM Secretariat, led by Janet Mukwaya.[43] The Directorate was to take charge of the political mobilization of all women (Boyd, 1989: 106–17) and Mukwaya saw her role as coordinating the work of all the women's organizations in the country. In the early years of her tenure in the Directorate, Mukwaya was known to call in leaders of women's organizations and question their involvement in various NGOs without her approval and that of the NRM. In one such discussion, Joyce Mpanga, who was chairperson of the steering committee of one of the first women's NGOs created after 1986, the Uganda Women's Effort to Save Orphans (UWESO), responded to Mukwaya's inquiry by saying: "I have my own freedom of association. It is written in the Constitution of Uganda and you cannot take it away from us. And as long as we want to carry on UWESO, we shall do so."

Mukwaya apparently informed President Museveni of Mpanga's rebuff and he then summoned Mpanga and informed her that the Secretariat had given her position in UWESO to Prime Minister Kisekka. She challenged him on this and Museveni eventually backed down, convinced that UWESO had an essential role to play. Ironically, Museveni's wife started the organization and is its leading patron (see Chapter 3). In the end Museveni committed himself to helping UWESO with transport and fund-raising.[44] Although the President has been a supporter of UWESO since then, the incident reveals the deep suspicion with which the NRM regarded NGOs, especially in the early years of the regime. It also shows how critical women's organizations were in softening the regime's position regarding NGOs. Nevertheless, many of the problems of autonomy persisted.

Although short on resources and not very visible in the women's movement, the Directorate maintained long-standing feuds with the Ministry of Women in Development and with the NCW. It first tried to get rid of the NCW without consulting the organization. But Mpanga, who was head of NCW after 1986, pointed out that the NCW had been formed by a parliamentary decree that would have to be repealed before the organization could be dismantled. She told the Directorate that the NCW wanted help in amending the 1978 decree, but objected to the extra-legal effort to dismantle the organization without parliamentary intervention. This led to clashes between the two. The NCW leadership invited Mukwaya to sit in on their meetings as an ex officio representative so that the Directorate would get to know what they were doing. These meetings involved numerous women's organizations which were trying to come up with a new structure for the organization. However, Directorate representatives actively sought to undermine the NCW by misinforming people in the villages that it no longer existed and that it had remained a UPC organization, thus creating general confusion among its local affiliates. The Directorate also sought to portray a defunct and discredited NCW to foreign donors.

The other key player at the national level was the Ministry of Women in Development, which had been formed in 1988 as a result of pressure from women's groups. The first minister was Joyce Mpanga. Because she was also president of the NCW, the differences between Mukwaya and Mpanga over the NCW unavoidably spilled over into a conflict between the Directorate and Ministry over questions of associational autonomy and even over the relative powers of the two bodies. In 1989 the parliament began to raise concerns about the NRM Directorate and the fact that it was acting as a parallel ministry while drawing funds from the national Treasury. Expensive political seminars were being held by the Directorate, using public funds but with little accountability. The Ministry of Women in Development raised the issue when the Directorate spent USh. 46 million on a one-week cultural event for women in 1989 with no long-term benefits, while the ministry was operating at the time on a USh. 26 million annual budget. The ministry began to withhold financing of the Directorate. In response, the Directorate went straight to the top NRM officials without the ministry's knowledge and got the go-ahead for projects which the ministry would have to include in its budget.

Even though Mpanga favored repealing the 1978 bill that had created the NCW, she felt the strong need for an independent co-ordinating body for women's organizations. To her mind, governments could come and go, and some might support women's mobilization while others might ignore it, or worse still, suppress it. Even the existence of a women's ministry could not be counted on since its existence depended on the regime in power. For this reason she wanted to see the continuance of a women's umbrella organization that would consistently look after the interests of women. As she put it:

> So when the ministry was formed in 1988, the first thing I told the National Council of Women was that as long as I'm minister I would not like the National Council of Women to disappear because it was working as an umbrella of NGOs and bringing women together . . . . I said the ministry is just an arrangement of the NRM. Tomorrow they may feel they don't want it or they may amalgamate it with something else. So I wanted the National Council of Women to remain but as an autonomous NGO body. And that's why in the ministry I started a section for NGOs, a section that could co-ordinate between government and NGOs, that could receive memoranda from NGOs and bring them to the attention of the government.[45]

The Directorate, however, felt that the NCW was responsible for mobilizing only a fraction of the women and that there needed to be other structures to mobilize the remaining majority. Mukwaya believed that women were not sufficiently involved in the local councils and needed their own institutions, which could be a training ground for leadership, creating a large pool of women who could become leaders. When the idea of national women's councils was floated initially, some women leaders like Mpanga expressed concern that they would dilute women's efforts to integrate themselves into the LCs because they would be more likely to involve themselves separately in the women's councils. The NCW, in turn, saw the NRM's efforts as politically motivated rather than based on a concern for women's economic development.[46]

Mpanga was soon thereafter replaced by Gertrude Byekwaso Lubega as Minister of Women in Development, and the NRM Directorate became more directive in its relations with the ministry, even resulting at several points in interventions by women's NGOs in defense of the ministry. In fact, at a September 1990 meeting of NGOs, the Ministry of Women in Development and the Directorate of Women Affairs in the NRM Secretariat, women's organizations asked for clarification of the relationship between the two and called for the same kind of relationship as existed between other directorates and ministries, suggesting the need for a less interventionist directorate. They also pressed for the total independence of all NGOs from the government and vowed to repeal the 1978 decree that established the NCW, arguing for a co-ordinating body to replace it that was totally independent from government.[47] They planned to bring the matter of Decree No. 3 1978 to parliament after extensive debate among women's organizations (Kabuchu, 1990b). The NCW itself wanted to relinquish its parastatal status for similar reasons, but also because it did not receive sufficient funding from the government and believed that as an independent body it would have a better chance of attracting donor funds. With the help of the United Nations Development Programme, it undertook a survey of its own groups throughout the country between 1989 and 1990 and discovered that most groups were in favor of amending Amin's decree. Educated women's groups in the NCW were especially concerned that the new organization assert its independence from the government.

Most small grassroots organizations wanted freedom to manage their own affairs, but did not want a complete break in their relations with government, for fear of a subsequent loss of funding. At the same time they expressed concern about being dictated to by the Ministry for Women and wanted the power to override ministry decisions regarding their organizations (National Council of Women, 1991: 8–9).

The National Women's Councils

After Mpanga left the Ministry, none of the subsequent ministerial appointments had strong roots in the women's movement. This made them less interested in protecting women's associational autonomy as a means of expanding the women's agenda. The weekly meetings Mpanga had with women's organizations were discontinued. With Mpanga's departure, many women leaders felt that the Ministry's commitment to strengthening independent women's organizations was weakened, making it harder to forge joint collaborative initiatives and to develop common agendas.[48] The strength of the Ministry, however, remained in the high caliber of most of its staff, their commitment to women's issues and willingness to work with women's organizations on legal issues, education about the constitutional process and other areas.

The Ministers who followed Mpanga were either too weak to stand up to the top NRM leadership or were uncritically loyal to it. For example, when it first was announced in parliament that the NRM was planning to establish Women's Councils to mobilize all Ugandan women, the Minister did not raise any questions about who had drawn up the plan, nor did she ask why they had not consulted the Ministry first, even though the plan involved ministry co-ordination and funding.

The Directorate pressured the Ministry of Women in Development to redraft and submit to the National Assembly the National Women's Council Statute repealing the 1978 decree that had created the NCW. The Bill was passed in 1993. This Bill would not have been controversial in and of itself, but it also replaced the NCW with a hierarchy of Women's Councils that were to be tied to the Local Council system and co-ordinated by the Ministry of Women in Development. Meanwhile, the Directorate had pressured the NCW to change its name to the National Association of Women's Organizations of Uganda (NAWOU)[49] and another "National Women's Council" was to be formed with a name almost identical to the former "National Council of Women". This appeared to be a deliberate attempt to confuse local women's organizations because the NCW had frequently been referred to as "the Council" and the new "Council" would be referred to in the same way. It caused a major uproar at the NCW's annual meeting. The NCW secretary general Florence Nekyon explained:

> Many women were cursing, saying how dare you [the directorate] change our name and some people said we should go and sue them. They said we had built up our name and now they are going to use it. We were told point blank that we had to change and some of the women in the Secretariat (Directorate) said, we have the power to make you change it.

The NCW was also bitter about the way the Directorate forced the Ministry of Women in Development, Youth and Culture to take over the organization of the annual 8 May International Women's Day celebrations, which used to bring together groups belonging to the umbrella organization.[50]

The new National Women's Council was to be made up of Women's Councils at the village, parish, sub-county, county and district levels under the direction of the Ministry of Women in Development, Youth and Culture, which would appoint the Secretary. The NRM claimed that these Councils would enable it to reach all women because the independent women's organizations did not mobilize the majority of women.

Even though most organizations, including the old NCW, supported the repeal of the 1978 decree and the creation of an independent umbrella organization, officials at the (now) Ministry of Gender and Community Development, NCW leaders, and other heads of women's organizations were critical of the way in which the Directorate intervened to get the bill passed and forced the Council to change its name. This campaign to deny legitimacy to the NCW continued after the Council had been transformed into the present-day National Association of Women's Organizations of Uganda (NAWOU), which was formed at a two-day meeting of the NCW in 1992.

The then Minister for Women in Development, Culture and Youth, Specioza Wandira Kazibwe, pointed out at a meeting of urban-based NGOs in 1992 that the women's councils were political structures, whereas NAWOU was to deal directly with NGOs and grassroots women's groups and clubs.[51] These kinds of statements led many to believe that the women's councils were really the NRM's version of a women's wing. Nevertheless, women's organizations took a wait-and-see attitude toward the councils but at the same time were wary of the NRM's apparent attempt to control women's participation. Some felt that the new development would divert the energies of women away from trying to work within the LC system and would create a competing structure. The MP from Mbarara Municipality, Winnie

Byanyima, echoed much the same criticism that Mpanga had made of Mukwaya's original idea of creating women's councils:

> I don't like them [Women's Councils]. I want them scrapped. I want women to go for real power. Any structure that is parallel, that takes them away from the real power and takes their time, which they have so little of, is diversional. The real place where women should be running and influencing is the local government.[52]

The Women's Councils also came under criticism for creating a structure parallel to the resistance/local councils without a clear delineation of authority between the local council women's secretaries and the Women's Councils. No sooner had the statute been passed than the Ministry of Women in Development, Youth and Culture was attacked at a meeting in Mukono in April 1994 by central government representatives, District Executive Secretaries, Town Clerks, RC5 chairpersons and RC5 women's secretaries, who expressed confusion over the relationship between the Councils and the LC system and how they fit into a decentralized system. They criticized the Ministry for not supervising the formation of the councils adequately and for distributing the statutes to the districts only a few days before the council elections without sufficient time to clarify their purpose and ensure their functioning (Businge, 1994). Others were confused about the difference between the Women's Councils and the LC women's groups and in some instances there was open feuding between the LC women's secretaries and leaders of the Women's Councils (Kwesiga, 1994).[53] At the first National Youth and Women delegates conference, there was fierce opposition to having separate leaders for the women's secretary and the Women's Councils because it was a set-up for conflict (Baguma, 1994; Nviri, 1994b). There was an extremely poor and unenthusiastic showing for the first elections for the Women's Councils, and in some cases (Makindye in Kampala and Masaka) the elections were wracked by religious and ethnic tensions.

Finally, a third criticism of the Women's Councils revolved around the threat they posed to independent organizations. As Byanyima put it:

> Another thing I don't like about them [Women's Councils] is that they are sort of a parastatal. To me any structure that is trying to put women into a structure under the government, I am suspicious about them. I don't want it. I want women to participate in government like men in the councils. . . . What implication does that have for the NGOs and independent autonomous action? Because now the NGOs in the particular areas do not have a free hand to operate and organize when there are these other structures of the state. That is my opinion. The NGOs should be active and should be the voice of women, which should be strong. NGOs should not be presided over by the ministry. . . . . It gives me the feeling of some kind of communistic state where women are being organized for the purposes of the government.[54]

This struggle over the NCW/NAWOU is indicative of the tensions between women's NGOs, the Ministry of Gender and Community Development and the NRM Directorate. At stake is the degree to which the NRM will tolerate organizational autonomy: whether independent organizations will be able to influence the Ministry and co-operate with it effectively; whether women's organizations will be able to pursue their own agenda free of interference from the NRM; whether the NRM will break from the pattern of previous regimes of using women's organizations for its own political purposes in garnering votes; and, ultimately, up to what point the NRM will tolerate a women's agenda that does not necessarily coincide with its own.

None of these struggles really came to a head for several reasons. First, the women's movement found that it could go ahead unimpeded because of its relative strength. Second, the NRM regime had been relatively accommodating of women's demands and there was no reason to antagonize them unnecessarily. And finally, the NRM simply had not committed the necessary resources to make the Women's Councils viable institutions that would seriously threaten the autonomy of women's organizations.

What also emerges from these struggles for autonomy was a change in the way the NRM Directorate became more directive in its dealings with the Ministry of Gender and Community Development, which in 1998 became the Ministry of Gender, Labour and Social Development. We have already seen how the NRM's influence over the Ministry had a direct impact on women's organizations. But there were other consequences of NRM control of the Ministry, some of which resulted in conflicts within the Ministry over its role. From its inception there were those who saw the Ministry playing more of a catalytic role with an emphasis on policy-making, while others saw it in its more traditional role of co-ordinating women's projects. This latter position was being pushed by the NRM in order to strengthen its control of women's organizations. The Ministry's shift from its original vision of being a catalyst to one of co-ordinator led to heightened tensions with NGOs (Bonnie Keller, personal communication, 1997).

The Paradox of Women's Associational Autonomy

Women's organizations in Africa, especially at the local level, have often gained a level of autonomy not enjoyed by other societal institutions. Authoritarian one-party states all too often incorporated trade unions, student and youth organizations, co-operatives, traders associations, and other such organizations into state and party structures, allowing them little freedom to maneuver outside these bounds. Other less fortunate organizations were eliminated or undermined. Certainly there have been national women's organizations and women's wings of ruling parties in addition to women's market and self-help associations that were incorporated into state structures, as described in Chapter 1.[55] But women have also always had their own independent informal savings associations, marketing networks, secret societies, income-generating organizations, and farming groups at the local level. These organizations were generally small, informal, localized, and usually invisible to the authorities. This has been as much by design on the part of the women as it has been a consequence of exclusion from mainstream institutions.

One of the main characteristics of women's associations in Uganda today is their autonomy from the NRM, in spite of enormous pressures for co-optation, both at the national and local levels. Paradoxically, women's organizations have been able to assert such autonomy under the NRM regime by taking advantage of previous and ongoing exclusions of women from most public arenas.

While women-only organizations are critical in advancing women's interests, there is a danger that they may be seen as reinforcing the marginalization of women because they can be taken as evidence that women have consented to an exclusionary political order that keeps them peripheral to political engagement (Staudt, 1986: 207). Thus, it is necessary to situate agency and subjective interests in the context of objective conditions within which agency can be exercised (Jónasdóttir, 1988). There are indeed exclusionary ideologies and beliefs that keep women confined in women-only associations and out of more influential institutions like the leadership of local councils. However, within these constraints it is important to look at how women are using their organizations to advance their interests.

The local-level conflicts in the case studies that are explored in the following chapters show clearly that women have not consented to exclusionary institutional arrangements. They are fighting to change those very structures through their own gender-specific forms of mobilization. What is even more significant – and not accounted for in feminist institutional analysis – is that they have adopted organizational forms that are seemingly based on a narrowly defined gender identity to challenge those very exclusions. In the process they are undermining the institutional bases of female subordination. They have taken institutional structures that constrain their mobilization and have creatively and actively turned them around in an attempt to expand their choices, opportunities and control.

The claim that I am making poses a number of dangers. Goetz has warned of the dangers of conflating "social or cultural identity with political opportunity and choice". She argues that this may quickly lead to "associating a rather limited sex-typed range of political and social interests with women" (Goetz, 1995: 7). However, in practice, the purpose of using gender-based associations to defend women's interests has often been more than simply a consequence of a culturally dictated norm and more than a manifestation of women's exclusion from male-controlled local governance institutions. Women used their organizations in the struggles described in this book to gain access to community leadership and to have a voice alongside men over the use of communal resources. There was nothing limiting or sex-typed about the women's goals for which they fought through the main organizations available to them. Clearly, resistance of marginalized groups necessarily occurs within organizations and fora that themselves are expressions of their isolation and political weakness. But it is important to look beyond these structural constraints to examine what people actually do within such limitations and what significance they themselves attach to their action. In other words, autonomy has to be understood in its particular historical and social context rather than in the abstract.

Thus, the autonomy of women's organizations in part grows out of women's marginalization, but has the potential simultaneously to become transformed into a political response to marginalization. It has the potential to incorporate agency and intentionality, depending on the context and circumstance. Autonomy thus embodies the tension between action and constraint which this chapter seeks to unravel and explore by looking at the ways in which women have advanced their interests through their own segregated, multi-purpose, locally based, small and somewhat invisible organizations.

Gender-Specific Organizations

There is no question that cultural traditions have resulted in highly gendered mobilization in Uganda, with women tending to work within their own associations independent of men. According to my 1993 survey, in Luwero, Mbale and Kabale women were much more likely than men to join a single-sex group and in Kampala they were three times as likely as men to be in such a group. Men, on the other hand were more likely than women to be in a group of both men and women (Table 4.2).

There are various factors that have contributed to these forms of mobilization. One historic explanation dates back to the early Community Development clubs, Girl Guides, the Mothers' Union, and other such organizations that were heavily influenced by the British experience of creating associations specifically for women (see Chapter 2). The practice of gender-specific organizations introduced by

Table 4.2 Gender Composition of Organizations (%)

	KAMPALA		KABALE		MBALE		LUWERO	
	Men	Women	Men	Women	Men	Women	Men	Women
	(n = 133)		(n = 140)		(n = 50)		(n = 50)	
All male	27	0	24	1[a]	43	0	0	0
All female	0	75	3[b]	64	0	68	0	70
Male and female	73	25	73	35	57	32	100	30

Notes: a) Sometimes a woman is brought in as treasurer in an all-male organization.

b) Men may try to run women's organizations on occasion (see Chapter 10).

religious organizations and donors corresponded easily with pre-existing patterns of gendered divisions of labor. Women in many parts of Uganda have farmed together in groups, taking turns in each others' plots. They also jointly carried out various domestic activities. These gendered formations were easily extended to more formal associations as British organizational influences asserted themselves on the Ugandan scene.

To this day, Protestant and Catholic churches have perpetuated these gender segregated forms of mobilization based on what were perceived as a "natural" divergence of interests having to do with women's traditional roles in the household. For example, the Catholic Church's work with women has emphasized nutrition, training in agriculture, child health, leadership training, provision of water supplies, music, drama and handicrafts in addition to spiritual concerns. The purpose of focusing on these particular activities is to improve women's contributions to the home as mothers and wives in raising healthy families (Guwatudde, 1987: 62). Ugandan and external donors, likewise, have a proclivity toward funding "women", some because they want to see women participate more actively in the economic, social and political life of the country, but all too often with the end result of reinforcing a particular set of stereotypical women's roles.

Yet another reason for mobilizing along gendered lines has to do with men's resistance to women's involvement in any form of mixed public life or associational activity. Given how threatening many men find even very benign women's associations, it has been easier to belong to women-only organizations in order to minimize suspicions of adultery that might develop in mixed organizations. Women have sometimes adopted organizational strategies to make their associations appear less threatening to men/husbands. They stress the less controversial aspects of their organizations to their husbands and emphasize how they contribute to the welfare of the home.

But even women-only organizations have proved to be too threatening to some men. My survey showed that women saw as a key problem objections from husbands who did not approve of their wives belonging to a group because they feared the women would gossip, the group activities would detract from housework, or that the women would come in contact with other men or with new ideas. In fact, these are not new problems. A study of women's participation in clubs in Kigezi conducted in the 1970s found that men generally disapproved of women's involvement in clubs for reasons very similar to those given today. They argued that women's clubs resulted in divorce because women had a tendency to gossip. They complained that their wives would be out too late in the evening, preventing them from completing their domestic responsibilities. They feared that their wives might surpass them in knowledge and use it against them; that they might learn rude behavior; or that they would leave them with the responsibility of looking after the children while they were out (Bagyendera, 1977: 36, 62).

Finally, women's marginalization from the local councils and other key community bodies has left them with little choice but to work within their own groups to influence public opinion and policy-makers, carry out community development initiatives, improve their own living standards and express their political views. One local council woman's secretary in Kasubi, Kampala, openly admitted this, saying that it was hard to mobilize women through the local council system and she was trying instead to mobilize established women's associations in her area such as a local Munno Mukabi group, local chapters of the Catholic Women's Guild and Mothers' Union, a women market vendors group, and several other local self-help groups. She put it quite explicitly:

> Women are not keen about the LC system but would easily come to a Munno Mukabi (self-help/burial society) meeting, one that involves issues pertaining to income-generation or religion. It is easier to organize women through their weak points by appealing to their values, to what they love and cherish rather than the LC system.[56]

Tabitha Mulyampiti also found in rural Pallisa that, because of the limitations of mobilization within the local council structure, women have formed organizations outside the system, often using local council women officials as mobilizers and leaders of clubs. She found 59 women's clubs in Pallisa district with approximately two clubs in each sub-county, involving about 9,600 women. The groups were involved in horticulture, vegetable growing, food and cash crop farming, brick making, handicrafts, music, dance, drama and other such activities. Like the women I surveyed, the main aim of the groups in Pallisa was to improve living standards, gain access to credit and property, earn enough to pay school and health fees, market their produce, learn better farming methods, and acquire new skills in cooking, handicrafts and tailoring. The groups were also fora for expressing opposition to various forms of oppression. They were used to appeal to policy-makers through dance, drama, and poetry, especially on issues concerning land, to which women had little access in this area. They also used these cultural forms to raise public awareness of problems of widows' inheritance and their lack of rights to keep their children (Mulyampiti, 1994).

Even though associations have historically been organized along gender lines, women have also used them at times as a strategy to maintain a sphere of action outside the purview of the authorities. Certainly, gender-based associations have been subject to manipulation and regulation by various regimes, but keeping the gender division has also made them less susceptible to outside interference. As the case studies in the following chapters show, this autonomy often gave women a critical space from which to fight for resources and to protect their interests. Most importantly, in all the case studies the organizations took on ideological dimensions which challenged the gender basis of the discrimination the women faced. In other words, the women transcended the cultural gender basis of their organizations and gave political significance to their gender-based mobilization.

Local Multi-purpose Organizations and Embedded Political Action

Women, unlike men, have generally organized themselves in multi-purpose organizations. In Uganda such multi-purpose women's organizations combine income generation, savings, social welfare, farming, cultural and other activities. This parallels patterns of female mobilization in many other parts of Africa from the Igbo Women's Councils in Nigeria to the Harambee groups in Kenya (Feldman, 1983: 68; Mwaniki, 1986: 215; Strobel, 1979). By emphasizing the multi-purpose nature of the organization, women can easily de-emphasize, when need be, those activities that involve community activism and mobilization that might challenge the status quo in terms of gender interests. The Kitumba women's group (see Chapter 7) transformed itself from a handicraft group into an association actively fighting for a community clinic and for women's right to lead such an initiative. Yet it continued to portray itself to the public as a rather innocuous organization when projecting such an image suited its purposes.

The classic example of such multi-purpose women's organizations are the dual-sex councils in West Africa, which are regaining their popularity. A dual-sex political system is one in which representatives of each gender govern their own members through a Council. In much of former Eastern Nigeria most communities have a broad-based Women's Governing Council that has sole jurisdiction over wide-ranging political, economic, and cultural affairs of women, from market issues to relations with men, and morality (Nzegwu, 1993). The decisions of these councils, according to Nzegwu, are binding, regardless of social status, education, or income level. Moreover, the local councils can represent women living as far away as Lagos, Kano, or New York. They are distinct from organizations modeled along Western patterns in that they promote a sense of "shared communitarian values rather than perceived divisive individualistic values", as Nzegwu puts it. Their leaders service a wide range of associations and therefore are multi-faceted in their approach, since they are concerned with social, cultural, religious, economic and political issues simultaneously, giving them a virtual "encyclopedic knowledge of their community".

Nzegwu argues that these women's councils are enormously important to local women because they have a strong community orientation and claim to legitimacy. Their diverse membership means that the council can draw on a wide variety of skills and know-how for advice. Accountability is maintained by a strict monitoring system where nothing is hidden and the threat of public humiliation and ostracism weighs heavily as a deterrent to violations of council norms. Accountability is tied to community validation, which is an extremely effective constraint on corruption in this context. The complex and efficient administrative structures that can also adapt to new situations are witness to the resilience of these associations.

Women's groups in Uganda adopt different functions as the needs of the organization change over time. In fact, one of the biggest problems in the survey was being able to make distinctions between women's groups, development groups, savings groups, digging groups, and even church groups, because their functions overlapped so much and were in flux over time. "Munno Mukabi" groups, for example, can be savings clubs, burial societies, digging groups, emergency aid associations, income-generating groups or some other type of organization. They may be defined as a burial group in one context and as a digging group in another or may fulfil a combination of functions. Moreover, some groups, savings clubs for instance, are embedded within other associations. I found, for example, numerous savings clubs operating within the Masese Women's Housing Project in Jinja. Similarly, Mothers' Union chapters contained unofficial sub-groupings of savings clubs nested inside them.

In a society where men often object strongly to women's involvement in any kind of associational activity, women may find it easier to justify their involvement by stressing less threatening aspects of their multi-purpose organization to their husbands, such as drama, handicrafts, etc. Thus, when Kitumba women in Jinja (see Chapter 7) wanted to start a health clinic and in so doing undermine the dominance men had held in community affairs, they worked through a drama group, which also carried out income-generating, farming, and other activities. At the time, their organization appeared innocuous, making it hard for their husbands to object to their involvement in the group. Had they said they were mobilizing to openly challenge gender relations in the community, they would undoubtedly have met with resistance from their male kin.

Just as women's lives are not always divided conceptually into discrete activities, so political action is conceived of as part of life and not a separate sphere. Household tasks, income-generating tasks, farming, caring for the sick and old, raising children, preparing and participating in community celebrations and community self-help activities are activities that blend into one another and make up life as a totality. Similarly, political action is often embedded in the activities of these multi-purpose organizations. This means that it is important not to decide a priori that women's organizations are not interested in political influence or in challenging institutional hierarchies along gender lines, simply because they are not established for those express purposes.

Modernization theorists might argue that Uganda is an agrarian society and simply does not have sufficient stratification to warrant specialized organizations. And indeed, the weak development of market activities and the lack of a clear separation of work and home for most women, urban and rural, gives rise to holistic conceptions of the sustenance of life in its many dimensions, minimizing the dichotomies found in Western industrial societies between public and private spheres, the market and the household. But I would argue that there is more to it than this. In fact, these multi-purpose organizations are also used as part of conscious political strategies. Embedding political action within multi-purpose organizations can serve numerous purposes.

It might be useful to provide a brief profile of one typical multi-purpose women's group in Kampala to illustrate the nature of this social formation and how women are able to maintain their independence of action by keeping the organization multi-purpose (see general data on marital status, religious affiliations, educational levels, ages and income sources of members of organizations in Kampala, Kabale, Mbale and Luwero in Tables 4.3–4.12). In 1988, a young 24-year-old Muganda businesswoman in Rubaga Division completed her Senior 4 education and decided to start Kigagga Kwekamba Women's Club. She got the idea to organize the group initially from her mother, who had been active in the Mothers' Union and the YWCA. The group, which had 35 members, 15 of whom were very active, was involved in crafts, weaving, rearing goats and chickens, cooking, looking after orphans and raising money to pay the orphans' school fees.

When asked about the association's major successes, one member recounted the building of feeder roads and a protected well and some brick baking they had done. Another thought the main success was the fact that they had encouraged women to clean their compounds so that the zone was the cleanest of all the zones in the vicinity. They raised money for the association through the sale of eggs and handicrafts, as well as music and drama presentations.

The members included Catholics, Protestants and Muslims. They also included Baganda, Banyankole, Acholi and Batoro, and admitted that at times

Table 4.3 Marital Status of Organization Members (%)

	KAMPALA (n = 133)			KABALE (n = 140)			MBALE (n = 50)			LUWERO (n = 50)		
	Men	Women	Total	Men	Women	Total	Men	Women	Total	Men	Women	Total
Unmarried	20	11	12	4	9	8	29	21	22	0	8	6
Married couple	80	70	71	86	62	67	71	58	60	80	60	64
Married polygamous	0	0	0	4	0	1	0	10	9	20	13	14
Divorced/separated	0	13	11	0	4	3	0	3	2	0	10	8
Widowed	0	0	7	4	25	21	0	8	7	0	10	8

Table 4.4 Marital Status of General Population Surveyed (%)

	KAMPALA (n = 552)			KABALE (n = 250)			MBALE (n = 206)			LUWERO (n = 135)		
	Men	Women	Total	Men	Women	Total	Men	Women	Total	Men	Women	Total
Unmarried	19	16	17	4	12	10	18	17	17	9	10	10
Married couple	75	68	69	84	63	67	76	63	65	78	63	66
Married polygamous	2	0	1	2	0	0	4	8	7	13	10	10
Divorced/separated	0	8	6	0	5	4	0	5	4	0	5	4
Widowed	1	7	6	4	19	16	2	6	5	0	11	9
Other	3	1	1	6	1	3	0	1	1	0	1	2

Table 4.5 Religious Affiliation of Organization Members (%)

	KAMPALA Men (n = 133)	Women	Total	KABALE Men (n = 140)	Women	Total	MBALE Men (n = 50)	Women	Total	LUWERO Men (n = 50)	Women	Total
Protestant	20	40	38	38	55	51	71	34	40	50	40	42
Catholic	67	32	36	52	38	41	14	29	27	10	40	34
Muslim	13	20	20	10	7	8	0	32	27	20	10	12
7th Day Adventist	0	6	5	0	0	0	0	5	4	20	5	8
Born Again Christian	0	2	2	0	0	0	0	0	0	0	0	0
Other	0	1	10	0	0	0	14	0	2	0	5	4

Table 4.6 Religious Affiliation of General Population Surveyed (%)

	KAMPALA Men (n = 552)	Women	Total	KABALE Men (n = 250)	Women	Total	MBALE Men (n = 205)	Women	Total	LUWERO Men (n = 135)	Women	Total
Protestant	38	40	40	43	56	53	42	46	45	65	47	50
Catholic	46	38	39	49	35	38	33	28	29	13	30	27
Muslim	11	17	16	8	7	7	16	23	21	13	16	16
7th Day Adventist	1	3	2	0	0	0	0	2	2	9	5	5
Born Again Christian	0	2	1	0	0	0	0	1	1	0	0	0
Other	3	2	1	0	2	2	9	0	2	0	2	2

Table 4.7 Education or Organizational Members (%)

	KAMPALA (n = 133)			KABALE (n = 140)			MBALE (n = 50)			LUWERO (n = 50)		
	Men	Women	Total	Men	Women	Total	Men	Women	Total	Men	Women	Total
No schooling	0	4	4	21	25	24	0	16	13	0	5	4
Primary[a]	13	36	33	52	48	49	14	53	47	30	63	56
Middle school[a]	7	7	7	14	4	6	14	3	4	10	8	8
Secondary school[a]	80	49	53	10	23	21	71	26	33	60	25	32
Tertiary education[a]	0	4	4	3	0	1	0	3	2	0	0	0

[a] Up to and/or including

Table 4.8 Education of General Population Surveyed (%)

	KAMPALA (n = 552)			KABALE (n = 250)			MBALE (n = 205)			LUWERO (n = 135)		
	Men	Women	Total	Men	Women	Total	Men	Women	Total	Men	Women	Total
No schooling	6	5	5	20	27	26	4	10	9	0	6	5
Primary[a]	32	43	41	51	44	45	31	46	43	44	56	54
Middle school[a]	9	4	5	7	3	4	4	3	3	4	4	4
Secondary school[a]	52	40	42	16	26	24	51	40	42	52	33	36
Tertiary education[a]	2	8	7	4	0	1	0	1	1	0	0	0
Other	0	0	0	0	0	0	10	1	2	0	1	1

[a] Up to and/or including

Table 4.9 Ages of Organization Participants (%)

| | KAMPALA | | | KABALE | | | MBALE | | | LUWERO | | |
	Men (n = 133)	Women	Total	Men (n = 140)	Women	Total	Men (n = 50)	Women	Total	Men (n = 50)	Women	Total
18–24	20	23	23	7	7	7	29	16	18	0	5	4
25–34	27	42	41	10	23	20	14	32	29	40	25	28
35–44	27	25	25	38	29	31	29	34	33	40	35	36
45–54	27	4	7	28	19	21	14	18	18	10	18	16
55–64	0	2	2	10	13	12	14	0	2	10	13	12
65–	0	3	2	7	9	9	0	0	0	0	5	4

Table 4.10 Ages of General Population Surveyed (%)

| | KAMPALA | | | KABALE | | | MBALE | | | LUWERO | | |
	Men (n = 552)	Women	Total	Men (n = 250)	Women	Total	Men (n = 206)	Women	Total	Men	Women (n = 135)	Total
18–24	15	24	22	8	15	14	4	18	16	4	18	16
25–34	45	41	42	24	27	26	52	32	36	52	32	36
35–44	16	21	20	31	28	28	26	26	26	26	26	26
45–54	16	7	9	18	13	14	9	15	14	9	15	14
55–64	8	3	3	8	10	9	4	6	6	4	6	6
65–	1	3	3	12	8	8	4	3	3	4	3	3

Table 4.11 Main Source of Income for Organization Participants (%)

	KAMPALA (n = 133)			KABALE (n = 140)			MBALE (n = 50)			LUWERO (n = 50)		
	Men	Women	Total	Men	Women	Total	Men	Women	Total	Men	Women	Total
Business	27	20	21	21	32	29	29	18	20	50	40	42
Employment	20	24	21	31	23	24	43	24	27	30	13	16
Farming	7	2	2	24	10	13	0	16	13	10	18	16
Spousal income	33	32	32	10	18	16	0	40	33	0	20	16
Other	13	22	21	14	18	17	29	3	7	10	10	10

Table 4.12 Main Source of Income for General Population Surveyed (%)

	KAMPALA (n = 552)			KABALE (n = 250)			MBALE (n = 205)			LUWERO (n = 135)		
	Men	Women	Total	Men	Women	Total	Men	Women	Total	Men	Women	Total
Business	29	28	28	23	27	26	33	22	24	52	36	39
Employment	27	16	18	33	19	22	31	16	19	22	8	10
Farming	6	2	3	20	6	9	16	9	11	22	19	19
Spousal income	28	38	36	8	21	18	9	46	38	0	30	24
Other	16	15	18	27	25	11	7	8	4	8	0	0

communication was a problem due to the many languages spoken in the group. Most were businesswomen and farmers and none were formally employed.

While the club was an income-generating group, the members also shared ideas about politics and had debated and disagreed on questions of multi-partyism versus a single-party system. They also had discussed and supported as a group the idea that women should take top positions in government, and agreed that men should not object to women's participation in clubs. The members pointed out that male resistance to their participation was one of their major problems and the leader had tried to talk to various husbands to allay their fears and persuade them not to restrict their wives. Members were required to be well-disciplined; no rumor mongering or backbiting was permitted; and women who were known to have committed adultery were not allowed in the club. This particular club was not on good terms with the LC1 chairperson and women's secretary. The two local council leaders had at one time laid claim to the association's drums and theatrical costumes. Finally, intervention from the LC3 leaders settled the score but tensions remained. The women vowed to oust the LC1 leader in the next elections, claiming that he was elected illegally by bringing in voters from other zones to vote for him. These experiences had made them protective of their independence from the LC.

Thus, women in multi-purpose organizations like Kigagga Kwekamba Women's Club are able to establish a basis from which to assert political influence. The case of this club, which is a fairly typical group, highlights the importance of not pitting domestic and public activities so sharply against each other. Even though the group was involved in income-generating activities and social service provisioning, group members discussed politics and were active in influencing the outcomes in local elections.

Small and Informal Groups

One way groups avoid the scrutiny of the authorities is by deliberately remaining small, informal, invisible and unregistered. Most local-level groups are not registered. The rest are chapters of a national body, or registered with the NAWOU, or they are a LC women's group. At the local level, being small and detached from larger intermediary organizations may have the consequence that organizations are not able to benefit from broader contacts and are unable to influence collective action at a higher level. Invisibility can mean being ignored by government policymakers so that one's interests are not taken into account. Informality (not being legally registered) has the potential consequence of not being able to access donor or government resources through legal channels.

On the other hand, smallness, invisibility and informality also mean that it is easier to evade potentially repressive measures leveled by the state against an organization in an effort to curtail its autonomy. They also imply a degree of self-reliance that has made many of these organizations at this level so durable. They have meant the capacity to determine one's own priorities and agendas under circumstances where states were only too eager to impose a national blueprint on local communities. Under authoritarian rule, autonomy of association in terms of smallness, informality, and invisibility has offered the benefits of a certain amount of freedom of association.

When I asked one member of a Kampala savings club why her group was unregistered when they might be able to apply for credit if they registered, she replied:

These organizations will collapse if they become formalized. We work so well informally. We have no office. Everything is nice and simple. The minute we become formal we will collapse. The minute we try to get credit, we will become a shambles. The group is based on trust, mutual confidence, flexibility. You do what you want, the organization is yours. What would we do if we registered? We would have to have a location, an office, and we can't afford that. We would have to get registered and do the proper paperwork. Who would have time to go around and do all that? We are all working women. Then they would want us to be a co-operative and we do not want that. They would want a fee and we can't afford that. We just want things nice and simple.[57]

Even then, only one half of all individuals in organizations surveyed reported being in groups that were registered in Kabale and Mbale. Two-thirds in Kampala said they were in registered groups, and three-quarters in Luwero. In almost all instances, few knew with whom they were registered and the respondents were generally confused about what it meant to be registered and whether affiliation with a national body implied registration. Based on this lack of clarity, I was left with the distinct impression from the survey that most organizations were not registered.

Conclusions

One of the main tensions in Ugandan state-society relations is the extent to which the women's movement and other societal groups can claim autonomy from the state. On the one hand, the Museveni government has made some concessions to women's organizations and has exploited the rhetoric of women's mobilization in order to win women's endorsement and votes. At the same time it has "engaged" society, in this case by seeking to curtail women's independent mobilization under the guise of co-ordinating their activities within the local councils, Women's Councils, and other such structures. Women's organizations have also "engaged" the state concerning numerous issues, including women's greater political representation, women's land ownership, rape and child molestation, girls' education and many other similar concerns. The main problem facing the women's movement is the government's lack of responsiveness and inability and unwillingness to address their key demands.

Thus, the central issue is not how to activate society to engage the state, but rather how to keep the state from crushing and co-opting the emerging associational life and instead become more responsive to the many new demands women and others have put on the agenda. The women's movement provides a fascinating glimpse into this dilemma because it has been able to maintain considerable autonomy. Moreover, some of the fiercest and most vocal critics of Museveni on corruption, land, Women's Councils, and other such issues are also leaders of the women's movement. At the same time women and women's organizations are generally supportive of the NRM government because of its anti-sectarian stance and verbal endorsement of women's concerns. But women have seized on the NRM's language of emancipating women and pursued these goals in ways Museveni never intended, as the four case studies in this book illustrate.

This chapter has described some of the main characteristics of women's organizations in Uganda and has shown why associational autonomy is a key factor accounting for the gains made by the women's movement at both the national and local levels. The following chapter will explore additional factors that need to be taken into account in explaining the rapid growth of the movement and its impact.

Notes

1 Think Tank Public Seminar, 8 July 1994.
2 Interview with Expedit Ddungu, Kampala, 9 March 1993.
3 United Nations World Conference to Review and Appraise the Achievements of the UN Decade for Women.
4 *New Vision*, 26 September 1990.
5 Interview with Sarah Ntiro, Kampala, 18 March 1993.
6 Interview with Joyce Mpanga, Kampala, 1 July 1995.
7 Ibid.
8 Interview with Maxine Ankrah, Kampala, 19 June 1992.
9 After the 1996 parliamentary elections, ministerial posts went to Janat Mukwaya, Minister of Gender and Community Development, Syda Namirembe Bbumba, Minister of State and Alternate member of Cabinet in the Office of the President, Rebecca Kadaga, Minister of State, Ministry of Foreign Affars, Catherine Mavejina, Minister of State, Ministry of Public Service and Cabinet Affairs, Jane Kuka, Minister of State, Ministry of Gender and Community Development.
10 Interview with Christine Lalobo, "Men are Using the Gender Bias to Run Down Women," *Sunday Vision*, 6 February 1994, p. 13.
11 Specioza Kazibwe (Iganga/Kigulu), Capt. Janet Mukwaya (Mukono/Mukono South), Dr. Maria Nakyanzi (Mukono/Ntenjeru South), Dr. Sophie Musana (Mukono/Buikwe North), Rose Nadiope Kadhumbala (Kamuli/Bugabula North), Winnie Byanyima (Mbarara/Mbarara Municipality), Mrs. Rhoda Kalema (Kiboga/Kiboga West), Cecilia Ogwal (Lira/Lira Municipality), Victoria Sekitoleko (Jinja/Bugembe).
12 Specioza Kazibwe (Kigulu South, Iganga), Winnie Byanyima (Mbarara/Mbarara Municipality), Fiona Egunyu Asemo (Ngora, Kumi), Juliet Kafiire Rainer (Kibuku, Pallisa), Tezira Jamwa (Kisoko, Tororo), Salaamu Musumba (Bugabula, Kamuli), Cecilia Ogwal (Lira Municipaity), Hajati Janet Mukwaya (Mukono South).
13 "Women Issue Their Own Manifesto," *All Africa Press Service*, 14 May 1996.
14 "Museveni Fights LC Bill in 6-Hour Night Meet with MPs," *The Monitor*, 1 February 1997.
15 "Museveni Wins Easily, 'O' Level Thrown Out," *The Monitor*, 26 February1997; 'O' Level Requirement Divides Sexes," *The Crusader*, 25 February 1997; "Women MPs Slam Bill as House Starts Hot Debate", *The Monitor*, 25 February 1997.
16 Interview, RK, Erina Muherya, Masindi, 19 November 1992.
17 Interview, RK, Pumla Kisosonkole, Kyambogo, Kampala, 14 October 1992.
18 Interview, RK, Joyce Mpanga, Kampala, October 1992.
19 "Women Sweep Law Society Top Jobs," *The Monitor*, 30 January 1997.
20 Anglican Communion News Service, 2 September 1996. Edited from an article by David Musoke in *Ecumenical News International*.
21 The conference was entitled "ACFODE Follow-up Seminar of Women's Decade Conference".
22 The former Ministry of Community Development, Youth and Culture was divided in half, with Community Development being merged with the Ministry of Local Government and Youth and Culture with Women in Development.
23 *New Vision*, 14 September 1988.
24 The ministry is made up of a legal department, an education and training department, and departments for research and communications, project implementation and NGOs, headed by a commissioner, who also supervises women in development officers assigned to various parts of the country, divided up into ten units.
25 Interview with Joyce Mpanga, Kampala, 1 July 1995.
26 *Women's Vision*, 31 May 1994.
27 The current law is being debated because it assumes that a girl under 18 years of age cannot consent to sexual intercourse. Some argue that this does not distinguish between a 17-year-old who may be in a common law marriage and a 6-year-old victim of sexual abuse.
28 Letter to the editor, "Sex Abuse Matter Trivialised," by Rebecca Kadaga, Chairman [sic], Women Against Sex Abuse, Kampala, *New Vision*, 23 December 1991.
29 Letter to the Editor, "Women Will Never be Equal to Men," by M. C. Kasibante Mayuanja Ntwatwa, Kampala, *New Vision*, 10 October 1993.
30 See Note 28
31 *New Vision*, 26 November 1993
32 Interview with Miria Matembe, Kampala, 16 July 1993.
33 Interview with Evelyne Nyakoojo, Kampala, 12 July 1993.

34 *New Vision, 19* May 1993.
35 *The Monitor,* 2–6 July 1993, p. 4.
36 "UMWA Revived," *New Vision,* 6 June 1990, p. 10.
37 Interview, RK, Florence Nekyon, Kampala, December 1992.
38 Interview with Hilda Tadria, Kampala, 26 June 1996.
39 ibid.
40 Interview with 1.3, Kampala, 26 June 1992. Number given to preserve anonymity.
41 Interview with Maxine Ankrah, Kampala, 19 June 1992.
42 Examples of the more activist organizations include Uganda Association of University Women, Association of Uganda Women Lawyers (FIDA), and ACFODE itself.
43 Janet Mukwaya became Minister of Gender and Community Development in 1996.
44 Interview with Hon. Joyce Mpanga, Kampala, 1 July 1995.
45 ibid.
46 Interview with Ruth Kisubika, Kampala, 8 June 1992.
47 To give a picture of the kinds of NGOs active in this period, the NGOs attending the meeting included World Vision, the YWCA, Uganda Girl Guides Association, Fellowship of Christian Women, Uganda Muslim Ladies Association, Salome Brotherhood, Women and Reproductive Health Network, Tree Planting Movement, Association of Uganda Women Lawyers (FIDA), Uganda Women's Effort to Save Orphans (UWESO), Action for Development (ACFODE), Foundation of African Development (FAD), Uganda Co-operative Alliance, Uganda Women's Finance and Credit Trust (UWFCT), Uganda Credit and Savings Union, Women Entrepreneurs Association, Makerere University Students Union, Disabled Women's Association, Association of University Women, and Wanyange Group, and of the umbrella organizations the NCW and the Development Network of Indigenous Voluntary Organizations (DENIVA).
48 Interview with Hon. Miria Matembe, Kampala, 16 July 1993.
49 National Association of Women's Organizations of Uganda was its old name prior to 1965.
50 Interview with Florence Nekyon, Kampala, 21 May 1993.
51 "Minister Challenges Women's NGOs", *NCW Newsletter,* 1992.
52 Interview with Winnie Byanyima, Kampala, 8 July 1995
53 "Conflict Grows between Women RC Groups," *Daily Topic,* 6 September 1994.
54 Interview with Winnie Byanyima, Kampala, 8 July 1995.
55 Umoja wa Wanawake wa Tanzania (UWT), Organização da Mulher Moçambicana (OMM), the Women's League in Zambia, the League of Malawi Women, etc
56 Interview with Ssebawato, Kampala, 18 June 1993.
57 Interview with 1.1, Kampala, 2 June 1992.

5

Why the Women's Movement Expanded under the NRM

Togaya kye zinze.
(Do not underestimate what appears to be insignificant like a rolled up piece of paper.)

Luganda proverb and name of women's group

The previous chapter demonstrated how autonomy was critical to the growth of the women's movement in Uganda and to its ability to influence policy. It showed how at the national level women's associations became an increasingly important force for changing political culture and political institutions through their efforts to seek gender inclusiveness in public leadership and in promoting policies that advanced the interests of women in society. This chapter explores other reasons that account for the new-found capacity of the Ugandan women's movement, which in less than a decade began to distinguish itself on the African political scene as one of the most vital societal movements.

In Uganda the proliferation of women's groups both at the local and national levels occurred around the mid-1980s and especially after 1986 when the NRM came to power, bringing with it considerable stability. The growth of women's organizations paralleled that of non-governmental organizations in general, which had increased to the point that a Development Network of Indigenous Voluntary Associations (DENIVA) was formed in 1988 (Musheshe, Jr., 1990: 4; National Council of Women, 1991). In Kabale, which had the highest concentration of associations of the four towns I surveyed, there were almost five times as many associations formed in the five-year period 1988–1992 as in the previous five years 1983–7.[1] In Luwero only one organization was reported to have been formed during the years of turmoil (1983–7), while half the organizations in that area were established in the following five years. One leader of a Mpigi rural women's group, Akiika Embuga Self-help Association, explained how in the past insecurity had destabilized the area and their possibilities for action, so that they were "running off every time a military vehicle was sighted". By 1990 they had been able to build offices and a meeting place for their organization, a store, a tailoring room, sheds for their poultry and numerous other projects (Kabuchu, 1990a).

The national organizations that existed prior to the mid-1980s tended to be either religious,[2] professional[3] or welfare associations.[4] Moreover, they were usually linked to a larger international body. After the mid-1980s the national associations differed not only in their variety but there also appeared a greater number of strictly indigenously based associations.

While some new groups reflected women's continuing interest in welfare concerns, like the Uganda Women's Effort to Save Orphans and the Uganda Disabled Women's Association (both started in 1986), many others represented a shift in women's status and interests and a broadening of their agendas. For example, women's heightened involvement in business was reflected in the formation of organizations like the Uganda Women Entrepreneurs Association Limited (created in 1987), which in 1993 became a national umbrella association for all women's business groups in country. Others revealed women's increased involvement in new professions, for example the Association of Women Medical Doctors (1987), the Association of Women Engineers, Technicians and Scientists in Uganda, and the Media Women's Association. Women's rights associations became visible for the first time in Uganda, including Action for Development (1985), the Uganda Global Network on Reproductive Rights (1988) and Human Rights Women Activists. Many worked to improve the status of particular groups of women, like the Second Wives and Concubines Association of Uganda (1996), Women in Development and Widows' Association, and the Single Mothers' Association. Others emerged in response to civil service reform, which involved major retrenchments of women, for example, Retired Mothers' Efforts for Survival (1996) and the Demobilized Women Civil Servants Association (1995). Regional development associations for women were also a new phenomenon, linking urban and rural women together in common cause to improve the welfare of their home regions, for example West Nile Women's Association, Mbarara Women's Development Association and Women's Action for Karamoja Development. Finally, associations emerged to reflect women's new social interests, like the Uganda Women's Football Association.

These patterns of mobilization were borne out at the local level as well, even though the organizations were smaller in size, generally with a membership of between 20 and 30. My survey showed that women in Kampala, Kabale, Mbale and Luwero who belonged to organizations started prior to 1985 were overwhelmingly involved in religious associations. After 1985, multi-purpose women's associations (usually with income generation at the core of their activities) and credit associations stood out as the main forms of women's mobilization in Kampala, Kabale and Mbale. Similarly, a 1977 study showed that women in Kabale were primarily involved in either the Mothers' Union (48 percent) or the Kigezi Catholic Women's Association (42 percent) (Bagyandera, 1977: 55). By the 1990s, however, the pattern of associational involvement was quite diverse in Kabale. In 1993, only 11 percent were involved in religious organizations in contrast with 90 percent in the 1970s. The remainder were divided among multi-purpose women's groups, credit and savings and burial associations, self-help, farming and other varied forms of mobilization.

Religious organizations remained an important arena for women's mobilization in all four towns. But religiously based associations themselves also began to assume many of the functions of women's multi-purpose associations. The older formal women's associations like the Mothers' Union, YWCA, and Catholic Women's Guild were formed prior to independence, primarily to socialize women into traditional roles, provide educational opportunities, serve welfare functions and promote religious concerns. Even today, the main aim, for example, of the Mothers' Union is to promote social, economic and political conditions that are conducive to stable Christian family life.[5] However, there have been some changes from the past. In contrast, today it is providing training and other assistance in starting income-generating projects.[6] According to Helen Wangusa, the leader of the Mothers' Union, who co-ordinated the activities of chapters throughout the 23 dioceses in Uganda, the Union had taken up women's political leadership as one of its main concerns and was proud of the fact that many women local council leaders were also Mothers' Union members. Even parliamentarians like Lois Bwambale, Miria Matembe, and Catherine Masaba had gained their initial experience in leadership through the Mothers' Union, according to Wangusa.[7]

Nevertheless, these religious associations faced continued constraints on their autonomy from church authorities in ways that served to limit their agendas. For example, the Catholic Bishop of the Kampala diocese, the Rt Rev. Matthias Ssekamanya warned that the Catholic Women's Guild should not fight for equal rights for women and that Guild clubs should not be used by women to overpower their husbands lest they break up their families. He asked the Guild to regulate women's moral behavior by combating prostitution and other bad habits and encourage women instead to become involved in income-generating projects (Baine, 1993).

In addition to these aforementioned forms of mobilization, women in the 1990s were heavily involved in handicraft and cultural (music, drama, dance) associations at the local level. They participated in welfare groups that assisted orphans and in associations for the physically disabled. They were also involved in cultivating groups, especially in areas like Kabale, where two-thirds of the urban dwellers farmed. Many of these associations participated in community self-help initiatives of various kinds, such as building roads, wells, and assisting rural women's groups with their skills. Almost all groups were multi-purpose, combining these various activities in different ways. Men, on the other hand, were more likely to be in single-purpose organizations, and, in particular, co-operatives, sports clubs and burial societies. They were also less inclined to be in religious organizations.

At the local level many of the associational forms were not new. Historically women had come together in both formal and informal or ad hoc arrangements to carry out joint weeding, harvesting, and planting, or to make preparations for ritual or celebratory functions (funerals, weddings, etc.) or to provide community services. Many of the new organizations focused on income generation, savings strategies, family planning and pre-natal care (e.g., Safe Motherhood), environmental tree planting, and the provision of services to orphans and AIDS victims. But these groups were, in fact, based on older organizational patterns which were now in the service of new functions.

The newness of many of these associations is reflected in their names. For example, in Kampala I came across groups with names like *Basoka Kwavulu ne Balyoka Batambula*, which translates roughly to "they must crawl before they walk," and *Togaya Kye Zinze* or "do not underestimate what appears to be insignificant like a rolled up piece of paper". In Pallisa, Tabitha Mulyampiti found groups with names like *Lugwere Tetete*: When a baby is learning to walk, falling and picking itself up it is encouraged with the word *"tetete"*, which means "move on".[8] Other Pallisa groups were called *Tulamuke* or "we should wake from our slumber",[9] *Twesowoileyo* or "we are emerging", Yet another group, *Asimba Asanyi*, refers to sowing millet and the importance of scattering seeds for better results lest the plants grow in clusters.

"When the jaws do not come together they cannot bite"

In explaining the growth of associational life in Uganda it is useful to start by considering women's own reasons for joining associations. The three most frequently mentioned reasons women gave in all four towns in the survey had to do with the need to improve their standard of living, learn new skills/educate oneself and get united (Tables 5.1 and 5.2). Women also mentioned that they wanted to socialize, gain new ideas, and meet like-minded people. The strong ethos that in order to succeed one must work together with others is reflected in the names of organizations. For example, one Pallisa group was referred to as *Agali Amo*, which is an abbreviation of a proverb, "when the jaws do not come together they cannot bite" (or in Luganda *Agali awamu, gegaluma enyama:* "if you have all your teeth, you can bite the meat properly"). The acronym of another group, West Road Women's Association (WEWA) means "give yourself". One of the members of this group explained that under difficult circumstances "It is important that you first give of yourself and think of others and then of yourself . . . . You cannot survive if you only rely on yourself, we all need one another." This view was shared by many we interviewed along with the concern that today it may be one group member who needs help, but tomorrow it might be you; you therefore need to be connected with people you can rely on. In the urban setting many of these connections are extensions of kinship obligations to non-kin, sometimes referred to by anthropologists as "fictive kinship ties".

Apart from these important subjective reasons for mobilization, there are several key reasons that explain the new growth in women's associations. Women did not start mobilizing from scratch. They had had decades of experience in religious and community development associations that gave them organizational and leadership experience to draw on (see Chapter 2). This explains why they were able so quickly to seize on the new openness of the NRM regime to mobilize in ways not evident among other sectors of Ugandan society. In addition, women took advantage of the stability brought about by the NRM takeover which made it possible for the first time in a long while to contemplate activities which required planning for the future.

The following pages describe other reasons for the increase in mobilization: (i) Women's new participation grew out of the transformative effect of the years of civil war on gender roles and expectations. (ii) General economic decline similarly affected household relations and put particular burdens on women to find collective solutions to securing new sources of income and food. (iii) The erosion of the state also meant that it could no longer carry out the functions it once had, similarly placing new pressures on community responses to social and welfare services (Kabukaire, 1992: 40). (iv) The new influx of donor support, initially after the ousting of Idi Amin but mainly after the NRM takeover, also had some impact on the formation of new organizations, although I shall argue that the impact is less than generally imagined. (v) Moreover, the new NRM regime encouraged women's mobilization and women were quick to respond to the new openness. (vi) Finally, although women's lack of education and literacy remained a constraint on continuing mobilization, the improved levels of education among women helped account for the strengthened capacity and viability of many organizations, especially those at the national level.

Impact of Internal Conflict

Ten years after independence Uganda plunged into years of civil war, internal conflict and institutionalized violence beginning with Idi Amin's takeover in 1971. Instability in most of the country (apart from the North) lasted roughly until 1986 when the NRM came to power after waging a prolonged guerrilla war. Fifteen years of conflict left over 800,000 people dead, 200,000 exiled and millions displaced within the country (Watson, 1988: 14). Out of these crises, new spaces for associational life emerged.

Table 5.1 Why Members Joined an Organization (%)

| | KAMPALA | | KABALE | | MBALE | | LUWERO | |
	Men (n = 133)	Women	Men (n = 140)	Women	Men (n = 50)	Women	Men (n = 50)	Women
Learn skill/gain education	6	22	5	12	0	20	0	12
Improve family's standard of living	11	14	49	22	57	16	9	21
Get united/help each other	16	11	8	16	0	20	9	11
Socialize	6	5	3	14	0	2	0	2
Gain new ideas/share ideas	6	3	0	1	0	12	0	11
Meet like-minded people	11	7	8	6	0	6	9	2
Develop women	0	6	5	9	0	6	0	7
Support goals of organization	22	9	0	2	0	0	36	9
Other	22	23	22	18	43	18	37	25

Table 5.2 Perceived Benefits of Being in Organizations (%)

| | KAMPALA | | KABALE | | MBALE | | LUWERO | |
	Men (n = 133)	Women	Men (n = 140)	Women	Men (n = 50)	Women	Men (n = 50)	Women
Learn skills	8	43	28	37	33	52	22	38
Obtain income	23	16	35	20	33	17	22	17
Socialize/foster togetherness	23	18	9	13	0	20	0	15
Other	46	23	28	30	33	11	56	30

The years of internal warfare had a profound effect on women's self-perceptions and on men's perceptions of women. Most importantly, it gave women activists leverage in pressuring the NRM to put women in top leadership positions. It thrust women into new roles and situations that fundamentally transformed their consciousness. Rural women found themselves talking to Tanzanian soldiers, harboring and feeding soldiers, and hiding their weapons in their homes during the war in which Tanzania helped the Ugandans oust Amin. Because they were women, Amin's troops did not suspect them. In the cities, husbands sometimes taught their wives to drive and how to run their businesses in the event that they themselves might have to disappear into the bush.[10]

At the beginning of the armed resistance to Obote's second regime in 1981 there were only a few women involved in the military aspects of the struggle, including Captain Olivia Zizinga, Joy Mirembe, Janet Mukwaya and Gertrude Njuba. According to Zizinga, women were assigned some of the most challenging tasks, like fetching supplies from Kampala and taking them back to the Luwero Triangle, from where the resistance was being mounted. Women dressed in ordinary clothes so as not to draw undue attention to themselves. They also treated casualties during this early period of the fighting, but by the end of the war they were fighting alongside the men. Zizinga said it was not easy for men to take orders from women, but since obedience in the army was not optional, the men had no choice but to learn (Chibita, 1996). Some, like Gertrude Njuba, were in the high command. The notion of women having men under them was an entirely new phenomenon. As the Hon. Joyce Mpanga pointed out: "It surprised men to see women in uniform commanding men when they were taking over Kampala. It was an eye-opener".[11]

Women who joined the National Resistance Army (NRA) fought side by side with men. The sight of women carrying both a gun and a baby on their back left an indelible impression on many. Women soldiers were impressed by the fact that women were treated the same as men in the NRA, which was markedly different from their experience with previous armies. Many women soldiers found the army a refuge from the problems they encountered at home, including poverty and oppressive husbands. Interviews with women soldiers indicated that many believed that the army would provide them with educational opportunities, and calculated that if they could survive the war they would eventually have a job in the army (Kagoro, 1989).

While the fighting did not have a direct impact on women's associations, it contributed to the psychological effect of women's changing overall perceptions of their capabilities and their roles (Ankrah, 1987; Watson, 1988). It also had an effect on male perceptions. As one woman put it:

> Men saw what women could do. They saw women firing guns, they saw women moving with a baby and a gun on their back. Men were scared and after the war tried to get women back into their traditional roles. They feared for themselves. They feared that women could no longer be manipulated. Even my husband when he was in the bush was astounded that he had not been able to eat or sleep because of the shooting and his stomach was upset all the time. One night they heard sounds and when they went out, the first person to have gone out and start shooting was a young woman of 16. She was there holding a gun firing away. This profoundly affected him.[12]

Economic Pressures

An important factor contributing to the increase in women's associations has been the economic crisis that began in the late 1970s, which put additional pressures on women to expand their income-generating activities and consequently to seek collective means of coping with new economic constraints. Clearly the internal unrest in Uganda had exacerbated the crisis. One of the factors that affected the livelihoods of urban households was the dramatic drop in real wages, which fell by a staggering 26.4 percent a year between 1980 and 1983 (Jamal, 1991; Mamdani, 1990: 438). Urban areas were also hit hard by civil service and factory lay-offs, cutbacks in social and welfare services, and the imposition of austerity measures as part of economic reform programs.

Thus, women's economic strategies assumed greater significance in the 1980s and 1990s because of their key role in sustaining the household. Women have often been the last line of defense, and have ultimately been the ones in the household responsible for providing food and clothing for the family and for paying school and health fees. Urban women have subsequently expanded their involvement in urban farming and small businesses through self-employment or joint ventures. This has necessitated an array of collective coping strategies, giving rise to new women's associations and networks (National Council of Women, 1991: 1).

As one ACFODE leader, Margaret Kikamphikaho, pointed out in explaining why women are more likely to be involved in voluntary organizations than men:

> Women are the ones who have been left out of development, politics, and the economic sector. It is only after Amin that women went into the informal sector. Before, men were the bread-winners. If he was a civil servant, he was producing for consumption, that was all. The children were not going to school. Before, we [women] never used to dress ourselves [pay for our own clothes]. Even me, one of the educated, I expected my husband to dress me (*laughter*). So . . . everybody's awareness has really increased. Women are paying for things today. They are in business. They are looking after everything themselves. Men were not the oppressed . . . they did not have to struggle, there was no need. They have always been there. Women were down there (*gesturing toward the ground*) and said, "Why must women always be down there?"[13]

The role of urban women in informal and private enterprises has been in large measure determined by the fact that women have been less tied to the formal economy than men, in other words, they have not had access to jobs in the formal wage sector because of a lack of education and discriminatory hiring practices. According to the 1991 national census, women make up only 20 percent of the employed labor force. This has meant that, as formal incomes have declined, there have been increasing pressures on women to seek informal and alternative ways to sustain the household. In urban Uganda this shift from reliance on formal incomes to reliance on informal and private sector incomes occurred in the 1980s.

Similar patterns were evident in rural areas. For instance, one woman who had grown up in Kamuli district said that in the past in her home village there had been only emergency-based self-help groups and religious and welfare associations. Since 1989 women had become involved in savings, income-generating, marketing, farming and animal husbandry groups, which formed, as she explained, because "The economic situation forced women to think about their needs, to raise money and to take matters into their own hands."[14]

In more general terms, women have entered many occupations and sectors of the informal economy that in the past had been solely the domain of men, such as tailoring or brick-making. For example, *Women's Vision* carried a story about Nakanyike Amina, aged 22, who followed her three brothers and four cousins into becoming a car mechanic (Kyambadde, 1996). In other areas like markets, the number of women has increased significantly. Today, women constitute the majority of vendors at the largest markets in Kampala. At Nakasero, three-quarters of the stalls are owned by women and two-thirds at Owino (Kabuchu, 1990a; Ssemirembe, 1993). Women have also become involved in new enterprises, such as mushroom and pyretheum farming (Kabale), silk farming (Kampala), vanilla growing (Mukono), papyrus handicraft development (Jinja), growing sesame seeds (Kitgum), soya beans, ground nuts, sun flower seeds and engaging in oil milling. Without an empirical baseline, it is difficult to pin down a precise measure of the change that has occurred as a result of women's new-found economic independence. However, the large number of new organizations tied to income generation is one indication of the change (see Table 5.3).

Survey respondents in all four towns reported that one of the biggest changes that had occurred since the NRM takeover was that they could now engage in all kinds of occupations and that they had started their own businesses and become financially independent of men (see Tables 4.11 and 4.12). Many reported that, as a result of this economic emancipation, they had also found a voice in the home. They felt they had freedom of movement and of association and could now stand up to men. The answers to the survey were open-ended but the pattern of responses was striking and consistent. They conveyed an overwhelming sense of accomplishment since 1986, stating that "women had developed", "they were no longer backward", "they had more confidence in themselves", "they had started their own businesses", "they had become financially independent of men", "women worked harder than they ever did", "women could involve themselves in any kind of occupation", and "they were no longer restricted as they had been in the past". Men were more tentative about the changes women had experienced. In Kampala, for example, four times more men than women saw no change in the position of women.

Many urban women have been involved in small businesses, ranging from hairdressing to making and selling pastries and other foodstuffs, running vegetable and fruit stalls, and brewing and selling beer. But there is also a growing class of large-scale entrepreneurial women. In Kampala some of the most successful women are involved in retail trade, which was largely taken over by female entrepreneurs after the expulsion of Asians from Uganda in 1972 by Idi Amin. Some are engaged in trade with the Gulf states and are popularly referred to as "Dubai traders", a term which carries it with it the derogatory but erroneous implication that all women involved in this trade also engage in sex work while abroad. In Kabale, women who used to retail used clothes have now shifted to the wholesale end of the business as a result of support from the Uganda Women's Entrepreneurs Association (Tanzarn, 1996: 15). Although individual women entrepreneurs have benefited from patronage networks, businesswomen generally have not had access to patronage and personalistic networks tied to the state. They tend to be part of the emerging bourgeoisie in Africa that is not based on extracting and diverting state resources.

In many rural areas, women have also pursued these kinds of economic activities because of increasing land pressures and customary land inheritance and ownership patterns, which discriminate against women holding land of their own. In Uganda only 7 percent of the land is owned by women in a country where the majority of the population obtains its sustenance from agriculture and where women grow 90 percent of all food crops and 60 percent of all cash crops (Tamale and Okumu-Wengi, 1992; Watson, 1988).[15] Single, divorced, and widowed women without options to own and reap the benefits of smallholder land tenure, and women who want independent sources of livelihood, often enter into trade or small-scale production. In rural areas, women are also major traders, especially those living in border areas. Take, for example, one of the most important commodities traded by women: smoked and salted fish from the Albert Nile. Not only does it bring in enormous profits, but the trade in this fish is extensive. The fish are obtained from Panyimur, Wanseko and Rhino Camp on the Albert Nile, Pawar and Jinja and are transported as far as Congo in the west, as far north as Yei in Sudan and on to Juba in the east (Meagher, 1990).

The emergence of this new business class whose wealth was not *primarily* based on the diversion of resources from the state is a phenomenon that has been described most extensively by Janet MacGaffey in the context of Congo, where women also have been especially prominent in such activities. MacGaffey calls this class of business owners "an indigenous local capitalist class", which invests in enterprises that produce for the internal and external markets. Their wealth is not based on holding political office or from activities based on fraud or extortion, but rather on business (MacGaffey, 1986: 162–3). As in Congo, women in Uganda have less access to formal institutions than men and therefore have tended to remain within the second economy.

Linked to this private sector and informal economic activity in Uganda are a growing number of organizations of varying nature. For instance, women are increasingly joining small groups set up specifically to assist in generating income (see Table 5.3). In Uganda these groups are varied and are involved in farming, animal husbandry, tailoring, fishing, trade in small household items, making and selling of foodstuffs and alcohol, providing services, etc. Women surveyed reported that the main successes of their groups included the provision of tangible benefits to members in the form of income, services or equipment with which to generate income. At the same time, providing education, assisting the needy and developing their local area were also seen as major accomplishments.

Rotating savings associations emerged as one of the most important types of business-related organizations that became especially popular in Ugandan and other African urban centers during the economic crisis of the 1980s and 1990s. These associations have served as a means of saving money to reinvest in businesses, to get new businesses started, and for major purchases, school fees, building houses or medical expenses. In Uganda savings clubs go by various names: *kilab* (club) in Lusoga, cash round, *munno mukabi* (mutual help, wealth, investment) in Luganda; *kalulu* (throwing lots) or *emigabo* (shares) in Runyankore.

The importance of new economic resources for women's mobilization is borne out in the case studies in this book. While many of the women's activities described did not require large sums of money, economic resources often provided the women with a feeling of independence that they could make decisions and act on them without constraint. For example, the Kitumba women (Chapter 7), who were small businesswomen and farmers, clearly had sufficient resources to support a school-teacher who conducted a baseline survey of the health needs in the parish. The women also contributed furniture and other materials to the health clinic, and carried out fund-raising among other women's groups for the clinic. Similarly, Joyce Muhire, whom the Kampala City Council (KCC) considered the "ringleader" of the opposition to the World Bank project in Kawaala (Chapter 9), had several businesses and as a widow owned a large beautiful well-built house that had been targeted for demolition in the Kawaala project.

The Kiyembe market women (Chapter 8) had had their ups and downs, but most had done quite well considering their many setbacks. One Kiyembe woman proudly told me how she had put all her children through secondary school and one had made it to Makerere University. Most of the Kiyembe women owned land

Table 5.3 Activities of Organizations (%)

| | KAMPALA | | KABALE | | MBALE | | LUWERO | |
	Men (n = 133)	Women	Men (n = 140)	Women	Men (n = 50)	Women	Men (n = 50)	Women
Income generation & business promotion	17	39	8	23	26	50	24	38
Cultural	8	27	6	11	0	24	0	16
Farming	0	7	18	11	0	7	4	14
Savings & loan	17	3	38	18	37	3	44	5
Welfare & public services	17	3	14	6	0	4	8	13
Education	0	8	1	7	0	4	4	5
Religious	8	5	3	9	0	1	0	3
Social	21	2	6	11	0	4	8	2
Other	12	6	6	4	37	2	8	4

and had other businesses they were operating simultaneously as individuals and as a group. Their economic gains were similar to those of other women market vendors in Kampala. For example, Grace Mbabazi, the market administrator at Nakasero, observed of market women, "Most of them made fortunes, they have built permanent houses and some of them drive cars" (Mugisa, 1994).

Retreat of the State

Another impetus for the growth of women's welfare and social service provisioning associations has to do with the government's relinquishing of its official responsibility in these areas (Kwesiga and Ratter, 1993: 13). Thus, much of women's service orientation has come out of necessity, where the state is not in a position to provide these services. Schools in Uganda were basically run until 1996 by Parent Teacher Associations that paid for school supplies and teacher salaries. Virtually all new health clinics in many areas of the country are started by private individuals or by local health groups. The care of orphans, the elderly and the sick has always been the responsibility of women in the community, but the AIDS epidemic has placed new pressures on women to care for orphans and AIDS victims.

Frequently the welfare provisioning arrangements involve a combination of collective assistance and individual income generating strategies (see Table 5.3). Some groups support one another as the need arises, for example, in securing an income-generating project, a job, housing or capital. One Kampala savings group located in a complex of 24 government-owned apartments was formed when one woman in the complex lost her husband as a result of an accident. As is customary in some parts of Uganda, the husband's family laid claim to her children and put pressure on her to marry her husband's brother to put an end to compensating for the bride wealth payment. The neighboring women got together and found her a job as a waitress. They also helped her start a business selling second-hand clothes, called *kunkumura* in Luganda (which literally translates into "shake and see"). The woman rented a meter of counter space in a shop from which she sold the clothes.[16] The group's joint efforts thus enabled her to maintain her financial independence and related individual autonomy. When a second woman in the group lost her husband to AIDS, the group intervened and persuaded the housing authorities to let her keep her apartment for an additional six months until she could relocate. They also helped her with transport. She eventually had to leave her apartment but she remained part of the group. When this second woman was widowed, the women realized how precarious their own positions were and consolidated their organizational structure in a savings club.

The main purpose of the group was to share contacts, exchange business and other ideas, provide financial assistance for income-generating activities, and give financial and other help in emergencies. The women saved money to pay for school and health fees, and to reinvest in their businesses. One woman used the money to complete a house that she was building.

Other groups combine income-generating projects with caring for the disadvantaged such as orphans, pregnant young girls who have been expelled from school, the disabled, and the elderly. Turihamwe Women's Group in Kabale aimed not only to assist its 14 members in their income-generating activities but also to serve the local community by providing storage facilities and markets for their agricultural produce. In addition, they also stipulated that each member take in two orphans and care for them. Uganda has particularly high rates of maternal mortality. More recently the AIDS scourge has left unprecedented numbers of children without parents, to the extent that the extended families can no longer absorb their orphaned kin. The government discourages the setting-up of orphanages because so many have ended up being money-making schemes at the expense of the welfare of the children. Therefore, people with the means have been encouraged to take responsibility for children in their own homes and women's groups have been active in sponsoring such arrangements.

Another typical pattern of social service provisioning involves urban groups or individuals who reach out to rural or disadvantaged women's groups because they believe they have something to offer them. For example, in Kampala, one woman who had been involved in several savings clubs with friends and a *Munno Mukabi* (farming group) was able, through her savings and a small grant from a women's organization, to start a "Mother and Child Center" in Wabigalo, a low-income part of Kampala. It was a day-care center for market women, but it was also a place where various groups of market women could meet to discuss their trade and marital problems, and child-rearing issues. Other groups met to learn how to manage their accounts or how to read.

Another group, A Stitch in Time Women's Association, was formed in Kabale in 1989 for women involved in tailoring, crocheting and making carpets. But they also had as an objective to help other women become involved in income-generating activities and to assist other women's groups. Their styles of carpets and bags were new in the area and had thus given them new markets. The leader of the group had been a pioneer in setting up a successful credit and savings society and she was encouraging others to join this group or form other savings clubs of their own. One of the members of a Stitch in Time had joined another women's group in the neighborhood where she lived. It was made up mainly of 34 uneducated small businesswomen who had a savings club that had worked extremely well on an informal basis. As an educated woman, her intention in joining the group was to help them connect with other women's groups in Kabale, get registered and open a bank account, thereby giving them access to training for small-scale entrepreneurs. She was very impressed by their successes without any help from anyone, and she felt obligated to share with them her knowledge and contacts.

Yet another small Kabale organization was made up mostly of market women but they called themselves the Professional and Skilled Women's Association for Development (PROWAD) since they once had been, or still were, involved in professions as businesswomen, teachers, nurses, and other occupations in the civil service. The PROWAD members spent time and their own limited resources visiting two rural women's groups in Kitogota and Rwakaraba on weekends to offer them training in sewing and knitting. The PROWAD members themselves had just learned how to grow mushrooms and were anxious to share this new-found skill with the rural women. Peace Sabiiti, one of PROWAD's members who sold handmade knitwear at the market, was particularly eager to help groups of rural women. She felt a special need to teach them what she knew because she had grown up in a remote area of Kisoro and had had the advantage of an education. Even though she would have liked to help the women she had grown up with, she was happy to do something for the rural women with whom PROWAD worked. She mainly taught them knitting, but also nutrition. As she explained:

> Infant mortality here happens because of the ignorance of mothers. They have plenty of food. They have chickens, potatoes, vegetables, but because of traditional beliefs women refuse to eat chicken, goat's meat and eggs. Men eat eggs and goat's meat. We are now trying to educate

them. . . Sometimes they don't know how to prepare nutritious food for their kids. The children get sick due to ignorance. We feel we should give them a light. We should help them because we had a chance of education.

Finally women come together to find ways to provide their own community with a service like a health unit or day care center, or to help find markets for goods produced in the community. These are service functions that benefit not just disadvantaged community members but a broad section of the population. The struggle of the women in Mutai and Kitumba to establish health units, as described in Chapter 7, is an example of these kinds of efforts.

In the case of the war widows' and orphans' associations which cropped up after 1986, many were phony organizations formed simply to gain access to donor funds. Gradually, it became evident that many associations were fraudulent scams, while other organizations like the War Widows' Foundation and the Uganda Women's Effort to Save Orphans (UWESO) emerged as legitimately concerned with the plight of widows and orphans.

Availability of Increased Donor Funds

The new availability of donor funds, channeled through international NGOs and religious bodies, embassies, international foundations, and also through government bodies, has been yet another factor in spurring the growth of indigenous organizations both at the national and local levels (National Council of Women, 1991: 1) (see Table 5.4). Major supporters of women's NGOs include DANIDA, SNV Novib, Oxfam, UNICEF, European Development Fund, World Vision, Konrad Adenauer Foundation, Ford Foundation, Swedish International Co-operation Agency, American Embassy, and the British Council.[17] Local donors include organizations like the Uganda Women's Credit and Finance Trust, which was formed in Kampala in 1984 and expanded branches to Masaka, Jinja, Mbarara, Iganga and Mbale.

Some attribute the increase in organizations almost entirely to these new resources. However, by the mid-1990s funds were drying up even for successful national organizations like ACFODE that had relied heavily on outside funding, forcing the organization to reconsider more self-sustaining strategies (Ankrah, 1996: 23). More importantly, at the local level funds for associations have always been scarce. In my survey not one woman mentioned the availability of donor funds as an incentive for forming an association. In fact, most of the groups surveyed did not have access to foreign or local funds. The main way they raised funds was by collecting dues from members, selling products, performing at cultural events, and in Kabale, from digging other people's fields (see Tables 5.5 and 5.6). In Mbale assistance from outside the group was negligible. In Kampala and Kabale one-quarter of the groups received outside assistance, while in Luwero almost one-third obtained outside funding. Religious-based organizations were the main ones receiving funding, which generally came from the national church body with which they were affiliated.

There does exist, however, at one extreme the phenomenon of "briefcase" organizations, most of which are based in Kampala. They were created simply to access donor funds, and they generally exist on paper but not in reality (the case of Kiribawa in Chapter 10 goes into this type of organization in depth). A more common problem, especially at the national level, is the existence of organizations that lurk in the border area between being a scam and being simply an inefficient organization with poor leadership and a weak constituency. As one ACFODE leader put it:

Table 5.4 Do Organizations Receive Outside Financial Assistance? (%)

	KAMPALA Men (n = 133)	Women	KABALE Men (n = 140)	Women	MBALE Men (n = 50)	Women	LUWERO Men (n = 50)	Women
Organization does not receive assistance	66	71	30	57	33	66	29	67
Organization receives financial assistance	27	23	17	16	66	4	71	15
Not known	7	6	53	27	0	30	0	18

Table 5.5 Organizations' Sources of Outside Assistance (%)

	KAMPALA Men (n = 133)	Women	KABALE Men (n = 140)	Women	MBALE Men (n = 50)	Women	LUWERO Men (n = 50)	Women
Church	0	10	0	8	33	81	75	70
Non-governmental organization	20	45	33	52	33	9	0	10
Local government	20	14	17	8	17	0	0	0
Bank loan	20	0	0	0	0	0	0	0
Other	20	21	50	13	17	0	25	10
Not known	20	10	0	17	0	8	0	10

Table 5.6 Fund-raising Mechanisms of Organizations (%)

| | KAMPALA | | KABALE | | MBALE | | LUWERO | |
	Men (n = 133)	Women	Men (n = 140)	Women	Men (n = 50)	Women	Men (n = 50)	Women
Membership dues	56	31	37	47	30	54	36	35
Selling products made by members	0	27	18	16	10	16	18	13
Cultural performances (drama, music)	0	20	2	3	0	5	0	8
Interest on loans to members	0	0	15	10	0	2	0	0
Farming to raise money	0	0	4	12	0	0	0	0
No fund-raising	0	1	2	0	10	5	0	0
Other	44	17	22	11	50	13	36	27
Don't know	0	4	0	1	0	5	9	16

I'm concerned that a lot of organizations have no constituency at all, but they have a three-year budget and an executive. And therefore they are as much driving the donors as the donors are driving them, in the sense that if there is no constituency you are not sure there is a mandate. And also there are agendas of the donors that they pay for. So it's easy to find someone and get that person and make her a superstar. I think a lot of that is happening and for me that is politically frightening, especially for women.[18]

This ACFODE leader feared that the donor agendas tended to be politically destructive because so much donor support focused on narrow short-term one-item agendas rather than support for women's advocacy around an agenda focusing on structural impediments to women's progress, for example, on legal change and changes in the education of girls. Donors favor smaller discrete projects because funding tends to be limited and the results may be more visible or directly related to their particular funding initiative. In contrast, support for advocacy is more of a gamble for donors because the results are often intangible, long-term and more diffuse.

Finally, in examining the impact of donors it is worth considering that the three most frequent responses to the survey question about the problems that associations faced were (i) lack of funds, (ii) difficulty in getting members to pay dues and (iii) difficulty in finding donors (see Table 5.7). Regardless of the perception that donors are dominating associational life in Uganda, most organizations do without such external resources most of the time (Tables 5.5 and 5.6).

NRM Encouragement of Women's Mobilization

In part, the new levels of participation have stemmed from a sense of entitlement that has been encouraged by the NRM practice of promoting women into political leadership positions at both the local and national levels. In the case study based in Kitumba, Jinja (Chapter 7), a woman contrasted the behavior of the male councillors in her village with that of the NRM, saying, "We as women, we have been oppressed . . . and they still want to oppress us further in this government of enlightenment". The women in her organization, Ekikwenza Omubi, seized on government rhetoric encouraging women to mobilize and used it as justification to pursue their own goals by starting a health clinic. These perceptions are in line with the survey findings, which reveal an overwhelming sense that things have dramatically changed for women since 1986 and that they have the possibility of realizing their political, economic and other goals now that they have the government's backing. In this same Kitumba case study, the government's encouragement of women was enthusiastically and actively endorsed by the sub-county chief, the deputy District Medical Officer, the District Administrator, and other key administrators, who felt their own work was enhanced by the leadership and participation of women in the communities. While this kind of support was not forthcoming across the board (for example, the District Medical Officer aggressively opposed the women's group), the backing was substantial enough to give further impetus to the women in this village to pursue their activities even in the face of LC resistance.

Ironically, the NRM's encouragement of women's participation has even benefited women in the opposition indirectly, putting pressure on them to demonstrate an interest in women's concerns and leadership. In the 1996 elections, the UPC-DP coalition, Inter Political Forces Co-operation (IPFC), presidential candidate, Paul Ssemogerere, appointed Mary Mutagamba as his campaign manager and likewise the third candidate, Mohammed Kibirige Mayanja, also had women like Grace Nulukenge on his campaign strategy team. Mutagamba, who is the women's parliamentary representative for Rakai and the former Constituent Assembly

Table 5.7 Main Problems Faced by Organizations

	KAMPALA Men (n = 133)	Women	KABALE Men (n = 140)	Women	MBALE Men (n = 50)	Women	LUWERO Men (n = 50)	Women
Lack of funds[a]	29	24	40	52	38	30	18	42
Disagreement among members	3	11	2	5	0	0	10	4
Other	52	28	51	25	25	25	36	37
No problems	3	31	7	8	12	30	18	13

a) Includes difficulty accessing donor funds and getting members to pay dues

women's representative for the same area, credits Museveni with her involvement in politics:

> If he [Museveni] had not empowered us, I wouldn't have thought of entering politics. He empowered the women, but they should be given the liberty to say what they want, not to follow him or NRM simply because he did it for them (Mwesige and Lupa-Lasaga, 1996: 7–8).

Many women seized on the NRM's rhetorical encouragement of women's mobilization to justify their local battles over their right to participate in public affairs and claim resources. Others used the government's position as a point on which to stand in arguing with their spouses and other male members of the household who might otherwise have objected to their involvement in organizations. In these instances, women entered the public realm to be on a better footing to fight their private battles, or as Susan Geiger (1998) put it, women entered politics to politicize the personal rather than simply to make the personal political. As a result of the initial gains described in the previous chapter, women were inspired to press for greater demands as the NRM appeared increasingly accommodating. They took advantage of these new openings to assert themselves both at the national level, as Chapter 4 showed, and also at the local level, as will become evident in subsequent chapters based on the case studies.

Increasing Levels of Education

Finally, one of the main factors contributing to women's heightened activism has been their increased access to educational opportunities (see Tables 4.7 and 4.8). While education is an important factor in explaining action taken at the national level, it has also been a factor in local-level struggles. For example, in the community struggle to reject the World Bank infrastructural rehabilitation project in Kawaala, some of the most active opponents were well-educated businesswomen. The women's leader, Joyce Muhire, a former school-teacher, claimed that the fact that she was educated (and widowed) allowed her to play a more active role in the struggle and to give encouragement to other less educated women in her neighborhood.

The role of education in organizations reflects broader changes in society. The education sector has witnessed faster growth than any other social sector, largely due to efforts by communities, which have prioritized education. The number of primary schools doubled between 1978 and 1987 and secondary schools increased even more, jumping from 120 to 515 in the same period (UNICEF, 1989: 61). In 1970 the ratio of girls to boys in primary school stood at 65 percent, compared with 89 percent in 1990. For secondary school the percentage of female to male students in 1970 reached only 31 percent compared with 63 percent in 1990 (UNDP, 1995: 53). This means that 45 percent of all girls were enrolled in primary school, 30 percent in lower secondary and 20 percent in upper secondary school. Thus, these rises in women's educational levels contributed to their efficacy as participants and leaders in their organizations and in politics.

Conclusions

The previous chapter explained how associational autonomy was key to the political impact and expansion of the women's movement in Uganda. This chapter has presented additional factors that are needed to explain these social transformations. In part, the expansion of women's participation was due to the structures facilitating opportunity presented by the NRM regime, namely, women's confidence-building experiences during the 1980–86 guerrilla war; the fact that associational and community strategies had increasingly replaced state provisioning of welfare and social services due to the state's retreat; and the NRM's encouragement of women to mobilize, which has legitimated women's beliefs that they have defensible rights based on claims to equality. At the same time women brought their own resources to bear, many of which were new. Women had pre-existing organizational bases which could be expanded and used to organize in a variety of ways. They also had a growing financial base, which provided them with new resources to draw on in their struggles. The new availability of donor funds has also been a factor in explaining women's mobilization. Moreover, increased access to educational opportunities has enhanced women's capacity to mobilize more effectively. Thus, in addition to associational autonomy, the combination of shifting political opportunity structures, changes in women's capacity to mobilize resources, and critical timing in negotiating leadership positions accounts in large measure for the vibrancy and success of the women's movement after the mid-1980s.

Notes

1 51 percent of all organizations were formed from 1988 to 1992, whereas only 11 percent were formed from 1983 to1987, according to my survey.
2 YWCA formed in 1952, the Mothers' Union formed in 1908, the Uganda Catholic Women's Guild started in 1963 and the Uganda Muslim Women's Association established in 1949.
3 Uganda Association of Women Lawyers (FIDA) formed in 1974, National Association of Registered Nurses and Midwives began in 1964, Uganda Association of University Women started in 1975.
4 Family Planning Association of Uganda founded in 1957.
5 Interview, RK, Helen Wangusa, Mothers' Union, November 1992.
6 Interviews with Florence Nekyon, Kampala, 21 May 1993; and Joy Kwesiga, 30 May 1993.
7 Interview, RK, Helen Wangusa, Mothers' Union, Kampala, November 1992.
8 Interview with Tabitha Mulyampiti, Kampala, 26 March 1993. Mulyampiti was conducting research in Pallisa for her MA thesis "Political Empowerment of Women in the Contemporary Uganda: Impact of Resistance Councils and Committees", Women's Studies, Makerere University, 1995.
9 This term is also associated with the cock crowing at 6 am, at which time villagers are supposed to wake up.
10 Interview with Ruth Kisubika, Kampala, 8 June 1992.
11 Interview with Joyce Mpanga, Kampala, 1 July 1995.
12 Interview with Ruth Kisubika, Kampala, 8 June 1992.
13 Interview with Margaret Kikamphikaho, July 1992.
14 Interview with Lucia Kiwale, Kampala, 26 June 1992.
15 Legally any Ugandan, male or female, can purchase or acquire title to land according to Land Reform Decree No. 3 of 1975.
16 Most of the stores in downtown Kampala that have not been returned to their original Asian owners are occupied by several women, who rent space by the meter. Rarely does one woman own an entire store.
17 Funders of women's activities in Uganda more generally have included Ford Foundation, Rockefeller Foundation, Konrad Adenauer Foundation, Oxfam, ICHRD (Canada), Panos, UN Fund for Population Activities (UNFPA), FINCA, the McKnight Foundation, KULU Women (Denmark), ICCO, Development and Peace (Canada), HIVOS, Canada Fund, NURRU, Danish International Development Agency (DANIDA), Swedish International Development Agency (SIDA), Royal Netherlands Embassy, Global Fund for Women.
18 Interview with Maxine Ankrah, Kampala, 19 June 1992.

6

Going
against the Grain

*Women's Challenges
to the Politicization
of Ethnicity & Religion*

Few would dispute that Uganda's post-independence history has been virtually defined by the politicization of ethnicity and religion. But ethnic identities are highly fluid, with blurred boundaries between groups that change over time (Kasfir, 1976: 53). Ethnic and other communal identities increase and decrease in their salience, depending on political and economic conditions. Much of the literature on Uganda's recent political history focuses on how communal tensions have characterized the rule of Obote I, Amin, Obote II and increasingly even of Museveni, who tried to distinguish himself from previous rulers by adopting a policy of "non-sectarianism". Few have taken note of countervailing societal tendencies that minimize the importance of difference in Uganda. These tendencies have arisen in the context of an emerging civil society that has taken stock of Uganda's history and is rejecting ethnicity and religion as the basis of political mobilization.

The women's movement is one such movement that has engaged in this type of political learning, but it is not alone. As Winnie Byanyima, Chair of the Women's Caucus in the Constituent Assembly, explained to the Assembly:

> . . . what I observe is that ethnicity is being used to provide platforms from which the amenities of modernity can be competed for. In fact, ethnicity is beginning to play a perverse role in our political development. Groups like women, youths, farmers, traders, workers, interest groups and lobbies are organising themselves and trying to articulate and to protect their interests. The current political atmosphere, I must say, is encouraging society to grow . . . but it is threatened by the growth of ethnicity which we politicians are sometimes promoting for narrow self-interest.[1]

Thus, the efforts to build societal organizations around new bases of commonly shared interests represents an important break with the past.

If one accepts the fact that identities can be constructed and molded by political and social agents, then it is plausible that they can also be reshaped and reconfigured. For example, when the British drew up the colonial administrative districts, several related groups were brought into Busoga; several smaller chiefdoms came under Ankole jurisdiction; fifty warfare units coalesced to become the Acholi; Nyoro secessionist elements separated from Bunyoro to become Toro district; and residents of Kigezi district, who are similar in identity to Rwanda's Hutu population, formed a new Bakiga identity (Young, 1976: 229–30). Clearly none of these identities were immutable and they were fairly easily molded by new administrative configurations. The colonial administration strengthened ethnic affinities by

Table 6.1   Uganda's Governments

Years	Ruler	Title	Party/movement of leader
1962–71	Apollo Milton Obote/Obote 1	Prime Minister (1966) President (1971)	UPC
1971–79	Maj. Gen. Idi Dada Amin	President	
1979 (April–June)	Yusufu Lule	President, Provisional Government	
1979–80	Godfrey Binaisa	President	UNLF
1980 (May–Dec)	Paulo Mwanga	Chairman	UNLF
1980–85	Apollo Milton Obote/Obote II	President	UPC
1985–86	Tito Okello	President	NLA
1986–present	Yoweri Museveni	President	NRM

drawing administrative borders along the lines of traditional political systems in the case of the four kingdoms, even giving salience to the Toro kingdom, which had ceased to function as a political entity for several decades. Linguistic and cultural differences became bases of administrative division in the North among the Nilotic and Sudanic groups. Christian missions, especially the Anglicans, used the administrative units as bases for their own divisions, thus heightening the importance of ethnic demarcations. By establishing schools that used local languages as the medium of instruction, the missions helped enhance ethnic differences, often giving them salience over clan, kin, and age differences (Hansen, 1977: 38–40).

This chapter first outlines the various communal tensions that have persisted to this day in Uganda and examines some of their origins. It then goes on to explain why women's organizations in particular eschew sectarianism, how they have struggled against it, and how they have created organizations along new inclusive lines as a break from past exclusionary bases for women's mobilization.

Communal Tensions in Uganda

Religious divisions were among the main lines of polarization in Uganda's post-colonial period, although they have diminished somewhat under the NRM government. Catholics have frequently been associated with the Democratic Party and Protestant non-Ganda were affiliated with the Uganda People's Congress (UPC), as evidenced as far back as the 1958 Legislative Council elections as well as in subsequent elections (Young, 1976: 251). In fact, the Democratic Party's acronym came to stand for *Dini ya Papa* (religion of the Pope), while the UPC letters stood for "United Protestants of Canterbury" (Mittleman, 1975: 69). Even though the largest number of Ugandans are Catholic (44.5 percent), political power has eluded them. At the same time it has given them more cohesiveness and made them more critical of the state. In contrast, the Church of Uganda, which accounts for 39 percent of the population, was tied to the colonial establishment prior to independence and both Obote and Museveni have been Protestants (see Tables 6.2 and 6.3 for religious and ethnic make-up of Uganda). Nevertheless, the Church's relationship to the various regimes has been more ambiguous (Ward, 1995: 72–3). In spite of the differences the churches have had with various political parties and governments, the parties themselves have sought to build their support along religious lines, creating deep schisms in society.

Second, fault lines have emerged between the non-Baganda and the Baganda, especially between the northerners and the Baganda. Martin Doornbos (1978) has shown how, in the Ugandan context and more generally, ethnic differences alone do not result in conflict. But if privilege and power coincide along ethnic lines then tensions are inevitable. This is what happened in Ankole when the colonialists elevated the Bahima to function as the rulers in their region, creating pronounced inequities between the Bairu and Bahima Ankole castes. It was not until the Bairu elites gained in power that ethnic friction declined in this part of Uganda, although these tensions have resurfaced once again in the context of NRM politics.

Doornbos's instrumentalist argument applies even more forcefully to relations between the North and South in Uganda. Baganda institutions, wealth and political cohesiveness led them to dominate the rest of the country under British rule (1894–1962). Various factors came to play in Baganda dominance, starting with the way in which the British built their administrative system by aligning themselves closely with the Baganda and by privileging the Baganda through special concessions enshrined in the 1900 Uganda Agreement. Buganda was granted several counties from the neighboring Kingdom of Bunyoro, which laid the basis for a dispute over what have been called the "lost counties". Moreover, the other three kingdoms of Ankole, Toro and Bunyoro were not granted the same privileges as Buganda when they were brought into the British colonial administrative system (Hansen, 1977: 38).

Since that time, the Baganda have been perceived as a major political force to contend with, in spite of the fact that they have not had direct political power since independence. The main export crops (coffee, cotton, tea, tobacco) and most of the country's food were grown in Buganda, because of its favorable climate, giving the area economic dominance as well. The region benefited from being the seat of the colonial administration, from having the best infrastructure, the most commercial enterprises, and the most schools and hospitals, many of which were run by church missions (Wrigley, 1988: 29). Because of Buganda's political and economic strength,

Table 6.2 Population by Religion (1991 Census)

		%
Catholic	7,152,289	44.5
Church of Uganda	6,300,439	39.2
Muslim	1,687,618	10.5
Other	900,063	5.6
Not stated	32,139	0.2
Total	16,072,548	100.0

Table 6.3   Population by Ethnicity (1991 Census)

Baganda	3,015,980
Banyankole	1,643,193
Bakiga	1,391,442
Basoga	1,370,845
Iteso	999,537
Langi	977,680
Bagisu, Bamasaba	751,253
Acholi, Labwor	734,707
Lugbara, Aringa	588,830
Banyoro, Bagungu	495,443
Batoro, Batuku, Basongora	488,024
Alur, Jonam	395,553
Bakonjo	361,709
Karimojong, Dodoth, Tepeth, Suk	346,166
Banyarawanda	329,662
Bagwere	275,608
Badama, Japadhola	247,577
Banyole	228,918
Bafumbira	203,030
Samia	185,304
Madi	178,558
Bahororo	141,668
Kumam	112,629
Sebei	109,939
Other	104,086
Barundi	100,903
Kakwa	86,472
Baruli	68,010
Baamba	62,926
Bagwe	40,074
Nubian	14,739
Bachope	12,089
Lendu	8,600
Batwa	1,394
Total	**16,072,548**

the British decided to keep the South demilitarized, and enlisted in the army the Nilotic Acholi and Langi and the Nilo-Hamitic Itesot. These patterns of economic, political and military polarization laid the basis for many of the conflicts in the post-independence period (Mazrui, 1975: 35).

A major crisis between northerners and southerners occurred in 1966, when the president, Milton Obote, a Langi, suspended the 1962 Constitution and introduced his own constitution which undercut the autonomy of districts and federal kingdoms; divided Buganda into four districts; placed the district council finances more directly under central control; and took away the districts' right to appoint civil servants by staffing the district administrations with central government appointees.

Kings became ceremonial heads and Buganda lost its special prerogatives, including its right to elect members to the National Assembly indirectly (Kasfir, 1976: 200).
The Baganda were incensed by the suspension of the Constitution and gave the
Obote government an ultimatum to leave Buganda territory. Obote's army of northerners responded by attacking the *kabaka's* palace, which ended in Baganda defeat.
The king was forced to flee the country to Britain, where he remained until his
death in 1969. After 1966 Uganda's politics became increasingly militarized as Obote
claimed the presidency in addition to being prime minister. Thus, rather than
depoliticizing ethnicity in Uganda's political life, as Kasfir claimed (1976: 196–214,
288), Obote's first government played the ethnic card under the guise of trying to
minimize the salience of ethnicity and create a national identity. Rather than damp-
ening ethnic sentiments, his efforts to destroy Buganda's symbols served instead to
fuel Baganda ethno-nationalism.

Later under Obote II, North-South tensions manifested themselves as civil disor-
der set in. The National Resistance Army was fighting a guerrilla war based in
Ankole, Buganda and Toro. Obote launched a reign of terror against villagers even
worse than anything seen during Amin's time. Hundreds of thousands of Baganda
were slaughtered in the Luwero triangle, and hundreds of thousands of others were
tortured and displaced between 1982 and 1985 under the pretext that Obote's army
was targeting the NRA and its supporters.

However, some of the fiercest conflicts have been among northerners themselves.
Tensions after independence also began to mount within the army between West
Nilers and Anya Nya, on the one side, and Acholi and Langi supporters of Obote on
the other. Idi Amin, who was a West Niler and commander of the army under
Obote, manipulated these tensions. When it appeared that he might be killed by
rivals in the army, Amin carried out a successful coup against Obote in January 1971.
This resulted in the widespread killing of Lango and Acholi in the army, but also of
those West Nile officers who did not switch sides fast enough. These events set the
stage for further violence (Low, 1988: 45).

Amin sought to benefit northerners and Muslims, but it is doubtful that either
group truly profited from his rule, given the strong disintegrative tendencies at
work in the country. Amin briefly made a bid for Baganda support by permitting
the return of the body of *kabaka* for burial in Uganda. He also initially made
conciliatory gestures to the Catholic, Anglican, and Muslim establishments in
an effort to claim legitimacy. But these efforts were short-lived as Uganda
plunged into economic disarray and anarchy. Amin terrorized the population
and killed symbolic individuals from various communities, including the Chief
Justice of Uganda, Makerere's Vice Chancellor and the Anglican Archbishop
(Low, 1988: 48).

As it turned out, more northerners than southerners were killed during Amin's
time because he pitted the Acholi, Langi and Itesot against the West Nilers, only to
find himself at odds with his own Kakwa people. Similarly, in the 1980s Obote relied
increasingly on the Acholi to do most of the fighting with the NRA. Thus when Tito
Okello, an Acholi, was placed at the head of the army, he turned against his Lango
colleagues and carried out a coup in 1985, forcing Obote to flee (Low, 1988: 50–51).
This left the northern Okello army pitted against the southern NRA until the NRM
takeover in 1986.

These same tendencies of ethnic mobilization have become apparent with the
NRM regime, in spite of its non-sectarian rhetoric and attempts to build a broad-
based movement representing a wide range of interests. New patterns of govern-

ment appointments have increasingly led to accusations of domination by Ugandans from the west ("westerners") and, in particular, domination by Museveni's own Banyankole people. Museveni, like Obote and Amin, has had to be mindful of the Baganda presence. However, instead of the conflict being simply between northerners and southerners, under the NRM the fault lines shifted to westerners vs. the rest, and in particular the West vs. the North (see more on this in Chapter 3).

New Bases of Mobilization

Given this history of intensely politicized ethnicity and religion in Uganda, one would hardly expect the emergence of new lines of mobilization. But perhaps it is because of painful lessons learned over the past four decades that new forms of organization are being created and revived. Women's organizations have gone against the grain of these older patterns of participation and have sought new ways to build ethnic and religious unity.

National women leaders in Uganda recognize that to build a women's movement it is necessary to construct as broad a base as possible and this requires building bridges across ethnic, religious and class difference, much like the women leaders in the 1950s and 1960s found it necessary to build ties across race and religion. Some go so far as to deny that their groups are 'political' because of the way in which "politics" has been equated with what is popularly referred to in Uganda as ethnic and religious "sectarianism". These same individuals may be involved in a wide range of political activities, including electoral politics, but they do not believe they are involved in "politics" because of the way they define "politics". While there are many men who oppose sectarianism, it is not clear that they equate it in the same way as women do with politics and with political parties. Women generally oppose multi-partyism to a greater extent than men, as this chapter will show, because it is associated with sectarianism. One of the consequences of this stance was that women to a greater degree than men threw their support behind Museveni and his no-party anti-sectarian policies in the 1996 elections.

In a country like Uganda where "politics" has clearly been the domain of men and where it has been associated with the military, repression, civil war, and sectarian fighting, women find it politically expedient to disassociate themselves from the term "politics". Women are so vehement in insisting that their groups are based primarily on economic or other concerns and not on ethnicity or religion that even groups like Action for Development (ACFODE), which have been active politically in advocating women's rights, in supporting women running for office, and in the constitution-making process, deny that they are in any way engaged in "political activity". When asked whether ACFODE was politically active, one of its leaders explained:

> We do not want these organizations to become terribly political. It would hurt too much. There would be too much pain, too much tension that we do not need right now. Everything has been so politicized along tribal, religious and party lines. Women through these organizations are rejecting that. We know the divisions exist among us, but it is more important right now to survive and to help each other out. We do not want to go back to the way it was, back to the repression, back to having to escape to the bush for fear of one's life. These organizations are non-denominational, non-tribal, non-partisan. They do not exclude anyone. The reason they are generally organized around sex is because of the gender division in our culture.[2]

This kind of position was reiterated by other women leaders as well. When asked whether multi-party politics would help or hinder an organization like ACFODE, which has been especially active in promoting female leadership in government and in promoting women's rights, its general secretary at the time, Margaret Kikamphikaho, was quick to reply: "We don't talk about things like that. We are not into politics." As far as she was concerned, party affiliations along with their related ethnic and religious affiliations were seen as too divisive to raise in her organization.

This position is consistent with the strategies laid out at ACFODE's national meeting in 1986 in which the organization adopted as part of its initial program a view that "women should talk to fellow women as women, not in terms of religion, political parties or conflicting organizations so as to avoid disunity" (ACFODE, 1988: 64). Miria Matembe, ACFODE's chair from 1989 to 1993, pointed out that ACFODE formed itself as an organization that embraced all women and as distinct from "sectarian" organizations that had predominated up to that time, like the Catholic Women's Guild, Mothers' Union, Muslim Women's Association. "ACFODE therefore came in to fill this gap where all women irrespective of tribe, religion, class or education levels could work together for the good of the Ugandan woman. What mattered was the woman" (Matembe, 1996: 25).

Another ACFODE leader remarked that it even took them a while initially to convince women that as a national body they were not political because of the ways in which other national women's bodies like the National Council of Women had been used by politicians in the past (see Chapter 3). Clearly, even though women may be intensely involved in public activities, many will define politics as a divisive activity that women do not engage in because it is associated with parties, which in Uganda still tend to be organized along religious and regional lines.

What is especially striking is how consistently women's groups are *not* based on ethnicity or religion, especially in the urban context, even when possibilities exist for organizations based along such lines. Women do participate in ethnically based cultural and burial groups and ethnically based urban associations that are concerned with the development of a rural hometown or home region, but the members of these groups tend to be both men and women, not exclusively women. According to the survey, virtually none of the women's mobilization in the four towns surveyed was based on ethnicity or religion, apart from those associations that were explicitly formed for religious purposes (Tables 6.4 and 6.5). The fact that this is so is interesting in itself.

For example, in Kabale where 83 percent of the respondents reported that they were Bakiga, as many as 77 percent of women were in groups that included multiple ethnicities (compared with 59 percent of the men). This is especially significant given the small numbers represented by other ethnicities in Kabale, which included the Banyankole (7 percent) and Banyarwanda (8.5 percent). Similarly, 53 percent of the respondents were Protestant, 38 percent Catholic and 7 percent Muslim, yet as many as 80 percent of women were in religiously mixed organizations. The remainder were in religious-based organizations (Mothers' Union, Catholic Women's Guild, etc.). In other words, *none* of the women's organizations that were not formed for religious purposes were made up of women of only one religion.

Similarly in Luwero, which had the highest concentration of a single ethnicity, (87.5 percent of the population surveyed was Baganda), *all* women were in multi-ethnic groups, whereas 20 percent of men were in groups of one ethnicity. Likewise, in the Luwero survey, 50 percent were Protestant, 27 percent Catholic

Table 6.4 Ethnic Composition of Organization (%)

	KAMPALA Men (n = 133)	Women	KABALE Men (n = 140)	Women	MBALE Men (n = 50)	Women	LUWERO Men (n = 50)	Women
Mixed ethnicity	87	94	59	77	100	100	80	100
One ethnicity	13	6	41	23	0	0	20	0
chi square		p=.327		p=.05		na		p=.005
Dominant ethnicity[a]	Baganda 65%	Bakiga 83%	Bagisu 46%		Baganda 88%			

[a] Survey results similar to 1991 census

Table 6.5 Religious Composition of Organizations (%)

	KAMPALA Men (n = 133)	Women	KABALE Men (n = 140)	Women	MBALE Men (n = 50)	Women	LUWERO Men (n = 50)	Women
Mixed denominations & religions	100	78	100	80	100	95	100	84
Single denomination[a]	0	22	0	20	0	5	0	16
chi square		p=.106		p=.004		p=.535		p=.361
Protestant[b]		39		53		48		50
Catholic[b]		38		38		38		27
Muslim[b]		19		7		2		16

[a] These are almost entirely religious groups, e.g., Mothers' Union
[b] Survey results similar to 1991 census

and 16 percent Muslim. As in Kabale, all Luwero women surveyed were involved in organizations with a multi-religious make-up except for those in religious associations.

However, these gender differences in organizational make-up were not as striking in Kampala and Mbale, which had a more diverse ethnic constituency to begin with. In my Kampala survey, for example, the Baganda constitute 64.5 percent of the population, Banyankole 5.5 percent, Basoga 5 percent, Banyarwanda 3.5 percent along with 18 other ethnicities. At least 94 percent of women in organizations were involved in multi-ethnic associations, compared with 87 percent of men. The survey yielded a population divided evenly among Protestants (39.5 percent) and Catholics (39 percent), with 16 percent Muslims. If one excludes the religious organizations, once again no organizations of both men and women were based on religion.

It would be a serious distortion to infer from this that ethnic, religious, and other kinds of politics based on particularistic ties fall along gender lines. But the sentiments of the women cited here do suggest that many women, in particular, are pursuing through their new associational activity a kind of politics that is more inclusive in its orientation. Because women are generally more involved in organizations than men, women's strategies of mobilization are especially noteworthy. What is important is the significance that women attach to these new bases for association.

Needless to say, these kinds of countervailing tendencies in women's associations have enormous implications for Uganda, where considerations of the country's political future raise questions of how to resolve the seemingly intractable conflicts over religious, regional and ethnic difference that have had devastating consequences in recent history.

Why Do Women's Associations Eschew "Sectarianism"?

There are several reasons why women's groups, in particular, have challenged the status quo that defines politics so strongly in ethnic and religious terms. At the national level the common cause of women's rights unites women of diverse backgrounds. Women have found that it is impossible to mount an effective struggle relating to legislation affecting women without building a broad-based movement.

At the local level women see economic necessity and survival strategies as bases for organizing along more inclusive lines by forming new communities and affiliations. The deepening economic crisis has placed greater pressures on women to become key providers within the household, necessitating new organizational strategies. Economic survival and the belief that one's own survival is contingent on the survival of others is the basis of women's associations, rather than an ascriptive affiliation. To cope with unprecedented hardship, women have joined to form groups to facilitate income-generating activities, savings, and the provision of social services, such as day care.

Another reason for these non-sectarian tendencies is that urban areas by definition have brought together people of different ethnic groups, clans and religious affiliations. Intermarriage between couples of different ethnic groups has become much more common since the 1970s. New associations are thus formed in the workplace and in neighborhoods creating new bases for community beyond particularistic interests and primary affiliations.

A less important factor, but nevertheless one worth mentioning, that may explain why women's groups tend to cut across particularistic ties is that married women from patrilineal societies often find it easier than men to form associations that cut across ethnic, clan and kinship ties. This is because once they are married they effectively cut themselves from their blood kin because they are expected to join their husband's clan, and yet are never entirely accepted into that clan and may be considered outsiders. They are restricted from membership of clan and kin associations. Unlike men, who are more likely to be involved in such associations, women from these societies find it easier to associate with people outside of their primary affiliations and can extend what anthropologists call "fictive kinship" ties to other women who are not blood relations. It is the kind of societal arrangement which forces women to establish closer ties to non-kin (Harriet Birungi, personal communication, 1992). However, while this provides an ongoing societal basis for such cross-cutting affiliations, it does not explain the changes that occurred after the mid-1980s with respect to forms of women's mobilization.

An interesting parallel exists in war-torn southern Sudan, which is embroiled in conflict between the main rebel group in the South Sudan Peoples Liberation Army (primarily made up of the Dinka) and the smaller faction, the South Sudan Independence Movement/Army (primarily made up of the Nuer) which is allied with the Khartoum regime in the north. In this conflict, the women have been critical to maintaining stability and cross-line contacts, often through marriage ties that bridge the Dinka and Nuer. They have become critical to efforts to secure peace in this area because their ability to access food, water and other staples is contingent on their ability to cross factional lines. Women in Lakes Province have met with paramount chiefs and the District Commissioner and argued against taking revenge on the Nuer, although to no avail. Women's groups have also met among themselves to discuss issues of peace (Center for the Strategic Initiatives of Women, 1996: 31). Clearly, women in southern Sudan as in Uganda have taken advantage of the connections they embody through intermarriage between groups consciously to strengthen cross-cutting linkages.

Strategies of Organizational Inclusiveness

Because the new non-sectarian-based groups cannot fall back on traditional kinship obligations or the other patterns of establishing trust that work within ascriptively based groups, many are struggling to establish new mechanisms to ensure accountability. The push for greater inclusiveness and accountability continues to be a painful learning experience for many groups, but there are, I believe, some small and important changes taking place. This is not to minimize the difficulties that persist, but rather to acknowledge the changes that have occurred and to recognize that they may form a potential basis for institutional reform that would stress greater accountability, pluralizing society and instituting more democratic procedures.

While women have pressed for greater inclusiveness within the public sphere, they have also sought greater inclusiveness within nationally based women's groups, often with tangible success. The Executive Committee of the Muslim Women's Association during Amin's rule was made up almost entirely of Nubians. Today the same body includes Batoro, Nubian, Banyoro, Banyankole and Baganda women.[3]

Unlike political parties, many women's associations are explicit about their rejection of the politics of sectarianism. Organizations like the Mothers' Union, the YWCA, Girl Guides, and other such groups that tended to have a Baganda leadership in the 1950s and 1960s, were noticeably multi-ethnic in composition by the 1990s.

I found women in many parts of the country who in recent years had deliberately loosened or severed their ties to organizations based on religion (for example, local chapters of the Protestant Mothers' Union) to join with women of other religions. For other women's groups the struggle has been an internal one to stem accusations of favoritism based on ethnicity. One leaflet supporting a candidate as chairperson for the prominent women's group Action for Development (ACFODE) appealed for unity in the face of such rumors, arguing that:

> Friend, if you find yourself dividing up the ACFODE membership into subgroupings like: . . . "Westerners" "Easterners," etc. stop and think because you are then killing the ACFODE spirit of single mindedness and substituting for it cleavages, cliques and factions – the hallmarks of anarchism and disintegration. We in ACFODE have always maturely worked together, side by side, without bothering to find out one another's nationalities or other sectional tags. All genuine lovers of ACFODE should by all means wish to uphold the original non-sectarian spirit.[4]

Indeed, ACFODE saw itself as a model for other organizations in its avoidance of "sectarianism," because "its rich mix of members helps unify Ugandan women, in a country where ethnicity, religion and regionalism are still strong", according to an article in its *Arise* magazine (Kwesiga, 1996a: 5).

Even women's organizations formed along religious denominational lines have begun trying to work together. For example, in Tororo District, a seminar was held by over 100 women representing the Catholic Women's Guild, the Muslim Women's Association and Mothers' Union chapters in West Budama. Its purpose was to create awareness about unity among women in the area who had continued to uphold intense religious and political differences. One speaker, Mrs Beatrice Joyce Owor, chairperson of the Mothers' Union, commented that it was sad that women in West Budama only came together for funerals, and as a result had formed many women's funeral associations, but had neglected to form joint income-generating organizations. She felt this was a loss for women in the area. "We have missed a lot of good things and opportunities because we lack unity, co-operation and love for one another", she lamented. She argued that hatred and bickering had bogged down the country and that it was time for women to forget the past, wake up and join women in the rest of the country in the process of economic and social emancipation. She also addressed another debate within the Mothers' Union that has caused many divisions and much suffering: She criticized the exclusion from the Mothers' Union of divorcees and women who are not married in the church and condemned the negative and conservative attitudes of Mothers' Union members towards these women (Jamwa, 1993).

More generally, among the women we interviewed in Kampala, Mbale, Kabale and Luwero, issues of religion and ethnicity were not seen as problematic in their organizations. While they reported problems of husbands objecting to their participation, problems of raising funds, attendance at meetings, collecting dues, mismanagement of funds, problems arising from age and education differences, virtually all denied that religion and ethnicity/language had given rise to problems in their group.

When confronted with ethnic and linguistic differences, women's groups have sought ways to work around potential problems that may arise from such diversity. The example of the savings club in Kampala mentioned in Chapter 5 illustrates this phenomenon. The club was formed by 13 women coming from several ethnic groups and included both Christians and Muslims. The women represented a wide range of occupations and wage levels. They included a nurse, secretary, university professor, waitress and several "housewives". They all had additional primary sources of income, most of which were informal (untaxed and unlicensed). They had individual businesses selling beer, beans, soap, second-hand clothes and books. One was a consultant for foreign donor agencies and non-governmental organizations, gave private French lessons, and did French-English translations for extra money. Another had a poultry shed, another ran a canteen, and yet another owned a private clinic. The main organizing principle was economic survival and mutual support rather than a primary affinity.

Because the women had different religious affiliations, they went to great lengths to accommodate these differences. The group had two funds, one regular to which they contributed and the other an emergency fund, which they built up by catering for the local Resistance Council and other organizations holding social functions. They deliberately chose to do the catering on non-religious holidays like New Year so that their activities would not interfere with the various religious festivals of the different group members. If they had to meet on a Friday, the Christian members would consult with the Muslim members to make sure it was all right to meet without them. Because the women are of different ethnic affiliations they conduct their meetings in English and translate into Luganda for the non-English speakers. Similar translating arrangements were reported by other savings clubs in Kampala. English is spoken fairly widely among the educated classes in Kampala.

Women have sought to bridge other kinds of differences with the same goal of inclusiveness in mind. In Busoga, women's organizations generally ignored a conflict in the mid-1990s within the Church of Uganda over a controversial Bishop Bamwoze – a conflict which in the past might have divided them. Previously it was Bamwoze's Diocese (Iganga Archdeaconry) that used to organize training for women, and women from there were said by others in Busoga to be "easily bought by cheap tokens given by Bamwoze". Women, however, were mobilizing throughout Busoga, irrespective of whether they were for or against Bamwoze. The NAWOU chapter, for example, went out of its way to bring in women of different backgrounds with different dialects so that they could not be accused of supporting one faction.

Similarly, in the past in Busoga there had been differences between women affiliated to the Mothers' Union and women who had not been married in church. In the 1990s groups were leaving their affiliation with the Mothers' Union because of this kind of exclusivity. Similarly, Catholic women's groups that did not work with non-Catholics subsequently suffered in their membership, while non-religious groups gained in numbers. As the NAWOU co-ordinator in Kamuli explained to me:

> I think there is a general tendency to throw away those identities like Kisozi Asaaba Awabwa opposed to Kisozi Mothers' Union group. People don't want to hear about sectarian segregation today . . . . Because in the past there were so many killed by divisions between the DP and the UPC. So people are disillusioned with sectarian religion. Today they can benefit from each other.

Finally, some women see sectarian-based partisan politics as having held back women's formation as an interest group and kept the women's agenda too narrowly focused on domestic, religious or economic issues without challenging the fundamental legal and other bases for their subordination. It tied them to political parties and in doing so depoliticized them. These women are critical of the Mothers' Union, the former National Council of Women and other such organizations, which they feel played important roles as precursors of the current women's movement, but nevertheless promoted women in their traditional roles without disturbing the status quo. They argue that women's involvement in economic, religious and welfare issues was being carried out at the expense of advocacy for women. Supporting women's income-generating activities, they claim, has not fundamentally changed their overall economic dependence. Among some leaders there is a clear sense that there needs to be more of a break with the past and that the women's movement needs to make stronger demands on the system. Others suggest that women's involvement in economic and welfare activities, in particular, is a route to empowerment in and of itself.

Multi-partyism vs. Movement Politics

Some of the clearest manifestations of women's resistance as a group to sectarian politics became evident in the 1996 presidential and parliamentary elections. Women candidates in the parliamentary contest frequently ran on anti-sectarian tickets. For example, one aspirant, Beatrice Byenkya, who ran for the women's parliamentary seat in Hoima, addressed a crowd in her constituency, arguing that "Those old politicians who want to represent you are more interested in religion and tribes and we, the young blood, we want unity" (Yunus, 1996).

However, the most obvious indication of anti-sectarianism was the strong endorsement women gave to Museveni in the elections, largely on the grounds that of the three candidates he was believed to be less likely to promote sectarian politics. Many observers and leaders of women's organizations attributed Museveni's victory to the women's vote. This perception was so strong that some husbands even retaliated against their wives to the point that women's defiance of their husbands at the polls became raised as a human rights issue, as numerous incidents of wife beating and harassment were reported in relation to women's electoral preferences.

The Alert Group of the Uganda Women's Network (UWONET) made appeals to Museveni and the Interim Electoral Commission (IEC) to stop the increasing incidents of intimidation and harassment of wives by husbands over differing political opinions. They argued that violence by husbands against their wives over political views should not be treated as domestic violence but as a serious crime, and that women's rights are human rights. Reports from Kampala, Iganga, Masaka, Apac, Mukono, Luwero, and Mpigi had indicated that women were facing increasing intimidation after the presidential elections. They were threatened with withdrawal of family support. Some were killed, beaten, thrown out of their homes, and some had their voters' cards grabbed from them or destroyed. Moreover, after the presidential election, women as a group were being accused, harassed and assaulted by different groups for having voted the way they did (Musoke 1996). Steve Akabway, Interim Electoral Commission Chairman, finally issued statements on TV and radio and in the press sternly warning husbands to stop harassing their wives over the election outcome. One of the consequences of this experience was that women did not turn out to vote in the parliamentary elections in such large numbers. As Christine Lalobo explained: "So some of them were saying, 'If I can't exercise my rights in my own way and freedom, then I shouldn't go there at all. Otherwise I am going to risk going out with a swollen eye".[5]

Table 6.6   Poll results of Presidential Elections, 9 May 1996

	Registered Voters	Actual Votes cast	Mayanja	Museveni	Ssemogerere
Luwero	210,116	150,127	2.4%	88.4%	9.2%
Kabale	198,229	181,913	0.2%	98.5%	1.2%
Mbale	362,316	20,686	2.0%	81.2%	16.7%
Kampala	130,000	65,000	NA	54.0%	NA

Women's views on sectarianism were also manifested in their perceptions of multipartyism, which tends to be equated with Uganda's history of sectarianism and instability. On multi-partyism women and men tended to have similar views, except in Mbale. In my survey, I found that three-quarters of the residents in Kabale were against multi-partyism and two-thirds in Luwero, while in Mbale not even half rejected it. In Kampala roughly one-third of all residents were for and another one-third against multi-partyism, with 16 percent undecided. In Kampala and

Mbale more men than women supported multi-partyism, while women were more likely to say that they were undecided. Mbale registered the strongest difference between men and women: 44 percent of male respondents supported multi-party- ism compared with 14 percent of female respondents. In Kampala, women and men differed on the issue but not to the same degree as in the other three towns, i.e., 45 percent of the men endorsed multi-partyism, while only 34 percent of the women were of that opinion (Table 6.7).

When it came to party politics, women and men both registered a lack of endorse- ment of any party, with women even less inclined than men to offer support to any party in Kampala, Kabale and Mbale (Table 6.8). There is substantially greater male backing for the Uganda People's Congress in Kampala and Mbale as compared with women. Similarly, men are more supportive of the NRM in Kabale. It is interesting that women as a group neutralize these divergences: in Kampala and Mbale by offering much less support to the UPC than men, while in Kabale they offer signif- icantly less backing to the NRM than men. Apart from these areas of male-female party difference, there were few other significant gender differences in party alle- giance, with strong ambivalence characterizing both sexes.

In Kampala, the NRM/Uganda Patriotic Movement (UPM) claimed a fraction more overall support (14 percent) than the Democratic Party (DP) (11 percent) with minimal (5 percent) support going to the Uganda People's Congress (UPC) and over half undecided or with no party allegiance (Table 6.8). Respondents tended to treat the NRM as a political party, while others thought of the defunct UPM as the NRM's political party. Women were four times less likely to support the UPC than men in Kampala although they supported the NRM and DP roughly to the same extent as men. According to the survey, while the NRM obtained proportionally most of its support from the Baganda in Kampala, the Baganda tended to support the DP (16 percent) slightly more than NRM/UPM (14 percent), with the majority (54 percent) remaining undecided or unwilling to respond. The 1991 Census indicates that Kampala is made up of 39 percent Catholics, 38 percent Protestants and 19 percent Muslims. The survey showed a fairly similar breakdown of religions. Of those Protestants in Kampala who had a preference, 53 percent supported the NRM/UPM while only 29 percent supported the UPC; 45 percent of the Catholics supported the DP, with 34 percent support- ing NRM/UPM, and 70 percent of Muslims supported the NRM/UPM. The incon- clusiveness of some of these survey results were replicated in the 1996 elections in which only half the registered electorate in Kampala voted, giving Museveni a 54 percent rate of endorsement.

In Luwero, where the Baganda predominate, we found no UPC supporters and only a handful of DP supporters. Roughly 44 percent of the women and 35 percent of the men supported the NRM/UPM (Table 6.8). The Protestants made up half the population in Luwero, Catholics one-third and Muslims 15 percent. All the religious groups were divided roughly in the same proportions politically, with less than half backing the NRM and the other half undecided. In the elections, 88 percent of reg- istered voters in Luwero voted for Museveni.

In Mbale, once again gender played a role in determining party preference, with one-third of the population undecided. Women were almost three times less likely to support the UPC than men. In Mbale, the Bagisu predominate, making up 46 percent of the population. They overwhelmingly supported the NRM, while the UPC gained much of its backing from the Langi, Acholi, Bagwere and Iteso. In Mbale, 48 percent of the population was Protestant, 38 percent Catholic, and 2 per-

Table 6.7 Attitudes Towards Multi-partyism of General Population Surveyed (%)

	KAMPALA (n = 552)			KABALE (n = 250)			MBALE (n = 205)			LUWERO (n = 135)		
	Men	Women	Total	Men	Women	Total	Men	Women	Total	Men	Women	Total
For	45	34	31	14	15	14	44	14	21	9	11	10
Against	38	38	33	73	72	72	33	46	43	78	67	69
Undecided	9	21	16	10	7	8	9	13	12	4	17	15
Other	0	1	1	0	0	0	0	0	0	0	0	0
No answer	6	6	5	4	3	3	7	23	19	9	5	6

Table 6.8 Political Party Allegiance of General Population Surveyed (%)

	KAMPALA (n = 552)			KABALE (n = 250)			MBALE (n = 205)			LUWERO (n = 135)		
	Men	Women	Total	Men	Women	Total	Men	Women	Total	Men	Women	Total
UPC[a]	16	4	5	6	7	6	24	9	12	0	0	0
DP[a]	15	13	11	8	7	7	7	1	2	9	3	4
CP[a]	2	2	2	0	0	0	0	1	1	0	1	1
KY[a]	1	0	1	0	0	0	0	0	0	4	3	3
NRM[a]	9	10	9	63	38	43	36	37	37	26	38	36
UPM[a]	9	5	5	0	3	2	0	0	0	9	6	7
None	28	56	45	24	40	37	22	39	35	52	43	44
Other	7	3	3	0	1	1	4	1	1	0	1	1
Don't know	9	7	8	0	5	4	2	11	9	0	5	4

[a] UPC (Uganda People's Congress), DP (Democratic Party), CP (Conservative Party), KY (Kabaka Yekka), NRM (National Resistance Movement), UPM (defunct Uganda Patriotic Movement).

cent Muslim. The largest number of Protestants (30 percent) supported the NRM, with 16 percent supporting the UPC, and 40 percent undecided, while half the Catholics supported the NRM. In Mbale, less than 6 percent voted and of these 81 percent voted for Museveni. Moreover, in the *Monitor* poll, 70 percent had supported Ssemogerere, with most of the remainder backing Museveni.

In Kabale, the NRM claimed support from roughly half the population, with one-third not supportive of any party and the remainder with allegiances that fell evenly between the UPC and the DP. Women and men did not diverge significantly in their support for parties, with the exception that women were twice as likely not to have decided which party to support. Not surprisingly, 98.5 percent of the electorate in Kabale voted for Museveni in the 1996 presidential elections.

Thus, in areas like Kabale and Luwero where there was fairly strong support for the NRM, there was not only a good voter turnout but, most importantly for this study, the differences between men and women were not great regarding multi-partyism and the political parties. Where support for Museveni was weaker, as in Kampala and Mbale, women were considerably more supportive of the NRM than men. Nevertheless, the high rates of indecision and refusal to answer the questions need to be noted and understood both as genuine indecision and uncertainty about what the future holds, and also as an indication of fear about answering such a question in the context of a survey. The political situation in Mbale was especially tense at the time of the survey because prominent UPC leaders had been visiting the area and were in dispute with the District administration. Regardless of the high undecided figures, the patterns regarding gender do emerge fairly clearly and were borne out in the 1996 elections.

Given the lukewarm support for the NRM and Museveni, women's organizations have not surprisingly been wary of efforts to co-opt them. One of the clearest examples of this kind of autonomy was evident after the 1996 elections, which brought in their aftermath disappointingly few women into ministerial positions. ACFODE, for example, wrote a letter to the Speaker of the National Assembly, James Wapakhabulo, protesting at the small number of ministerial appointments, arguing that women were completely let down in spite of the fact that it was "public knowledge that the women of Uganda were most vital in pushing" the Movement's agenda. The letter stated clearly that there "cannot be democracy where half of the people are sidelined".[6] The stance women parliamentarians have taken against the top NRM leadership regarding corruption and patronage and concerning key pieces of legislation (for example, the Land Bill) are further evidence of the ways in which the women's movement has simultaneously distanced itself from the regime.

Conclusion

The experience of the women's movement in Uganda shows how women have challenged the politicization of ethnicity and religion, especially when it has led to violence. At the national level women have sought to build linkages around common gender concerns in the interests of creating a broad women's movement. They have seen their ability to transcend difference as a way of challenging the corruption and divisiveness of patronage politics that has all too often been built upon narrow ascriptive lines. At the local level, working together for economic survival and the provision of social and public services becomes an added impetus for cross-cutting collaborations. Thus, women's movements have sought to minimize difference as part of their contribution to a process of reconciliation, and of healing the wounds of ethnically or religiously based violence and conflict.

Notes

1. Proceedings of the Constituent Assembly, Official Report, Wednesday, 3 August 1994, p.1490.
2. Interview with No. 1.1, Kampala, 2 June 1992.
3. Interview with Hajati Nantongo, acting Chairperson of the Uganda Muslim Women's Association, Kampala, 27 March 1993.
4. Letter by Dr R. G. Mukama in support of Joy Kwesiga as Chairperson of ACFODE in the 1993 election.
5. "Politician Hubby Snatchers Should Be Censored", *Monitor,* 8 May 1996.
6. "Letter to the Speaker", *Arise,* 19, (October–December) 1996, p. 53.

7

Reconfiguring
the Political

The Story
of a Jinja
Health Clinic

*Women wanted to manage [the clinic] with men at the back. Men wanted control with
women at the back.*

Headmaster of secondary school in Kitumba

How and *why* do women's political interests differ from those of men? What constraints do institutions themselves place on women's participation that undermine
women's best efforts? What implications do these limitations have for the way in
which women mobilize? These issues are explored in the context of a women's organization in a Jinja village, Kitumba (a fictitious name), which fought to initiate and
control a non-profit-making health clinic and ran up against the opposition of
wealthier, better educated and more powerful male elders in a local council. The
terms on which the male elders would permit women to participate in establishing
and running the clinic were such that the women's input would have been reduced
to nil. In order to have any say in running the clinic, the women knew they had to
have substantial control of the entire operation. It was not enough just to have a few
female faces on a committee. They needed control of the *process* and the capacity to
shape the clinic to suit the needs of the community. Given the limitations of existing institutions like the local councils, women could only give expression to their
interests through their own autonomous organization.

When women enter the public arena, they often bring with them new concerns
and ways of thinking about issues. Women parliamentarians in Sweden and Finland,
for example, focus on education and social policies more than their male counterparts. In Britain, women MPs are more likely than the men to introduce Bills having
to do with women, children and consumer issues. Similarly, in Uganda, women parliamentarians have tended to focus more than men on issues pertaining to health,
education, child welfare, sexual assault and gender equity. Women legislators in general around the world have brought into the political arena relatively new issues
having to do with child care, sexuality, and family planning – issues which were once
confined to the private sphere. Women tend to adopt this different emphasis in their
concerns, regardless of party affiliation (United Nations, 1994: 207).

Also women's political concerns do not always boil down to interests in the same
instrumental way that other societal interests are expressed. Birthing, raising

children, caring for the household, attending to the elderly and sick in the household, carrying out subsistence farming and income-generating activities, involvement in voluntary community service, and other such responsibilities fall
disproportionately on the shoulders of women in Uganda. In Jinja District, where
the following case study is situated, a recent study showed that women spend
16 hours a day working and engaged in domestic work, while men spend only five
hours working, with few domestic responsibilities. Men in this district have
19 hours for sleep and leisure time, while women have only 8 hours (Achieng, 1998).
These patterns of labor are typical throughout Uganda.

The aforementioned responsibilities often make women more attuned to the
ways in which the public and private are intricately connected. It is no accident
that it was a women's group that determined that health care was the number one
priority of the Kitumba community, given the fact that women are the primary
health care providers in Ugandan households. As the household members with
the primary responsibility for taking family members to health facilities, participating in health education workshops, caring for the sick at home and being
responsible for paying for the health care, women had a lot at stake in the success
of the clinic. They felt that women had been most actively involved in health care
provisioning. Their group had taken the initiative to improve health care in the
community and for these reasons they felt women should control the clinic and
its management.

Diamond and Harstock (1981: 720) argue that taking women's lives seriously
would have major consequences for our understanding of what is political and
the relationship between public and private would be seen as much more inter-
connected. Because of the way labor is divided in the household, women in
Uganda are generally more interested than men in pursuing collective community
strategies, in ensuring that the most vulnerable members of the community are
protected, and in placing the welfare of people above profit, power, patronage
and other considerations.

As Kathleen Jones (1988: 25) puts it:

> Re-defining our concepts of politics, activity, and community necessarily challenges the
> assumed bifurcation of the public and the private into two radically isolated realms. It also pro-
> vides a foundation for a theory of political activity that could include women, "female" virtues,
> and "female" interests, without having to adhere to an ahistorical or essentialist reading of
> women's lives.

Jónasdóttir (1988: 53) puts it another way, arguing that

> Women should be able to act on the strength of being women and not mainly despite being
> women. They must be visible politically as women, and be empowered to act in that capacity,
> because there is the continual possibility (not necessity) that they may have needs and attitudes
> on vital issues which differ from those of men.

Thus, while women may share similar interests with men, they often have distinct
concerns which may not always be embraced with the same enthusiasm by men.
Moreover, what is at issue here is not only the idea that "women's" concerns would
be given greater expression in the public realm if there were more politically active
women. The point is that male politicians would more readily adopt these concerns
themselves were the division of labor to change. Eventually "women's" demands
would lose their gendered nature. Thus, the problem is not simply one of getting
more women into legislative bodies or public fora. The problem is also one of getting more men to take up domestic/caring responsibilities and thus heightening
their appreciation of a broader range of issues.

Many themes common to the other case studies will be revisited in the concluding chapter of this book (for example, the marginalization of women from local councils, women's autonomous association). However, this chapter will highlight the issue of women's interests that arises out of their position in the division of labor and their heavy household responsibilities. The sensitivities women bring to politics should not be essentialized or seen as innate. There is nothing inherently "female" about these proclivities. To the extent that men engage in the daily care of other household members, they too will generally adopt these same concerns. Women's interests are a product of their private roles, responsibilities and experiences, which men need to share with them more.

In the Kitumba example, women's interests differed from the interests of men in the community in a way that made the notion of simply adding women and their concerns into the equation an inadequate solution to the problem of representation. The case study also shows the limitations of gender awareness among men. While gender awareness is important, men in the public arena can also easily dismiss women's concerns because they delude themselves into thinking that all that is needed is sympathy and a few token gestures on their part. The Kitumba example is a good one because the male elders in the local council, who stood in the way of the women's group, prided themselves on their gender sensitivity and the way in which they had championed women's rights in other contexts.

When mechanisms for protecting women's interests are not institutionalized, a disproportionate amount of weight rests on the acumen and forcefulness of individual leaders to press their cause. Although having women in key positions in the government and within the LC system has been important and has permitted gains, it is no guarantee that women's interests will be represented consistently. For example, Mutai, another town in Jinja District, saw a similar conflict over the establishment of a health clinic. Fortunately for the Mutai women, the LC5 general secretary at the time, Ruth Owagage,[1] also known as the "Iron Lady of Jinja", came from their town and was able to intervene and persuade the LC3 representatives to support the women as leaders of the health clinic. Both Kitumba and Mutai women's groups experienced similar kinds of opposition from the LC3 leadership, but the big difference between the two outcomes was the intervention of Ruth Owagage in the Mutai case. When it came to the Kitumba conflict, she claimed that she did not understand it as well as her own case in Mutai and therefore did not support the women's group. It appeared from conversations with her that she had been persuaded by the male LC authorities in Kitumba to oppose the women. So even key individual leaders may be inconsistent in their support for women's causes, demonstrating how much depends on individual leaders when institutions have a dominant male ideology and physical presence.

The Kyoyenda Women's Group in Mutai had started out as a group that raised pigs and was involved in a joint savings club. They then decided to start a clinic because they realized that health was their main problem, and the main government hospital was 19 kilometers away. They also wanted cheaper health services than the private clinics nearby were able to provide. One member donated a house and garage and her husband donated the land around it. The group raised money for furniture and repairs to the house and latrines. They petitioned for and obtained a medical assistant and three drug kits (needles, injections, medicines) from the District Medical Office. They also received four local helpers, guards, a porter, two midwives and a nurses aid. They built the maternity ward with their own hands.

In spite of their hard work and diligence, however, the women's group came under attack first from the women's husbands, who thought they were devoting too much of their time to the health clinic without any tangible benefit for themselves. Then they came into conflict with officials from the local LC3 committee, which had held elections for a local health committee behind their backs. The women bitterly objected to this move and called for a re-election. A second election was held and the women won the top three positions in the local health committee that governed their health clinic. But they would probably not have been able to obtain this second election without the intervention of the LC5 general secretary.

Another very similar struggle took place in Mitiyama, where a Japanese NGO was funding a health clinic run by a group of women. The nearest hospital was located 35 miles away, so the clinic brought in a doctor and other medical personnel to treat people once a week. The Japanese funding provided for free services for the first year, with a small service fee starting in the second and third years to help sustain the project after the Japanese funding pulled out in five years. The LC3 committee ended up in a tug of war with the steering committee of the clinic, demanding that the LC3 health committee take control of the clinic and charge fees. The women running the clinic went to see Hon. Joyce Mpanga, their MP in Kampala, who had helped them get the NGO started, to complain about the attempted LC takeover of the clinic. Mpanga intervened to prevent the takeover and helped preserve the independence of the clinic. She explained:

> As I told you, for me I don't get pushed around much. So I told the LC5 chairman "Look, this was a pure NGO that had come here to work like any other NGO . . . We want to build a separate independent project that will give most of these people medical assistance because it is a service." The women asked me after the struggle [was over,] "But why should this man [LC3] want this?" and I replied: "It is because they want to eat that money."

As in Mutai, the intervention of a person with some political clout, in this case a member of parliament, made the difference in being able to keep the clinic autonomous.

These examples, along with the Kitumba case, suggest that a more far-reaching redesign of institutions would be necessary to institutionalize women's access to resources so that they are not entirely dependent on the strength and inclinations of individual women or even men leaders. This would require a reconfiguration of politics itself in a way that would make it possible for women to participate fully and be heard. But, as the case studies suggest, the process of change is not an easy one, nor is it without struggle between conflicting interests.

This book has outlined some general patterns in the kinds of concerns women have brought to the political arena in Uganda, but it cannot be assumed that all women share all of these concerns, nor can it be assumed that men do not. Moreover, it cannot be assumed that the issues will not change or that men will not come to see the women's concerns as in their own interest. However, what we are looking at in this case are interests that at this particular point in time tended to fall along gendered lines because of the different experiences of Jinja men and women in work, the household, church, education, politics and other key institutions.

By calling this a gender conflict, I am not suggesting that this was a conflict simply between men and women, since many men and male government officials supported the women, including the District Administrator, the sub-county (*gombolola*) chief, the District Security Officer, the District Medical Officer (until he changed his position), the deputy District Medical Officer, the Director of Medical Services in Entebbe, and the Local Council heads in neighboring villages. The conflict was gendered in the way that women's interests were identified, represented and fought for by both men and women. In fact, Ekikwenza Omubi had the support of most men in the community and key male leaders in the district administration and in several ministries.

The story of how the health clinic was established illustrates how women made use of changing opportunity structures to gain access to and control over community resources. The Kitumba women had taken advantage of the government's new openness to women's mobilization and to the privatization of social services. In this sense, Ekikwenza Omubi is an organization that reflects part of the unfolding changes in Uganda's associational life.

The new spaces for associations like Ekikwenza Omubi emerged partly as a result of changes in government policy, but also partly because the government did not have the capacity and resources to fulfill many of the social service functions it once carried out. For example, in the area of health services, in the 1960s Uganda had one of the best medical delivery systems in Africa. Government health facilities were well stocked with medication that was provided free of charge to users. With the disruptions of the Amin regime in the 1970s, the government health services deteriorated rapidly, medical professionals diminished in number and medicines became scarce. Today, voluntary, private and local healers are the main sources of health care in the country as a consequence of the decline in government facilities (Brett, 1991: 297–309; Whyte, 1991: 130–48). Since the government has increasingly relinquished control of the medical system to private and community initiatives, it has made modest sums of money available to the sub-county administration to assist in the establishment of such units. Already 37 community-run health units (outpatient clinics) like the one started by the Kitumba women had been established in Jinja District by 1993, compared with 8 units in 1989.

In Jinja, as in other parts of the country, women have responded to the government's active encouragement to mobilize and its reliance on women's involvement in development. In the Ministry of Health, for example, the policy on primary health care has been directed at women, who are looked upon as the key health care providers in the household. Ekikwenza Omubi seized on these government encouragements to justify their leadership of the health clinic. Since the NRM came to power in 1986, women in Jinja have made significant gains in becoming more active in community affairs and in achieving leadership positions.

Moreover, several prominent female national leaders, including the Vice-President and former Minister of Women in Development, Specioza Wandira Kazibwe, the former Minister of Agriculture, Victoria Sekitoleko, and parliamentarian Rebecca Kadaga, come from the Busoga area where Kitumba is located. In the March 1994 elections for the Constituent Assembly to debate the new constitution, Busoga had more female contenders than any other region in the country. Jinja has also had a number of prominent local women leaders, including Hope Mwondha, who was the Chief Magistrate of Jinja, Annet Nalwanga Kibirango, the District Administrator appointed in 1993, and Ruth Owagage who was General Secretary LC5 and in 1996 became a Member of Parliament.

Although women in Jinja have taken advantage of these changing opportunity structures, they have predictably met with resistance along the way. Their experiences with the Local Councils have been uneven and follow patterns established in the following case studies of Kiyembe and Kawaala (Chapters 8 and 9). Because the LC leadership reflects local power structures based on gender, class, ethnic, religious and political party configurations, community members who challenged

these existing power structures, like Ekikwenza Omubi, ran the risk of antagonizing the LC leadership. Thus, because of these limitations of the LC system and, in
particular, its male elder bias, women in Kitumba pursued their interests through
their own independent economic, cultural, religious, and welfare organizations.
In fact, the conflict in Kitumba convinced many women of the importance of
forming their own organizations. As one woman put it, one of the main gains of
the conflict was that women found the courage to organize and start many groups
in the area.

The Conflict

Kitumba village on the outskirts of Jinja municipality had been a relatively peaceful
community that knew how to pull together when it came to initiating major projects like the building of a senior secondary school in 1990. This seeming tranquility
was shattered in 1991 when male village leaders refused to sanction the establishment and management of a parish health clinic by a women's group called Ekikwenza Omubi Women's Project. The name of the association comes from the
Lusoga proverb *"Ekikwenza omubi – omulungi takimanyha"*, which roughly translated
means, "when someone falls in love with an ugly one, the beautiful one keeps won-
dering why" or "beauty is in the eye of the beholder".

As far back as people could remember, men and women had co-operated fairly
well in parish projects, with some exceptions. Male and female football (soccer)
clubs even competed with one another, with women frequently winning the
matches. Like the members of Ekikwenza Omubi, the men who opposed
the women's initiative had in the past made contributions and sacrifices to improve
the welfare of their parish. Both the men and the women embroiled in the conflict
were for the most part respected and exemplary citizens. Many of these men even
claimed to support women's emancipation. How, then, did Kitumba become transformed into a community divided bitterly in a gender-based conflict over the way
in which community interests were to be expressed?

The conflict in Kitumba revolved around two key issues. The first was over Ekikwenza Omubi's insistence that they as women should run the health clinic. The
women's group had come to the realization that they needed to control the clinic
and that the community's health care needs would not be served adequately were
they to let the male elders in the community take over the leadership of the project.
The Kitumba case shows that in order to maintain control of the clinic, the women
had openly to challenge existing gender biases and definitions of community that
had favored male leadership in local politics, in the church and in most public activities in Kitumba. Thus in the struggle that unfolded, women transformed a fight for
a community service into a battle for female leadership and, in the process, they
developed critical analyses of power, gender relations, and gender identities which
this chapter will explore. They also discovered new methods of asserting their collective interests.

In addition to the issue of leadership, the second point of contention was over
the size and function of the health clinic. The women wanted a modest health
center that included an outpatient clinic and maternity unit, which they felt was
feasible given the available resources. The men leaders wanted a big dispensary
and some even wanted facilities that would provide better services than the main
hospital in Jinja.

Background to the Conflict
Before going further with the story, it may be helpful to give some background to the people in this part of Uganda. Kitumba is situated in Butembe county outside of Jinja, the second largest city and the most industrialized center in Uganda. Jinja District is located in the western part of Busoga, where the majority population (65 percent) are known as Basoga who speak Lusoga. Other ethnic groups in the district include the Baganda (8 percent), Iteso (5 percent), Banyole (4 percent) and Bagisu (3 percent). With a population of 65,169, Jinja has the highest population density of any district in Uganda (428 people per sq. km.), with the exception of Kampala. Kitumba village is in Mafubira sub-county, which has about 50,384 residents. Like Jinja, it is primarily Protestant (Church of Uganda), although there are also Catholic and Muslim residents. In Jinja District, 48 percent of the population is Protestant, 28 percent Catholic and 22 percent Muslim. One-third of the rural population is literate, with women having literacy rates of 53 percent compared with 69 percent literacy rates for men (Statistics Department, Jinja District, 1992).

The published historical record on women in Busoga is extremely thin. One Ugandan historian, writing between 1921 and 1938, detailed the duties of Basoga men and women, revealing a strictly gender-based division of labor, much of which appears to have been sustained to this day. Men were at that time in charge of marketing cash crops, manufacturing bark cloth for sale, animal husbandry, hunting wild animals, preparing wooden tools and making pottery, in addition to ruling the country and fighting "if there was war". Women were to grow food for consumption, look after all domestic affairs, gather firewood, fetch water, prepare food, look after children, buy and sell articles in the markets, look after the sick, build roads, and "cry bitterly for the dead" (Lubogo, 1962).

In one brief mention of relations between husbands and wives based on research carried out in Busoga in 1950, Lloyd Fallers describes a similar division of labor and characterizes the Soga household as a male-dominated one. Women, he observed, worked much harder than men, yet the men controlled and dispensed the household resources as they wished. Men were free to travel and sit around the beer pot with friends discussing village affairs, while the "good woman" was expected to work hard, bear children and not travel away from home unescorted. She could not own land or property and had to be represented by her husband or father in court. She was to kneel in the presence of her husband, whom she addressed as *ssebo* (sir) or *mukama wange* (my lord). However, in reality, Fallers found that this was more of an idealized picture of gender roles and women had more control than they were said to have. Women did, in fact, market eggs, chickens and even cotton from their own plots, thus obtaining cash which they could use as they pleased. In some homesteads, he found "open revolt", where women felt unduly restricted and rebelled by resisting their husband's authority or by taking lovers. Women of childbearing age were more restricted than elderly women, who had considerably more freedom to travel, trade and carry out other such activities. Fallers observed at that time that "female deviations from the norms of submission . . . are not fundamentally new developments in the Soga social system" and that the husband's dominance had in practice been rather tenuously maintained. At the time he was writing women began to gain greater opportunities to escape male authority by seeking employment in Jinja or Kampala (Fallers, 1965: 76–9). As in such earlier periods of transition, women today in Uganda are taking advantage of the newly emerging opportunity structures to mobilize themselves around broader community concerns.

Ekikwenza Omubi, which was made up of about 30 women, emerged out of a Mothers' Union group within the Protestant Church of Uganda. Like other women in the village, the women in the group were involved in smallholder subsistence farming and animal husbandry, growing staples like cassava, beans, and maize in addition to fruit and vegetables. They also included women involved in handicraft production, in trading fruits and vegetables, and in other forms of self-employment. The leader of Ekikwenza Omubi, Gertrude Kisozi (a fictitious name), was a trader in second-hand clothes and ran a restaurant that catered to union workers at a nearby coffee factory. The women in Ekikwenza Omubi reflect very much the general range of economic activities that women engage in district-wide. In Jinja most women (54 percent) are engaged in subsistence farming, 10 percent in trading, and 16 percent are wage-employed.

The women in the group were mostly over 45 years of age and a large number were widowed or divorced and were raising children on their own. The organization's objectives were aimed at improving the welfare of the community and, like organizations in other parts of Uganda, it had a strong social service component to it. The members' particular aims were to provide education for needy children, especially orphans; to provide poor parents, the physically handicapped, and refugee parents with sources of income; to promote the economic status of women; to promote the social welfare of children, their families and the community as a whole; to build health care centers; to improve women's health; to provide services to improve the care of children; to collect statistics and information concerning the health of women and children in the community and to establish small-scale industries and promote income-generating activities (poultry farming, arts and crafts, brick-making, weaving, etc.) (see Appendix C). The organization was completely self-sufficient, with its finances coming from membership fees and the proceeds from sales of products made for the group.

Kisozi had been thinking of establishing a clinic since 1985, but her plans did not materialize until 1992 and then only after her group had surmounted several obstacles. The group identified the lack of health services as the most pressing concern women faced. Since many in the group were poor widowed and divorced mothers, they were especially burdened by the long distances they had to travel to obtain medical care for their children and the high medical fees they had to pay. Moreover, women in all families were primarily responsible for maintaining the health of the household and faced similar problems. Therefore the women's group decided to set up a health clinic for the parish, which included four villages with a combined population of roughly 25,000.

Kisozi first tried to work through her local chapter of the Mothers' Union, but the chairperson rejected her application for funding for a health clinic. As chairperson of the parish church council, she then asked for funding for a clinic and land from the diocese, whose officials told her to go to the LC2 officials to raise funds. After a brief debate over whether they should get all taxpayers or all church-going Christians to make a donation, the LC2 representatives finally took no action on her proposal.

One of the Ekikwenza Omubi members introduced the group to a local NGO called Africom, which had already been involved in provisioning community health care services in Jinja District. Kisozi, together with a woman teacher from Africom, carried out a three-month baseline survey of Kitumba parish to determine the health care needs of the community. They listed the numbers of people, the ages of the residents, the most common illnesses and the general health care problems in Kitumba parish. To determine existing sanitation standards, they asked residents about the protection of local water sources and how they prepared their food. The survey was intended to help them make a case for establishing a health center in ·the area.

Africom was about to bring medical personnel to Kitumba when the District Medical Officer (DMO) forced it to close down its operations because it had been following unauthorized medical procedures.[2] Having lost the support of Africom, Kisozi went to the Director of Medical Services for the country.[3] He advised her to contact the District Medical Officer in Jinja, which she did, armed with a project plan and data about community health needs. The DMO told her to contact the LC1, LC2 and LC3 leaders in order to follow the proper procedures for establishing the health clinic.

The Conflict

At this point several of the women in Ekikwenza Omubi cautioned Kisozi about working with the LC leaders, pointing out that because the LC executive was predominantly male, women's control of the initiative might be undermined. Some disagreement emerged over tactics at this point. The members argued that they would rather take longer building the facility on their own than lose control over the project. But Kisozi, having already decided that she was prepared to sacrifice some control in the short run to get the clinic off the ground, did not heed their warnings, and went with the male LC leaders to the DMO's office in April 1991 to discuss the clinic.

She then went back to the church to ask for land on which to build it, and this time they agreed to provide the land as long as she worked with LC1 representatives. Elections for members of a Health Unit Management Committee (HUMC) were held in co-operation with local LC1 leaders. The lay "Leader of Christians" in the parish nominated Kisozi, arguing that the head of the committee should be someone who would not be "prevented by her husband", and "who was democratic" and "kind to everybody".[4] Kisozi was elected leader of a nine-member committee – thus resembling the LC structure – composed of 6 men and 3 women to oversee the establishment of the health clinic. It was generally understood that it would be a women's project with men acting as advisers.

The LC1 chairman lent the women a building for temporary use until a permanent clinic could be built. The DMO agreed to give assistance to the health clinic as a women's project, and at a ceremony presented the HUMC with staff, including a medical assistant, a dresser, two nurses, five nurses aids, and a midwife. The clinic was established and proceeded to operate quite smoothly. Almost all those we interviewed in 1993 who had made use of the clinic (both supporters and detractors of the Women's Project) were on the whole pleased with the services provided. Since its establishment, the clinic had been serving at least 14 neighboring villages, with up to 30 patients a day.[5] It was involved in the provision of emergency services, the immunization of children and community outreach programs for education on child rearing, family planning and other public health issues.[6] It also served the local primary and secondary schools, which no longer had to transport the young people all the way to Jinja for treatment. However, it still lacked adequate facilities and had experienced drug shortages.

Meanwhile, the DMO advised the LC3 leader to help the women with their project. It soon became apparent to the LC leaders that the DMO wanted the women actually to manage the clinic. This realization triggered the trouble that followed.

Gradually the LC1 (Kitumba) and LC3 chairman began to withdraw support from the project, arguing that it was not a community project but rather Kisozi's personal affair. The local clergyman eventually withdrew his promise of land for the same reason and gave it to the LC3 chairperson for him to use to establish a clinic. In anger, Kisozi left the church council. The LC1 chairman chased the women out of the building he had originally given them for the clinic.

A campaign to discredit Kisozi's integrity began as rumors circulated that she was a money-hungry schemer and was employing witchcraft against her opponents. She was said to be a murderer, a cheat, and "half-baked" (i.e., uneducated). She even received letters insulting her for her lack of education, for not having gone to school but "stopped at the window of the classroom". The opponents of Ekikwenza Omubi accused the DMO and his deputy of being partial in siding with the women.

When the DMO was informed about all this, he threatened to remove the clinic if the LC3 leader continued to try to "hijack the project from the women". The women's group called on the District Administrator (DA) to intervene to prevent bloodshed. The DA tried in vain to settle the dispute. He supported the women's project and told the LC leaders that he had never seen people as self-sacrificing as the women in this parish. He urged them to help the women and dismissed the efforts of some of these local leaders to discredit Kisozi for her lack of formal education.

The sub-county (gombolola) chief[7] also tried to mediate in the conflict without success. He felt that the clergyman and the LC leaders had betrayed the women, and advised the LC leaders to leave the women alone. He remarked: "I do not know why they [the LC leaders] take an interest [in the project]. After all there is no money in it. In reality it is just unfairness. Gertrude Kisozi has initiated the project. After bringing it up they want to grab it from her, which she does not allow. She has mobilized women, who have responded." He described Kisozi as exceptional and said that he had never seen a woman leader with such intelligence and strength in his subcounty.[8]

At one point, the LC1 chairman of Kitumba met with Kisozi and acknowledged the sacrifices she had made to establish the clinic, but asked her to step down from her position as chairperson of the HUMC and allow a male elder in the community to take over, while she remain a committee member. Backed by the women's group, Kisozi remained firm in her refusal to relinquish her position. When she resisted, she was reminded again that she was a poor illiterate woman. Subsequent efforts to unseat her failed since the leaders of the other LCs in the parish continued to support her.

The District Administrator allowed a building committee to be set up. At this point Kisozi suggested that representatives from all sides be put on the committee, hoping that this would mollify the male leaders. With time, the campaign to discredit Kisozi and the women's group gained larger numbers of followers in the community, including some women, leaving the community bitterly divided. In fact, many believed the intensity of the conflict to be unprecedented. The sub-county chief had never seen a community conflict as divisive as this one in the eight years he had held his post.[9]

The conflict came to a stalemate when the DMO, who completely reversed his position under pressure from the LCs, tried on three separate occasions to get the police to arrest Gertrude Kisozi's husband for failing to transfer the Kitumba Health Project and its equipment to the LCs and the District Medical Office. According to a letter of 5 May 1995 from the District Security Officer the arrest was "not carried out",[10] because there was no warrant; Mr Kisozi told the police to go away. Meanwhile, Gertrude Kisozi went into hiding for three days, but after the third failed arrest, she went to the District Security Officer, who appeared to sympathize with the women and told the police not to arrest Kisozi. In a letter he advised all parties, including the LC5, LC3 and the District Medical Officer, to come to an understanding.

The District Medical Officer meanwhile confiscated the clinic money, equipment and supplies that belonged to the women, and transferred the clinic to the primary school. When he found out that the women had gone to the DSO, he forced the medical staff at the school to go on leave and as of July 1995 Kitumba had no operating clinic. Without government support, the women began to seek private and NGO support for their initiative.

The District Security Officer tried in vain to get the feuding parties to work out their differences, but was outmaneuvered by the LC3, LC5 and the DMO, who ignored his request. The DMO told the women to get a licence and open a private clinic (without government assistance) if they still wanted to have a clinic. They objected to this since their clinic was a non-profit-making institution and should therefore not be subject to the same regulations as profit-making clinics. The women made a last-ditch attempt to appeal to the NRC Women's representative from the area, Irene Wekiya, who advised them not to let the DMO take the clinic equipment and supplies. She promised to look into the matter but they never heard from her again. The women approached the central government representative, who clearly did not understand the role of the LC3 in funding local health initiatives, and reprimanded the group for going through the LC system, arguing that they should have worked directly with the DMO.

Community Divided: The Meaning of "Community" Contested

An important part of the debate was over how "community" participation and interests were to be defined. Everyone was ostensibly in favour of promoting "community interests" and "community participation in development." But "community" did not carry the same meaning for the women in Kitumba as it did for the male village leaders. Both the LC leaders and Ekikwenza Omubi believed that the whole community would benefit from the health clinic. But for the women, community control in this case would have to mean control by women because they had the most at stake in establishing the health clinic. To let men lead would be tantamount to giving up any control women had, a lesson they had learned in previous community initiatives like the building of the senior secondary school. Ekikwenza Omubi identified their parish as the main population that would be served by the health center and gave special preference to women and children. Women were to manage the clinic, according to the project description, in order to "facilitate parish community initiative, develop and maintain health care, develop and cultivate income generation sources in order to support the *gombolola* [sub-county] community based activities and more so to support themselves as individuals and their respective families in both public and private capacities".[11]

The men, on the other hand, felt unjustly pushed to the side. The headmaster of the secondary school in Kitumba explained that when they first called a meeting in 1991 regarding the health clinic: "As men we were observers and not active in discussions." He found this unsettling since men usually do most of the talking at public gatherings. He also thought that women would fail if they were in the leadership of the clinic.[12]

The right to control the health clinic escalated as the women became increasingly active in getting it established and, as a result, felt that the men were trying to take over something to which they had not contributed. Kisozi pointed out that with other women in the group they had been doing all the work to establish the clinic with little help from the men:

> Now me as a woman, I saw the problems of the lack of health facilities and I stood up. I did not even get a shilling from them [the LCs and other opponents of the Women's Project], not one chair, not one table, nothing. . . . . I never got anybody to help me with the baseline survey. Why should they now ask to take over? I will not allow anybody to lead me. I am still firm and I pray that it is over. It may mean that I die but I do not mind.

Her husband added, "Men just want to take over what is not theirs. . . . She is in line with government policy. All women have been called to wake up. That is why I have supported her and I even think the government will help the women."[13]

One woman expressed the same sentiment with a proverb: "*Omulimi mulimi, nomuli muli*" meaning "One digs [farms] but another one eats [the farmer's produce]."[14] Another woman trader in sweet potatoes said: "I think the problem is just the issue of being a woman. How can a woman lead? Since when did women own things?"[15]

Yet another reason the women felt they should be in control of the project was that historically women had been the main ones who had involved themselves and succeeded in community efforts. As Kisozi put it:

> As far as the men of Kitumba are concerned, they are not used to community work. So no man will be willing to start such a group. In my life there has been only one man from a neighboring village who had started such a group, but he never even managed to get support.

She felt that those who were better-off were even less inclined to involve themselves in community work because "they think that a person who goes out to help others is a redundant person. After all, when does that person find time to care for his/her family?" The main constraint on women getting involved in such community efforts, she felt, was that "they are socially oppressed by men and they are not allowed to move out on any venture".[16]

Building Alliances

In the course of the conflict, the women's group learned how to build alliances and coalitions of supporters in their community, in other parts of the country, with local government officials and even with national leaders. In trying to overcome the resistance from the LC1 chairman and local church leaders, the women in Kitumba sought the support of members of their community, leaders of neighboring village Local Councils, and women's groups in neighboring villages. Ekikwenza Omubi rallied support for their cause even as far as Entebbe, through drama and singing performances. At one point, the group won an award for having written the best song about AIDS in the sub-county. Women in neighboring villages donated money and their labor to help keep the clinic clean. The women's group even got male villagers to donate furniture for the clinic.

The women not only drew support from other women's groups but they also gave support to other associations. Gertrude Kisozi went to Bugandi in Iganga and tried to get them to start a health clinic. She also spent time educating them on various matters since she found the women in "that remote place" in "a poor state".[17]

The women gained support from highly placed political figures at the national level, including the Minister of Agriculture (who visited the group), the Minister of Women in Development, and the parliamentary women's representative from Jinja, not to mention the national Director of Medical Services at the Ministry of Health. The fact that the women even approached many of these individuals with their problems, defying commonly accepted proscriptions on behavior determined by gender, class, education and social position, suggests the kind of confidence they had developed in the course of the struggle. But it also shows how the government's affirmative policy towards women had made a difference in opening up new possibilities for women to assert themselves in public affairs.

Many government officials at the district level also supported Ekikwenza Omubi and saw the women as important allies in their efforts to accomplish various goals. The District Security Officer backed the women, providing them with legal advice. The sub-county (*gombolola*) chief had seen some of the biggest advances in his sub-county in women's economic activities, including a tree planting project in Namulesa, a ceramics project in Buwenda, and a heifer project in Bugembe. For him too, supporting women made good political sense because of the visible pay-offs.

Similarly, the deputy District Medical Officer told us that he had become aware of the importance of women in carrying out various preventative health care programs through his involvement in the day-to-day provision of health services. He felt that women were more receptive than men to preventative educational initiatives and were more likely to attend seminars. In other words, the women made his work easier. Unlike the DMO, the deputy DMO was anxious to see women in charge of such a health center because, as he put it, "women and children are the government's target population for health care" and because "women are oppressed" and they need to be supported in their efforts to "uplift their status as women".[18]

These male government officials were openly sympathetic to Ekikwenza Omubi and found creative ways to help the women. As the conflict unfolded, the deputy DMO and the District Administrator, in particular, raised important questions about the role of female leadership, strengthened their commitment to women and made clear their own reasons for supporting women in the district. For example, the deputy DMO, who was acting DMO for much of 1991 and 1992, helped establish the health clinic by redefining policy. His goal was to raise the consciousness of the local community members to support the idea that women can be good managers. As he put it:

> I call the women my fellow health workers. And indeed, I think they are. I have refused to recognize the male-dominated management. I take cognizance of collective participation. Male domination at any one stage negates those objectives, for they are now used to subordinating women. They cannot envisage a change.

One can certainly attribute the positive support the Kitumba women received from these leaders to a government orientation that generally encouraged women's mobilization. But whether government officials acted on these new enabling institutional changes depended largely on individual inclinations. The official policy of the Ministry of Health has been to promote women's participation in health care, and, indeed, the Ministry has developed many programs in which women receive particular attention, including primary health drives for immunization, maternal and child health, family planning, nutrition, AIDS programs and clean water campaigns (Kakwenzire, 1990). Nevertheless, the DMO in Jinja was not convinced that this policy was upheld by all individuals working in the ministry. As he remarked, half jokingly, "The Ministry of Health does not care about anything other than their Pajeros (fancy cars) and their allowances. They don't care about women."[19] In other words, having a progressive policy was not enough; individual leaders like the DMO and his deputy did make a difference. Even the DMO had been a supporter of the women in 1993 but by 1995 had succumbed to pressures from the male elders and LCs in the community, when the Director of Medical Services at the Ministry of Health, who had backed the women, died suddenly. The DMO reasoned that since the policy of decentralization was in effect, he was under no obligation to the Ministry and could let the LCs act as they saw fit.

Thus, much of the interpretation of policy was still left to individual male leaders who were not bound in any way to take women's interests into account. Those who did, did not necessarily support the women because they were women or because there was a personal political advantage in doing so. They did so because it made sense to them in their efforts to promote good community health and community development. Women were active participants in preventative health care and had been critical to the changes that had occurred in the local economy. On this basis, the leaders saw that it made eminent sense to support the efforts of Ekikwenza Omubi.

Constraints on Women's Mobilization in Kitumba

The Local Councils

While in general the women had support at the national and district levels, the main opposition came at the local level where they faced fierce resistance from the Local Council leaders. The general national encouragement of women's mobilization did not automatically translate into policies adopted at the local level. As Kisozi put it:

> It is specifically very difficult for women at lower levels because whereas the president has a very good will for women, the people at lower levels, especially the LCs, spoil things and you end up not even enjoying the good policies of the government.[20]

It is interesting to note that of the 37 health units initiated in Jinja, the only two that resulted in community disputes were started by women, including that in Kitumba. In both these conflicts the main resistance came from local LC leaders. The Kitumba women's group explained that even other dealings with the LCs had been problematic for women, for example, when it came to signing documents. In an incident in 1993 the women had started, with the help of the Ministry of Agriculture, a fish pond to raise fish because many children in the community were suffering from kwashiorkor due to economic difficulties. Three months later, when Gertrude Kisozi was away at a training seminar in Nairobi, the LC officials poisoned all the fish. The women drained the pond and started all over again with the help of the Ministry, which gave them 200 additional baby fish. Earlier when the women had sought assistance from the District Administrator, the LCs made sure he bypassed the women's group when visiting the village.

Similarly, the lack of female leadership in the LC system had consequences when the women attempted to take the initiative. There are two dimensions to this problem. First, because, for social and cultural reasons, women rarely run for office, the chances of elected women officials having a collective impact are slim. Secondly, those women in LC positions, especially those who hold the position of women secretary, have been elected primarily by men, who dominate the electorate. They may not necessarily be the most active women in the community, especially where men have deliberately decided to select a woman who will toe their line. Thus, Kisozi was not able to enlist the support of the LC1 secretary for women. "The LC1 Women's Secretary was helpful at the beginning but she began to fear men and has advised us to leave the project for men to take over so we can start on something else," she explained.[21] Even the women's secretary in the neighboring village of Buwekula was unsupportive of Kisozi because she was antagonizing the men. She felt women needed to stay in men's good graces in order to have access to land; she said she did not support the men in the LC who opposed the women, but reasoned that "If they refuse to give us land, where will we women go?"

The class dimension of the LCs also worked to the women's disadvantage. Those in leadership tended to be better situated, and this further impeded women's representation. As Kisozi pointed out:

> Having more women on the LC executive would help us if we know what we are doing. In our village, we elect somebody because she is rich. Like, for example, they cannot elect me because they want somebody from a well-built home irrespective of her intelligence, thinking that because of her well-built home she will have understanding.[22]

Other Constraints

Ekikwenza Omubi met with resistance not only from the LC leaders, but also found that the local Church of Uganda and Mothers' Union chapter were not supportive of their initiative and refused to help in their quest for land for the clinic. The clergyman sided openly with the village leaders. Since Protestants have dominated the community numerically, Protestant religious interests were also reflected in the LC leadership.

Thus, Kisozi found that her willingness to align herself with non-Protestant women was used by some church members and LC leaders to discredit her. Although not central to this particular conflict, religious differences manifested themselves when Kisozi left her involvement in the local Mothers' Union chapter. Although some of the Ekikwenza Omubi members remained in the Mothers' Union, the group broke away in order to gain greater autonomy in its activities. In breaking away, they were able to link up with Catholic and Muslim women who were interested in broader community concerns. The anti-sectarian principle behind the formation of Ekikwenza Omubi is typical of the way in which women throughout the country are finding new bases for collective mobilization around economic and community concerns. It is especially significant in a country where religious differences have played a major role in the country's turbulent history (Tripp, 1994).

Yet when Kisozi started working with women of other religious orientations she was labeled a supporter of the "Democratic Party", the party associated with the Catholic Church, although there was no basis for this rumor. Nevertheless, her break with past practices showed that, even though the regime has banned party competition, the religious sectarianism that accompanied it in the past is not far below the surface and was used as a basis for opposing the women's group.

Yet another challenge to the women came when the clinic issue was seized on by contenders in the 1996 parliamentary race. At one point the candidate who eventually won the election tried to intervene in the conflict to make it appear that he was behind the clinic in order to gain support. He tried to contribute money to the clinic but the women refused his assistance because he wanted to take credit for the clinic as a way of garnering votes. In the end his plan failed because, as Kisozi put it: "He found it difficult to influence the decision of the women. So what he has done is now to pass through the LCs and since the LCs can talk to the DMO it is very easy for him to have influence."

Transformations in Consciousness

As women learned how to build coalitions, they also developed critical analyses of women's gender subordination in their community. They saw clearly that their own experience of trying to claim leadership had parallels elsewhere, including the case of Mutai. They also saw the link with male views about women in national politics. As Kisozi pointed out:

> The mere fact that, even when you are traveling in a minibus, you will hear remarks by men that Museveni is a fool, he doesn't understand. How can he pick a woman to lead? [a reference to the Vice President]. So that one [example] shows the type of thinking they have about women.

They found, for example, that the issue of who had the right to control the clinic had strong class dimensions that were intricately tied to their gender position. The economic status of women was seen as inseparable from men's objection to women in leadership. "With men, especially the rich who are the sole breadwinners, they regard women as just rubbish", argued Kisozi.

Much of the women's analysis also focused on the issue of poverty and education in justifying why women had the right to manage such a clinic. What especially irritated the male leaders was that Kisozi and most of the women in Ekikwenza Omubi were illiterate and poor. The headmaster of the primary school in Kitumba said:

> Would you like to be ruled by an illiterate person? It would be ridiculous to allow this woman to lead women around here who are educated. You see that woman [Kisozi] is very bright and if she had formal education she could move mountains.

The men opposing Kisozi included high ranking civil servants, retired headmasters, and wealthy farmers and businessmen. The men were educated, spoke English and some had even traveled abroad. One of the women in the group explained: "For us, we do not have education. We as women, we have been oppressed . . . and they still want to oppress us further in this government of enlightenment." Another woman in the community explained:

> Sometimes the rich have a feeling that once poor, always poor and if one is poor you lack insight. So now how can she [Kisozi] from down here come up with such a bright idea . . . The woman was the first to move and then the clinic was as good as established . . . Now they say she is poor and if she spends time in managing the clinic when will she work for her family?

One older woman, Rachel Katawera, put the gender-based conflict in historical perspective, telling one of my research assistants (who is her niece) that lack of education had never been an obstacle to male leadership in the past. For this reason she argued that it should not be used to hold back women's leadership:

> You see, my father and my brother started this battle [for women's emancipation] long before anybody knew that any government could allow women to participate in public life. Men for a long time, and in fact up to now, are desirous of keeping women under them. They reason like fools. Okay, so Kisozi did not go to school but even my father, your grandfather, did not go to

school. But he ruled [as county chief *saza*] and people respected him. When Nviri [speaker of Busoga District Council under British colonial rule] appealed to the Basoga to send their daughters to school, they said he wanted to employ women in his office, so he could gain access to them [womanize]. My child, support Kisozi. She has given birth to an idea and I do not see why she should be discouraged. Even your uncle here is bitter about the whole issue. "This land belongs to me," he says. "I am the one who gave the school and the church part of it. Why are they behaving like this against that woman?"

As for you, we say *"Embwa telekaawo musuntumalire gainyhayo."* "A dog always squats like its mother." . . . If your [fore]fathers had discriminated against you [young educated women/girls] would you be feeding us now? They gave fees to all children and that is why even girls can now work and earn. If they [the LCs] are sure there is nothing to gain, let them just build and leave the management to Kisozi. Does one need to be a chairperson in order to move things? Let them leave the woman to enjoy her glory. She is not asking for too much. She is leaving all the seats on the executive [of the building committee] to the men.[23]

Kisozi herself challenged the discrimination against her based on her lack of education and being a woman:

What do they [the LC leaders] mean when they say I am illiterate, and a woman then? They talk about themselves having nothing to gain from [running the health center] as though it would not be there for them but it would be there for me. Surely, if there is nothing to gain, let them work along with me. They have several times tried to persuade me to step down. I am sticking to only one post, that of chairperson, so I can be introduced as the founder. It makes a difference when you are at the forefront. . . . If it means nothing, let them leave me in the chair.[24]

Many residents in the community were not troubled by Kisozi's lack of education since she had sought help from others who could read, for example, from the teacher, in carrying out the baseline survey. Kisozi and the women realized that not being educated was a limitation, but it was no excuse for staying out of public service in the community. They felt they needed to start from where they were and do what they could. Some pointed out that many with education had done little for the community, while others without education had accomplished a lot. As one woman in the community said:

We have supported Kisozi . . . She is a good leader, dedicated. As for me, I gave cassava [to feed the teacher conducting the baseline survey] but those men did not do that. Now they say a woman who does not read cannot lead. She cannot read or write. But I am talking about wisdom, inborn ability.

At one meeting with the LCs, a member of the Kitumba Women's Association argued that, simply because a person has not been to university, they should not be disqualified from leadership and that mechanisms could be found to deal with this disadvantage. She argued that if a founder is illiterate, then you select a secretary who will be educated, but leave the founder to lead.

Gertrude Kisozi's husband also pointed out that his wife had kept meticulous records of the organization's correspondence and other important documents. He went on: "Just look at the way she does her business, especially her filing system. It makes all their arguments defective, because even though she is uneducated, she knows the value of keeping information well filed and the file looks like it is kept by someone who knows the value of documents."[25] I read Gertrude Kisozi's files and was also impressed at the care with which she had saved all the organization's documents.

Lack of education, low class status and gender, wrapped into one, were thus seen by better-off community members as obstacles to leadership, while for the women themselves, these identities had little to do with capacity for leadership. After the clinic had been removed from the Ekikwenza Omubi, the gender and class dimensions of their struggle and their organization became even clearer to them. The LC leaders tried to split the organization along class lines, telling the better-off members to leave the association and form another group since the lower-class women were too difficult to deal with. The well-to-do women formed a new group and the LCs tried to get the new organization to manage the clinic. But, interestingly enough, the better-off women in this new LC-backed group continued secretly to support Ekikwenza Omubi. They reported to them on what the LC leaders were up to and complained about demands made on them by the men. "It shows that they still have a feeling that they still belong with us", said Kisozi. This secret alliance shows both the way male influence constrained the women, kept them separated along class lines and forced them to exhibit their false allegiance to male interest, and also the women's capacity to overcome these differences, suggesting that gender interests proved in the end to be the overriding uniting concern in this struggle. In an ironic twist to the story, the wealthier women's own lack of economic status, according to the Ekikwenza Omubi women, is what kept them from asserting their common gender interests. For the poor women, it was their economic autonomy from men that had permitted their involvement.

The women in Kitumba learned a lot about the relationship between gender and class in the course of their struggle and were clearly able to engage in sophisticated sociological analysis about their situation. But they also learned the benefits of resistance. As Gertrude Kisozi put it:

> I learned to be committed and not to be afraid just because people are talking. Women who have gone through such an experience should teach others that with commitment things will move. It will also be very exemplary for the young ones who see you suffer. Because they will grow up knowing that there is nothing on a silver plate.[26]

When Women's Participation Matters

This chapter draws on one case study of a struggle by a women's organization to establish a health clinic and take advantage of the decentralization of health funds to the village level. The women found their efforts thwarted at every step of the way by those who had historically held the reins of power in the community. The women were constrained, among other things, by pre-existing cultural norms and patterns of authority that were biased towards wealthier male elders and against poor women. The case study shows just how difficult it is for women even to be allowed to contribute to community development, not to mention lead an initiative. Even with representation, women do not have the same access to and control of local government resources as men. They find it difficult to be heard in local council meetings and even more difficult to claim leadership in these local government institutions. Gains for the "community" may not be translated as easily into gains for women. When women do attempt to redefine community interests in broader terms, they often encounter resistance, as this study demonstrates.

This chapter has shown how and why the Kitumba women's group defined the issues differently and autonomously from the Local Council leaders. Ekikwenza Omubi's notion of participation was far more inclusive than that of the LC3 leaders. The women believed that the only criteria for leadership should be commitment and ability to get things done. While education might be desirable, they did not believe that lack of education was a sufficient excuse not to participate in community work. Unlike the LC3 leaders, they felt that neither education, nor wealth, nor gender should be considered as criteria for leadership. They also vigorously opposed mobilization along religious and ethnic lines and were vilified by the LC3 representatives because of the inclusiveness of their organization. These concerns of inclusiveness and reconciling differences follow patterns of women's mobilization throughout Uganda.

Ekikwenza Omubi, like other multi-purpose women's organizations in Uganda, aimed to give assistance to orphans, parents who were poor, the physically handicapped, and refugee parents. They had also taken up other social service concerns, including addressing the problem of malnutrition (kwashiorkor). In the case study of the clinic, the women identified the lack of adequate health facilities as the key problem facing the Kitumba community. Men had usurped control over joint male-female projects in the past and therefore the women felt that sharing control would mean relinquishing leadership entirely to the men, as had been the case in the past. This record of male domination had left the women in a zero-sum situation in which they would either have complete control or none at all. Sharing power would, in effect, have taken any assertion of women's interests entirely out of their hands.

Voluntarism is also a key characteristic of women's organizations in Uganda. In Kitumba, women had a history of organizing voluntary associations and activities. Not only were they active in their own village, but some of the women had gone to help women's organizations in other parts of Busoga. The women therefore especially resented the LC takeover of the clinic when the men had not contributed to the project, arguing that men were not used to community work.

But for women in Kitumba, voluntarism was, in fact, a political solution to a community problem. It was a solution that required collective efforts, mobilization of resources, sometimes a struggle for access to resources, creation of community support, and assertion of influence. Clearly, this way of carrying on politics in this arena was an implicit expansion by the women of the way local politics was to be conceived. It challenged the strictly utilitarian notions of political influence and competition that have characterized much of Uganda's political life and replaced it with a model that emphasized not only self-interest, but also co-operation, sharing, and sacrifice.

Thus, for women's interests to be taken into account, it is not sufficient simply to have more female faces in various public institutions, in the same way that other interest groups are represented. Much more is at stake. To incorporate women's interests, the basic rules that drive these bodies need to be re-engineered, along with the conditions under which women enter the political/public arena. This will require nothing short of a change in the relationship between the public and private spheres.

Notes

1. Owagage became the Jinja women's representative to the NRC in the 1996 elections.
2. The DMO regretted having to take this punitive action against Africom since he felt their general program was sound and in line with the goals of his office and the needs of the community.
3. The Director of Medical Services was Kisozi's cousin, and he advised her to follow regular procedures to establish the health clinic. This relationship roused suspicions in the community that he had intervened on her behalf but we found no evidence of this in discussions at the District Medical Office and with other government officials.
4. Interview with Gertrude Kisozi, Kitumba, 3 April 1993.
5. Kitumba Health Center 1993 Log book.
6. Interview with GWL Medical assistant, Kitumba Health Center/Women's Project, Kitumba, 19 April 1993.

7. Sub-county chief is strictly an administrative position. The political counterpart of this position is the LC3 chairperson.
8. Interview with 2.1, Mafubira, 19 April 1993.
9. *ibid.*
10. Letter from District Security Officer Mike C. Okirya, JJA Central to LC3 Chairman, Mafubira regarding Conflict between LCs/DMO's office and the Kitumba Health Project, 5 May 1995.
11. Kitumba Health Center/Women's Project Statement of Purpose, January 1992.
12. Interview with 2.2, Kitumba, 19 April 1993.
13. Interview with Gertrude Kisozi, Kitumba, 3 April 1993.
14. Interview RM, Rachel Katawera, Mafubira, 27 April 1993.
15. Interview RM, Irene Mutesi, 29 April 1993.
16. Interview with Gertrude Kisozi, Kitumba, 7 July 1995.
17. *ibid.*
18. Interview with Dr. Balyeku, Deputy District Medical Officer, Jinja, 2 April 1993.
19. Interview with David Kitimbo, Jinja, 19 April 1993.
20. Interview with Gertrude Kisozi, Kitumba, 7 July 1995.
21. Interview with Gertrude Kisozi, Kitumba, 3 April 1993.
22. Interview with Gertrude Kisozi, Kitumba, 7 July 1995.
23. Interview RM, Rachel Katawera, Mafubira, 27 April 1993.
24. Interview with Gertrude Kisozi, Kitumba, 3 April 1993.
25. Interview with Mr Kisozi, Kitumba, 7 July 1995.
26. Interview with Gertrude Kisozi, Kitumba, 7 July 1995.

8

The Practical
& the Political

A Battle
for Market Stalls
& Power

Although the government insists on the rights of women, men do not want us to have freedom. The war between men and women is still on.

Kiyembe market woman

The following case study explores why women in Uganda often find that they have to organize along gender lines to protect their interests. The Kiyembe market conflict reveals the depths of male bias against women in society and how quickly this bias becomes politicized when women attempt to make even small claims on resources. It also shows how institutions like the local councils, regardless of efforts in design and intent to equalize gender relations, reinforce pre-existing gendered power relations. In this particular case study, the local council leaders colluded with the Town Clerk to evict women market vendors from a market controlled by a women's co-operative, which in turn struggled to regain its market stalls.

At first glance it might appear that women's organizations are constituted along gender lines because of cultural prohibitions on women's public participation and because of the marginalization of women from dominant institutions. Interestingly, women have often transformed these manifest exclusions and put these gendered but independent organizations to new uses that may be quite subversive of the status quo. No longer are they simply innocuous groups raising pigs, marketing vegetables or making bricks. Today we see small heretofore invisible women's groups engaging in more politically significant forms of mobilization. In all four case studies in this book, women were able to use their associations to assert their autonomy and challenge institutions that limited their political, economic and social participation as women in their respective communities. Moreover, women's own explanations of why they engaged in women-only groups revealed sophisticated understandings of gender subordination.

Much like other women in Uganda, the Kiyembe women had experienced a loss of control and resources when they had been in organizations with men. They felt that the only way to protect their interests as individuals was to keep their organization exclusively female. They even restricted the women's employment of male vendors through a clause in their constitution that required women to ask permission from the Co-operative if they wanted to hire male vendors. No such

161

stipulation was made for hiring females. To an outsider this might have seemed like an unnecessarily cautious measure, but in retrospect, given the way events unfolded, the bylaw revealed the women's keen understanding of gender relations in the business environment.[1]

The women were also aware that they were being subjected to the kind of harassment that other market co-operatives did not face. They knew that it was because of their success that the male vendors moved in to take what did not belong to them. The LC5 chairperson openly declared that he had never seen a market completely owned by women and saw no reason why it should remain that way.

Similarly in Kitumba, Jinja, Ekikwenza Omubi struggled to start a health clinic and ended up having to fight to hold on to their control of it as women (Chapter 7). Like the women in Kiyembe, the Kitumba women found that there would have been no way for them to exert any measure of control had they been working jointly with men in the same organization. Past experience had taught them that the men they had worked with would eventually try to take control of their resources and authority.

Thus, organizations which appear superficially to be perpetuating a more traditional division of labor may in fact be quite subversive of the status quo in male-female power relations. Some, like the Kiyembe Co-operative, assumed this identity from the outset, while others like Ekikwenza Omubi were transformed in the course of defending their interests as women from outside threats. Even though the women in all four case studies were aware from the start that their activities threatened male authority, as the struggles unfolded their awareness of the gender dimensions of their conflicts grew.

The way in which the Kiyembe women theorized their own struggle and related their experiences in the market to the broader societal subordination of women was indicative of the profound awareness they had acquired in defending their rights and interests as women. The women linked the men's takeover of their market to other forms of oppression, including wife beating, attitudes of male superiority, and political domination. For example, when I asked some of the Kiyembe women what they had learned from their struggle, one explained:

> I want to say that it appears some men can never be considerate towards women. Although the government insists on the rights of women, men do not want us to have freedom. The war between men and women is still on. Some men are not sympathetic to women. They do not regard women as fellow human beings. That is why they beat us. Don't you think it is very shameful for a man to take a stick and beat his wife? That shows they do not regard us as fellow human beings.[2]

Another woman explained:

> One thing I learned is not to trust someone immediately because we trusted men and brought them into our market and the result is what you have there in your paper [this chapter]. These are people we employed. They turned round and grabbed our things. They were not even kind enough to pay us some money. They actually took away our rights to the market.

Thus, as in all the case studies, the Kiyembe women I describe below, were organized along gender lines not only in accordance with cultural practices, but also because they found they had common interests as market women that could only be addressed through a women's organization. This is not to say that women have not successfully used mixed organizations to fight for their rights. The leading national women's rights organization, ACFODE, is a prime example of an organization that actively includes men as members and on its staff. Similarly, at the local level in the Kawaala case study (Chapter 9) the residents' committee that opposed the World Bank rehabilitation project included both men and women. But the general experience has been that women have found it necessary to work in women-only organizations.

This brings us to one of the paradoxes of the women's movement: the strong gender-based lines along which women mobilize in Uganda's women's organizations not only reflect the marginalization of women in Ugandan society and cultural predispositions, but they have become a source of autonomy and a key resource in women's fight for advancement.

Transforming the Practical into the Strategic

In the Kiyembe case and the following case studies I describe how women used their existing gender-based associational forms which often took on forms of invisibility, informality, and smallness in response to structural constraints on women's mobilization. I show how women transformed these potential constraints that marginalized them and took the autonomy this afforded them to seek positive institutional change. In order adequately to explain how this use of autonomy was critical to women's attempts to transform a subordinate status, it is necessary to convey the consciousness that accompanied these struggles and how it affected attempts at institutional change. It is important to identify how women perceived their struggle for access to resources.

All too often, women's, especially poor women's, struggles over access to resources are seen simply as attempts to realize their interests in narrowly defined domestic roles, rather than also seeing the conflicts as being simultaneously manifestations of gender consciousness and identity. A priori assumptions are often made and women's struggles over land, water, housing, health care, and other such non-gender-specific issues are rarely seen as arenas in which women challenge the status quo in gender relations. These struggles, important as they may be to women themselves, are frequently not recognized as on a par with feminist mobilization, because the women do not represent themselves in the language of feminist discourse, and the struggles are not seen as politically transformative for women, nor as undermining the bases of women's subordination. Moreover, these kinds of strategies have even been said to reinforce an oppressive gendered division of labor.

As Amy Lind has argued, rarely is discussion focused on how poor women "negotiate power, construct collective identities and develop critical perspectives on the world in which they live – all factors that challenge dominant gender representations" (Lind, 1992: 137). In other words, in spite of the extensive literature on women's resistance, relatively little has been said about the process of transforming gender identity and expression, especially among poor uneducated women. The field of autobiographical personal narratives is an important exception to this generalization.

There is an emerging feminist literature concerning Africa that poses a very rigid understanding of gender interests based on Maxine Molyneux's distinction between practical and strategic gender interests. Molyneux (1986), in a frequently cited essay, makes a distinction between two types of women's interests, namely, strategic and practical gender interests, to help delineate how women as a group act in complicated and sometimes contradictory ways because of their varying class, ethnic, gender and other identities. Strategic interests are based on an analysis of women's subordination and from the creation of alternative arrangements that help in overcoming the "sexual division of labor, the alleviation of the burden of domestic labor and childcare, the removal of institutionalized forms of discrimination, the establishment of political equality, freedom of choice over childbearing, and the adoption of adequate measures against male violence and control over women". A "feminist" level of consciousness is required to struggle effectively for these "real" women's interests.

According to Molyneux, practical gender interests arise out of women's position in the division of labor. Having primary responsibility for domestic work, women are likely to mobilize in response to economic necessity and to immediate threats to their ability to provide basic needs, including housing, health care, food, clothing and water. Women may also organize for better access to community services and sources of income-generation. Although practical gender needs are a consequence of gender subordination, they do not challenge male domination because they arise out of everyday needs. Practical interests, argues Molyneux, are integral to the formulation of strategic interests, but feminist political practice requires the politicization of practical interests and their transformation into strategic interests (1986: 284–5). Drawing on Molyneux, numerous scholars have questioned the transformative capacity of the new forms of association that are emerging not only in Africa but in many parts of the world where political liberalization is occurring. They argue that these organizations are geared towards meeting immediate needs and do not have the wherewithal to bring about fundamental changes in the constitution of society and the state.

Distinctions similar to that of Molyneux have been made in the literature on women's organizations in various contexts. Bujra, for example, distinguished between women's organizations based on active solidarity against exclusion from male society and those based on passive solidarity, i.e., women forming collectivities to carry out tasks associated with biological or social reproduction (1979: 31). This suggests that women's groups based on common domestic duties do not have the capacity to challenge gender inequities. March and Taqqu, likewise, contrasted defensive women's groups that mobilized as a response to crises with women's groups that were active in creating separate resources, alternative social conditions and autonomous influence (1986: 33–5). Again, it is not clear from an empirical standpoint why groups dealing with the effects of economic crises cannot simultaneously be active in asserting autonomous influence.

But Molyneux's characterization of this dichotomy has gained most currency in the recent comparative literature on women's political and economic mobilization both in Latin America (Barrig, 1989; 135; Feijoó, 1989; 92; Jaquette, 1989; 192–3; Pérez-Alemán, 1992; 251–2; Stephen, 1992) and increasingly in other parts of the world, including Africa, even Uganda (Wakoko and Lobao, 1996: 309). It has also been adopted in the literature on women and the state and in discussions of approaches to gender planning in the Third World by international, governmental and non-governmental donor agencies (Charlton et al., 1989; Moser, 1991; Waylen, 1996). Some have argued against the dichotomy and prefer the notion of a continuum between strategic and practical gender interests (Marchand, 1995: 64).

Although Molyneux's dichotomy has come under some criticism, it continues to be used not only in scholarly discourse but also by some feminist activists, leaders of non-governmental organizations and donor representatives in various African countries. It is being used in a way that I fear will minimize the knowledge, consciousness and activities of low-income uneducated women without sufficiently appreciating their experiential understanding of gender subordination, not to mention their capacity for analysis of their own conditions.

This distinction between practical and strategic gender interests, which now permeates much of the comparative feminist literature in the social sciences, first gained currency in the early years of Brazilian feminism. It was expressed most clearly at the 1975 *Encontro para o Diagnóstica da Mulher Paulista* (Meeting for the Diagnosis of the Situation of Women in São Paulo), which was a citywide meeting of people from neighborhood associations, unions, church organizations, political parties, and research and academic institutions (Alvarez, 1989a: 28–9). More generally, in the 1970s and 1980s, it also came to characterize a demarcation between "feminist" and "feminine" movements in Latin America, with feminine groups fighting for day-care centers and better health services for women and children, while feminist organizations were said to question existing gender power relations (Alvarez, 1989b: 210–11, 245). Indeed, much of the history of the feminist movement in Latin America in the past two decades has been not just a theoretical debate over how to define feminism, but a conflict that had practical implications and often became extremely heated between women representing different classes. Middle-class feminist groups were considered more concerned with "abortion, domestic violence and sexual and reproductive freedom" in contrast to popular *movimientos de mujeres* that mobilized around improving basic community services, according to Sternbach et al. (1992: 230). Feminists often argued for a space where they could prioritize gender-specific issues, while popular organizations called for an agenda for women that was more inclusive and broad-based.

One of the problems with these distinctions, apart from revealing a narrow perspective on what constitutes political activity, is a view that underestimates the impact of these economic organizations on the consciousness of women, a consciousness that is critical in mobilizing women around broader political issues. The change in women's economic position and organizational involvement has had a profound and unmistakable impact on their consciousness, as the four case studies demonstrate.

The dichotomization of strategic and practical gender interests is problematic for a number of reasons. It tends to be elitist in outlook, assuming that poor women cannot transform everyday struggles for the betterment of their communities into struggles that challenge sexual subordination without the help of "more enlightened" outside feminist influences. Molyneux's view is reminiscent of the position that only when workers have been educated by the Marxist vanguard to be able to identify and understand their true class interests can they organize accordingly along class lines. Some scholars have been explicit about the class dimensions of consciousness, placing "lower-class women" in the category of women who only struggle for economic survival and need to be educated by middle-class feminists about gender oppression and strategic gender interests. Barrig (1989: 118–19), for example, writing on Peru, argues that communal kitchens and local organizations were unable to change the way in which women valued their "potential as citizens or as dynamic agents of change in their own communities". Moreover, she suggests that participation of this kind has not brought about a new awareness of women's gender identity.

While it is true that not all such mobilization leads to a new awareness about gender identity, one cannot assume this a priori without knowing the particulars of a struggle. Indeed, as Barbara Nelson (1993: 8) has also argued in reference to Molyneux's dichotomy, "There is no intrinsic reason why class, problem definition and tactics must be so tightly bound" so that "practical gender interests arise in the popular classes from the immediate problems of women," while "strategic gender interests arise in the old and new middle classes."

Molyneux allows for the possibility of politicizing practical interests and transforming them into strategic interests. Others like Chinchilla argue that "women of different classes and sectors are likely to come to feminism in different ways." Depending on their class, ethnicity and other factors, some come to feminism through practical gender interests, others through strategic gender interests and others through general social consciousness (Chinchilla, 1992: 46). But because of the rigid dichotomization of practical and strategic interests, these conceptualizations do not account for situations where struggles over practical interests can be *inherently* struggles against the subordination of women. In the Kiyembe struggle, for example, women were fighting not only for market space but also to maintain their control of the market. This involved creating a collective female identity and the realization that in order to meet their "practical gender needs" the women needed to overcome a particular form of gender discrimination. As the Kiyembe case shows, gender subordination is overcome in real world contexts. It does not happen in imagined or theoretical worlds, but rather in real relations between men and women. It occurs within negotiations, accommodations and conflicts over access and control of resources and power and it is within this process that new identities are forged.

Some proponents of the strategic vs. practical gender interests dichotomy have argued that fighting for access to water or better health care or food provisions does not alter the basic gender division of labor but simply facilitates women's domestic work and hence their further subordination (Feijoó, 1989: 92). In this view the Kiyembe struggle could be seen as a fight to assist women in pursuit of an income to support their children without changing the fact that the bulk of the responsibility for maintaining the household still falls on women. To look only at this aspect of the issue misses an important recognition that the struggle in itself can be a transformative experience. The way in which it is transformative is, of course, highly contingent on the location of that struggle and the context. The Kiyembe women found themselves fighting for the right to control the market they had started, pushing to eliminate constraints that had in the past prevented women's economic clout. The very fact that women were seeking to protect their interests in a public way was a transformative experience in gaining new-found confidence and courage to take action, and in developing new ways of thinking about their problems. In the context of a regime like the NRM, the attempt to test the effectiveness of a newly implemented government orientation that purports to be more inclusive can also be a learning experience.

It is striking that, in all four case studies, the conflicts over resources and resource management were in *essence* struggles to alter the gendered character of power relations in the community. In fact, what became evident in the Kiyembe struggle was how the women themselves framed the conflict almost entirely in gendered terms and based it on an analysis of women's subordination in Uganda. In other words, the strategic/practical duality was non-existent because the way in which they struggled to attain what could be called a "practical interest" – market space – was inherently a struggle for a "strategic" end – women's control of the market.

Background to the Conflict

Kiyembe Women's Co-operative Savings and Credit Society (KWCSCS) was formed in 1983 by Mary Kaikara, a *muluka* (parish) chief. Part of her impetus in organizing the women came from attending a meeting of the National Council of Women at which they were encouraged to become active organizing women. She encountered a group of women traders who were selling clothes illegally off the verandahs of large Kampala shops like Mukwano Enterprises. Most of the women were widows, many had fled the war in Luwero, and others were poor residents of Kampala. Because they sold their goods illegally, they were subject to City Council harassment and imprisonment. They had tried to obtain licenses but their requests were denied because they did not have an approved location from which to sell. Shopowners were not going to sanction vendors selling off their verandahs. Therefore, the women's main goal was to gain legitimation of their business in the eyes of the authorities and this necessitated finding their own place to sell from. They explained in a letter to me: "As this trade was illegal, the authorities like Kampala City Council were against it and from time to time the women were arrested and taken to court. As this was conflicting with the law, we decided to organize ourselves and formed this Society which was recognized by the authorities . . ."[3]

Kaikara felt sorry for the women and decided to approach them slowly, fearing that they would not trust her because of her position as parish chief and as one who collected taxes from vendors for the City Council. She gradually gained their confidence and together they discussed strategies to change their situation. As one of the original members explained: "After the problems we faced as women trading in places not agreed to by the City Council, when this woman made a call to us to get together and work in a proper particular place, we were happy and joined her effort."[4] Kaikara organized a meeting between the Town Clerk, the District Commissioner and the women and registered the group with the Co-operative Society. At the time of formation there were 10 original members, by 1985 when they were registered with the Co-operative Society they had grown to 72 members and by 1986 they had 107 members with a total of 290 market sellers, some of whom were employees of the Co-operative members.[5] Their main objective was to "unite the members to do business together", but they also sought to improve their living standards and create employment opportunities for women by hiring women to help them in their trade.[6] From the outset they had ambitious plans. In addition to running the market they planned to construct a building for their organization, to start farming (which they did eventually), and to purchase a minibus which they would rent out to earn income for the organization.

In 1984 they applied to the Town Clerk for a plot of land to start a women's market and were granted plot No. 18 on Market Street as a temporary allocation.[7] Originally the plot had been the site of a house owned by an Asian, who had been a victim of Amin's expulsion of Asians in 1972. The house was then bombed in 1979 during Obote's takeover from Amin and all that was left on the plot was rubble. The women rented a tractor, and leveled the rubble. They brought marram and water and stamped on the ground to level it. Finally they built the stalls.

Many organizations which appear to be formed simply along customary lines have adopted a more deliberate rationale for the gendered basis of their organization. From the outset, the Kiyembe Women's Co-operative was formed explicitly to address the particular needs of women vendors because they were acutely aware that these needs would not be adequately addressed in a co-operative that included both men and women. Women traders were at a disadvantage at the time they formed and had difficulty in obtaining legal places to sell. The Co-operative gave them organizational strength to negotiate a place for their market and also an institution through which they could improve their position as businesswomen, gain access to loans and support one another.

The Co-operative's leader, Mary Kaikara, explained why the Co-operative had to be a women's organization:

> Even the men had their own co-operatives which included women also. But for our case, I had registered the Kiyembe Co-operative under women only, because I had foreseen the problem. Earlier on, whenever I organized anything in the company of men, they would try to exclude me after seeing that I had set up everything for them. So having this in mind, I knew that if we included men in our co-operative they would cheat us and take our property.[8]

Another Kiyembe woman underscored the need for them to form a women's group:

> It started as a women's and widows' organization, meant for females only, not to include men. Men are troublesome . . . We wanted to co-operate together and make an organization as women. Also to save money and start business projects to help women.[9]

The organization was multi-ethnic and also included Catholics, Protestants and Muslims. In their organization the women went out of their way to accommodate religious and ethnic differences as they affected their activities. For example, they used English, Swahili and Luganda to communicate with one another, using interpreters when necessary. They also took into consideration each others' religious holidays. They did not run into any problems because of religious or ethnic differences. The only membership criterion was that one had to be a businesswoman and pay USh. 2,000 to join ($1.80 in 1993). Some had education up to the seventh grade and some had secondary education up to form four. Their leadership included a chairperson, secretary, treasurer and six committee members, who were elected every three years by members lining up behind the preferred candidates. Decision-making was collective, especially concerning money issues. The Co-operative would have to meet to agree before money could be released from the bank for a particular purpose. The members we spoke with could not recall any financial disputes in their history. The money collected could be used for joint business ventures but also to help women who fell sick or needed funds because of a death in the family.

The bylaws of the Co-operative drawn up by the KWCSCS reveal a concern for maintaining good relations between members of the group. The association assumed the responsibility for taking the body for burial if a member died, members were to behave well at work or in any "responsible place" (i.e., not drink, flirt openly with men, use bad language), they could not slander a fellow member of the group or steal items belonging to another seller. Moreover, they had an interesting anti-competition clause: members were forbidden to call customers to their stall – a common practice in other markets – and instead had to let the customer find the item on his/her own.[10] They felt that, without such a clause, sellers would create confusion and even hatred among members resulting in quarrels and misunderstandings. The women mentioned that another reason for such stringent bylaws was their desire to set a good example as a women's co-operative, especially to male market sellers, whom they sought to impress with the high standards they set for their membership. As Kaikara put it, they wanted to show men that women can be co-operative. "People think that women can't co-operate and they are jealous. We wanted to show how women do co-operate."[11]

The women took enormous pride in their organization. They enjoyed attending functions for women's organizations and dressing up in their uniforms. One woman explained: "People would say 'This is a strong group. They look like angels in their uniforms.' Even after the NRM came to power we continued to be active and would not miss attending national ceremonies."[12]

Initial Disruptions

The women's problems began in 1985 when the Okello regime took over in a coup and soldiers were rampaging around. On numerous occasions the women had to flee their stalls, returning to find all their goods and money stolen. Even those who placed their goods in nearby stores lost everything because the stores were broken into as well. The Co-operative itself lost a lot of its money, office equipment and important documents during this period. The members borrowed money and struggled to get their businesses going again.

When the NRM came to power later that year, they were able to save and rebuild their businesses. But the losses they had incurred put them in a vulnerable position when they faced their next hurdle. Wasswa Ziritwawula, chairperson of the executive council of LC5 (i.e. head of the Kampala City Council), called together all the members of market groups along with the employees of the stall owners. The KCC is responsible for administering the markets in Kampala. At the meeting, which the Kiyembe Co-operative attended, Ziritwawula announced that the KCC was taking over all the city's markets.

He gave them an ultimatum. If they remained members of their co-operatives, each individual had to pay USh. 300 a day per stall in taxes (a sixfold increase from the previous sum of Ush. 50 per day). Otherwise they must abandon their co-operatives. The audience was stunned. Kaikara recalled: "After disturbing people's minds like that he went on to say that those in the co-operatives are thieves. Imagine that all our employees and members were listening to this! Anyway, when all these events took place I was not afraid because I knew that I was on the right side. I remained firm." After the meeting was over there was a commotion in the hall and all the members of Kiyembe Co-operative pleaded with Kaikara to disband the group so that they could be exempted from paying Ush. 300 a day. This caused the first major disruption in the group, leaving it intact but badly divided.

The second major disruption came when Ziritwawula announced in 1988 that each market seller could have only one stall. The women suspected that some young male vendors had made a deal with Ziritwawula in order to take over their stalls. It would be impossible to ascertain the truth of these allegations, but suffice it to say that such accusations of KCC corruption are not uncommon in Kampala markets (Gombay, 1993). One man, George Kaddu, proudly described himself as the leader of the rebellion against the women. He had been a hawker who had previously worked in Tukoze Bukoze market until 1985 when he moved to Kiyembe because sales were not good at the former location. Kaddu was a member of the Kampala Area Hawkers Association and rented a stall from Kaikara. He first tried to assert control of the market through the LC structure at the time the LCs were being set up, but failed. He then changed his strategy to work through employees of the market women. He began the rebellion on 25 May 1987, claiming that the women had removed his brother from a stall he was sub-renting. He went to Kaikara and told her that they would remove the women administering the market. He met with Ziritwawula and the Member of Parliament from Kawempe at the offices of the acting Town Clerk, and complained about Kaikara to them. Shortly thereafter in what purported to be an "equalizing" measure, Ziritwawula announced that whoever was tending a stall was the owner, regardless of whether they were an employee of the women, a sub-renter or stall owner. Kaddu claimed that the men won the rebellion and got "our independence, free of her power". Kaddu was able later on to win the chairmanship of the LC from 1987 to 1991.

This devastated the Kiyembe women: many of them owned several stalls and a few had women relatives, but most hired young men to tend the stalls for them as employees or sub-tenants. Women were often not able to tend the stalls themselves because they had to care for sick children, attend to other business or farming, or go on maternity leave. Some had to appease their husbands who did not like them to work. As a result of this new regulation, all the women with employees lost their stalls, while those who were seated at the stalls on the day the announcement was made were able to keep them.

Ziritwawula told the male vendors to report to him if the women tried to reclaim their stalls. The women were certain that Ziritwawula had benefited financially from the new arrangement between the City Council and the markets. The women lost not only their stalls but their property as well. Even more significant, they lost their control of the market. For the women, this was as important as the loss of property. As Kaikara explained:

> They took our property because we were women. I say so because they accepted money from all the other groups that had assembled with us at the City Hall, but they didn't take their authority. Those people are in the markets, organizing the vendors and working hand in hand with the City Council. But because our market is for women they assumed that they could claim our authority as well.[13]

When the announcement was made by Ziritwawula allowing men into the market, other Kampala women's associations like the Uganda Muslim Women's Organization, women market sellers at Owino, and the National Council of Women, held fund-raising efforts and rallied to their support.

Male Vendors' Perceptions

Several of the male vendors who benefited from the takeover agreed that the women had not been treated fairly, but then went on to justify their eviction. One who supported the takeover argued that the women's co-operative should not have been destroyed and even suggested that the male vendors should give them money. But most argued that the Kiyembe women market sellers, and in particular Kaikara, had been oppressive and exploitative of the male sub-tenants and needed to have their powers limited. They admitted having complained to Ziritwawula that they did not want the market under the control of women and they credited him with having removed Kaikara and the women's co-operative from controlling the market.[14] Ziritwawula himself presented this argument, saying that there was bribery involved in obtaining stalls from the KCC and no formal application process. His intention was to get some of the vendors off the streets and into market stalls.

> Some cunning women had many stalls. We did not like the women having many stalls so we suggested they give some out and remain with two. There were only 100 stalls registered with the KCC but in fact Kiyembe had 400 stalls. The women paid for only 100 stalls and kept the

balance. I told the women that on a certain day those who were there could register as permanent stall holders. Some women leaders extracted money and gave only some to the KCC. On one stall there were three in it but only one was paid for. An investigation made us realize there were stalls registered in ghost names and one woman had 20 stalls.

Ziritwawula argued that the women were charging stall renters USh. 15,000 or three times the actual rate per stall including a commission for dealing with the KCC.[15]

The women market sellers responded to this charge by saying that the subrenters paid a tax of USh. 800 per month to Kaikara, who took it to the KCC, for the use of their stalls. After Ziritwawula became LC5 chairperson they paid USh. 7,200 per month to the KCC tax collectors, a sum which they felt was exorbitant, and eventually the Co-operative complained to the Town Clerk and got the fee reduced to USh. 2,600–3,000 per month. When we asked a group of women (not in Kaikara's presence) whether Kaikara extorted money from the vendors they strongly denied the accusations and argued that these kinds of problems began after Ziritwawula took office.

The LC1 chairperson had a very different analysis of how it came to be that men had taken control of the market. He downplayed the intervention of Ziritwawula and the male vendors and laid the blame on the women themselves and their business failures. "As you know, women are not aggressive in business and lack persistence. It is not that men do not like women. Others even work with their husbands. Others get married or fail in business and go away."[16] This view that women left the market because of a lack of business acumen was repeated by the sub-LC chairman, Charles Ssenfuka, who said, "There were many women but then women had not developed a lot of aggressiveness in business until men took over and now the men are the majority." One market woman responded to this accusation, explaining that

> By the time the men came to the market, they found we were doing very well in our businesses. If they were more active and serious than we were in business, why didn't they start their own businesses? Why did they have to grab ours? Those allegations are intended to deny us our rights and they use them to grab our things. There is no woman that ever abandoned her stall anyhow, but we failed to raise money to re-establish ourselves after we had been evicted. We had never failed to raise money to pay KCC dues.[17]

Ziritwawula, who was himself associated with the Democratic Party, spread the rumor that the women were UPC supporters in an effort to discredit them. He argued that even in 1983 the women had fallen prey to a UPC effort to control various institutions like markets, hospitals, and schools as sources of revenue for the UPC, pointing out that Kaikara was a staunch UPC supporter. Markets like Kiyembe had been established during the UPC regime in 1980–1.

Virtually all the male vendors we spoke to mentioned the UPC connection. Some of them had informed Ziritwawula that the women's co-operative was a political organization, not a women's organization, which outraged the women market sellers as did the claim that they were UPC supporters.[18] Kaikara was a parish chief during Obote's time and remained parish chief throughout the NRM period of rule. In a political environment where little could be gained without personal connections, the fact that Kaikara had personal ties to some UPC leaders and was able to obtain the market during Obote's rule was used against her. In an effort to delegitimize the claims of the women to run the market her detractors argued that her UPC connection was the only authority on which she had claimed the market. Because the UPC was no longer in power they reasoned that her claim was no longer valid. But in fact, party affiliation had nothing to do with the women's basis for forming the market. They all supported different parties and explained that they all had different political opinions. Regardless of their individual party sympathies they agreed that the NRM government had opened up new possibilities for women, and as one Kiyembe woman put it, "women are becoming politically active and involved in the same affairs as men". She added, "Women are so effective as leaders and work harder than men so as not to be counted as failures. We attend political education training together with men. Women can even lead the men in this."[19]

Open "War" on Kiyembe Women's Co-operative

When the women tried to regain their stalls in 1987, the young men beat them with sticks and bars, threatening to kill or imprison them if they approached their old stalls. Some men even called in their brothers who were soldiers from Lubiri barracks to harass the women. The secretary of the Co-operative was dragged out of the Co-operative office and they tore her dress and beat her. Although other markets experienced similar conflicts, the women felt that the harassment by the young vendors far exceeded that in other markets because they were women, but they refused to back down and be intimidated. When Kaikara arrived on the scene after the secretary had been beaten up, people at the market told her what had happened and told her to run away, saying that the boys would surely beat her.

> I went to the office, but as soon as they saw me, they started shouting "there she is, there she is." I deliberately walked slowly to the City Council office, we came back with City Council men and sat in our office. The boys shouted at us, saying "Leave the office, the market was given to us by Ziritwawula. Why are you hanging on to it?" These boys didn't want us anywhere around this market. But we were still around, I was still organizing my women, trying to find a way I could protest or find another working place where I could take my society. I wanted to protest because I knew I was right. I thought Ziritwawula had just been misled. I had hoped that in the future he would regain his senses and return our market to us.

The woman confronted Ziritwawula directly and explained how they as women had acquired the market. He responded to them, according to Kaikara, "Ah! I have never seen a market owned by women. Why is it that it is only women who shared in this place?" He told them once again that he could not reverse his decision. Not surprisingly, the women put the blame fairly and squarely on Ziritwawula for causing "division" and "chaos" in the market by bringing in the men. He had undermined the cohesion of the organization, which had fallen into debt because the members were having a hard time paying back their loans since they had lost everything in the eviction. Others who were thrown off the stalls left altogether and could no longer be traced.[20] Ironically, years later at a function for women's co-operatives, Ziritwawula was handing out certificates of achievement and when presenting a certificate to the Kiyembe Co-operative, he apologized publicly to them, saying that he had been wrong to try to disband the organization.[21]

The women approached the Town Clerk and his deputy, the District Administrator, the Minister of Women and the Kampala Central Business and Workers Committee for assistance but found that many officials doubted the truth of their story and some believed them to be "mad". According to Kaikara, "We tried to complain to various responsible people . . . . but we failed because they all feared the person who had given the orders. An RC5 chair is someone very important."[22]

The blow to the organization was even more bitter when they witnessed the male vendors starting up their own organization called the Kiyembe Vendors

Association. They claimed Kaikara's stalls and printed their own identity cards. The women wrote to the Town Clerk in protest, calling on him to intervene. They framed the issue as a gender conflict.

> There is a splinter group of vendors (*bayaye*). All have failed to fulfill the set of objectives of the society and are in the process of forming another society (men only), which will disrupt the smooth running of this market in particular, and the society in general. As you will observe, this market was allocated solely to women because of the calamities that had befallen them during the period of misrule . . . . These *bayaye* have mobilized themselves into a group, seized the office, chased away the pioneer members and their executive committee and reallocated stalls to non-members . . . The terms of reference in an allocation letter from your office clearly stipulates "Women Savings and Credit Co-operative Society" and not "Men's Society".[23]

The men's group was one of three sub-units of the local council that oversaw the market, dealt with minor issues like disputes over money, and had responsibility for the cleanliness of the market. It was supposed to liaise with the KCC and settle conflicts between traders and between sellers and buyers. To this day the Kiyembe Vendors Association operates as a dual structure alongside the Kiyembe Women's Co-operative, with little if any contact. They both intervened separately on behalf of their constituencies when faced with a common threat, for example, the National Enterprise Corporation (NEC) takeover.

The women continued to face harassment from the male vendors and even from some female vendors. As I began to inquire about the Kiyembe Women's Co-operative Savings and Credit Society, I was told by numerous people that it no longer existed. As I learned later when I met with women in the co-operative, the male vendors deliberately spread misinformation about the group when outsiders came looking for them. It was not surprising that enormous hostility existed between the male and female vendors. When I visited the market to talk to the women we talked at the stalls and the women physically barricaded the walkway between the stalls to keep the male vendors from passing through, fearing that they were spying on us.

A Dead-end

The women's problems did not end with the LC5 chairman's efforts to crush their organization. The lease on the property expired in 1991 and the Custodian Board (for departed Asians' properties) put the property on which the market was located up for auction. The Kiyembe Vendors Association (consisting of male vendors) also made a bid for the market, offering USh. 15 million or USh. 50,000 per stall in a market of 300 stalls.[24] The women were not notified and only found out by chance when Kaikara was visiting the offices of the Ministry of Women and happened to mention the Kiyembe market to the Minister. The Minister advised the group to make a bid for the property, even though the deadline for the bids was only three days away. They made the deadline, having to move quickly to get together the processing fees, contact a lawyer, and meet to decide on how to bid.

They lost the bid to the National Enterprise Corporation (NEC), a parastatal which the army had run since 1989 to make funds for itself by manufacturing bread, mattresses, pharmaceuticals, and lime. NEC wrote to the market sellers in 1992 informing them that they would be evicted. It then started trying to extract money from both the men and the women vendors. The Kiyembe Co-operative approached the head of a Kampala business association, the head of the market at the City Council offices, and the Ministry of Women in Development. The Ministry found out that the NEC had no authority to collect money from the stall owners because it had not yet paid the Custodian Board for the plot. The KCC and the LC1 also contacted the NEC to discuss the problem with them; the NEC promised the LC1 chairman that it would leave the traders alone. Soon thereafter, it was charged with gross mismanagement of funds, not having submitted audited accounts since its formation,[25] and by 1995 it had been disbanded.

No sooner had the NEC disappeared from the scene than new rumors surfaced that the original Asian owner of the property had returned to claim his plot; the Custodian Board had returned the property to him, as it was mandated to do. The women wrote to the Town Clerk asking him to return the market to the women so that they could control it, leaving the Asian to collect taxes and fees from them.

By 1994 it was clear the Kiyembe Co-operative had done all it could on its own to reclaim the stalls and was taking steps to find a new market for the women, who had appealed to the Town Clerk, the District Administrator, the Minister of Women and most recently the Ministry of Community Development – but to no avail. They had also sought legal assistance from the National Council of Women and the Uganda Women Lawyer's Association (FIDA), with no success. Worse still, the most active women's rights organization, Action for Development (ACFODE), wrote a satirical piece in its newsletter making light of their struggle, commenting that "here [in Kiyembe], the dignified battle between the sexes amused us" (Mirembe, 1990). The organizational weakness of these intermediary organizations made them incapable of supporting the cause of the Kiyembe market women, even though representatives of the NCW and FIDA made it clear that they thought the women had a just cause.

But the real letdown was the LC1 and the way it was used by dominant interests to undermine the women vendors. The market council's job is to promote cleanliness and settle disputes between buyers and sellers and among sellers themselves. Yet according to the LC1 Chairman, the society's activities were outside the council's areas of jurisdiction and they did not relate to them formally, although the women did send the LC1 chairman copies of their correspondence and inform him of their seminars and other activities.

The Local Council sided with the male vendors throughout the struggle. The chairman had asked Kaikara repeatedly to remove the iron sheets from the Co-operative's office because they wanted to use the space. She told him that the office was not hers and that it was for the society and the women, "thus a government office", she explained. "For me as an individual, I can't accept because the office isn't mine. I am answerable to other people." She refused to consider his request to remove the office until he put it in writing, which he never did. When asked about the LC's role, one of the women replied: "We are only waiting for the day when they tell us to stop coming to this place and that will be all."

Unlike the women, the men felt that the LC was helpful in solving problems and the male vendors had good working relations with the LC. The chairman of the sub-LC at Kiyembe, Charles Ssenfuka, did not feel that there was any conflict between the LC or the sub-LC and the women.[26] He was not concerned about the conflict because Kaikara had moved back to the village and was focusing on the association's income-generating activities.

By 1993, some women who had once owned several stalls ended up renting stalls from male vendors who had originally been their employees. There were more men than women owning stalls at Kiyembe, even though there were more women sellers than men, because the non-Kiyembe women vendors were looking after stalls owned by their husbands.

After the evictions, Kaikara lost all her stalls and by 1993 was managing a farm for the co-operative in Luwero, although she visited the women every week. Other women became servants, farmers or fell destitute. The group continued to meet into the mid-1990s, although it had been reduced to 40 members, but they were very close and relied heavily on one another. Old members still visited them. They jointly owned a farm in Luwero and planted cassava and sweet potatoes because they wanted to do something that would unite them. They have also been pooling their money to start cultivating silk moths. Although they were renting, their plans were to buy their own land and build a house so that any woman who fell ill or ran into financial difficulties could go and settle there.

Although the co-operative had suffered the many blows recounted in this chapter one member explained why the organization persisted: She attributed their success to the fact that "we never let our fellow women down", referring both to women in the group and to the interactions they had had with other women's groups. In addition to her market sales, she also sold knitted and crocheted products she made herself. The woman, 44 years old, was a Muganda Catholic. She had children and had no formal education. She saw her fellow women as a source of business and other kinds of advice "because they understand gender issues and are always ready to listen to me".[27] She continued:

> We appeal to many women to join because we tell them about the shares one can hold and how many heads can act better than one. They can get together to sell uniforms to a school and get more money than if they were selling as an individual. . . . Women are more likely to join such organizations than men because women like being noticed and are more enthusiastic about joining together to fight male dominance. This is so because women have become more active now that they see the government helping them move forward in society.

Rethinking Women's Interests

In thinking about Molyneux's "practical versus strategic gender interests" dichotomy in the light of this case study, it becomes evident that one cannot a priori disregard the impact of women's mobilization concerning day-to-day issues without looking at the particulars of a conflict or considering the consciousness women bring to the struggle and how that consciousness evolves. By consciousness, I am referring to women's capacity to analyze critically the forms of domination they confront and to find ways to change these relations creatively.

A starting point that assumes that only middle-class or educated feminists have the wherewithal to bring critical analysis to bear on gender relations is flawed from the outset. It betrays unmitigated hubris. To define "real" feminist struggles as ones concerning strategic interests and then to contrast them with "practical" women's interests runs the risk of narrowing the scope of the feminist movement and of predetermining the terms of reference. This dichotomy lends itself to portrayals of poor, uneducated women as incapable of analyzing, strategizing and changing their local conditions. The view that poor women only organize around economic issues in a passive or defensive way, in reaction to crisis or new economic hardship, denies them agency and consciousness. It fails to recognize that they may be perfectly capable of analyzing their conditions in their own language and style, taking independent action, and actively transforming their consciousness and environment.

When the terms of the feminist debate are so narrowly defined, one wonders how the voices of many women, like those in Kiyembe, could ever take part, let alone be heard on an equal basis in a feminist dialogue. Where is the entry point for such women into a discussion in which feminists would genuinely have something to learn from them? How can women from diverse cultural, ethnic and economic backgrounds – some of whom have never even heard the term "feminist" but might have a lot to say about gender domination – engage in such a discourse *on their own terms*?

A more useful line of inquiry would start by distinguishing between women's interests, opportunity structures, and their identity as Barbara Nelson and Amy Lind have begun to do in their work (Nelson, 1993: Lind, 1992). Already a growing literature has begun to appreciate the way in which women have used domestic images of their power, such as, motherhood, as vehicles to assert their interests in the public arena (Bouvard, 1994: Martin, 1990). In the case of Buena Vista in Mexico, Martin found that the images of women's role in childbirth and mothering subordinated women but at the same time provided a basis for their entry into the political arena. Women, who are thought of as self-sacrificing mothers, had been "called" to enter the political arena to save the community from corruption and abuse of power (1990, 471). Similarly, Las Madres de la Plaza de Mayo in Argentina and the mothers of disappeared relatives in other Latin American countries drew on their role as mothers, wives and grandmothers and their claim that they were not political to legitimize their struggle and openly to challenge authoritarian regimes.

Understanding women's interests was one dimension of the Kiyembe struggle, because this was more than simply a women's struggle for access to resources. The Kiyembe struggle, like the other case studies in this book, shows how women challenged the very premises of the way in which politics is carried out, namely, the very structures that limited their participation, leadership and control. This involved forging new collective identities by "challenging dominant representations of gender and incorporating this into their politics", as Amy Lind puts it (1992: 144). The example of the Kiyembe conflict (but also Kitumba and Kawaala) illustrates that women were not just interested in meeting everyday needs. In the final analysis these were power struggles between men and women over resources and leadership in which women transformed and politicized their identity.

Notes

1. Bylaws of Kiyembe WCSCS, 2 January 1985 (in addition to Co-operative Society Constitution).
2. Focus group discussion with Kiyembe market women, Kampala, 27 June 1995.
3. Letter from Kampala Central Business and Workers Committee to Aili Mari Tripp 27 May 1993.
4. Interview JK, Juliet Kakooza, Kampala, 10 February 1993.
5. Letter from Mary Kaikara, Chairperson, to Chairman, Kampala Central Business and Workers Committee, 27 February 1990; Focus group meeting with 15 members of Kiyembe Women's Co-operative Savings and Credit Society, 27 May 1993; Brief on Kiyembe Women's Co-operative Savings and Credit Society to the National Secretary, National Resistance Movement, 22 April 1986; Letter to Ministry of Finance from WCSCS 29 July 1987.
6. Letter to the National Secretary, the National Resistance Movement, 22 April 1986.
7. Letter from S. Ochieng, Acting Town Clerk to Kiyembe Women's Co-operative Savings and Credit Society, 17 December 1984.
8. Focus group discussion with Kiyembe market women, Kampala, 30 May 1993.
9. Focus group discussion with Kiyembe market women, Kampala, 22 and 30 May 1993.
10. Bylaws of Kiyembe WCSCS, 2 January 1985.

11. Focus group discussion with Kiyembe market women, Kampala, 27 June 1995.
12. *ibid.*
13. Focus group discussion with Kiyembe market women, Kampala, 22 May 1993.
14. Interview RM, Charles Ssenfuka, Kampala, 16 July 1993.
15. Interview with Wasswa Ziritwawula, Kampala, 18 July 1993.
16. Interview JK, James Kapere, Kampala, 16 July 1993.
17. Focus group discussion with Kiyembe market women, Kampala, 27 June 1995.
18. Focus group discussion with Kiyembe market women, Kampala, 22 May 1993.
19. Interview JK, Juliet Kakooza, Kampala, 10 February 1993.
20. Focus group discussion with Kiyembe market women, Kampala, 22 May 1993.
21. Focus group discussion with Kiyembe market women, Kampala, 27 June 1995.
22. *ibid.*
23. Letter from WCSCS (M. Kaikara) to Town Clerk, 2 December 1988.
24. Interview with George Kaddu, Kampala, 16 July 1993.
25. *The Monitor,* 11–18 December 1992.
26. Interview with Charles Ssenfuka, chairman of sub-LC Kiyembe, Kampala, 16 July 1993.
27. Interview JK, Juliet Kakooza, Kampala, 10 February 1993.

9

Resisting
Patronage Politics

The Case of
Kawaala Housing Project

They say Museveni brought peace, but Kawaala residents never got peace. What kind of peace is this, kicking us off of our land? . . . We are crying, crying, crying. Museveni will lose support if he does not heed our calls. He will find us not supporting him if Kampala City Council treats us this way . . . . Can the President hear the voices of the people of Kawaala? We want development very badly. The Kampala City Council has frustrated our efforts.

Woman resident of Kawaala, Rubaga Division

The first chapter of this book described two kinds of competing societal influences: one that corrodes state legitimacy from within through forms of patronage and personalized rule and the other consisting of cross-cutting societal interests that seek accountability from the state. The following story describes a battle in which the most active opponents were women, who as a group had the most to lose from a new development scheme that was being fueled by patronage.

Certainly these kinds of struggles are not peculiar to women. Susan Dicklitch (1994) documents a strikingly similar struggle in Jinja in the late 1980s and early 1990s in which patronage ties between the highest RC levels and the Jinja Municipal Council (JMC) resulted in the resignation of the Walukuba East Parish LC2 council. They were protesting at the collusion of LC3 and LC5 with the JMC that had prevented the residents from getting access to water for several years in spite of having paid their water bills to the JMC. Unable to work through the LC system, the LC2 leaders were forced to organize outside of the system and form a Walukuba Tenants Welfare Association (made up of a board of trustees that included a Protestant, Catholic and Muslim religious leader). This organization was promptly banned by the Jinja District Administration but was later permitted to apply for registration as a NGO. It succeeded in getting the water turned on but was unable to recover all the money that had been "eaten" (Ugandan euphemism for corruption) along the way.

Thus, the issues raised in this chapter have significance for civil society more generally, beyond women's struggles. But patronage poses particular constraints on women as it remains one of the main obstacles to women's political participation. In the post-independence period, women have generally been excluded from holding patronage positions. This exclusion, in turn, has limited their possibilities for participation in formal politics because they do not have the leverage and resources to exert influence through such informal channels. Thus, one of the key consequences of women's organizational autonomy is that it has positioned many women in a way that makes it easier for them to challenge various destructive norms in the culture and practice of politics. Chapter 7 argued that women need different institutional arrangements in order to be able to participate fully in politics and public life. Part of this demand is aimed at removing the hidden informal political networks that rarely benefit the poorest members of society.

Indeed, one of the big obstacles preventing women from getting involved in politics is the perception among women that it is a "dirty game". As outspoken Ugandan women's activist and Member of Parliament, Miria Matembe, put it: "In Africa, the main challenge is to make politics clean and thus attractive to women. Reject nepotism, corruption, and cynicism."[1] While this perception of politics remains a major reason why women hesitate to get involved, women politicians themselves often remark that it is not sufficient to decry corrupt politics and that women need to involve themselves more actively in politics in order to change the political culture. As Zimbabwean women's activist Tsitsi Kuuya pointed out:

> How can women make politics a clean game? This will be a challenge for the women who enter politics . . . Politics is said to be a dirty game and women do not want to be associated with dirty games and have not explored ways of cleaning up politics. Alternatives for women have not been explored. The women of politics need to take this as a challenge and work hard to have more than 20 women in parliament (Kuuya 1995: 7).

This same theme of politics being an unscrupulous activity resonates in many women's circles throughout Africa and has become more of a concern as women have increasingly sought political leadership in the 1990s. Charity Ngilu, who ran for president in Kenya's 1998 elections, openly challenged the clientelistic electoral practices of buying votes and playing the ethnicity card. She discouraged the electorate from seeking money from political candidates with the refrain "Kenyans are not beggars!" In contrast, the ruling party candidate and president, Arap Moi, was said to have spent freely in her home region. Although she won the parliamentary seat in her Kitui Central district, the fact that Ngilu, who is a Kamba, lost so many Kamba votes in the presidential contest demonstrates not only the difficulties women political aspirants face, but also the fact that there can be real political costs to challenging entrenched clientelistic practices (Githongo, 1998).[2] In Uganda, women have also begun to challenge the clientelist practices that infuse institutions. But this has been a dangerous and uphill task, as Winnie Byanyima, a member of parliament from Mbarara Municipality, discovered when she attacked corruption and patronage in her constituency.

Women as individuals are not any less prone to the lure of clientelistic practices, especially in a society where patronage is sometimes the only route to power. At the same time, women as a group have been outsiders of these informal networks and have very little to gain and much more to lose from the continuation of such practices. Women's distaste for patronage politics, therefore, is not intrinsic to being a woman. Rather, it arises out of political, economic and social marginalization, which has often allowed them to distance themselves from patronage politics and challenge it, especially when it has infringed on their interests as we see in the case of the Kawaala Housing Project.

The following case study shows how patronage influenced the design and implementation of a World Bank-funded project to improve infrastructure in the community. Patronage politics undercut constructive offers of voluntary community participation and self-help and excluded community participation and input. It resulted in policies that offended the local Baganda cultural sensibilities. It perverted the local council system through the use of bribes. It led to unnecessary

physical intimidation of residents and blatant disregard for the legal system. Moreover, patronage was responsible for the implementation of a project that overlooked
the concerns of women, widows, the elderly and others who shouldered enormous
responsibilities in supporting the household yet had minimal resources at their disposal. Because women had so much at stake in how the World Bank project was for-
mulated and expressed the strongest antipathy towards it, they also became the
targets of City Council carrot and stick measures to win their endorsement of the
project.

In this case study it becomes apparent that women, more than the men, objected
not only to the project's goals, but also to the way the Kampala City Council
attempted to force the project on the residents, to manipulate local councils, and, in
particular, to exert unwelcome pressure on women's organizations. As in the previous case studies, women found it even more difficult than men to influence the LCs
from within and to find avenues to express their opposition. They sought not only
independent organizations from which to assert their interests but also a quiet invisible network that was active in building public opinion especially among women.
This network demonstrated simultaneously both the marginalization of women,
who could not mobilize in open organizations for fear of antagonizing their husbands, and also their action within the constraints in which they found themselves.
They used autonomous forms of mobilization to create public opinion against the
effects of patronage politics that had permeated formal political channels. Women,
who had the least to forfeit from maintaining patronage networks and the most to
gain by getting rid of clientelistic practices, were among the most vocal opponents
of the World Bank project itself.

Background to the Conflict

The initial planning of the Kawaala Housing Project (KHP) started on 12 July 1989.
By August 1990, the Town Clerk of the Kampala City Council (KCC) launched the
first phase of the KHP by distributing a document in Kawaala to explain to residents
the nature of the project.[3] The aim of the project funded by the World Bank as one
component of its Uganda First Urban Project, was to provide Kawaala with piped
water, improve sanitation in densely populated areas, provide market places, repair
roads and install electricity. The project was to be financed by the World Bank
through the Ministry of Finance. The Bank was to provide a loan of US$4.5 million,
which would be paid back over 20 years, starting 5 years after the completion of the
project.

According to the project document, the aim was to help "low income groups"
construct "modern" houses which fit the City Council's policies for Kampala. One
thousand plots were to obtain piped water and electricity. While the document
admitted that some "squatters" would face eviction, the KCC felt the project was
necessary because no such project had been carried out by the KCC since independence. The Council also hoped to gain experience from the implementation of this
trial project for administering similar projects elsewhere. In addition, the project
was to provide jobs and income for the local residents.

The project would cover 140 hectares on which 1,031 houses would be built to
accommodate 21,500 people. Three-quarters of these houses would be small two-to-
four room accommodations of 200–225 square meters, 15 percent would be of

medium size (225–300 sq. meters) with 3–5 rooms and 10 percent would be large (300–400 sq. meters) two-storied houses. The plan also included the building of four primary schools, four nursery schools, two secondary schools, one community center, one dispensary, one post office, one shopping center and a market.

The document indicated that the World Bank wanted to ensure that both the people and the government supported the project. The KCC indicated in the document that, since the government had committed itself to taking a loan for the project and the Local Councils were in favor of it, this objective had been met. It claimed it had sought and won approval for the project from the LCs, including LC5, and was carrying out "education of the masses about the project" using radio, TV and the press.

Kawaala Residents' Responses to Project

No sooner had the KCC document been distributed than popular pressure led to the formation of an ad hoc residents' committee to respond to the proposed project. Women residents were especially influential in spurring the formation of this group. Residents in Kawaala elected an 11-member Abataka (Residents) Committee to investigate the project and gather community views. The committee drafted a report and submitted it to the Local Council.[4] The report clearly set out the issues that were a source of contention in what was to become a four-year battle between the residents and the City Council.

Among the most important issues was the lack of consultation with residents before drawing up the plan. This lack of consultation, as will be shown later, was a consequence of patronage obligations that did not allow for community input. The residents' report is worth quoting at length because of the centrality of the issue of consultation to the conflict:

> The residents were surprised by the [KCC] document and the lack of consultation before the project plan was drawn up . . . The residents were amazed at the City Council plan, which shows lack of feeling for the people. There is nothing to show that the plan will go through. Residents do not think the KCC will manage to carry off the project directive . . . Anything to help the residents needs the involvement of themselves. They resent policies being forced upon them by the KCC and World Bank. . . The residents saw no reason for destroying the present houses in the hope of building new ones.

There were cultural issues involved as well. Kawaala land belonged to the Kabaka until 1966 when the state claimed it. The area was settled primarily by Baganda, for whom the land, and the fact that many had ancestors buried in the area, were closely tied to questions of identity. Similarly, notions of space and the style of houses are part of this identity. Baganda pride themselves on their individuality and several told me they could not imagine living in an area with rows of small similar looking houses. In the report the residents claimed that dividing larger plots into smaller ones would be tantamount to creating a slum and would destroy tradition (obuwangwa). Taking land away from families to divide the plots into smaller units "would create enmity and division among families". Because people usually live in large and extended families, the residents asked, "How can they plan 2–3 rooms for such families?"

They also challenged the idea of building 1,000 plots, four primary schools, four nurseries, one secondary school, a community center, hospital, market place and trading center all on 300 acres. "This shows that town planners don't first visit the site before drawing a plan", according to the report. Had the KCC consulted with residents they would have discovered that the area already had four primary schools,[5] a secondary school,[6] a nursery and a dispensary. Moreover, the area had power, running water, and tarmac roads, but they needed upgrading. Among the most important requests the residents made in the report was to be given leases on the land they occupied.

They concluded that "The aims/objectives of the project are to benefit the KCC and not the Kawaala people". There was already a sense that personal gain through the offices of the KCC was at work. But they added that "If there is an aim to develop the area, a real leader and residents should be involved. The residents would like the KCC and World Bank to hold a meeting with them," hinting that the local LC leadership was posing its own set of problems through their connections with the City Council. Finally, "The residents do not support the Government's ideas of getting loans from the World Bank for this kind of project of developing Kawaala area."

Women's Interests

From the outset, women in the community were the most vocal opponents of the project and as such were critical in shaping public opinion on it. As the main household members responsible for providing food and caring for the children, the women often felt more immediately threatened than their husbands by the changes and, in particular, by the proposed KCC eviction of 675 households. One of the reasons women tended to be more fiercely opposed to the project had to do with their involvement in farming and income-generating activities, which depended on their connections with the land and their homes. In fact, almost all the women we interviewed in the area were involved in farming and small business. They knew that if they were evicted, it would be almost impossible for them to re-establish themselves on their own somewhere else at an affordable cost. Women with income-generating projects had come to rely on local markets, resources and networks that had been built up over time and could not easily be replaced. They included shopkeepers, seamstresses, waitresses, and sellers at markets like Owino and Shauri Yako. Some sold second-hand clothes, others charcoal, or vegetables. Others said they made and sold bricks, crafts, pancakes, table cloths and a variety of goods.

Of the 23 women we interviewed in Kawaala II, the majority farmed, most of them in Kawaala itself and the remainder in other parts of Kampala or in rural home villages. They grew crops and subsisted from farming, either through consumption or sometimes the sale of crops, or by selling foods made from their own produce. If evicted, they would not only lose a place to live but also a source of livelihood. Recent studies show that over one-third of Kampala residents are involved in agricultural production and that 45 percent of their food comes from their own activities (Maxwell and Zzizwa, 1993). Kawaala was no exception.

For the women who farmed in the vicinity, it would be hard to find farm land elsewhere in the city because land was becoming increasingly scarce. Poor widows simply did not have the wherewithal to move from where they had lived all their lives. One 77-year-old woman, who had lived in Kawaala since childhood, was worried about being evicted from her plot. She had outlived her husband and children and was living off the rent of houses she owned on 2 acres of land that she had inherited from her mother. These houses were being targeted for demolition. She was too old to farm and had no one to support her. "Now I am doomed . . . I do not want to go away from here, I am already too old. How many days have I got left?"[7]

Breaking with the convention of silence in public, women were more vocal than men at public meetings regarding the project. As one woman leader put it:

While men were shying away, women were able to say anything in public meetings in front of government officials. Women were more vocal because they were directly affected. It is very hard for women to stand without any means of income. In most of the cases at home women are thought of as property . . . most of these women are people who basically support their children and without any income and food they cannot do it. . . . You come and take their peace and income and they are going to fight, not because they want to, but because they have been oppressed and suppressed.[8]

Abataka Committee

The Abataka Committee wrote to the Member of Parliament for Rubaga, Damian Lubega, in September 1990 asking him to call a meeting of the KCC and members of the committee. In the letter the residents underscored the importance of involving local residents in the planning of such a project. "If there is an intention to develop Kawaala as a Council Planned Project, priority should be given to the social good-will of the tenants, grassroots leadership, the elders and local residents. Anything short of this will be unsuccessful even if forced on us."[9] The letter received no response.[10] Finally, a meeting was convened on 30 May 1991. At the meeting the Town Clerk agreed with the Abataka Committee that the KCC should work with the people in planning the project, but argued in the KCC's defense that the project had been thoroughly discussed and studied by the KCC before it was introduced to Kawaala residents. He warned the residents of the dire consequences that might result from their continued objection to the project. For their part, the residents made it clear that they "severely detested the way the project was introduced from the beginning," evoking an apology from KCC officials. The KCC authorities agreed to the residents' demand for leaseholds on their plots of land to be based on the size of the plots, ranging from one-eighth to half an acre. They also agreed that any further steps would be taken in consultation with the Abataka Committee.

But soon afterwards the KCC began to renege on what had been agreed. Without consulting the Abataka Committee, it changed the size of the plots and made them much smaller than had been agreed previously. The smaller plots would involve breaking up family houses that had already been built. Moreover, the residents had heard nothing about the leases for which they had applied, and they disagreed with the Council's new resettlement plans.[11]

Meanwhile, the KCC decided unilaterally to create its own ad hoc Steering Committee to oversee the implementation of the Housing Project in Kawaala and did not invite any of the Abataka Committee members to the meeting. After raising objections at having been excluded, they were invited by the Town Clerk, Patrick Makumbi, to a meeting to nominate members of the committee.[12] The Abataka Committee refused to participate in the Steering Committee. Wilberforce Sserwaniko, secretary of the Abataka Committee and chairman of LC2, wrote to Makumbi, arguing that he opposed the steering committee because it was set up by the government and not by the people of Kawaala. He pointed out that the Steering Committee consisted only of government officials and LC chairmen from LC2 upwards, ignoring the people most directly affected by the project. Only one member of the affected area would be represented on the committee. Sserwaniko's letter continued: "In my view it would be disastrous for the people of Kawaala to let their coach be steered by a group of people with no purpose or interest in their destination."

Sserwaniko also objected to the terms of reference of the Steering Committee, which, according to a KCC document, stated that the Committee was to formulate guidelines in conformity "generally but not always specifically with the public good

of the residents in the project area". He wrote that this painted "a clear picture of
the authoritative and oppressive Kampala City Council authorities who designed
this committee to act as a rubber stamp and not in the interests of the alleged beneficiaries". He flatly refused to participate in the Steering Committee, stating that "If
I joined hands with you in your committee, I would be working against the interests of the people of Kawaala and I would be an oppressor too."[13]

Between September 1991 and May 1992 the KCC held meetings with residents and
Local Councils, registered the *bibanja* (plot) holders, finished surveying the area, valued the structures and crops, and completed the final layout for the project. It was satisfied that "the project has now received the full support of most residents including
the LCs".[14] Nothing could have been further from the truth. Residents argued that
they were not informed about what was going on, nor did they fully comprehend
how the project would affect them. Many were unaware of the consequences of taking the compensation money. Moreover, they were not given prior notice when the
engineers and technicians came to measure their plots, and evaluate their houses,
crops and trees. They objected to the fact that in many cases they evaluated the size
of the plots without even measuring them and assessed the value of the houses without going into them. The residents saw these intrusions as a violation of their rights
and privacy and in many cases they chased the KCC vehicles away. "It is not that they
do not want development, but they are insecure. They do not know exactly what was
happening. If the City Council would have involved us, we would have mobilized
people for them," as one resident put it.[15] Another resident even went to court seeking a court order to arrest the LC members who were helping the surveyors.[16]

Land issue

The residents had seen similar "development" projects take place in other parts of
Kampala, such as Namuwongo (a Ministry of Housing, Lands and Urban Development project), where the poorer residents were evicted and their houses were sold
to non-residents, often through patronage ties. They believed the same was about
to happen in Kawaala. Moreover, they strongly objected to KCC references to residents as "low-income people" and "squatters", implying that they did not have the
right to live on the land they occupied, most of them for their entire lives. As one
woman put it: "If a person can build houses and feed children, why call that
poor?"[17] These labels clearly served to distance the residents from the planners and
objectify them into categories of people who could be manipulated, rather than
respectable human beings who wanted to participate in the future of their community.

In Kawaala the houses targeted for eviction did not have leases. However, of the
two dozen residents interviewed almost all were born and had spent their entire
lives there, some since 1930. Technically, "squatters" are people who occupied the
land after the 1975 Land Reform Decree, without permission from the KCC. However, the overwhelming majority of tenants had, in fact, settled on the land prior to
1975. Moreover, the residents had paid taxes to the KCC and the KCC had willingly
collected the taxes without challenging the legality of their occupancy.

Kawaala was originally owned by the Kabaka (King of Buganda) and other
Baganda officials and chiefs, to whom the tenants of plots (*bibanja*) paid rents (*busu-
ulu*), which served as a form of payment for their public duties. This *mailo* tenure
system, which began with the Buganda Agreement of 1900, introduced the concept
of private ownership of land, undermining traditional bases of ownership. When
the Kabaka was deposed by President Obote in 1966, the land was taken over by the

state and later came to be administered by the Kampala City Council. Under the 1975 Land Reform Decree the residents then became "tenants on sufferance" of the state. Although they were permitted to obtain lease holdings on the land, few did so because of cost considerations and bureaucratic procedures. The land technically belonged to the Kampala City Council and according to the 1975 Land Reform Decree could not be bought and sold, but in practice *bibanja* rights to mailo land continued to be bought and sold (Maxwell, 1993: 33–4). In 1993 the land was returned to the Kabaka as part of the return of properties (*Ebyaffe*) and, even though the KCC was to administer the land, it now had to do so in consultation with the Buganda Land Board.

The residents argued that recognition of cultural preferences and practices was an important part of local government-community relations. Unlike other parts of Kampala, the people in this community were predominantly Baganda and the fact that the land belonged to the Kabaka was significant to them. The residents of Kawaala are the descendants of people who received plots of land in exchange for carrying out duties at the Kabaka's palace in Mengo and Kasubi. They did not want to be evicted from this land, not only because their livelihood depended on it, but also because they would be cutting themselves off from a cultural heritage and community. Land has significance far beyond property and even politics. According to Holly Hanson (1994), it expresses moral and social relationships among the Baganda. This, she argues, explains the enormous emotional intensity of land controversies in Buganda, which are often interpreted as violations of a moral relationship or order.

First, many Baganda have ancestors buried in Kawaala which in part explains why land is of central importance to the Baganda. One way of asserting a claim to one's land is through burial of one's kin. In the past if there was a dispute over a piece of land, one of the ways of proving land ownership was whether one had ancestors buried on the land, because one could only bury one's dead on one's own land.

In a letter to the Kabaka requesting his assistance, residents reminded him that the land included the burial ground of Mugema, the great-grandfather of the Buganda; Senkezi and Bawala-enkedi of the Mamba clan; Mukangula, who was Mutesa's gate-keeper; Sabaganzi Mwakiri, who was the maternal uncle of Kabaka Mutesa and Bubasuula of the Ngeye clan.[18] Even Baganda from other parts of Kampala expressed frustration over the evictions because their ancestors were buried in Kawaala and they needed to return to Kawaala for funerals and other family celebrations.

The KCC project director, a Muganda herself, recognized the importance of land to the Kawaala residents: "The Kasubi tombs are located near here, they say it is the Kabaka's land and the community does not want to part with the land."[19]

Nevertheless, she claimed that the Kawaala Baganda were conservatives who did not want to part with their land. She also argued that they were violating the law by burying their dead in an urban area, contravening the city bylaws even though many of their ancestors were buried there before any such laws were enacted. Similarly, the Minister of Information had summoned one of the members of the Abataka Committee and made him look out of his window overlooking the railway station. He pointed to the station and said "You people, why do you tie yourself to dead bodies? People had bodies and graves here and they were moved [to build the station]."[20] Needless to say, these kinds of insensitive remarks incensed the Kawaala residents. For the Baganda, transfer of graves can take place under special circumstances, but even then one can only bury one's kin in one's own home area.

Second, the residents rejected the KCC idea of small houses as not being part of their customary way of living. As one woman put it, "We like beautiful things, beautiful houses, we do not want to live in small quarters (*mizigo*) that all look the same. We need space for our funerals and celebrations. Why should we be squeezed, put into a post-industrial way of living when we are not accustomed to that?" Several objected to the KCC's categorization of houses into three incrementally larger groups and feared that in building the new houses they would in effect divide the village into one area for the poor and one for the rich. They felt that artificially dividing people in this way would destroy the village communal spirit in which people of different means lived and shared together.

In an alternative proposal for the project, the residents mentioned more than once the importance of observing cultural prerogatives. "The overall objective of the project is to promote the social, cultural, political and cordial relationship between plot/*bibanja* owners." They also envisioned that the project, if carried out along lines more acceptable to them, could potentially enhance a sense of community of a kind experienced in rural villages by working together to improve Kawaala. The residents would rebuild the village in the city and in doing so they would deepen their sense of ownership and cement "the community spirit and belongingness". "Kawaala will turn out a model planned serviced urban community in which the African village perspective will be portrayed," the alternative proposal read. These non-material goals were clearly as important to the residents as the physical improvements.

Compensation Issue

One of the arguments the KCC used against the residents was the fact that some of them had agreed to receive compensation for their plots and houses and in doing so were agreeing to give up their rights to the plots and thereby indicating their "support" for the project. Many people were unaware of the full consequences of their actions at the time. Most were never compensated. Some were given blank forms and told to sign them. One woman, who was made to sign, received a check but it bounced. Those who did receive compensation sometimes received as little as USh. 30,000 ($30), which was grossly insufficient to buy another plot of land and rebuild a house; it would not even buy a door to a house in Kampala. One resident had been given USh. 49,000 ($49) for his house and one and a half acres of coffee and some other crops.

Some accepted the money, worried that, if they did not accept it, they might lose their plots anyway and be left with nothing. Others were approached when they found themselves in a tight financial situation; they decided to accept the money to ease themselves out of an immediate crisis and worry about the consequences later. One woman's husband had just died and she found herself in dire financial straits; in desperation she accepted the money to pay the school fees for her children.

Some husbands and wives fought among themselves over whether or not to accept the meager compensation fees, especially in households where the husband was without a source of income. In most cases, the woman resisted accepting payment, while the husband, who legally owned the house, would claim the money without her knowledge. He might then spend the money, which was minimal, without telling his wife. If the wife objected to the husband's actions, she would risk provoking him. It was not uncommon for husbands to refuse to let women make decisions on family property, even if the wife was the main breadwinner in the family and the primary individual responsible for tilling the land.

By the middle of 1993, out of 675 residents 174 had agreed to have their crops valued and of this number only 8 picked up their checks. Three women and five men had even taken compensation cases to court, claiming they had not been fully compensated.[21]

Alternative Proposal

In the midst of the conflict in 1992, the Abataka Committee came up with its own alternative proposal, "Developing Kawaala Through Participation Self-Help by the local Current Plot/Bibanja Owners and Kampala City Council: The Proposed Kawaala Land Development Project" (see Appendix D). Even though the proposal was flatly rejected by the KCC project director, as were subsequent suggestions presented by residents, this document is useful in understanding the position of the residents. It also reflects the new norms they were trying to institutionalize, not just in Kawaala but in the way the City Council interacted with local communities more generally.

The proposal was based on community participation in the project, which meant that the project was to "have neither a principal, nor an inferior implementing partner. All the participating partners shall be on a par." A basis for a new relationship "of trust" between the residents, the KCC and the World Bank was outlined in which the terms of reference for the project ensured security of land tenure for the residents in return for their co-operation with the authorities. The residents would directly "participate, be consulted and involved in the project proposal, planning, implementation, monitoring and evaluation" because they were the prime beneficiaries of such a project. They would pay the KCC for the leases of their plots and the services provided, and would co-operate in paying taxes introduced by the City Council to pay for the services. The City Council would provide lease offers to plot owners, improve or install new infrastructure, and carry out surveying and land planning in consultation and full participation with the plot owners. The World Bank would refrain from importing and imposing unacceptable plans on the people of Kawaala and would limit its relationship to the City Council to providing financial assistance for infrastructural improvements that the community residents themselves would decide.

Instead of evicting residents and building new schools, roads and clinics the proposal called for the restoration of telephone services that once existed in the village and of the piped water supply which had broken down due to the negligence of the Water Board. Residents also called for the improvement of two existing privately owned schools and of the traditional road system. The only new constructions they would have liked to see were a sewage disposal system and the expansion of an existing dispensary for which land was available from a *bibanja* owner who was willing to move if compensated.

Thus, through this proposal the residents were pressing for some recognition on the part of the authorities that people's land and dwellings are not disposable and cannot easily be replaced. They were suggesting that Kampala should be planned to accommodate the realities of people's lives and not an idealized version of what a city should look like. The residents not only lived in the houses, they obtained income from renting rooms out, they were involved in farming that was critical to sustaining them, they had income-generating projects that were tied to their locale; moreover, they had belonged to the community most of their lives. As mentioned earlier, many also had buried their ancestors on their properties and they could not be moved for cultural reasons. For the residents, especially women, with limited means, education and opportunities, their survival literally depended on remaining in the area. For these reasons they demanded security of land ownership in the form of leases for their plots.

Patronage, Foul Play and the Local Councils

As the opposition to the Steering Committee mounted, the KCC shifted gears and brought the LC1 Executive Committee into the fray to try to bolster support for the project and the Steering Committee. At the same time, members of the Abataka Committee and other residents joined the Steering Committee, apparently to keep an eye on its activities. As far as the residents were concerned, the events that followed were evidence of patronage networks at work.

The issue of plot size became increasingly contentious, because so many (women in particular) obtained a living by farming the land. The average size of a plot is half to three-quarters of an acre, some are as large as 2–3 acres, while a handful belonging to princes are 3–4 acres. The Steering Committee proposed to keep plots at a size that could accommodate farming but the KCC objected. From then on, the KCC completely bypassed the Steering Committee and took unilateral decisions in implementing the project. This only served to heighten suspicions in the community that KCC officials were personally to benefit from the allocation and selling of plots, because preserving larger plots would leave them with fewer plots to sell. These moves by the KCC and the Abataka Committee effectively shifted the focus of the conflict to the LC1, LC2 and LC5 Executive Committees.

The other change in KCC strategy involved a plan to influence women's organizations in the community, because women had been so outspoken about the project and were influential in creating public opinion. The LC Women's Secretary explained that she and the project manager came up with an idea to get women's groups together and try to influence the women, who in turn would influence the men in the community. They would try to get women involved in the project, for example, making bricks for the houses, and at the same time find out what they were doing.[22] She admitted that it had been hard to mobilize women through the LC system and that she needed to reach them through organizations that were relevant to their concerns.

In April 1993 a seminar was planned by the City Council with the theme "Women's Roles in Developing Nations". All the major groups in the area, including the Munno Mukabi Kasubi Kawaala Group, the Catholic Women's Guild, the Kawaala Women's Club, Kasubi/Kawaala Women Market Vendors, and the Kawaala Mothers' Union[23] were invited to a program that featured presentations on the Munno Mukabi experience, the role of women's clubs in a developing area, "the business lady in development through market acquisition and management" and other such topics. The speakers included the LC1 Women's Secretary, a co-operative officer, a KCC official and the director of the Kawaala project, Ruth Kijjambu.[24] The meeting was a deliberate attempt to draw women into a debate on the housing project and the future of the area through their own organizations on their own turf. However, it was postponed several times and finally never took place because of the levels of hostility among women in the community toward the KCC. Kijjambu admitted she was tipped off about a plan to disrupt the meeting and it was therefore canceled.[25] Women questioned why Ruth Kijjambu was organizing women in

Kawaala when she was not a resident. "Here we say we should develop ourselves. So why is she coming?" one woman asked. She continued, "The seminar was about duping women."[26] When they finally held a seminar, it was in Ndeeba, not in Kawaala, and it was attended by what residents considered to be handpicked peo-ple who would "easily dance to Kijjambu's tune".[27]

Two months after having been elected, in about May 1992, the LC1 Executive Committee came under sharp criticism from local residents, who decried the way KCC officials were allegedly using the project to feed their patronage networks and for "enriching a few at the expense of the people of Kawaala". They felt that if they, as residents, were involved in the implementation and monitoring of the project, the KCC would be accountable to them, the beneficiaries, rather than simply to the World Bank. Women in the community accused the Committee of having lured peo-ple to line up behind them through "foul play", using alcohol and money to bribe them. Their suspicions had been roused when the women discovered that there were more votes than registered voters. Many residents suspected that some of the committee members had obtained bribes from the KCC. It was also widely claimed that various counselors were illegally asking for money from residents in exchange for application forms for leasing land and even for a simple identity card. In the past, the Committee had held meetings every Wednesday for local residents to bring their problems and disputes. These meetings were discontinued. One of the reasons the women suspected the LC1 leaders found it so easy to dismiss the residents' objec-tions was that they themselves had nothing to lose. Many were unemployed, and they were not land owners but rather tenants who could rent as easily in Kawaala as anywhere else. Further up the LC hierarchy, many of the counselors did not live in the affected areas and similarly did not have anything at stake personally.

On 20 May 1992, residents of Kawaala II informed Kasubi Parish LC2 Executive Committee that they had decided to withdraw their confidence from their LC1 Executive Committee. They asked for the election of a new LC1 Executive Commit-tee to be arranged for a meeting slated for 24 May 1992, on the grounds that the LC1 Executive had conspired with the KCC to evict them from their land.[28] The LC5 Executive Committee canceled the meeting, setting off a series of appeals and counter-appeals by both the residents and the LC1 Executive Committee to the Dis-trict Administrator, the NRM Secretariat, LC3, and Nakulabye Police. Residents told *Ngabo* reporters that they wanted to get rid of the LC1 Executive because they had not explained why some of the houses in Kawaala were to be demolished, they had not attended residents' meetings to discuss the matter, they had instructed the police to arrest residents without just cause, they had failed to account for money collected from residents, they had embezzled money from residents and they did not show proper respect toward the residents.[29] When the Deputy District Admin-istrator of Kampala, Louis Otika, met with residents of Kawaala Zone II in July 1992, he asked them to group themselves into supporters and opponents of the LC1. The overwhelming majority (517 out of 537) opposed the LC1.[30] After the meeting, Otika accused residents of throwing stones at him and the accusation was published in *Ngabo*. Both men and women residents of Kawaala were incensed that such lies were published and went to the *Ngabo* offices to protest the article.

In response, three members of the LC2 Executive Committee intervened and set up a sub-committee to investigate the problem, but used their report as a not so veiled attempt to unseat the LC2 chairman, Sserwaniko, accusing him of under-mining development in the area.[31] The Vice-Chairman of LC2 Kasubi called a parish meeting and informed the residents that the LC II Chairman Sserwaniko had resigned, which Sserwaniko flatly denied.[32] The sub-committee then convened a meeting on 26 August 1992 of LC2 executives without Sserwaniko's knowledge and announced his resignation, according to the Luganda-language paper, *Ngabo*. Sserwaniko responded that he was not against the project or the development of Kawaala, but rather he believed that, if the project was to succeed and be implemented, it should benefit local residents; the KCC should go ahead as long as the residents "are deeply listened to, consulted and involved".[33]

Residents objected to the way the local LC officials at various levels were tied to the KCC through patronage and were therefore not accountable to the people in the communities. The counselors consistently saw it as their mission to try to persuade people of the value of the KCC project rather than trying to make sure that the project was implemented in a way that met the needs of the residents. Moreover, the LCs acted as a constraint on independent action and mobilization that was outside their jurisdiction.

The authorities also often treated the residents in a condescending and paternalistic manner. Moreover, the residents faced numerous threats and even physical intimidation. The LC5 Chairman of Kampala, Christopher Iga, advised the LCs at a KCC seminar to show the people what was right and wrong and sternly warned the residents that "If you commit wrongs on the pretext that what you are doing is right, the long arm of government will get you."[34] Residents bitterly protested these remarks in interviews with *Ngabo* reporters and felt they had the right to talk about issues concerning their area.[35] The lack of consultation and information the project was threatening to undermine it completely. By 1993 the level of hostility had grown to such proportions that the KCC representatives could no longer talk to residents without incident and tempers flaring. The minute Ruth Kijjambu, the director of the project, would stand up to talk at a meeting, she was booed and chased away. "Go away, we don't want to see you here," people shouted at her. Kawaala residents were angered even further by the fact that she had used Radio Uganda to insult them.[36]

The KCC and LC1 then convened a meeting in March 1993 and brought along soldiers and police. Angered by this display of intimidation, the residents refused to talk to the KCC and the militia started harassing them. The meeting broke up as it turned into a riot and police and militia drove the residents away. From then on, the KCC was unable to convene a meeting without armed security. Several times the LC5 chairman also threatened to use the "long arm of the law" against those who opposed the project. "Is that peace?" one woman opponent of the project asked. "We just stood our ground, but we said if there is to be death over this project, let it come for we already have seen a lot."[37] Residents openly questioned why this project was so important to the KCC that it would resort to violence to see it implemented. The KCC authorities argued that, if they abandoned the project, this would set a bad precedent and would prevent the implementation of other such projects and World Bank support for them.[38]

Residents bitterly complained that none of their LC leaders were standing by them in the face of such intimidation. In fact, the March 1993 incident made many believe that the District Administrator, the LC5 chairman, the Member of Parliament, the Town Clerk, and the KCC project director were all working "under the same umbrella," as one woman put it. She continued: "All they want is to cheat us, nothing more. . . . What kind of LC system is this when it hurts people?" She was particularly upset by the LC1 Women's Secretary, who at one meeting told the soldiers to go after some of the more vocal people and gave them their names. This made it abundantly clear to the residents that she was "not fighting for the people but for her own gains".[39]

Many residents suspected that money was somehow involved. One KCC official more or less admitted this to one of the women leaders, telling her that "If you don't want the project, we'll put it elsewhere. We'll get our 'commission' elsewhere all the same." When she asked whether there really was a commission involved, he kept quiet. Another woman resident wondered out loud why the LCs brought in soldiers to meetings "if there is nothing to gain".

Court Injunction

Notices were sent out on 6 May 1993 from the Town Clerk to those who would have to be resettled, giving them six months notice to move from their locations.[40] The letters were brief and vague. According to the KCC letter of notification, those affected would be those whose structures did not conform to the minimum building standards and the ones which were located in areas planned for infrastructure services, public utilities, community facilities, markets and open spaces. From the letter it was not clear if the recipient of the letter would be affected or what alternative plans were being made for those who would have to move.

Less than a week after the eviction notices were sent out, over 80 residents sought an injunction to restrain the KCC from evicting 675 families and violating the initial terms of the project, which did not include evictions. The injunction was also to bar the KCC from threatening and harassing the complainants. One of the sworn affidavits by a complainant cited one such case of harassment, claiming that on 20 February 1993, the project director with the help of KCC law enforcement officials threatened to use violence against the applicants if they did not accept the meager sums of money in exchange for their plots (bibanja). The residents also sued the Town Clerk and the project director, whom they accused of being motivated by self-interest and attempting to sell the plots to individuals without offering the residents the first priority to obtain leases, as required by law.

The residents' lawyer, Godfrey Kibirige of Mayanja-Nkangi Co. Associates, argued that, according to the Public Land Act, if an outside resident wanted to occupy land by obtaining a lease, he/she needed the consent of the current resident. According to Kibirige, the law supports customary tenants and the KCC should therefore desist from selling to outsiders without the consent of the residents.[41] The defendants' lawyer argued that the judge should ignore the suit because the number of residents bringing the suit was small in number. In spite of the defendants' pleas, the Uganda High Court issued a six-month injunction against the KCC on 15 May 1993 restraining it from "threatening, harassing and evicting the applicants from their bibanja at Kawaala II village . . ."[42]

Ignoring the injunction, the KCC refused to halt the project and continued cutting holes through people's hedges, and placing markers on their property without informing them of what they were doing. People in the community were devastated and felt that even the courts, their last recourse, were of no use. A quiet protest swept the area. Women stopped going to farm, they did not clean their compounds and they stopped burning garbage and, instead, let it collect in heaps. As one woman put it: "There is a general feeling of disturbance, people are in a panic. Psychologically, people are sick."

I went to visit an elderly woman who had lived in the area since 1930 and who was facing eviction. She had been in bed for three days since KCC road engineers

had come and placed markers on her land. She had been told they were building a
road through her home. She explained to me how she felt:

> Women are of no concern to the City Council. . . . I would rather die than face what is to come.
> I am not working for a living now and am doing badly. I am sick and worried. Old as I am, how
> can I go to my children for help? I am not well but I do not want to go begging and face such
> humiliation. This is the only thing I have in my life, this property, you see. There is no point in
> going to the LCs, I am too old to be told lies.

This widow was supporting five grandchildren on her own in Kawaala off the land
she farmed. A friend had given her land nearby on which she grew potatoes, yams
and cassava for subsistence. She also owned a house on one acre of land and rented
it out, keeping one room for herself. From her rent she was able to buy paraffin and
soap. At first she was told she would be compensated for the land but then later the
KCC told her it would not give her anything because she and other Kawaala residents had delayed the project. There was no plan to resettle her or assist her in any
way. She said that, frail as she was, she had fought to stop the project, even though
she wanted development. It was clear that without her house to rent and field to
dig there was virtually no way for her to sustain herself and the five grandchildren
if she was evicted.

This woman, like many others, had been told different things at different times.
At first, residents had been told that the plots would be divided up and everyone
would obtain a lease to a plot. Later they were told that, instead of obtaining plots,
they would be given compensation for their crops and houses and would have to
find new plots and houses on their own. Some were told improved houses would
be built for those being relocated and then they were told this would not be the
case. After the injunction, the project director told me there would be no evictions,
only relocations. But at the same time, the KCC was going ahead with the road construction without informing people of its plans. It was finally stopped when people
exerted physical force and threats to oust the engineers and their assistants from the
area. The ongoing battle between LC1 of Kawaala I and the residents also came to
a head when the residents dropped the entire LC1 committee and elected new
leaders.[43] Opponents of the project like Wilberforce Sserwaniko and Joyce Muhire
were brought back to the executive of LC1.

World Bank Complicity

Finally, the World Bank withdrew support from the Kawaala Housing Project on the
grounds that the KCC failed to meet the deadline of 15 January 1994 for compensating residents.[44] The injunction and the conflict that had precipitated it undoubtedly played a part in the decision not to postpone the deadline but rather to cancel
the project altogether. World Bank representatives never publicly acknowledged
their responsibility. They saw themselves merely on the sidelines as a financial institution serving as the financier of the project. Yet residents saw matters differently.
"The World Bank was one of the forces that was aiming at displacing us. Their
pulling out was welcome," said Sserwaniko, the newly elected chairman of LC1
Kawaala.[45] Certainly Bank funding and then its withdrawal made all the difference
to the lives of Kawaala residents affected by the project. Without promises of Bank
funding, the project would not have been set in motion, turning the lives of residents upside down, while disrupting and dividing the community. In the end, the

residents remained without adequate electricity, water supply, roads, or houses. The involvement of the Bank clearly raised issues of accountability to the people affected by their funding. It also raised questions about the "partners" it chose to work with and the extent to which it investigated the feasibility of projects it was funding by directly consulting the so-called beneficiaries. The Bank's lack of concern about the patronage politics that infused the project was quite remarkable to the residents.

World Bank officials had been concerned since 1990 when they started hearing different stories. The residents' group briefed them on its side of the matter. The KCC assured the Bank that this was its first project and it was understandable that people would be apprehensive about it. It told the Bank officials that this kind of trouble was to be expected and reassured them that it was not the majority who were against the project but just some trouble makers. The Bank vowed not to release any money until the construction was complete. In January 1993 road construction started.

The World Bank's team leader for the project, Aulikki Kuusela, argued that the Bank pulled out because the KCC was unable to meet the conditions the Bank had set, namely, the land was not free for development as a result of the dispute and people had not been resettled. The Bank team had the impression that the people "disrupting" the process were only a handful and it was clearly unaware of the widespread opposition to the project, the complexity of the issues involved and the depth of feeling regarding the removal of burial grounds. It had worked with the KCC project manager, relied on her information and never directly consulted with the local residents. Kuusela felt that the conflict was primarily "between the KCC and the people" and not between the Bank and the residents. Rightly or wrongly, she laid the blame on the KCC for its blueprint approach of superimposing a ready-made plan on the residents without consultation. She suggested that it was engaged in an "old kind of planning". At the time, Kuusela personally considered that the project would never work without local participation. When asked what she had learned from the Kawaala fiasco, she said that "such projects need to be conceived in conjunction with the major stake holders."[46] Regrettably, this insight came six years too late to help the residents of Kawaala.

When at a public seminar I asked the then Vice-President of the World Bank, Edward Jaycox, why the Bank did not see itself as accountable to the people of Kawaala in addition to its own board, he replied that the Bank did not want to give any credence to the impractical "cult of participation" that had emerged in development circles. He dismissed the residents' motives, explaining that in his experience of past urban projects, when community groups opposed development projects, outside political forces could generally be uncovered because these groups were easily manipulated by such people with ulterior motives.[47] Clearly no such outside forces were visible in the Kawaala conflict.

Aftermath of the Conflict

The new LC1 committee wanted to take the former LC1 Executive to court over their demand for USh. 1,000 bribes when residents applied for leases. The LC5 and the central government representative retaliated by trying to divide Kawaala LC1 into three sub-divisions. This was purportedly on the grounds that Kawaala II was too large, there was excessive insecurity in the area, and because of political tensions. Once again, the residents were not consulted on the subdivision although the authorities claimed that public meetings had been held to discuss the matter. Moreover, the residents complained bitterly that the sub-county (*gombolola*) chief had moved through their zone demarcating the sub-divisions with 20 armed personnel. Residents wondered why armed personnel were necessary if the decision had been taken by the residents. Numerous letters were sent to LC5 and the Ministry of Local Government, the Minister of State for Presidential Affairs and other authorities protesting at the lack of consultation.[48] All these pleas were ignored and on 15 January 1995 elections were held in the two newly created sub-divisions. Representatives were simply handpicked and nominated by the Office of the Central Government Representative in violation of LC statutes. Once again, residents protested in writing to key authorities but to no avail.

The Kawaala conflict did, however, have ramifications in the 1996 parliamentary elections. NRM supporter Bakayana Kityo, who had been LC II Chairman of Kasubi in 1992, lost to multi-partyist and federalist Wasswa Lule in Rubaga North division. This was due in large measure to what residents considered his betrayal of Kawaala residents when he sided with the KCC and the World Bank in the conflict (Malaba, 1996).

Conclusions

The City Council, the World Bank and the LC authorities were unable to make a positive difference to the welfare of the residents of Kawaala when they had the chance because they were incapable of listening to the residents and working with them as equal partners. But it was more than just a lack of will. Patronage networks that linked the Kampala City Council with the local councils made it impossible for them to work with the residents and represent their interests. They undermined trust between the leaders and the residents and made the notion of accountability redundant. This made a mockery of the legal system and led to the physical harassment and intimidation of residents by the authorities.

Stepping back from the events of the conflict, it becomes evident that the residents, especially the women involved, were trying to institutionalize some new norms for community mobilization, not just in Kawaala but more widely in providing a model for other community projects. They had a vision of a more collaborative effort that took the needs of women, widows, children, and the elderly as a starting point and recognized their dependence on the land for survival. Without adequate compensation, these people had few options. They also sought to preserve a moral and cultural order that valued the centrality of land and revered the ancestors who were buried on the land. They sought to maintain the cohesion of the community and the sense of belonging by rejecting a plan that would have given undue salience to class difference and obliterated the particular characteristics and the individuality of the Baganda houses. None of these norms could be implemented as long as clientelism poisoned channels of accountability and representation.

In the broader picture, the Kawaala struggle is in many ways a microcosm of some of the changes that are occurring in Uganda as people are seeking new forms of autonomous mobilization outside of the state. For the women involved, the struggle was more than one over the fate of Kawaala: it was also at a very personal level a conflict that involved their husbands as well as the local authorities over the conditions of their participation in local politics.

Thus, women's exclusion from formal political channels forced them to rely on their own autonomous associations to oppose the influence of patronage in their community. Marginalization had its costs and it limited their mobilization to informal groups, but it also meant that the women had less at stake than other groups in perpetuating the patronage networks. With their own independent mechanisms of mobilization, they were well positioned to oppose the project, offering their own alternative vision of how the initiative could be established along self-help co-operative lines.

Notes

1. Miria Matembe, Plenary Speech, "Approaches to Governance, Citizenship and Political Participation: Strategies," NGO Forum '95 in Beijing, 3 September 1995.
2. "Ngilu is First Kenyan Woman to Run for Presidency," *The Guardian,* 17 December 1997.
3. "World Bank's Plan on Kawaala Housing Project".
4. The report, *"Enkola Etegekebwa Bank Yensi Yonna Ku Ttaka Ely'E Kawaala,"* was signed by the entire Abataka Committee and was sent to the Town Clerk, the President and Vice-President of Uganda, the Ministers of Local Government, Finance, Lands and Surveys, Housing and Urban Development and Planning and Economic Development. It was also sent to the Chief Advisor to the World Bank and the KCC, the RC5 Chairman, Kampala, the NRC member for the Rubaga Division, the LC3 chairman, Rubaga Division, RC2 Chairman, Kasubi Parish and RC1, Kawaala II, chairman.
5. Nakyekoledde (Kasubi Family School), Kawaala Parents School, St Andrew and Daniel Primary School, Kasubi Church of Uganda Primary School
6. Namungoona Orthodox Church S.S.S.
7. Interview with Dolotia Nakibuka, Kampala, 18 June 1993.
8. Interview with Joyce Muhire, Kampala, 26 June 1995.
9. Minutes. Special Meeting 30 May 1991. Land Development at Kawaala/Kawaala Development Project.
10. "Residents of Kawaala Accuse KCC of Hypocrisy," (trans.) *Ngabo,* 25 August 1992.
11. Letter from W. Kaddu, Chairman of the LC I Resistance Committee, to the Town Clerk, Kampala City Council, 22 May 1992.
12. Letter, 15 July 1991, Patrick Makumbi, to Chairman, Abataka Committee.
13. Letter from W. Sserwaniko, 19 July 1991.
14. Summary of Progress on Kawaala Project, 27 April 1992.
15. Interview with Joyce Muhire, Kampala, 18 June 1993.
16. Interview with Ruth Kijjambu, Kampala, 13 July 1993.
17. Interview with 1.4, Kampala, 18 June 1993.
18. Letter from I. K. Kibirige, Chairman of the Kawaala Abataka Committee, to His Highness the Kabaka, 9 March 1993.
19. The Kasubi tombs are the burial ground of the last four Baganda kings.
20. Interview with Wilberforce Sserwaniko, Kampala, 26 June 1995.
21. Interview with Abdu Segane, LC1 Secretary of Information, Kampala, 16 June 1993.
22. Interview with J. Ssebawato, Kampala, 18 June 1993.
23. The Mothers' Union is a Protestant Church of Uganda organization for women who have been married in the church. In Kawaala the group was involved in education around how to manage homes, child care, and concerns of adolescent girls. Of the two dozen women we interviewed in Kawaala II, most were Protestants, but there were also some Catholics, Balokole (saved), Muslims and Pentecostals.
24. Program, Kawaala Site and Services Women's Mobilisation Workshop, City Council of Kampala, 17 April 1993.
25. Interview with Ruth Kijjambu, Kampala, 13 July 1993.
26. Interview with 1.4, Kampala, 18 June 1993.
27. "Residents of Kawaala Accuse KCC of Hypocrisy," (trans.) *Ngabo,* 25 August 1992.
28. "Residents of Kawaala Appeal to Museveni and Ssabataka" (trans.), *Ngabo,* 28 May 1992.

29. "Residents of Kawaala Have Explained Why They Moved a Vote of No Confidence in their RC1 Executive" (trans.) *Ngabo*, 4 July 1992.
30. "Kawaala Residents are Looking Forward to Electing a New RC1 Executive" (trans.), *Ngabo*, 7 July 1992.
31. Report of Kasubi Parish Sub-Committee on Kawaala II, 23 July 1992.
32. "The RCII Chairman Sserwaniko Refutes Allegations that He Had Resigned" (trans.) *Ngabo*, 21 August 1992.
33. Letter to RC2 Sub-Committee from Wilberforce Sserwaniko, 18 August 1992.
34. "Iga Strongly Accuses Residents of Kawaala Who Do Not Want to Develop Kampala," (trans.) *Ngabo*, 22 July 1992.
35. "Residents of Kawaala Disagree with What Was Reported by the Deputy DA Kampala," (trans.) *Ngabo*, 28 July 1992.
36. "Residents of Kawaala are Fed Up with the Project Manager," (trans.) *Ngabo*, 18 September 1992.
37. Interview with 1.5, Kampala, 18 June 1993.
38. Interview with Ruth Kijjambu, Kampala, 13 July 1993.
39. Interview with 1.6, Kampala, 18 June 1993.
40. Notice 6 May 1992 to residents from Patrick Makumbi, Town Clerk
41. Interview with Godfrey Kibirige, Kampala, 13 July 1993.
42. *Monitor*, 30 April – 4 May 1993; *New Vision* 15 May 1993.
43. "Kawaala RC1 dropped," (trans.) *Ngabo*, 23 August 1993.
44. *New Vision*, 10 February 1994.
45. Interview with Wilberforce Sserwaniko, Kampala, 26 June 1995.
46. Interview with Aulikki Kuusela, World Bank, Washington, DC, 27 July 1995.
47. Seminar on "African Development Reconsidered" hosted by the Africa Bureau of the World Bank and James S. Coleman African Studies Center, University of California-Los Angeles, Lake Arrowhead, CA. 14–15 June 1994.
48. Letter from Wilberforce Sserwaniko, Chairman RC1 Kawaala II, to Chairman RC5 Kampala, 5 December 1994.

10

Anatomy
of a Deception

"Something is Fishy
in Kamuli"

Most of this book has focused on women's associational autonomy from the state and the ways in which women have used this autonomy to express their interests and bring about institutional change. Autonomy, which involves the capacity to make decisions independently of external pressures, can also be expressed in relation to foreign and domestic donors. This is not to say that state and donor influences are similar or that they have the same consequences. The influx of donor resources in Africa poses a threat to associational autonomy different from the challenge to autonomy posed by the state. Donors create new relationships of dependency and conditionality. Donors may also introduce new imbalances in community access to resources, thus giving rise to healthy competition but possibly also conflict, corruption and new patronage networks. Clearly, the cost/benefit relationship in donor funding is something that always needs to be scrutinized to determine when support becomes more of a hindrance than an asset.

Much of the literature on associational change in Africa suggests that the impetus for the formation of organizations comes from the increased availability of donor funds. Even many donors themselves make this easy assumption, perhaps because they are most in contact with groups pursuing funding and not with the many groups that do not apply for support. My survey showed that most organizations were unable to secure such resources, and that the majority of associations relied on their own funds. Nevertheless, there is sufficient donor money available to have an impact on various sections of the NGO community. Certainly this donor-NGO nexus exists and has become an increasingly important phenomenon as bilateral and multilateral donors and international NGOs pump more money into local NGOs, especially into apex level NGOs (Gariyo, 1994: 6).

These resources introduce new shifts in community and even gender dynamics, some of which have the potential to benefit recipients and some of which are quite disruptive. Donor funds may have equalizing consequences, empowering groups of people such as women who previously have not had access to various resources. The availability of donor funds may create a new basis for co-operation along associational lines, if the criteria for funding require group rather than individual or household collaboration. This impetus for group formation may be positive, but it may also be a less efficient use of resources in cases where it might be more appropriate to fund successful or promising individual entrepreneurs rather than opportunistic groups formed for the sole purpose of gaining access to donor funds.

At one extreme there is evidence of the emergence of a considerable number of "briefcase" organizations with little else to show for themselves beyond a chairperson and a treasurer (Dicklitch, 1998). At present, there is no way of assessing how many such organizations exist. However, it is unlikely, despite claims by politicians and even some scholars, that most NGOs are corrupt. More commonly there are intentions to create a sustainable organization while at the same time tapping into the available donor funds. Where the middle and educated classes might once have sought resources through government jobs, today the emphasis has shifted more toward donor-funded NGOs as a potential source of livelihood. Initiators tend to combine two very different motives: one, to advance a particular development goal by starting a NGO and two, to make a living by running a NGO. While there is nothing wrong with either intention, the economic situation in Uganda is such that the latter ambition may easily supersede the developmental goal.

Mamdani (1994) has observed that NGOs are not accountable to the people they intend to benefit, but rather to their financiers abroad. He suggests that they fragment public life and spread "a culture of charity and dependency, not democracy and sustainability". This is in general an exaggerated assessment, but it does accurately describe some NGOs. Kiribawa, the NGO described in this chapter, is a case in point. It was formed by an opportunistic woman as a money-making scam. Its members, not content simply to be the victims of a deception, fought hard to make it a real organization and to give it legitimacy. The process of creating legitimacy required asserting autonomy from donors. In a few years Kiribawa grew into the largest network of women's associations in Kamuli, with a network of 35 organizations and a membership of 5,600 women spanning five sub-counties. The groups were involved in agriculture, adult education, training of traditional birth attendants, operating a nursery school, making handicrafts and bricks, carpentry, beekeeping, tree planting, and drama.

From the outset, local and foreign donors, the NRC women's representative from Kamuli and the District Administration tended to treat the women's network as though its only reason for existence was to obtain external resources, thus in effect helping to foster a relationship of dependency with the network. It is instructive to examine a case from Kamuli because this district has the greatest concentration of both local and international NGOs in Uganda, according to Development of Indigenous Voluntary Associations (DENIVA) (Drata, 1994).

Thus, the availability of donor funding to NGOs and local organizations has created new struggles over accountability and donor dependence, not just among groups competing for these scarce resources, but more importantly *within* the organizations themselves. The possibility of obtaining funds is a powerful lure not only for well-meaning people but also for opportunists. It also takes on class dimensions since those most likely to apply for these resources are the better educated, better connected and better informed parts of society.

Strategies for Ensuring Accountability

The Kiribawa case study provides an example of how women sought autonomy and accountability through an internal leadership struggle. It illustrates poignantly the close connection between dependence on donors and corruption, i.e., how easily NGO dependence on donors can be turned into a situation where individual leaders benefit at the expense of the membership. It shows that there is a fine line between useful support and funding that is destructive of the purposes of the recipients and the donor. For most organizations, the pursuit of accountability is less dramatic with fewer difficulties, but the dangers explored in this case study are present even in less extreme situations of dependence on donors.

Nevertheless, uncommon as the Kiribawa case is, similar situations have emerged in other parts of the country where a more educated woman tried to take advantage of rural women to appropriate the group's donor assets. For example, in an almost identical story, Kyeijanga Women's Group in Kinkizi, Rukungiri, had started out in 1987 as a farming group in which women grew crops commercially and shared their profits. They also farmed on each others plots to help each other out. The group leader, who was the most educated woman in the parish, used her organizational ability to register the group and helped them get funding from the European Development Fund (EDF) Micro-projects Program for a grain milling machine. She kept the mill at her house, leading to accusations that she was trying personally to claim the mill. As in the Kiribawa case, the women had to struggle to get the chairman to repay the EDF, which in turn contributed 16 percent of the expenses towards a new mill, while the women paid the rest of the USh. 1.8 million to purchase the mill. In no time, the 35-member group had expanded its assets to several million shillings (Kahera, 1993a; 1993b). Another well publicized case is that of the Kiboga Women Sunflower Project, which booted out one of its leaders who was also the LC5 Women's Secretary, after discovering that she had diverted over USh. 21 million they had obtained as a loan from the Uganda Co-operative Bank (Kayizzi, 1994: 11).

One of the consequences of the fact that groups are based less on affective ties, on familial, clan, ethnic or other close ties, than in the past has been that new forms of accountability have had to be developed to replace or accompany older associational bases of trust and reciprocity. The National Association for Women's Organizations of Uganda (formerly the National Council of Women) has reported a significant rise in the number of women's groups seeking assistance in drafting constitutions, suggesting a greater need for establishing structures to guarantee accountability.[1] These trends fit patterns of proceduralism found in other parts of Africa, including the holding of regular elections, operating under constitutional guidelines, and having clear-cut mechanisms for changes in the administration (Chazan, 1982; Little, 1973).

Even most informal savings clubs in the four towns I surveyed had created mechanisms, including drawing up constitutions, to strengthen accountability. This was the case regardless of how much the members emphasized the importance of trust, and irrespective of the size of the club. For example, one Kampala savings club of 13 members had a chairperson, deputy chairperson, treasurer, secretary and deputy assistant who comprised the Executive Committee. They needed at least two present from the Executive Committee in order to make a decision, and at least four to approve the application of a new member, which had to be made in writing.

Namasuba Pinda Zone Women's Club in Kampala was another example of a typical informal (unregistered) group. It was made up of 16 members representing several ethnic groups, in addition to Protestants, Catholics and Muslims. The women varied in their levels of education, with occupations ranging from secretaries to housewives, traders, and teachers. The group, which was involved in drama and singing, handicrafts, farming and animal husbandry, was formed in 1986 by a woman who, according to the members, thought women should be self-sustaining and develop independently. The group had a chairperson, general secretary, information secretary, secretary for mobilization, sports secretary, head of the weaving section, project manager and treasurer. Elections were conducted annually by lining up behind the person preferred. In spite of the organization's informality, it was governed by several bylaws, which one member elaborated to us:

> Number one, a member must be trustworthy. Number two, well, if there is anything to be done and it involves large sums of money, we don't let an individual handle it alone. We choose three members to assist in carrying out the task. It is hard then for one person to waste the money. We keep our money with the treasurer and she banks it. There are another four members who sign checks if the money is to be released by the bank. Third, there is the discipline law, a woman must behave like a woman [not commit adultery, drink a lot, etc.]. If you are not behaving well, then you face the disciplinary committee for punishment. The final bylaw concerns dress: women must dress decently in our club.

Thus as associations become more plural and less tied to immediate kin, they move away from simply relying on social sanctions to seeking different forms of accountability that are more formalized, e.g., based on a constitution. Their plural make-up also makes these associations less likely to fall prey to the same kind of ethnically based favoritism that pervades public institutions, especially in the way appointments are made and resources distributed. This has had consequences beyond the issue of ascriptive ties. For example, in the 1980s many organizations of physically disabled people were monopolized by individuals who used them to enhance their own position. Today, members are demanding greater accountability, and throwing out corrupt leaders, while others have formed new groups because the old ones did not serve their purposes. One woman we interviewed, for example, left a physically handicapped women's group and joined the Disabled Women's Association of Mukono because, as she put it, "the leader was unfair and gained a lot from us. She took all the foreign trips and offered herself the aid meant for us."[2] This pattern has been repeated in countless instances.

Background to Kiribawa

The story of Kiribawa that follows is one of a major deception, the architect of which was a wealthy educated women who sought to create a women's organization solely for the purpose of obtaining personal funds. Every step of the way the women in the organization tried to create a genuine self-sustaining organization, but found themselves thwarted by her schemes. In the end, she fled the country with a lot of money and thus in monetary terms the women lost their battle. But they were left with some important lessons. Through their struggles they discovered their capacity to restructure the organization, to establish mechanisms of accountability, and to give the organization legitimacy. Above all they gained courage to deal with educated wealthier people who had initially intimidated them. In the course of the conflict between the members and the organization's founder and later between the members and a male co-ordinator, the women began to assert some other organizing principles that would allow them to operate in a more democratic and self-sustaining fashion.

Background to Kamuli

Kamuli District is situated in Busoga, in southeast Uganda. The district has a population of 485,214 according to the 1991 census. The main food crops include soybeans, maize, sorghum, cassava, sweet potatoes, finger millet and rice, and the main cash crops include cotton, coffee and sugarcane. According to the 1991 census, the district is populated predominantly by Basoga (76 percent) with lesser numbers of Iteso and Banyoro. Membership in the Church of Uganda (51 percent) is greatest, with a strong Catholic (28 percent) representation and a small Muslim population (12 percent). Women in Kamuli are primarily involved in agricultural production, with 94 percent of economically active women farming. Only 33 percent of the women are literate, compared with 49 percent of the men in Kamuli and 41 percent of women in Uganda more generally (Statistics Department, Kamuli District, 1992). In most cases, women were unable to inherit or own property and found many obstacles to their advancement. They were disadvantaged when compared with men in terms of opportunities for political leadership, economic advancement, and access to education.

Start of the Group

Sara Igoyola, the YWCA co-ordinator in Bugulete, had attended a function in Kamuli in May 1988 in honor of the then Vice-President Kisekka. There she was approached by a young man who told her that he knew a woman in Nairobi, a secretary to the donors working with the African Medical and Research Foundation,[3] who had assigned him to organize women in Kamuli. Igoyola inquired about the woman's ethnicity and nationality and was assured by the young man that she was a Musoga and a wealthy woman from Kamuli township. The woman, Miriam Bikumbi Ndimu (commonly referred to as "Milly"), came to Kamuli regularly and was building a house in town. The man persuaded Igoyola to form a group and gave her a list of names of individuals to include in the group. She told him that since he was a man, he would not be needed in the women's group.

Igoyola brought ten women together in 1989 to form a network called Kiribawa. Some of the women were willing to contribute their land for the activities of the new organization.[4] Many of the organizations that came to form Kiribawa had been in existence since the 1960s.[5] Igoyola wanted the organization to be formed to include a cross-section of women of differing social status, from illiterates to university graduates. The Kiribawa women got a banker to serve as treasurer, reasoning that donors would require considerable accountability and she would be able to provide this.

Rebecca Kadaga, the National Resistance Council women's representative for Kamuli, was on the co-ordinator's list and was brought in as a member *in absentia*. When contacted, she readily agreed to join, saying that her interest was to help create a model that could be an example to women living in other parts of the district. She belonged to many such organizations, symbolically rather than with the intention of participating actively. As she characterized her role: "I look at myself as somebody who links the women to opportunities because one of the problems we have in that district is lack of exposure. I mean, people are born in Kamuli, they grow up in Kamuli, they never go anywhere."[6] The members were grateful to have her join since she was a lawyer and this would save them the hassle of having to find a lawyer if necessary. The women did not attach any particular importance to the fact that she was a member of parliament.[7] "We never looked at that [her Council Member position] at all in that we never wanted to identify her with that. But rather that she was a woman from Kamuli district, her parents are here and we thought we could easily approach her," remarked Igoyola.

The founder, Milly, was different from the other Kamuli-based members. She impressed the group with her worldliness, knowledge of organizations elsewhere, and her donor contacts. When it came to electing a chairperson the choice of Milly was self-evident.[8] Milly was visibly pleased to take over the position of chair. When she visited the group, she briefed them on developments and wrote out minutes of the meetings in English. In 1990, Milly obtained their registration certificate from the NGO Board at the Ministry of Internal Affairs and the women celebrated with what one member said was a "grand party".

The group initially planned to expand their marketing activities and process food for sale. Members each contributed USh. 10,000 in addition to USh. 700 for stationery, documentation and organization-related transport; they pooled their resources and opened a USh. 40,000 bank account.[9] Initially, they decided to focus their activities on the strengths of the individual members. Kiribawa started a carpentry workshop on property owned by one of them and with the money they had in their joint bank account.

It was not long thereafter that it became evident that Milly had formed the network simply to lure donors. She advised them to use this carpentry project as bait to attract donors. Her intentions were also evident from the initial constitution, to which she added the handwritten clause: "The organization is to depend largely on donations from outside or inside Uganda."

Kiribawa approached the Uganda Women's Credit and Finance Trust and was successful in obtaining a loan of USh. 800,000. The women were under the impression that the funds were to go to the entire group, but instead USh. 200,000 went to the woman on whose property the carpentry workshop had been established and another woman allegedly received funds for a piggery. The rest of the funds disappeared into thin air. Sara Igoyola had started a weaving group, Kyebajja Tobona. When she asked Milly for USh. 100,000 to purchase supplies for her group, she was rejected. Suspicion began to mount in the organization because of the undemocratic way in which the funds were disbursed.[10]

A pattern of disappearing donor contributions began to emerge. The group was visited by a representative of the Japanese Small-Scale Grant Assistance Scheme who gave the group a check for $24,039 (USh. 23,318,000) for a tractor and trailer but the chairperson never informed the group about the money. Groups in Bujumba, Bukamira, Nawango and Butende did manage to get one bicycle per association as part of the Japanese donation. According to the man who was appointed co-ordinator by Milly, the funds for the tractor were placed in her personal account. Similarly, a representative of an American religious NGO, the Methodist Global Ministry, came to visit Traditional Birthing Assistants (TBAs) in the area. Kiribawa members took her around and showed her how traditional medicines were used in labor and in the event of birthing complications.[11] The women heard later that the Methodist Global Ministry had sent a check for $10,000 to the TBA members of Kiribawa. The check was never seen. According to Kadaga, this was when the women began to get suspicious since they could not trace the funds. Relations began to cool between the members and the chairperson around this time.[12]

Prayers, Lies and Videotapes

The women's patience was tried when the chairperson wanted to hold a breakfast prayer meeting of traditional birth attendants. She came with a Kenyan guest and they taught the women a song. Then Milly said that, if she went into a trance, they would know that the Holy Spirit had descended on her. She asked the women to close their eyes and hold their hands together in front of them while a man photographed them. She talked very little about delivery complications, but preached a lot, according to the women. She gave them sodas, bread and popcorn and videotaped the event. She also tried to give money to the RC5 leader and the District Administrator, but they refused to take it, saying that the money should be given to the women at the meeting.

The parallel between this event and a popular African joke was not lost on the women and was recounted by several of them in the context of the deception that occurred at the prayer meeting. As the joke goes, the European missionaries came and told the Africans to close their eyes and bow their heads and pray. When they finished praying the missionaries had taken their land away from them. One woman explained that, just like the missionaries, Milly, in feigned piety, made the women bow their heads. When they were finished praying they opened their eyes and discovered that she had taken their property from them. By the time the meeting ended the women were annoyed and complained that she was turning them into a worship group.[13]

Their suspicions were heightened when they witnessed the co-ordinator of the network giving her a letter he had collected at the post office and opened. Milly warned him sternly never to open Kiribawa mail, clearly suggesting to the women that she had something to hide. The women took the opportunity to ask her about the tractor and Milly said it had been purchased and was now being fixed.

About this time the women heard rumors that Milly had abandoned Kiribawa and started a second organization, hiring other workers, and had even established office premises. Twelve Kiribawa women traveled from Kamuli to the NGO board in Kampala to check the matter of registration. They found that, unbeknownst to them, their group had been registered under another name, Kiribawa RUWODEN, an acronym for Kiribawa Rural Women Development Network. In the registration application, the property of the organization, the fruit drier and the bicycle, were indicated as being held by "Kiribawa RWDN". This surprised and confused the women.

The parliamentary representative, Rebecca Kadaga, confirmed the women's suspicions. As vice-president, Igoyola convened a meeting of Kiribawa and invited Milly to attend. The members asked her why she had not convened a meeting to inform them about developments with the organization. They suspected that she had opened up offices of another organization, RUWODEN, with the UWCFT money but she told them that she had used her own money for this. Some members praised her "very good heart," but others wondered why she was using her own money on association activities. They wondered how she would account for it, but were afraid to ask her lest she asked them to contribute. When they inquired, she told them she had left Kiribawa and had founded RUWODEN.[14]

In creating this organization Kiribawa members discovered that she had used Kiribawa's name (albeit slightly altered), its registration, its finances, its letterhead and even a few of its members. One Kiribawa woman who did not know how to read, unknowingly signed all Milly's RUWODEN documents thinking they were Kiribawa documents. As it turned out, Milly had written to the Japanese donors and told them to send the check to RUWODEN, claiming that the organization had changed its name. The Japanese complied. Milly then told the women that there had been an error on the check and it had to be sent back to Japan, thereby causing a delay.[15] In fact, she had put the check in her own RUWODEN account.

Meanwhile, the co-ordinator informed Kadaga that Milly had an account in Barclay Bank's in Kampala from which she was drawing money. She had set this up ostensibly because Kamuli was too isolated to carry out foreign bank transactions. Milly later explained to Kadaga that she had not sought the approval of the membership in opening Kiribawa's account in her name because she was in too much of a hurry. The co-ordinator also explained to Kadaga how Milly had hurriedly drafted a constitution for Kiribawa and appointed a new board of directors without consulting anyone. She also penciled in an additional paragraph to the constitution, making herself the sole signatory of Kiribawa funds. "Where such accounts are opened the director general will be the *sole* signatory and the accounts here will be to act as the parent accounts for the one in Kamuli. Accounts can be opened in Jinja, Kampala, Nairobi, London and at all other areas where it is of value to operate them. In such cases, one signature will suffice."

Kadaga confronted Milly and told her the women wanted the money and the tractor back. She replied that she had already paid for the tractor but still needed USh. 600,000 for repairs. Kadaga offered to foot the USh. 600,000 repair bill on condition that Milly handed over the account to her and opened up a new account with RUWODEN signatures. Milly did not come to their planned meeting the next day, having apparently fled to Kenya. Kadaga went to the police but found that they were very slow in going after Milly. "I suspect that part of the money in the account was paid to them, because after some time they ran out of steam, so to speak," she said. Kadaga went to the Ministry of Foreign Affairs to investigate a course of action, but no action was taken.

From Kamuli to Interpol

The women went to Kadaga, who advised them to sue Milly. Since Milly had by this time left for Kenya, the women went to the District Administrator, who advised them to contact Interpol. Interpol caught Milly and returned her to Kamuli, where she reported to the police. Kadaga and the women went to the police. Milly, in her defense, argued that the money was not enough to buy a tractor after it had been changed into local currency. She produced a receipt for USh. 16,000,000 written out to Kiribawa for the purchase of what she claimed was an old tractor and a request for more money to cover inflation. The police advised the Kiribawa women not to press charges and send the woman to prison, otherwise the organization would get nothing.[16] And so Milly was released from police custody by the Officer in Charge of the Criminal Investigation Department. Most of the women suspected Milly had paid off someone in the police department to negotiate her release.

The women's suspicions increased. They took the receipt for the tractor to Akamba Company, which was supposed to be repairing the tractor and they said they knew nothing about a tractor. The women then discovered that the receipt had been forged. They also sought to verify Milly's claim that she had placed the organization's funds in a foreign exchange bureau in Jinja. The owners of the bureau said she had approached them but they had refused her their services because of the way she presented herself.[17] The women returned to Interpol, but by this time Milly had vanished.

European Development Fund and the Solar Fruit Drier

After Milly disappeared numerous problems remained to be sorted out. The European Community's European Development Fund Micro projects program[18] was beginning work in Kamuli and had approached Kadaga to obtain lists of groups for possible support. Through Kadaga they were introduced to Kiribawa. EDF staff visited Kiribawa three or four times, largely as a result of Milly's initiative. They gave the group a solar drier, a slab of chimney, and bags of cement. They erected it on Milly's own property, whereupon she "personalized" it, as one member explained.[19] Neither the EDF nor Milly ever consulted with the organization's members about locating it on Milly's property. The Kiribawa women then consulted with the Ministry of Justice and the NGO registrar at the Ministry of Foreign Affairs, only to find out that the drier was the property of RUWODEN.

After realizing what had happened, the members contacted an EDF representative, who promised to get the drier back to Kiribawa. The organization purchased a plot of land worth USh. 270,000 from the town council on which they built a structure to house the drier, which was subsequently moved there. Some of the Kiribawa members went for training on how to use the drier.[20]

However, their problems did not end there. With Milly out of the picture, the coordinator had effectively taken over leadership of the group and had created a new set of problems for the women. The members alleged that the co-ordinator was selling their dried fruits and pocketing the money since they saw little of their returns. This was confirmed by a VSO volunteer working with the group who went to Kampala and checked with their distributor, Fruits of the Nile company, and found that the co-ordinator had indeed been selling the fruit without compensating the women. The women themselves also complained to the company.

The co-ordinator sowed divisions among the women, used small bribes to keep them in line, appointed to the leadership several with whom he was involved personally, dispensed with leaders who challenged his authority, and sought out illiterate women as leaders whom he felt he could more easily dupe. It took the women two years to gain the courage to expel the co-ordinator, which finally occurred at a public meeting in April 1995. A new executive body was democratically elected in a general election.

Lessons Learned

Although the whole experience left the women demoralized, they persevered in trying to inject genuine accountability into the organization. In the process a number of important lessons were learned and incorporated into the revitalization of Kiribawa, which has been a slow process.

Leadership

One source of problems was the gap in educational background between Milly and the rest of the women and the ease with which she was able to take advantage of them because of this, for example, the Kiribawa woman who unknowingly signed papers for RUWODEN.[21] One suggestion that was made was to include younger educated women in their activities and rely on them to read the documents.

Rebecca Nsimbi, loan officer at UWCFT in Kampala who had worked with Kirib-awa, saw the case as an unusual one because the gap between Bikumbi and the women was so great.

> The rest of the groups, they are normally all the same, they have the same income, the same beliefs, the same understanding. But this group was unique in that the leadership was too much above the group members . . . There were a lot of women who couldn't even challenge the chair-person.

The co-ordinator confirmed this: "She [Milly] never liked the women, illiterate women, to make any decisions – she had the final word on all issues."

After Milly had left, the women had a similar problem with the co-ordinator, who blatantly manipulated the organization's leaders, whom he had deliberately selected because they were illiterate, while keeping the educated women away. Some women felt they would not be able to manage without him because he had connections in Kampala and spoke English. The distance from Kamuli to Kampala was also a problem. The members relied on Milly and the co-ordinator because they felt they were unable to travel the long distance to Kampala to take care of the busi-ness. However, the distance was more psychological than physical and had more to do with the isolation of rural life, lack of education and lack of experience.

As the women were forced to take their case to Interpol, the Ministry of Justice and the Ministry of Foreign Affairs and had to deal with the district administration, the police, the donors, the NGO Board, bankers and other authorities, they began to realize their own capabilities. The fact that the women did in the end confront their fears shows their determination and capacity to take on new challenges.

Several of them commented on the fact that women's groups should not be run by men, given the common tendency of men to try to lay claim to women's prop-erty, money and authority, and to manipulate women's feelings of inferiority to their own personal advantage. Right from the outset some of the women had opposed having a male co-ordinator, but Milly overrode their wishes.

Several women felt that it was critical to select leaders who were locally based with local reputations to maintain. The fact that Milly had an Ugandan identity (with the name Miriam Namudoli) and a Kenyan one (Milly Bikumbi) and was not well known by the residents meant that she had little at stake in terms of her repu-tation if things did not work out for her. Another member pointed out that "If you have people posted from elsewhere they may not have the interests of the people at heart. You need community staff to mobilize people." One consequence of not having a locally initiated project is that it results in poor design and weak prospects for success, according to a local NAWOU representative.

Internal Democratic Culture

The NAWOU co-ordinator, Irene Ereemye, explained that in Kiribawa most of the decisions were taken by a small clique and the rest of the membership was not con-sulted. If a member opposed an action taken by the clique, she would be ousted from the group by the Kiribawa co-ordinator. Thus no one ever got far enough to challenge the fact that there were no records, no accurate minutes, no accounts or other means of ensuring accountability.[22]

In many ways this lack of a democratic internal culture, which is typical of groups that experience difficulties, is not part of the more general associational culture of Kamuli. A 1991 survey of women's organizations in Kamuli found that in most groups (70 percent) the activities were decided on by all the members through consensus and that almost 80 percent of the members were satisfied with the content of their group's program. The criteria for leadership were based on the leaders' ability to communicate and mobilize. Leaders tended to have higher education than the membership (usually above the O level in secondary school). The women surveyed emphasized that they did not seek out elites as leaders, but rather individuals whom they could trust. Should the leader fail to carry out her duties, she could be replaced, and they felt there was no shortage of educated leaders to choose from (Kabukaire, 1992). Members felt they needed to participate in the selection of leaders. The Kiribawa leadership was not elected by a general assembly and thus only "the few who could read and write were given the upper hand," according to one woman.[23]

The women wrestled with other ways of ensuring greater accountability. In the aftermath of their problems with Milly, members felt they needed to be consulted on all major decisions, for example, where bank accounts are to be opened and who the signatories are, the organization's constitution, etc. They felt strongly that the members themselves needed to be involved in drawing up the constitution. One member said that donors should examine mechanisms of accountability before providing loans. She added that a mutually agreed constitution would help the women be "self-guarded". They needed to take pains to manage their organization seriously. A constitution, combined with seminars addressing the issue of accountability, would enhance the organizational capacity of the group and make it easier to monitor.[24] The Kiribawa constitution was in fact rewritten by the members in what they felt was a democratic process.

Others pointed out that by not requiring members to pay a membership fee, they were not giving them a sense of ownership of the network and a sense of belonging. The members had wanted to pay these fees and some had even inquired about where they should be making their contributions. All other women's organizations in Kamuli Parish paid fees (Kabukaire, 1992: 52). However, when a membership fee for Kiribawa was proposed, Milly forbade them from instituting such fees.[25]

Related to this was the observation that truly to claim a donor resource as their own, the women would first have to invest something themselves in the enterprise. Because of the way the organization was set up simply to gain funding, the women did not take greater responsibility to maintain accountability. Initially it was easy for Milly to get away with her stories because so much of the purpose of the organization at the outset centered around obtaining funds and she had taken most of the initiative to get them.[26]

Real Power Brokers in the Community

Already it appeared that one of the main forces that kept the women divided and supporting the co-ordinator was the male elders in the area. The elders exerted a very strong influence over the women, who were obligated to act in accordance with their wishes. At several junctures the women had agreed to expel the co-ordinator but then backed down because individual members would report being advised not to take such action by their husbands, uncles, and other male elders. Thus, getting rid of the co-ordinator also became a broader act of resistance against the key male authorities in the community.

One of the women leaders in Kamuli pointed out that one thing she had learned in the course of this struggle was the importance of getting the elders on their side prior to starting a new initiative that required political support in the community. The women, she felt, had underestimated the necessity of building alliances of this kind, and had found out too late when lack of such support left them divided. The elders were the real power brokers in the community, more so than the LCs, and convincing them that it was in their interests to back the women's initiatives was critical to the women's success.

Seeking Support from the Authorities

The women held the NRC women's representative for Kamuli, Rebecca Kadaga, responsible in part for the Kiribawa fiasco and demanded that she come and explain the situation. Because she was a lawyer, they felt that at several points she should have known some way of settling the matter. When she did not turn up at key meetings and was unable to stop the police from letting Milly go, suspicions were raised about her complicity with Milly.[27] It was not uncommon to hear comments like: "Rebecca Kadaga brought this thing [RUWODEN] to Kamuli. I am at war with her, Rebecca, because she brought it here. When she did, the set-up was a bit fishy."

A serious lack of trust emerged between the local women and the then NRC Women's Representative. Partly it had to do with the sense the women had that the representative treated them as though they had an inferiority complex. She did not treat them as equals. After Milly was out of the picture, the women continued to call on Kadaga on numerous occasions to come and explain the situation, but she failed to show up. By not coming, she left herself open to suspicion. They even appealed to her mother, who lived in the area and sympathized with the women, to put pressure on her daughter to come, suggesting that Kadaga's inaction could be politically costly. Indeed, it is possible that Kadaga's inaction had repercussions on her 1993 bid for a seat in the Constituent Assembly, which she lost when she decided to run in Buzaaya county rather than in her traditional base in Bugabula county, where Kiribawa had its base. Nevertheless, she was able to reclaim her political standing in the June 1996 parliamentary elections, winning a seat as a women's representative for Kamuli in spite of accusations by her opponent of vote buying (Caleb, 1996).

The District Administration and the Local Councils were also of little assistance in the women's problems with Milly and the co-ordinator. The women were concerned about involving the District authorities and the LCs too heavily in their problems because they feared that they would be asked for money. Several women pointed out that when they asked these LC or DA authorities for recommendations they were charged fees. They feared they would be charged if the authorities knew they had obtained financial assistance.

The District Administrator, however, said that NGOs should not only use the district offices for recommendations for loans, but should also report all incoming funds and give them copies of relevant correspondence. When problems emerge, if the District Administrator has not been informed about the funds, the local authorities claim they cannot be of assistance. "People think we want to handle their money but our interest is just to monitor," the District Administrator, Edward Masiga, stated.

The District administration, according to the NAWOU co-ordinator, was indifferent to the women. She explained: "I think if the district administration had put in a little bit of effort, this thing would have been rectified somewhere in 1992. These people were very slow and they did not bother because it concerned women."[28] In one instance, the women alleged that the Kiribawa co-ordinator had sold 120 bags of maize and beans picked from three communally owned gardens belonging to

Kiribawa. Some women saw the bags behind the DA's office awaiting transportation and went to complain to the DA's office but to no avail.

Donor Dependency

While the women learned many important lessons about leadership, about fostering a more democratic culture within their organizations, and about dealing with the authorities, some of the most important lessons of Kiribawa had to do with working with donors. One Kiribawa member blamed Milly Bikumbi and her associates for treating the women as though their only interest was in receiving outside assistance by any means. As she put it:

> Our women were told that unless you registered with Kiribawa you would get no assistance. Some of us open-minded people thought that one weakness is that every group that comes has to be opportunistic. Nothing then can come without plucking something. They wanted to get money from the outside. They had to have the group registered and so they had to bluff our semi-literate group so that they could benefit.[29]

Many of the problems associated with the donors had to do with the way in which grants and loans were disbursed. Several women felt that the donors relied too much on the leaders who came to their offices seeking support. The donors also relied on written project proposals and not sufficiently on talking to the parties involved. "Local people have a lot of vital information which would be helpful to individual donors. Donors depend too much on what is put down on paper," the NAWOU representative observed. One Kiribawa member put it bluntly:

> In my opinion the source of problems is that the donors may not know what we women think. They could be regarding Bikumbi [Milly] as a group member working for the group concerned and yet she is fighting for her own. . . . . . Milly, after receiving the things, had visitors, took pictures, made a video and she would go away leaving you just speculating. We thought she wanted to take pictures of members to give to them and yet she had other motives. So if those visitors [donors] want to help us, they ought always to talk to us and not only to the leaders. We would become familiar with them. . . . and we could even go and visit them when we have problems like now.[30]

In retrospect, the donors made obvious blunders that could have been avoided through closer consultation with the membership. For example, Dr. Madra, former director of the NGO Board, suggested that the Japanese donors were to blame for writing out a check without investigating why Milly wanted a check without the name of the organization on it. Others felt the EDF should not have given the solar drier without first ascertaining that there was a site for it. The EDF relies primarily on informants who visit the location and determine whether or not the recipient is creditworthy.[31] The women believed that many of these problems could have been avoided had the EDF representatives actually talked to the women in the group to find out how the finances were being handled. As one put it: "The literacy level is very low and is thus exploited by those who are educated. . . it is typical because always an educated woman is put as a torch to guide a group . . . These people think we are stupid and tell us to 'do this and that'."[32]

The women were also not prepared to manage the loans. They were not educated about bookkeeping, doing a needs assessment, or assessing their capacity to use the loan. For example, some used the funds for purposes they were not intended for (one bakery group ended up growing wheat and raising pigs and chickens). Even more common, although not such a problem in Kiribawa, is that sometimes poor women who have been given money for one purpose, for example, to assist in establishing a small business, may reason that they have other basic needs that are more pressing to attend to and use the loan accordingly.

In other instances, women would take the advice of men about which businesses to engage in after they had obtained a loan for a different purpose and the men were found to have taken commission for the advice or have been brought in as husbands, generally leading to a diversion of funds from their intended purposes.[33] Basically, as one put it, women might think that their problem was lack of capital but they might not be aware of the fact that money can bring problems.

Others point to the way the influx of donor funds has killed the voluntaristic spirit that used to prevail to a greater extent in women's clubs. One 90-year-old woman who had been a leader of women's organizations in Mpigi from her youth commented: "Nowadays people elect those with money to represent them but don't bother to see how they carry themselves in public. We used to work without money. We still need to work as volunteers."[34] The UWCFT representative, who impressed us as thoughtful and reflective about the role of her organization in Kiribawa, believed she should have disbursed the funds in smaller installments and monitored them each step of the way.

Yet another problem in Kamuli and elsewhere in Uganda is the lack of communication between donors working within the same district. In Kamuli alone the organizations disbursing funds include the Christian Children's Fund, the NAWOU, the EDF, the YWCA, Abesiga Mukama, the Uganda Community Based Association for Child Welfare more commonly known as UCOBAC, World Vision, Action Aid, Nabulizi, UWCFT, and many others. Lack of communication frequently results in duplication of effort and a repetition of mistakes. Had the EDF and UWCFT, for example, had greater contact, many mistakes could have been avoided in the Kiribawa case. This lack of co-ordination was later rectified through the formation of a NGO co-ordinating body in the district to encourage greater dialogue.

Individual Entrepreneurs versus Income-Generating Groups

One response to the Kiribawa fiasco was that some women began to focus on their own family businesses and felt safer applying for loans on their own rather than as a group. According to some members, this meant that they could be more sure of the gains from their efforts.[35] The ways in which donors tend to prioritize funding groups of women rather than individuals is also indicative of the way they attempt to define relations with recipients, especially women. For example, rarely are men asked to form groups to apply for funds, but women face this additional requirement, which may or may not be appropriate, when seeking loans. The same bias is apparent even in the terminology used to describe men and women entrepreneurs. Men who apply for business loans are referred to as "businessmen," while women are said to be involved simply in "income-generating projects," regardless of their scale or whether they are working individually or in a group.

I would caution against drawing the conclusion from Kiribawa that funding individuals is always more desirable than funding groups since what is advantageous is entirely context-specific. Nevertheless, the case study does raise some of the problems associated with the donor emphasis on organizations, although not the usual problems related to co-operative efforts that have to do with inefficiency, problems of managing and disciplining workers, and the costs of participatory decision-making structures (Brett, 1993: 288–91).

UWCFT, for example, prefers to fund groups even though the repayment rate of individuals is excellent, while groups have proved to have dismal repayment records. Nevertheless, it feels it can accomplish more in terms of training when it works with groups as opposed to individuals. Equipment can be shared, and marketing of goods produced by a group can be streamlined and combined. For women, who generally do not own property and land, collateral becomes a problem and it is easier to hold a group liable for repayment than an individual who does not have other resources. Moreover, group pressure for repayment of loans is great.[36] A more cynical way of putting the issue might suggest that from the point of view of the donors it sounds better to be funding a network like Kiribawa with a membership of 5,600 rather than one individual.

Nevertheless, there are pitfalls associated with funding groups in some contexts. Depending on the group's history and past record of working together, donor funds may end up going simply to those individuals who have invested most in the group because they have greater resources, as they did in the Kiribawa case with the carpentry business and the piggery.

Often the class dimensions of the group do not start out as antagonistic but they can become a source of friction, even when well-meaning wealthier women try to use women's groups to ameliorate economic differences between themselves and poorer women. While examples of opportunists like Milly in Kiribawa are rare, it is more common to find a slightly better-off, perhaps more educated or more resourceful woman trying to help women who are not doing as well. She may have access to resources through her husband or she may own some property of her own or be involved in a business. She may have better management and leadership skills and may be capable of initiating community activities. She wants to help and decides to do so by organizing a group so that she can help more than one individual. She may also find a way to make money of her own by helping women get started in a group income-generating project. In some cases, wealthier women who set out to help a local women's group with their own resources, skills and time, may understandably end up exerting excessive influence over the organization, thus resulting in tensions (Gariyo, 1994: 10). Other problems can arise as well.

I asked one such businesswoman in Kamuli who was involved in a brick-making project why she felt compelled to find ways of making the group project work for financially disadvantaged women. She commented: "When we work together, the weak can be helped by the strong. If you are a chairperson, as leader you can easily organize them." She noted that the size of the group was key to its success and that smaller groups did better. In her area of Bugulete, the most successful groups had been small with around 10 members, including Abeinani, one such group which was involved in dairy production, growing crops, brick-making and running a nursery. Abesiga Mukama carried out tree planting, wine-making, farming and operating a manual printing machine that made exercise books. And finally there was the Kyebaja Tobona Hand Loom project.

A similar problem between a group initiator and the members emerged in neighboring Bugiri district's Bukooli with less favorable results. Sarah Nakendo, the chairperson, started Bukooli Women's Oil Milling Project in 1988 along with nine active members. She was advised by a banker at Uganda Co-operative Bank Bugiri that there were women in the area who wanted to grow sunflowers but could not because there were no oil mills. So Nakendo applied for funding from

the EDF for an oil mill. She also helped 16 other women's groups to submit proposals for equipment as well. Two proposals were accepted, including hers and a
brick-making project.

Before being able to claim the mill, her group had to obtain land and construct
a building to house the mill. Her husband had a house he had failed to complete
so he allowed the group to use it. But the EDF said they feared her husband might
in the future hijack the project, so Nakendo approached the Town Board officials,
who gave her a plot. She paid half the price, and tried to get the rest of her group
to contribute equal shares of USh. 500,000 each, but they were unable to do so.
Eager to start building, Nakendo borrowed money from her husband and used
some of her own funds. She grew sunflowers on 70 acres but wanted to cultivate
at least 150 acres and was hoping to get the other group members to plant the
remaining acres.

In 1990 the LC5 secretary for women asked for all women in the area to be
brought into her organization. Similarly, the co-operative bank refused support
until she had a membership of at least 35 women. The UWCFT would not give support until the issue of the organization's size was resolved.

However, Nakendo was reluctant to bring more women into the group since they
were unable to contribute, although they wanted to benefit from the group. Even
of the core group of nine, only one woman had contributed USh. 80,000, another
USh. 10,000 and another USh. 15,000 while the rest had just contributed their physical labor. As Nakendo put it:

> I know I need them even in the provision of the raw materials. They are the ones who will plant
> the sunflowers and thus provide the seed for extracting oil. But they should pay. I have used all
> my savings to put up the building. In fact, for fear of binding them excessively, I have now
> resorted to asking for the loan as an individual.

As a consequence many women in the community resented Nakendo's not letting
them join the group and benefit from its gains.

Had this been a straightforward economic transaction, these problems would not
have emerged since Nakendo could simply have paid for the labor. But she wanted
to bring her fellow women along with her and give them some way to benefit from
her initiative. The various donors not only insisted that she apply through a group,
but differed in their stipulation on the numbers of women they believed should be
in the group. Few creative solutions have been found to resolve these kinds of
dilemmas that stem from inequality and mostly good intentions on the part of individual women. Even the purchase of unequal shares in a business with varying
returns may not be sufficient to satisfy both donors and recipients alike, but it might
be a step in the right direction.

Gender Inequalities and Donor Responsibility

Gender inequalities also pose particular challenges to, and constraints on, women's
associational activities in ways that require creative loan disbursment. Men respond
in different ways to the fact that donors give preferential treatment to women's
groups. Some, like Sarah Nakendo's husband who provided his wife with land and
a loan, are supportive of women's endeavors and see women's advancement as
integral to their own progress. Others, like the co-ordinator of Kiribawa, appear
sympathetic to women, but are in fact attempting to hijack women's organizations

for their own personal gain. Other men try to interfere in internal group decision-making, manipulating cultural beliefs of male dominance to influence decisions taken by a women's group.

The fact that men, not women, generally have access to land and property makes women especially vulnerable when applying for loans, since they rarely have sufficient collateral. This makes women more often than men dependent on groups to secure a loan because donors believe that the group as a whole has greater resources if things go wrong than one individual. Women generally do not have their own land on which to plant trees and cultivate crops of their own choosing and they may not have their own premises on which to carry out income-generating projects. By relying on their husband's land they subject themselves to the whims of their husband who might all of a sudden decide to claim the capital they have invested in their project, deciding to use the land or premises for another purpose or even to sell it.

Men may also feel threatened by women's groups out of jealousy, or competition, and because they believe women should not be so active outside the home since it detracts from their household duties. For example, in 1988, when Sara Igoyola opened the YWCA offices in Kamuli as a field organizer, she came across many women brick-makers working in isolation from one another on a family basis. Igoyola knew one of them, and asked her to convene the women brick-makers and their families. She met with them together with the chairperson of the Mothers' Union. They prayed together and afterwards Igoyola urged them to co-operate as a group and asked the men to allow the women to join together.

The men had their own organization, Buwanume Mukwaya Co-operative Group, which had become inactive according to the women. At the time Igoyola visited the women brick-makers in 1989, they decided to break away from Buwanume Mukwaya and form the Bugulete Women's Group because they felt that, as women, they had separate interests, or put more simply, the men's group, Buwanume Mukwaya Co-operative Group, refused to allow them to make bricks. The women wanted to make bricks and the men thought it was not worth it.[37]

The women's group had a profile not unlike that of others in the area. Bugulete had six active members out of a total of 10–15 members, many of whom were prevented from being active by their husbands. The group ranged in age from 18 to 60, and like other groups in Uganda, included a mixture of Catholics, Protestants and Muslims although all were Basoga. Their educational background ranged from second grade primary, which is what most members had attained, to the chairperson, who had reached her second year of secondary school. Even this small group had office bearers, including a chairperson, secretary, treasurer and two committee members who were selected mainly by consensus or, if necessary, by a show of hands. Leaders had two-year terms that were renewable. Members paid a USh. 1,500 fee and purchased shares of USh. 1,000 each with a five-share maximum.

One woman provided the land on which they could make bricks. They selected her as the chairperson. Igoyola continued to visit them and advise them. "They had told me about their lack of school fees for their children. So I advised them to stop hiring outsiders and instead hire their own children to do most of their work and give the money to their children," she explained. She also advised them to draw up rules about how much time they were to put in, how many bricks to make and how tasks would be divided, for example who was to prepare the clay and who was to lay the bricks. Most of the women farmed in the morning, made the bricks from 2 to 4 in the afternoon and then went home to do their chores and attend to other business.

Later in 1989, the UWCFT set up offices in Kamuli and Igoyola encouraged the women to apply for a loan. The whole idea was new to them and some at first feared that they would be imprisoned. Eight women applied for a loan and also obtained a market for their bricks at the district hospital, which was being built. The District Administrator agreed that the women's bricks should be used in building the hospital. The women worked hard and the group prospered to the point that even men brick-makers asked women to sell bricks for them to the hospital. But the District Administrator had stipulated that, unless all the women's bricks were sold, no one else could sell bricks to the hospital. In 1993 one member remarked that the members "can buy salt and paraffin at home, pay school fees for their children and when they get the loan, they use their own children who earn and buy exercise books for themselves. So Bugulete is doing well and we have almost finished paying the loan back."

Some men's groups became jealous of the women's group and started "decampaigning" them. They dropped the price of their bricks and even, though their quality was not as good as that of Bugulete, the hospital cancelled the account with the women's group and went over to the men. After that the women had to seek new markets and for a while their sales dropped. Thus, gender inequalities can easily sabotage efforts to provide assistance to women and need to be taken into account in the process of disbursing loans to women.

Conclusions

The Kiribawa case shows how women's associations need to stand aloof from pressures by politicians and other influential individuals to create organizations by top-down means in order to access funds. The creation of such an organization is frequently a set-up for failure since women may find themselves being used to accommodate someone's personal financial agenda. As the Kiribawa story shows, organizations hastily created for the purpose of seeking donor funds may not possess the necessary safeguards to ensure accountability and democratic process. They may not be established with the interests of the membership in mind because the impetus for formation comes from the top. The Kiribawa case also showed how the organization was susceptible to interference from the local male authorities, since it had not been formed with the interests of women at heart. From the co-ordinator to the male elders, the men posed numerous challenges to the women, preventing them from taking the organization in the direction they wanted to go. This brings us back to the centrality of associational autonomy and the necessity of autonomy not only from the state but also from donors and local power brokers.

Kiribawa's lack of accountability had disastrous consequences for the women who were drawn into the network. They lost time, money, and trust in each other as a result of the manipulations of Milly and the co-ordinator. Without mechanisms of accountability, there was little incentive for donors to be accountable to the recipients, to learn what the recipients' needs and potential difficulties might be, and to listen to the applicants themselves and not only the leadership. These measures protect not only the donors but the intended recipients themselves.

Notes

1. Interview with Florence Nekyon, Kampala, 21 May 1993.
2. Interview, JK, Olivia Kazibwe, Kampala, 8 February 1993.
3. In fact Bikumbi had been fired from AMREF for embezzlement.
4. Interview with Sarah Igoyola, Kamuli, 21 June 1993.
5. *ibid.*
6. Interview with Hon. Rebecca Kadaga, Kampala, 24 April 1993.
7. Rebecca Kadaga later become deputy speaker of the House.
8. Interview with Feibe Waigumbulizi, Kamuli, 21 June 1993.
9. *ibid.*
10. Interviews with Rebecca Nsimbi, Kampala, 12 July 1993; Sarah Igoyola, Kamuli, 21 June 1993; Feibe Waigumbulizi, Kamuli, 21 June 1993.
11. Over 90 percent of births in Kamuli occur in the home with the assistance of a TBA. Until 1993 Kamuli had no hospital and all clinics were private. Through their involvement in Kiribawa, TBAs received training and equipment. They charged a modest fee to the birthing mothers and 5 percent of the fee was returned to the organization (Kabukaire, 1992).
12. Interviews with Feibe Waigumbulizi, Kamuli, 21 June 1993; Moses Kyewalyanga, Kampala, 24 June 1993; Rebecca Nsimbi, Kampala, 12 July 1993; Monica Nayenga, Kamuli, 8 June 1993.
13. Interview with Feibe Waigumbulizi, Kamuli, 21 June 1993.
14. Interview with Sarah Igoyola, Kamuli, 21 June 1993.
15. Interview with Hon. Rebecca Kadaga, Kampala, 24 April 1993.
16. Interviews with Feibe Waigumbulizi, Kamuli, 21 June 1993; Moses Kyewalyanga, Kampala, 24 June 1993.
17. Interviews with Moses Kyewalyanga, Kampala, 24 June 1993; Feibe Waigumbulizi, Kamuli, 21 June 1993.
18. EDF is one of the major funders of small enterprises in Uganda. Other funders include the Canadian Fund, Dutch embassy, NOVIB, British Commission, American Embassy, Oxfam and the German Small Enterprises Development Foundation.
19. Interview with Grace Nanangwe, Kamuli, 21 June 1993.
20. Interview with Feibe Waigumbulizi, Kamuli, 21 June 1993.
21. *ibid.*
22. Interview with Irene Ereemye Balikuddembe, Kamuli, 7 July 1995, Kamuli.
23. Interview with Irene Ereemye Balikuddembe, Kamuli, 21 June 1993.
24. Interview with Grace Nanangwe, Kamuli, 21 June 1993.
25. Interviews with Irene Ereemye Balikuddembe, Kamuli, 21 June 1993 and Margaret Kazungu, Kamuli, 21 June 1993.
26. Interviews with Moses Kyewalyanga, Kampala, 24 June 1993 and Feibe Waigumbulizi, Kamuli, 21 June 1993.
27. Interview with Irene Ereemye Balikuddembe, Kamuli, 21 June 1993.
28. Interview with Irene Ereemye Balikuddembe, Kamuli, 7 July 1995.
29. Interview with Grace Nanangwe, Kamuli, 21 June 1993.
30. Interview with Sarah Igoyola, Kamuli, 21 June 1993.
31. Interview with Steven Hinde, Kampala, 14 June 1993.
32. Interview with Irene Ereemye Balikuddembe, Kamuli, 21 June 1993.
33. *ibid.*
34. Interview, RK, Deborah Kiwanuka, Bunamwaya, Mpigi, 11 May 1992.
35. Interviews, Kabali, Bugulete, Kamuli, 15 April 1993.
36. Interview with Rebecca Nsimbi, Kampala, 12 July 1993.
37. Interview, RM, A. Kirongero, Bugulete, Kamuli, 16 April 1993.

11

Gender
& Institutional Analysis

The Limits
of Political Representation

Having fought for and maintained a significant amount of associational autonomy, women's organizations in Uganda nevertheless faced important institutional obstacles that stood in the way of achieving their goals. While this study has adopted an institutional approach to the study of politics, it has gone beyond the general discussions of institutional development to show that expanding female representation is insufficient to serve women's interests adequately as long as institutions are configured in ways that continue to suppress the expression of those interests.

Much of the current preoccupation in institutional analysis of political change has to do with state-society relations: creating strong, responsive, effective representative/democratic institutions. Some have explored the effects of institutional change (Putnam, 1993); conditions for the development of democratic institutions (Rueschemeyer et al., 1992); how strong societies work against the development of strong states (Migdal, 1988); the effects of irrational and politically motivated government policy on economic efficiency (Bates, 1981); strengthening governance structures in the public realm (Hyden, 1992; Joseph, 1990); and strengthening local governance (Wunsch and Olowu, 1992). Others have focused on crafting or designing institutions that are viable and meet the needs of members or beneficiaries (Chambers, 1995; Leonard, 1991; Ostrom, 1992). While these and other institutional studies have provided many excellent insights into the processes of political change, many have not been as good at asking whether institutional changes benefit all members of society in the same way. Few disaggregate communities, constituencies or civil society in their analysis of the effects of institutional change, nor do they explore the macro-micro or local-national linkages. This is especially problematic where institutions consistently work to exclude particular groups within society on the basis of gender, class, age, ethnicity, race, and other such factors.

Much of the discussion of African civil society has treated it as a unified entity in relation to the state, reflecting this kind of elision of difference. Even though there is general recognition that civil society is not homogeneous or cohesive (Lewis, 1992; 36; Fatton, 1995), the debates around civil society in Africa frequently end up treating it as one entity when civil society is poised "against the state," "engaging the state," "existing between the household and the state," being "framed by the state" or defined in relation to the state. While it is important to be able to generalize about civil society, there are often assumptions of homogeneity and unity of purpose built into such unqualified characterizations.

Many institutional approaches, especially those looking at civil society, have not sufficiently appreciated the differential impact of rule changes on women and men, i.e., the gendered nature of institutions. As seen in the Ugandan case, women have had to deal with institutional constraints that have marginalized them politically and have tended to restrict their mobilization to independent, small, invisible, informal, gender-based associations at the local level.

Institutions set the parameters within which people co-operate, compete, and interact with one another. They are a set of rules and moral norms that constrain individual behavior through compliance procedures (North, 1989; 201–2). North divides institutions into three categories, including constitutional rules (fundamental written or oral rules that establish the terms and conditions of governance); operating rules or institutional arrangements (laws, regulations, associations and contracts); and normative behavioral codes, which legitimize the constitutional order and operating rules (Davis and North, 1971; Feeny, 1988, 171–6; Oakerson, 1988). Governance refers to the setting of rules and their application and enforcement (Feeny, 1988: 172).

Elinor Ostrom argues that viable governance structures involve rules that specify process, not content, and that the rules should be transparent and visible. Political development, according to Ostrom, should expand society's capacity to identify and mobilize resources in tackling problems, rather than concentrate it. Opportunity structures in a free society allow people greater latitude in pursuing their aspirations: to engage in collective teamwork to solve problems; to undertake communal efforts to provide essential public services; to have access to law-abiding governing institutions; and to share in the outcomes of joint efforts. This freedom requires constitutionally guaranteed rules of association (Ostrom, 1992: 62–4).

Decentralization has been seen as critical in providing resources to further these goals identified by Ostrom. However, many of the discussions of new institutional analysis have not adequately accounted for the *politics* of decentralization and an analysis of how existing power dynamics determine *who* can best take advantage of decentralization. All too often those who have traditionally wielded power at the local level, like wealthier elders, continue to do so, while marginalized groups like women continue to face obstacles to their increased participation. Ugandan women, emboldened by a regime that seeks to promote their leadership, have begun to demand greater voice at both local and national levels, but are finding their best efforts undermined by powerful entrenched interests.

Thus, if new institutions are intended to provide for the common good, yet work only to the advantage of some sectors of society, and consistently against the interests of others (namely, against a particular class, ethnic group, or in the case of this book, women), one is compelled to ask, good governance for *whom?* Granted, individuals cannot always have all their interests represented. Nevertheless a pattern of discrimination against one group of people based on their identity reveals limitations to institutional capacity to identify and pursue aspirations, to engage in collective action, to access government and enjoy the benefits of political and economic development. In the case of women, their initial resource endowment, their lack of access to political and economic power, and cultural constraints all too often hamper their ability to contribute to a communal undertaking of the kind referred to by Ostrom.

Aili Mari Tripp
Rethinking "Community"

This study also challenges an implicit view of "community" that has gained almost mythic proportions in debates on political and economic development institutions. In contrast to the earlier modernization thinking that regarded community as a manifestation of all that was considered traditional, parochial, backward and resistant to progress, today many scholars, multilateral and bilateral donors, private foundations, and NGOs almost uniformly see "community" as a critical locus of devolved power and meaningful participation. As scholars and practitioners of development became increasingly disillusioned with heavily centralized state-directed development models, they turned to community and non-governmental organizations as alternatives to corrupt, inefficient, centralized states that had little use for local participatory input. "Community" is seen as a repository of knowledge of local conditions and best management strategies for local resources. However, all too often, this view of "community" virtually assumes a homogeneous, egalitarian, ahistoric community, sharing common values, interests and goals. In this sense the idea of "community" has almost become universalized (Agrawal, 1997).

The case studies in this book have shown how problematic such idealized assumptions become in the context of real communities. Politics in the locales discussed in this book was animated by gender, class, ethnic, religious, age, and other societal divisions. Community tensions were far from static as they evolved over time out of specific historical circumstances. For example, the kind of local gender-based conflicts described in this book were not apparent ten years earlier in the same communities, having arisen in the context of the current regime. As the story of the conflict in Kitumba Health Clinic (Chapter 7) unfolded, it became evident that the community was in conflict because members did *not* share a common vision or similar interests. Moreover, one group of community women was challenging the status quo and norms that had historically kept women out of community leadership. Under these circumstances the very notion of "community" itself had become contested.

Many of the struggles described in this book show how difficult it is for women to be allowed to contribute to community development, let alone lead an initiative, even within an environment that is relatively supportive of women's mobilization. Women and women's organizations relate to the state very differently from men. The case studies reveal how women do not have the same access to and control of local government resources as men. They find it difficult to be heard in local council meetings and even more difficult to claim leadership in these institutions. Yet these are the same councils which, by most accounts, have brought a semblance of accountability to local government, involve considerable devolution of power, and are important institutions for local decision-making (Brett, 1994; 67–8; Ottemoeller, 1998; Tideman, 1994). Gains for the "community" may not be translated as easily into gains for women. When women do attempt to redefine community interests in broader terms, they often encounter resistance.

As new contenders for power and resources, women face serious limitations that have to do with the way in which deeply ingrained ideologies, pre-existing patterns of authority, and long-standing interests seek to maintain the status quo and keep political power in the hands of male elders. The problems of representation that women face even under such "favorable" conditions demonstrate how their difficulties in politics exceed simply issues of interest politics. Women experience the political system as one that is from the outset hostile to their involvement. Popular attitudes suggest that women's "proper" place is still in the home rather than in politics. Women often lack resources to run for office. Other more mundane constraints include the holding of lengthy meetings at hours that make it difficult for mothers with young children to attend. Thus, decentralization needs to be seen in its broader political, social and historical context without assuming that a change in the rules of the game is automatically a change in the rules for all the players. For these reasons, it is instructive to look at the consequences of decentralization for women at the local level, using the case studies in the last four chapters as a basis for this analysis.

This book has sought to grapple with the capacity of women to assert autonomy from the state amidst enormous pressures for incorporation both at the national level (Chapter 4) and the local level. The case studies examined different ways in which women used their organizational autonomy at the community level to change and challenge institutions that were working against their greater participation in economic and political life. The studies showed women fighting for new access to resources, which in the instance of Kitumba and Mutai (Jinja) involved health clinics. They also fought to protect resources they had lost, including control of market space in Kiyembe (Kampala) and a sunflower mill and financial resources in Kamuli. In addition, the book looked at a struggle involving women's attempts to have a voice in how community resources were to be used in the case of the Kawaala infrastructural rehabilitation project in Kampala. These struggles were more than efforts to bring about greater female representation. They were about changing the institutions themselves in ways that would make political action and public involvement more accessible to women by incorporating women's interests, needs, values, and political objectives.

Women and Institutional Change

The case of Uganda is an important one, because it brings to light a dilemma in institutional change: new players – namely women – are brought into the game, but the rules, structures, and practices continue to promote existing political and social interests, making it difficult for women to realize their interests. Instead of being able to rewrite the rules to meet their own or more gender-balanced aspirations, women are told to play along under the pre-existing rules which have entrenched particular male interests, usually of relatively wealthier elders and patrons. Moreover, women may learn how to make the pre-existing rules work for them and even to win at times. But rarely can they make the rules or make the rules work on their own terms. Usually it is at the expense of disguising their own particular and distinct needs (Goetz, 1995: 2–3).

This inability to tailor the rules to meet women's needs helps explain why even though the local council (LC) system has given reserved seats to women in Uganda, they have a difficult time asserting their interests in these structures. Kabukaire found in her 1992 study of women's mobilization in Kamuli that, despite the government's new openness to the formation of associations, women in this district felt they had not benefited from the government's policies vis-à-vis women. One of the lessons of her study was that it was not sufficient simply to have women's grassroots organizations, but women also needed meaningful mechanisms to translate this participation into policy-making within the state (Kabukaire, 1992: 60, 70). My case studies also bear this out.

In the four case studies in this book, where women challenged the pre-existing dominant interests and sought to change the rules of the game, they met with fierce resistance. In each case study, the women were unable to use the local council system to advance their interests and had to resort to their own gender-specific forms of mobilization.

This book shows how institutional changes in the real world are rarely tidy and complete. They rely on individuals with varying degrees of commitment to change or who may be opposed to the changes since they undermine their own personal interests. There may even be conflicts between various interest groups over the changes that undermine their effectiveness. Sometimes ideological beliefs can override incentive structures that would appear to encourage individuals to abide by a new set of rules. For example, in one of the case studies in which a women's group sought to start a health clinic, one of the sub-county leaders in the local council said to me: "I agree with the [government's] emphasis on women to go ahead. I am happy that women are now struggling with men. I am happy about women coming up. In fact, I am very happy about it."[1] Yet when it came to approving funds for the women's clinic he could not conceive of allowing the women in question to lead in this community endeavor because women had not participated in this way in the past. Even though the clinic would have improved the welfare of the community and would have made his leadership look good, he remained the most vocal opponent of the women's project, opposing the women simply by virtue of who they were, i.e., poor women. This sub-county leader saw no contradiction between his support for women's emancipation and his opposition to the clinic because he was not opposed to women's advancement in other areas, for instance in education. It is this kind of analysis of ideologies, perceptions, cultural beliefs and, ultimately, the politics of institutional change, that needs greater attention. As Apter put it in his critique of new institutionalism, it is necessary to pay more attention to the inner workings of social and political life from the perspective of those who engage in it (1991: 476). Institutional change involves more than simply a technical solution to a problem of incentive structures.

Thus, this book has shown how the marginalization of women into gender-specific organizations operating outside the local council system has paradoxically positioned women in a way that has often made it easier for them to challenge patronage and other institutions that serve to exclude women from politics. There are many marginalized groups that share the same characteristics of exclusion that women face (for example, immigrants, refugees and displaced people, the poorest members of society, youth). However, this book has shown that women are positioned somewhat differently in that they tend to have long-standing experiences in organization and to this day possess considerable associational capacities that allow them to challenge authorities and institutional arrangements that work to their detriment. Moreover, the informality, smallness and flexibility of local women's organizations have often provided them with the necessary autonomy of decision-making with which to challenge the status quo.

The rest of this chapter draws out the commonalities between the case studies and shows how they fit broader patterns of women's political behavior in Uganda. It explores the impediments to women's representation and participation at the local and national levels. Finally, it discusses the importance of autonomy and the increase in women's political activity at the local level, drawing on the case studies and paralleling the discussion in Chapter 4 of the national level.

Changing Forms of Women's Mobilization in Local Politics

There are certainly many examples in the past of women attempting to bring about institutional change (such as marriage law reform in the 1960s) or resisting institutional change (such as opposing taxation laws levied on women by local government in the 1960s). Nevertheless, the new levels of women's mobilization in Uganda since 1986 have made acts of gender-based collective resistance, especially at the local level, even more likely.

Emboldened by women's new visibility in politics, many local women felt encouraged to try to stake their claim for various resources and to defend their claims on resources in a way that was not so evident in past decades. For example, older residents in Kitumba village (Jinja) and in the sub-county could not remember women ever trying to control a community project in the past nor had they previously sought to start health clinics before Ekikwenza Omubi and the Mutai women's group came on the scene. Likewise, although women had sold in large numbers in Kampala markets, there had not been a market the size of Kiyembe exclusively run by women in recent memory. Similarly, the fact that one of the biggest hurdles in the large Kiribawa organization was getting over the fear of having to deal with distributors, donors, government departments, and other authorities suggests that in general the women's exposure to the world outside Kamuli was limited prior to the Kiribawa struggle. The fact that they were only beginning to realize that they would have to work with the elders and win them over was indicative of their inexperience in struggling for resources, suggesting that such struggles were infrequent in the past.

It would be an exaggeration to claim that the whole country has been rocked by a myriad of such small conflicts involving women. Nevertheless, they are common enough to attract attention. Moreover, it was also fairly easy to find other conflicts that paralleled the case studies even down to the finer details of the case. The story of the Kyeijanga Women's Group in Rukungiri is almost identical to the case study of Kiribawa in Kamuli (Chapter 10). Similarly, in Mbale, women's organizations belonging to the National Council of Women mounted a campaign in 1993 against the NRC women's representative because three years earlier she had appropriated a vehicle for her personal use that had been given to the women's groups by President Museveni.[2] The women's struggle to establish a health clinic in Kitumba bears an uncanny resemblance to the struggle in Mutai, a village located only 20 miles away (Chapter 7). The Hon. Joyce Mpanga related to me yet another story with identical proportions from her own constituency of Mubende.

The fact that the case studies were so easy to identify even without significant press coverage suggests that these kinds of conflicts are not rarities. I stumbled on to the Kawaala conflict in the course of conducting the survey when we found women respondents in this area unusually reluctant to respond to our questionnaires. Further inquiries in the community uncovered the fact that the residents erroneously believed we had been sent by the LCs and Kampala City Council to collect information about them. After clarifying our intentions, it was not difficult to uncover the role of women in the conflict and to learn what was at stake for them in resisting the authorities.

Similarly, various colleagues at the Makerere Institute for Social Research and the Women's Studies Department informed me of the other conflicts, which I investigated even though I had not initially sought to pursue such struggles as part of my research design. Nevertheless, it became immediately evident that these conflicts brought to the surface key societal tensions and, in particular, institutional constraints on women in a way that could not be captured through the survey or in in-depth interviews.

Clearly, not all conflicts take the form of full-blown organized struggles as seen in the case studies. More often, women's mobilization takes the form of everyday resistance to gender-based exclusions from political, economic and social life, but also to corruption, patronage and intimidation. Just to give one example, in Bukosa, Kamuli, during the elections to the 1993 Constituent Assembly, women heckled, booed and jeered the Member of Parliament, Dan Balawa, when he stopped to greet a group of them attending a meeting of their farming association, Agaiwamu. They said his presence was not welcome since they had not invited him to their meeting and accused him of intimidating voters and buying the support of the LCs. They were especially annoyed with him for telling them not to vote for his opponent because she was a woman.[3]

Women have seized on the regime's rhetoric of liberating women to fight for their rights inside the home as well. They have not only made the personal political, but they have also made the political personal. Daily individual acts of resistance easily escape notice. In one dramatic incident of this kind, a recently widowed woman, Noerina Mubiru, of Mubende, was confronted by her husband's relatives one Sunday morning before she left for church. They had come to grab her possessions, a customary practice in some patrilineal Ugandan societies. The ten relatives presented the widow with a list of things they intended to take back to their village. In desperation, she stripped naked and walked into the living room where the relatives had assembled. She stood in front of them, pointing to her private parts, saying: "You see, this was one of the properties my late husband loved most." She patted her behind and said, "This was the second item he loved. If anybody wants to remove his property, he will have to start with these and then I can show you the rest." The father-in-law fainted and the relatives fled as fast as they could.[4] These kinds of daily acts of resistance rarely receive recognition in the media or by scholars, and yet they represent an important way in which women have translated arguments of the women's movement into their personal lives, attempting to resist the oppressions that affect them most directly as individuals.

Finally, not all assertions of resistance have been focused on specific abuses or incidents of exclusion. Some local struggles have been directed at more general problems. One of the most dramatic examples of this kind of resistance was mounted by women in Gulu district in an April 1989 march for peace. Over 1,500 women marched through the streets of Gulu for five hours protesting at the "bitterness of the war". They wore their mourning dresses, tied scarves round their heads, and carried baskets as they wept, chanted funeral songs and blew funeral horns. Almost the whole town was weeping. Many of the women were half naked, lifting up their breasts to demonstrate the most vehement of curses against wrongdoers. They women carried placards in Luo that read: "We need peace"; "Anger escalates into trouble and death" (Kiniga kelo peko kitoo); "We do not condone the shooting/ambushing of cars" (Pe wamito celo motoka); "Sleeping in the bush has brought sickness and death" (Buto ilum okelo twoo kitoo). The women took their demands to the office of the Minister of State for the Pacification of the North, Betty Bigombe. Their protest was aimed at highlighting the ways in which women have borne the brunt of suffering as a result of the continued unrest in the North. It was as much an expression of resistance to the actions of their own menfolk as against the NRA.[5]

Constraints on Women's Involvement in Local-Level Politics

One of the consequences of associational autonomy is that women have increasingly sought to influence local politics through the LC system by running for office, but also, as in the four case studies, by trying to resist council actions that did not serve their interests as women. Even though the women in all cases generally supported the LC system, they were acutely aware that the councils could easily be manipulated by certain powerful men to their disadvantage with little recourse on their part. So powerful and tight-knit was the institutional apparatus they were up against that they were unable, even as an independent organization, to challenge it successfully. In all cases, although to a lesser degree in the Kiribawa case, the LCs were an active obstacle to their efforts. In Kitumba, the LC3 that controlled the funds for health in the area became the main opponent of the women's cause and sought to hijack their project. In Kawaala, the LCs at all levels refused to take the residents' viewpoints into consideration. In Kamuli, the LCs were not helpful in assisting the women in dealing with the criminal activities of the leader of the Kiribawa organization who had absconded with their funds.

In the case of Kiyembe market local male vendors aligned themselves with the Town Clerk, established themselves as local council market leaders and drove half the women market sellers off their stalls. The women fought to regain them, but to no avail. In Kiyembe, as in the other three conflicts discussed in this book, the main stumbling block for the women was the fact that those in control of the LCs were unwilling to allow women leaders any say when it came to asserting women's collective interests.

Limitations of LC System for Women

Problems of Representation

Many analysts of the LC system see it as enhancing community co-operation, political participation, political accountability and the resolution of social conflict (Nsibambi, 1990: 279). Certainly the system represents an enormous advance for local participation, when compared with previous regimes. But the conflicts in the case studies also reveal some of the weaknesses of the system and, in particular, the difficulty of including all members of the community, especially women. Nsibambi has argued that "LCs are more likely to capture the commitment of the people when they portray themselves as organs of the people and not as organs of the government". But being organs of the people does not guarantee that they will or even can represent *all* people. They will tend to represent primarily those who hold LC positions of power, who, in the case of Kitumba, for example, were middle-income male businessmen, farmers and civil servants.

Thus, one measure of the capacity of local councils to fulfill their participatory role would be the extent to which they can effectively represent competing interests within society. But critics have questioned how representative LCs can be for various sectors of society like women. The one position out of nine reserved for the Women's Secretary at the village level is elected by all citizens in the zone and therefore may not necessarily be representative of the interests of the majority of women in the area, especially where men still make up the bulk of the voters. Some have found instances where male villagers deliberately promoted younger more timid women, "a pretty face", or women who they knew would not challenge male authority, during campaigns for the women's secretary post. In the 1989 elections Patrick Kiggundu (1992) reported that the criteria given for electing women ranged from who would be the most controllable and who was the most beautiful, to who had the longest curriculum vitae.[6]

By the time one reaches the elections for the women's seat on the District Resistance Council and the women's NRC seat, the electorate is overwhelmingly male, meaning that women's representatives in such indirect elections are, as Mamdani (1993) puts it, "less likely to function as representatives of women at large, and more likely to function as representatives of NRM to women at large". Moreover, since the women are elected overwhelmingly by men, it can not be guaranteed that they will see themselves as advocates of women's concerns.

Makara Sabiti's (1992) study of LCs in Luwero, Kalangala, Kampala, Kasese, Arua, Bushenyi, Soroti, Tororo, Jinja and Lira found that many men supported their wives becoming LC1 chairpersons. However, those who opposed their wives did so giving the following reasons: "Because she will not perform her home duties efficiently", "she would think she is greater than me," "she would not be able to serve two masters – myself and the LCs," "I do not want to be under a woman," "I should be the leader since I am the husband."

Ingvild Burkey in her 1991 study of the Resistance Council system, found similar constraints on women, where husbands prevented wives from attending meetings, joining women's groups or getting involved in other political activities. Some women who were elected as Women's Secretaries were forced by their husbands to resign. Others veered away from participation because it was not worth the domestic quarrels that would inevitably ensue (1991: 24).

The net effect of these kinds of constraints on women's representation in the local councils has two dimensions: First, because for social and cultural reasons women rarely run for office, the chances of elected women officials having a collective impact are slim. Women's associations, like those in the case studies, which sought changes in the community found themselves blocked at every step of the way, in part because they did not have forceful allies (male or female) within the LC system. Secondly, those women in LC positions, especially the Women's Secretary position, have been elected primarily by men, who dominate the electorate. Frequently, although not always, the LC secretaries are not the most active women in the community, especially where male leaders have decided deliberately to select a woman who will toe their line.

Burkey (1991: 23) found in her study of the LCs in Luwero, Rakai, Mbale, and Nebbi that the Women's Secretary usually played a low-key, subordinate role in the committee, especially at the village and parish levels. She was responsible for providing refreshments and entertainment for official guests, while the male LC officials did the talking. Similarly, Expedit Ddungu found in Luwero that hardly any of the Women's Secretaries kept files, they had no defined targets of action, they regarded their job as more of an opportunity to sit on the LC executive, they maintained virtually no correspondence with the Women's Secretariat of NRM Secretariat and did not know or care why they were secretary for women.[7] Other observers suggested that the main task of the Women's Secretary boiled down to resolving domestic disputes and hosting visitors (Mwesigwa, 1994).

In three of the case studies in this book, the LC Women's Secretary worked actively against the women who were challenging dominant interests. In the fourth study of Kiyembe market, one of the women fighting to reclaim market space officially held the LC woman's seat but refused to claim it lest she be thought to be siding with the male vendors in control of the LC. The Kitumba women were not able to enlist the support of the LC1 secretary for women. "The LC1 Women's Secretary was helpful at the beginning but she began to fear the men and has advised us to leave the project for the men to take over so we can start on something else," explained the group's leader, Gertrude Kisozi.[8] Even the Women's Secretary in the neighboring village of Buwekula was unsupportive of Kisozi because she was antagonizing the men. The secretary felt women needed to stay in men's good graces in order to have access to land. She said she did not support the men in the LC who opposed the women, but reasoned that "If they refuse to give us land, where will we women go?"

In Kawaala, the Women's Secretary was one of the most outspoken supporters of the Kampala City Council (KCC) project and labeled the women who opposed the project as "anti-governmental". Her aggressive campaigns against opponents of the project made many women even more convinced that they had to organize informally rather than openly. Her complicity with the KCC project made women distrustful of her. The informal women's network wanted to become a formal organization, but could not do so without her permission. "How can you start a group? They may get you and say that you are convening anti-government meetings. But the LC meetings have not been convening. So how do residents convene?" said one woman opponent of the project.

While there are many dynamic women's secretaries, the aforementioned tendencies persist and contrast noticeably with the quality of leadership found in women's independent organizations. Even women who are active and outspoken in their own organization find their hands tied when they enter the LC system, as Kabukaire discovered in her study of Kamuli. These women councillors reported that they became reluctant to challenge the government, spending much of their time explaining why the government encouraged the formation of women's groups, and justifying the government's lack of assistance to women's organizations (Kabukaire, 1992: 60, 70).

But when it came to male representatives, women in all four case studies found it even more difficult to secure support within the local councils. Part of this lack of support has to do with the fact that the LCs were controlled by dominant interests that were not sympathetic to women's causes. In the case of Kiyembe the LCs were controlled by young male vendors who had previously been employed by the women or had been hawkers who sold goods that they carried around with them. In Kitumba the wealthier elders in the community worked through the LC to exert their influence, while in Kiribawa they held sway by indirectly imposing their views. In Kawaala, many of the most vocal councillors supporting the KCC were unemployed men who did not have deep roots in the community and had less to lose by going against the residents. What is interesting in all these cases is how permeable the LC system was to different kinds of male interests and yet how thoroughly impenetrable it was to women who wanted to exert influence. In three of the cases, the LCs became the key mechanism through which women's interests were suppressed.

Clearly community elders were the most important players in the Kiribawa and Kitumba cases, irrespective of the LC's influence. In Kiribawa the women learned over the years the importance of building alliances with these powerful elders and winning them over to their side. The elders' word could sway community opinions decisively and they were therefore key to the success or failure of the women's struggle. In the case of Kitumba the elders were leading businessmen, headmasters of primary and secondary schools, church leaders, landowners and men of royal descent. They were influential in the LC system at various levels and were able to pose serious challenges to the women as new contenders for influence.

In many cases there was a class dimension to the representation that also worked to the women's disadvantage. Those in leadership tended to be better situated, which worked further against the women. As Kisozi pointed out in the Kitumba struggle:

> Having more women on the LC executive would have helped us. But in our village, we elect somebody because they are rich. For example, they cannot elect me because they want somebody from a well-built home irrespective of her intelligence, thinking that because of her well-built home she will have understanding.[9]

Problems of Participation

Beyond problems of representation, women have mixed experiences participating in the LC structure. Around one-third of the women surveyed reported participating in all or most of the LC meetings, with Kampala having the highest participation rates for women. Men participated roughly twice as much as women. There were still many constraints on women, making it difficult for them to attend and speak up at LC meetings. Tabitha Mulyampiti found in rural Pallisa that women's attendance at the LC1 level made up slightly less than half the participants. The reasons given for not attending had in large measure to do with opposition from spouses. Those women who attended meetings tended to remain silent. Those who spoke up at the LC1 meetings attended by Mulyampiti did not have their concerns addressed. A Pallisa LC Women's Secretary said that at one time all the men in her council decided that women should not bother attending the meetings since it interrupted their domestic chores and that men should attend on their behalf. The woman LC representative was able to argue and convince them that women should attend the meetings and felt that her opinion was listened to. However, the fact that these men even contemplated such an action is evidence that they were not yet at a point where they could take the participation of women for granted. One Pallisa LC women's secretary commented:

> We are still neglected by our fellow committee members, the men. Many of them still think that a woman's husband should decide on her behalf. The committee is also dominated by men and usually when I talk, they think – before I can complete my sentence – that I am trying to oppose them. They have even stopped calling me to the meetings (Mulyampiti, 1994).

The fact that men had more time to meet than women served as yet another crucial constraint on women who were active in the LC system. Women leaders complained that men scheduled meetings at times inconvenient for women who had to attend to domestic chores, and came late to meetings, which meant they ended late, posing additional problems for women with children and suspicious husbands.

Another aspect of the problem of participation has to do with the direction of command, which remains ambiguous in spite of the intention of devolving power from the center down to the grassroots level. The council members[10] are to serve as a communication channel between the government and the people in the area.[11] They are at once representatives of the local residents and at the same time are required to answer to government. Wilberforce Sserwaniko, who had been the dissident LC2 chairman in Kawaala (Chapter 9), found himself torn: "You are caught in between, so who do you serve first?" he asked. "How can I be on the side of the government on an issue that I feel is oppressive. This is my constituency."[12]

The Kawaala struggle points to other limits of the LC system. It was indicative of the excessive influence of the City Council in micromanaging the affairs of people at the local level while ignoring their complaints and input. As one woman in the neighborhood pointed out: "We say they are KCC's LC officials because when we went to court to obtain the injunction against KCC, the LCs did not support us."[13] In the end, leaders like Sserwaniko had to abandon the local councils and form the independent Abalaka Committee and the informal women's network because they could no longer adequately represent the interests of their residents through the council system. The Kawaala case points to the difficulty of challenging abuses of the system from within and the necessity of autonomous mobilization.

And finally, it shows the local councils' limited capacity to entertain genuine initiatives from the grassroots. The local councils and the City Council continued throughout the struggle to ignore the demands of the Kawaala residents, consistently refused to communicate with them over key developments, misinformed the residents, went ahead with ready-made plans in defiance of a court injunction, and attempted to bypass the leadership. When that failed, the KCC tried to create its own committees, meddled in the LC elections, and tried to influence electoral outcomes. It intimidated residents physically and ignored their alternative proposals.

At the heart of the struggle was the issue of participation. The LC system was unable to accommodate any departure from plans that had been made by higher authorities. The residents emphasized that they wanted the project to be a joint undertaking in which all participating partners – the KCC, the LCs, the residents and the World Bank – were on an equal footing at every stage. As the beneficiaries of the project, they should not be "targets" of development, but rather full participants in the planning, execution, monitoring and evaluation of such a project. As we heard time and again in interviews with opponents of the project, they were not against upgrading the infrastructure in the community, but they were against the way it was carried out. As citizens, they had the right to be informed about what was going on, but, more importantly, they wanted to be included in the decision-making process. Had the residents' plan been incorporated, the project focus would have inevitably changed from one of evicting residents from their plots to one of upgrading their homes and existing roads, and extending electricity and water services rather than duplicating existing structures and provisions.

By participating in the project, paying for leases, paying the taxes for services provided, improving their homes and carrying out self-help projects, the residents felt they would have a greater stake in developing the area. The KCC would be obligated to come up with funding for the social and physical infrastructure. The pledge to pay taxes in exchange for services is a significant gesture in a country that has one of the highest tax default rates in Africa and where there is little social pressure to pay, especially among the self-employed, who make up the majority of the residents in an area like Kawaala.

But as this struggle showed, the residents were forced to abandon the LC system and rely on alternative forms of organization to articulate their demands because the LC became more of a recipient of City Council directives than a voice for residents.

Joyce Muhire and the Local Councils

It is perhaps instructive to examine one woman's experience working both within and outside the LC system in the context of the Kawaala conflict (see Chapter 9). Women had been especially influential and articulate in both informal and public debates about the fate of Kawaala. So influential was this opposition that one woman in particular, Joyce Muhire, was singled out by KCC project director Ruth Kijjambu as the "ringleader" of the movement against the project.[14]

A one-time primary school teacher, Muhire stopped teaching when she gave birth to a child with cerebral palsy. She continued to farm, however. Her husband, who had been headmaster of Makerere Secondary School, died in a plane crash a few years later, leaving her with full responsibility for their eight children, five of whom were young. To make ends meet, she started a poultry project of 200 chickens; bought a 10-seater minibus taxi that made trips to Kiboga, Hoima and Mbarara; and travelled regularly to the Middle East to purchase goods, such as electrical appliances, which she sold in Uganda. She was also planning to start a boutique. Joyce was proud of the fact that she paid her taxes "as they should be paid" and kept her books in order. She was training her teenage daughter to take over her businesses one day. After her husband died, she felt cut off from people and decided she "did not want to be in a cocoon". She became active in organizing women in the community and served as leader of the local Mothers' Union chapter for three years. She also became a member of the Kawaala Housing Project Steering Committee.

Having gained the confidence and respect of her fellow women, she ran in the February 1992 LC elections and won a seat on the LC2 executive committee as Women's Secretary. She was one of the most vocal women opponents of the Kawaala project, and the KCC intervened in the LC elections to prevent her being elected to the LC3 committee, which forms the LC5 council. An official from the KCC (name withheld) said she was troublesome, anti-developmental and that people should not risk putting her on the committee. She was hurt by this deliberate attempt to keep her out of office, but said, "I forgave him and don't hold a grudge." She suspected the Town Clerk was behind this move to edge her out of a higher position. As the struggle over the project unfolded, women like Muhire who tried to take public stands and organize against the project became targets of fierce intimidation and public humiliation by the City Council and the local leaders.

As LC2 Women's Secretary, she visited women's organizations, encouraged women to form new associations, organized education around family planning and AIDS, and encouraged women to be financially self-reliant. She also helped men and women settle domestic disputes, especially where women could not persuade their husbands to let them carry out income-generating projects or attend association meetings. Kawaala women expected a lot from her as a resourceful articulate educated person, and made many demands on her time.

Gradually Joyce Muhire saw her responsibilities as a single mother beginning to conflict with her LC2 work, especially when she frequently found herself returning home from meetings at midnight. Many of the men councillors did not "keep time". She would frequently go to a meeting scheduled for 5:30 pm which did not start until 8 pm because councillors would arrive late. She explained: "Where is the time for children? I wanted to give my love to my children. Why should I be in public when my children are suffering?" Overworked and her health failing, Muhire resigned from her post nine months later, but remained on the project Steering Committee. Later, the actions of the City Council regarding the project compelled her return to politics. In 1994 she was elected to the position of vice-chairperson of LC1 Kawaala II.

Even though the accusations against Muhire and her opposition to the Kawaala project mounted, she continued her campaign against the KCC. She continued to network and visit women in the community, mostly to keep them informed about the project, to see how they were doing and to comfort and support those who were afraid for their future. But because of her vocal position against the project, she no longer received invitations to KCC meetings regarding the project. Muhire saw it as her obligation to speak up. Many of her women neighbors were illiterate and were uncomfortable dealing with LCs, District Administrators, Town Clerks, and the KCC. "Some timid women cannot face the DA and others. For us who can, we went and faced them."

Muhire organized an informal women's network to oppose the project. Those who were active in this network were mainly widowed, divorced or married to men who sympathized with their resistance to the project. Even Muhire, whose husband had been supportive of her endeavors, found that it was not until she was a widow that she became active in mobilizing women. But in many households where the woman opposed the project and the husband was indifferent or supported it, women could do very little. In these cases, when women voiced their opposition to the project they were both physically and verbally abused by their husbands and by the authorities. Moreover, many husbands would not let their wives go to meetings. One Kawaala woman who had been involved in a 13-member women's credit and savings group for four years said that secrecy was a paramount condition of membership. At the age of 47, she had 8 children, farmed one acre of her husband's inherited plot (kibanja) and sold charcoal for a living. Her husband was employed as a driver at a downtown bank. "Ours is a savings club known only to people who save there. For some of us, even our husbands are ignorant about it. You know, some men do not want women to earn money."[15]

While, on the one hand, Muhire was able to mobilize women through a quiet campaign to influence public opinion in an unobtrusive way that was socially acceptable, she saw that these tactics also tended to relegate women unnecessarily to the background. By organizing more openly they would have risked being called "anti-government", which was a label women were not willing to accept because, as many pointed out to me, they did not consider themselves against the government. To organize in more visible fora many women would have had to confront their husbands publicly which was also too great a danger. In spite of these many constraints, the fact that women found ways to involve themselves in this protest had a tangible impact on its outcome.

Continuing Constraints on Women in National Politics

In spite of the enormous strides made by the women's movement in Uganda, women continue to face considerable obstacles to their full political participation even at the national level where women have greater public visibility. Here the obstacles to women's full participation in the political arena are daunting. For example, female parliamentary candidates face a myriad of cultural prohibitions on political activity not experienced by their male counterparts. Married women politicians often find it difficult to find a constituency to run in: if they run in the constituency where they were born, they are told to go to the constituency where they are married. When they run in their husband's constituency they are told: "You came here to marry not to rule."

Women candidates have to project an image of absolute devotion to their husbands and families and of being good wives and mothers to a degree not required of men. As Christine Lalobo, a 1996 parliamentary aspirant, put it:

If you are intending to become a woman candidate to contest a seat, you can't put on shorts or
trousers and go to the village. You have to wear a *gomezi* [formal women's attire], you have to
look like a good girl, mommy's good girl. For the men, they can go away and drink their *malwa*
[alcoholic drink] in the most unexpected places, they can run around with so many women and
nobody bothers. It's patriarchal.[16]

In media interviews, journalists tend to be preoccupied with questions of
whether the woman is properly married and how many children she has. Winnie
Byanyima spent much of her time during her Constituent Assembly election campaign having to defend her single status. Divorcees face similar suspicions (Kalebbo,
1996a; Mwesigwa, 1994). If a woman receives assistance from a man in a campaign,
almost inevitably some kind of implication will be drawn of a sexual favor, which
usually has no basis in reality (Kasente, 1994). This makes it difficult for women to
enter into male political networks, but it also makes it difficult for men to support
female candidates.

In general, women candidates running in the 1996 elections faced greater public
ridicule than men, were labeled "unfeminine" and some even risked their marriages
and public discrediting by their husbands. In one case a husband even nominated
his wife's rival (Mugambe, 1996). Female politicians are attacked for being elitist and
building their careers at the expense of rural women, while male candidates are
never berated for this (Ofwono-Opondo, 1993).[17]

Women are also disadvantaged because they often lack the necessary resources
to run. Candidates are expected to distribute beer, give small gifts and make contributions to fund-raising events, funerals, weddings and community projects. Since
women are usually not incumbents, they also are at a disadvantage. Incumbents
have had a chance to use their positions to build roads, bridges, hospitals, clinics,
schools and churches and in this way win votes.[18] Kasente (1994) found that in the
1993 Constituent Assembly race, some officials in charge of running the elections
were openly hostile to the women candidates.

Even in parliament where there are many vocal women representatives, women
experience discrimination. Loi Kageni Kiryapawo, NRC representative for Tororo,
put it bluntly:

In our case, when we are supposed to represent the interests of women, we are always shut
down by the men. In most cases their reaction is negative and since they make up the majority
of the House, their decisions are always paramount.[19]

One key consequence of having a critical mass of women in a body like the Constituent Assembly was that it began to change the political culture of the discourse.
One of the most dramatic incidents reflecting this change occurred when a male
member of the assembly accused women of not being straightforward and always
meaning something different from what they actually said. He was asked to withdraw his remark, but in doing so said that women were like frogs, who when peer-
ing out of a coffee cup see the sky and think they have seen all there is to see. At this
point, one of the delegates, Miria Matembe, walked out of the assembly in protest
and all but five of the women delegates followed her. They did not return until an
apology was made and the remarks retracted. No such insults were repeated during the remainder of the sessions and women came to be treated with greater
respect in the discussions.[20]

Women's Seats in Parliament

One limit on democratic participation is the method by which holders of the
women's seats in parliament are selected. The subject was debated vigorously in the

Constituent Assembly without resolution. It has divided women members of parliament and differences over the issue have been split across party lines.

In 1991 the legislature known as the National Resistance Council (NRC) had 270 members, 149 of whom were elected by an electoral college made up of LC2 committees. Nineteen members were selected by LC2 committees in Kampala City and 13 municipalities. One woman was elected from each of the 34 districts by the LC5 council. Seats were reserved for 38 historical members who formed the original NRC during the guerrilla war, 20 presidential nominees and 10 members of the NRA Council. The National Executive Committee (NEC), made up of 82 members, was the standing committee giving political direction to the NRC and monitoring government performance. Its members included the historical members, 10 presidential nominees, and representatives elected by the NRC from each of the districts (Burkey, 1991: 9).[21] As a result of the fact that so many representatives were either appointed or elected through an electoral college, many NRC representatives felt only minimally accountable to their constituents, and in many districts residents rarely saw them in order to confront them with questions of why they remained without clean water, feeder roads, clinics, etc. Moreover, unlike the LCs there was no right of recall of NRC members (Burkey, 1991: 39).

This lack of accountability in parliament changed with the 1996 elections, when constituents started voting directly for their representatives rather than relying on electoral colleges. For example, the residents of Kawaala (Chapter 9) were able to affect the outcome of the 1996 parliamentary elections in their division by ousting a candidate who had backed the Kampala City Council rehabilitation plan and bringing in a candidate who had opposed it.

According to the 1996 Parliamentary Elections Statute, women running for the reserved seats were to be elected by the LC2 and LC3 councillors in the district and all members of the parish and sub-county women's councils rather than by universal suffrage like other members of parliament.[22] However, unlike other parliamentarians, the women are elected on a district-wide basis, rather than in their own county, which means that their constituency is often ten or more times larger than that of other MPs (Kalebbo, 1996a: 16).

Most women running for election prefer the electoral college because they find that the district, which on average has 7,000 voters, is too large an area in which to campaign. Some suggest that an electoral college is easier to influence than an electorate, while others are convinced that the electoral college is made up of people who are better educated and informed than the general public and less easily bought off with little gifts of salt and sugar. They claim that the majority of people do not know what is best for them (Byanyima, 1996: 15). Women already face financial limits, domestic demands, cultural biases and therefore, according to this argument, should not be subjected to the broader electorate's vote (Kwesiga, 1996b: 26).

Others point out that the electoral college privileges wealthier women who have an easier time swaying a smaller electoral college. This lends itself more easily to corruption and the buying of votes (Waliggo, 1996a: 4). In the case of Kamuli (Chapter 10), the Bugabula women were able to affect the outcome of the direct election for the women's representative for the Constituent Assembly, forcing a well-known candidate, Rebecca Kadaga, to run in a neighboring constituency where she lost. However, when Kadaga ran for NRC women's representative for Kamuli in 1996, a vote that is district-wide and conducted through the electoral college, the women who had voted her out in the previous election had no impact.

Critics like John Waliggo argue that being elected by the whole district would give women representatives greater legitimacy and the capacity to challenge the Member of the Parliament in his/her constituency if necessary. By representing the entire district rather than a county, the candidate's authority would be enhanced to an even greater extent. In fact some male MPs fear universal suffrage for the very reason that they fear the women candidates might "interfere" with their constituency.

Another critic of the electoral college system for women's representatives, Winnie Byanyima, argues that the women MPs cannot legitimately speak on behalf of their constituents if they only represent the views of the electoral college (Byanyima, 1996: 15). She has adopted a third view, arguing that women should be elected by all the women in the district and not by the men. This would give them a mandate to make sure that laws take women into account and promote equal opportunity for all. Moreover, as Joy Kwesiga points out, other special groups like soldiers, people with disabilities, workers and young people all elect their own representatives while women's parliamentary representatives are elected by male and female LC representatives at the village, parish and sub-county levels, with the implication that women are too politically immature to vote for themselves (Kwesiga, 1996b: 27).

By having the Local Councils elect the women representatives, Kwesiga points out, it is not clear who these women parliamentarians are representing. If they claim to represent the entire district, they are often told that they represent only the women, yet they are elected by both men and women.

Multi-partyists raise yet another objection. They feel that the electoral colleges are primarily made up of NRM supporters and therefore would vote primarily for NRM representatives, even in areas made up mainly of multi-party supporters. They claim that the electoral college is especially susceptible to corrupt methods of persuasion. When the electoral bill was passed, the UPC-DP opposition coalition, the Inter-Party Co-operation, challenged the method of election in an IPC press release, which stated: "In a country where the local councils have become appendages and organs of the NRM, it would appear as if all the Women District Parliamentarians have been truly given to the NRM with both hands."

The other problem is that the electoral college is susceptible to corruption because it is made up of a relatively small number of people who can easily be bribed and influenced. Some men were careful to keep out candidates who explicitly took up women's causes.[23] Because there are only a few women on the electoral college, it is easy for the more powerful men to subject them to intimidation because it is not difficult to figure out how they voted. Thus, women who were not wealthy also found themselves at a disadvantage (Okurut, 1995).

One woman who ran unsuccessfully in the elections for women's representative came out of the experience disillusioned with politics, not simply because she lost but because of the extent of the corruption and the way people had come to expect politicians to hand out money. As she put it to me in a personal correspondence: "I did not give money since that is not my style of doing things. Secondly, I was determined to use the little money I had for printing posters and traveling only" (personal communication, 10 January 1997). This candidate, like so many, found the political culture of elections not only an affront to their sensibilities but also an impediment to women, who do not have such resources to begin with. Her experience was not unusual and was reiterated time and again. According to the Kisoro women's representative, Jeninah Ntabgoba, the problem had intensified. She had not used any money when running in the 1989 elections but found that in the 1996 elections money played a major role, especially in contests for general seats.[24] Another woman who lost by a small margin in the contest for the women's seat in Mbale, Irene Nafuna Muloni, argued, as did the candidate above, that "because there is so much poverty, people, especially the rural poor, were carried away by as little as 500/= for their votes."[25] Similarly, a former parliamentarian and Constituent Assembly delegate who ran in Mukono pointed out that "everybody was expected to use money. I did not have that much money to buy my way through. In any case, I was against it. I had done my best, serving as a woman representative. Little did I know that merit alone was not enough."[26]

Importance of Autonomous Mobilization at the Local Level

One of the most important factors facilitating women's new challenges in Uganda more generally but also in these four communities was the fact that women's organizations served as an independent autonomous base from which to operate. Ekikwenza Omubi (Chapter 7) in Kitumba was a base from which the women lobbied the local councils. The gains they made would not have been possible had they been forced to rely simply on the LC system itself. The LC1 Women's Secretary, cowed by the male elders, would not support Ekikwenza Omubi nor did the women receive support from the Women's Secretaries even at the LC5 level.

Similarly, in Kiyembe it would have been inconceivable to try to work through the LC1, which was the very institution that had been hijacked by the male vendors to launch what the men called "a war against the women". In Kawaala the LCs were under the influence of the Kampala City Council and failed to defend the interests of the community, leaving individuals no alternative but to form an independent Residents Committee and the women's informal group to oppose the World Bank rehabilitation project. In all three cases, the fact that women had their own organizations meant that they were ideally situated to pose challenges to the LCs in a way that would not have been possible had they not had these independent fora at their disposal.

Autonomous forms of association have had enormous ramifications for women in Uganda. They have meant that women could mobilize in organizational forms of their own choosing, with leaders and a membership that were not constrained by external political considerations. Greater autonomy permitted women to challenge the status quo and hold leaders accountable in ways that were not always possible during the Obote and Amin regimes. It has also meant that they could define their own interests and set their own agendas. Moreover, they could set bolder agendas than in the past, challenging gender subordination more directly. Women's organizations were no longer means of buying easy votes for politicians, but rather now had the potential to influence electoral outcomes.

Women found they could build broadly based organizations without external interference. For example, Kitumba's Ekikwenza Omubi had emerged out of the Protestant Mothers' Union, but, due to the nature of its activities, expanded to include a broad section of women in the community, including not only Protestants but also Catholics and Muslims. This permitted them autonomy from the local church, which sided with the LC leaders in opposing the women's group. However, it earned them the label of being supporters of the "Democratic Party," which is associated with Catholics, even though the majority of members of the organization remained Protestant. Similarly, the Kiyembe Co-operative represented a mix of religions and ethnicities with strong political leanings towards the NRM, but it also incurred the false label of "UPC supporters" in an attempt to discredit them. Kiribawa and Ekikwenza Omubi are both located in Busoga, which has been wracked by a long-standing and sometimes violent conflict between supporters and opponents of Bishop Cyprian Bamwoze. The women's organizations in both locations remained unaffected by the turmoil and have kept their differences over these issues out of the activities of their organization.

In Kitumba, the secret alliance between the wealthier women and the members of Ekikwenza Omubi also suggests ways in which gender interests were consciously used to override class differences in defiance of efforts by male elders to divide the women along class lines. In Kitumba, the women sought a form of organization that allowed poor and illiterate women a voice in community matters. This was distinct from the practices of the LCs in the area, who tended to favor the views of the wealthier members of the community and the elders. The male elders resisted the women's efforts to control the health clinic, while the organization's leader, Gertrude Kisozi, argued that women were "socially oppressed by men" and "not allowed to embark on any venture". The male leaders opposed the women simply because they were women, poor and uneducated. These patterns of mobilization follow more general trends in women's mobilization in the country (documented in Chapter 5) that have sought to build organizations at both the national and local levels along broad lines.

However, autonomy has also meant that women have been able to resist external pressures to mobilize in particular ways. Iganga District's Bukooli Women's Oil Milling Project, for example, had to resist numerous attempts by outsiders to determine the size of the organization (Chapter 10). The LC 5 Women's Secretary wanted the nine-member organization to include all the women in Bukooli, while a co-operative bank demanded a membership of 35 before it would grant them a loan. Even the Uganda Women's Credit and Finance Trust would not fund them until the issue of size was resolved. Nevertheless, the group insisted that to broaden it to members who would not be able to afford to buy shares would only lead to the dissolution of the group, which was already being strained by such difficulties.

Autonomy meant that the women could pursue specific goals which implicitly challenged the status quo. For example, the Kiyembe co-operative wanted a separate organization for market women, because it wanted to establish a different set of norms and standards for the behavior of vendors that minimized the divisive aspects of competition and emphasized co-operative strategies. But even in establishing their rules for market behavior, the women saw themselves as challenging some of the more unsavory practices of male vendors by trying to set a good example through their organization. As one woman put it:

> Men can be troublesome. When they see things going well for women they want to take over the whole thing. In my experience, businesswomen want to do things in a proper way, they don't want to grab things that are not theirs. Women are straight. I don't know, maybe men have more problems and needs and tend to want to get money as quickly as possible. Men may withdraw funds from the bank without telling the group, which women I know would not do.[26]

In the case of Kawaala, both men and women in the Residents' Committee drew up an alternative proposal to that of the Kampala City Council for rehabilitating the infrastructure of the area. As intended beneficiaries of the project, they wanted to participate directly in the decision-making regarding the project, but they also offered their own labor and co-operation as part of their contribution to its success.

They wanted all plans to take account of the realities of the way in which people, especially women, seek a livelihood, rather than simply following a blueprint for an idealized version of what Kampala should look like.

Thus, associational autonomy was critical in allowing the women's organizations the freedom to pursue new norms that challenged older less participatory forms of mobilization. Autonomy allowed them to broaden the membership of their organizations, to resist external donor and LC pressure to adopt various policies that in the long run would undermine their organizational viability, and to create new or alternative models of community participation.

Women's Challenges to Clientelism in Local Councils

In each case study, the women's struggles involved chipping away at a patronage network that had been the basis of women's exclusion from power and resources. In Kiyembe and Kitumba the patronage network was based within the LC system itself. In Kawaala, the network was between the various levels of LC councils and the Kampala City Council. In Kamuli, there was collusion and indifference at all levels from the LCs to the District Administration to the police, making it difficult to discern the contours of the network(s).

One of the main obstacles the women faced in their fight for accountability was the weak security environment that was subject to the manipulations of various authorities. In Kiribawa, the chairperson of the organization who had absconded with its funds was able to bribe the police to let her go, never to be seen again. In Kitumba, although the District Security Officer supported the women's group, the District Medical Officer was able to persuade some police to try to arrest the group's leader without an arrest warrant. They failed in this attempt only because she was aware of her rights as a citizen.

All but one conflict involved physical violence and intimidation on the part of the LC authorities. With the tacit approval if not complicity of the LCs, the male vendors at Kiyembe beat up the women and threatened to kill and imprison them. The co-operative leader deliberately walked slowly to her office after the organization's secretary had been beaten up, in a display of cool defiance and refusal to be intimidated by the young men. In Kawaala, security forces and police were used consistently to intimidate residents at meetings, sometimes leading to outbreaks of violence. Women protested quietly by not cleaning their compounds and by not burning their garbage. In Kitumba, the LC officials were said to have threatened Kisozi and her supporters with physical intimidation to the point that she was compelled to declare that she did not fear death, if it came to it.

The weak legal environment also worked against the women in all four cases. In Kawaala, the KCC went ahead with the project after the court issued a six-month injunction against the Council requiring that it stop threatening and harassing the residents and stop the evictions, which were not part of the initial terms of the project. This blatant disregard for the law by a governmental body left the residents with little recourse, forcing them physically to evict the KCC engineers and technicians from their area. Similarly, even though the residents complained to the central government representative and other authorities about specific cases of massive bribery in residents' dealings with the LCs, no legal action was taken. Again, the residents were left with little recourse in the face of such abuse other than to vote the LC leaders out of office, which they did.

All of these breaches of the law and abuses of the security forces contributed to a situation of instability and a feeling that the individuals in the government were above the law, that the law could be circumvented if need be by the authorities, and that the police and other security forces did not serve the public interest, but rather were in the control of individuals in the government.

The Kawaala leaders found it difficult to demand accountability within the council system. It was common practice in Kawaala as elsewhere in Kampala that councillors would illegally demand payment from residents asking for assistance. Nevertheless, the councillors are not paid and there is almost an expectation that they will use their positions to "eat". As Sserwaniko put it, "it has now become a culture to demand some money from whoever is looking for help. No one will take the councillors to court. The government regards the LCs as an extension of itself." The tightness of the patronage network makes it almost impenetrable for challengers to these arrangements. Attempts in the various cases to bring the issues of corruption to the attention of higher authorities fell on deaf ears. The fact that the issues extended beyond the rehabilitation project became evident after the World Bank withdrew from Kawaala and the LC5 and central government representative continued to try to isolate the individuals who had been trying to expose the corruption. They created three sub-divisions in what had once been a single sub-division, leaving the opposition leaders with only one-third of their constituency.

The abuses were so widespread that, in the view of the opponents of the project, were one to begin exposing a few breaches of the law within the LC system, it would be difficult to know where to stop. Nevertheless, when the Abataka Committee told the government that the LCs had illegally collected USh. 650,000 from residents applying for leases, the government refused to act, saying it did not have sufficient evidence. Instead, it sought to isolate the Abataka Committee by creating sub-divisions in Kawaala II and thereby minimizing the influence of the dissident leaders.

Part of the problem has to do with the fact that even well-intentioned LCs find they are expected to organize and attend meetings, adjudicate local conflicts, attend workshops and other public functions, mobilize people for a variety of functions, collect local taxes, and sign documents with no monetary compensation. Most have to dip into their own resources to conduct much of this business and the work of the LC1 chairman may also take time away from his own business or agricultural work (Burkey, 1991: 28–30).

It is interesting to note that, in all of the cases, not once did the women consider a strategy of trying to "buy" the allegiance of the authorities, even though such manipulations were evident all around them. Part of this inclination came from their long experience of being disadvantaged by such tactics. It also arose, at least in the Kiyembe case, from an impetus to change the political culture of local politics by establishing new standards and by setting an example for the LCs through their own thoroughly scrupulous behavior. But perhaps the most compelling reason for their disdain for patronage had to do with their intense desire to win their battles, which might have been further jeopardized had rumors surfaced that they were circumventing the proper channels and adopting less than straightforward means of obtaining their goals.

In fact, the women's groups heard no end of accusations from their opponents in the two instances where patronage was suspected to have played a role. In Kiyembe, the leader of the co-operative, who was also a *muluka* (parish) chief, had initially obtained the market from the authorities in the Obote regime. However, there was nothing untoward about the way the co-operative went about claiming the plot of land, which was lying idle. After consultations with the District Commissioner and the Town Clerk, it applied to the Town Clerk for a plot of land. Similarly, in the Kitumba case, the leader of Ekikwenza Omubi sought advice from a relative, who was the national Director of Medical Services at the Ministry of Health. He advised them to work through the LC system and there was no evidence of his intervention on her behalf after that initial consultation. Thus, autonomy was critical in situating the women in a way that would allow them to challenge the abuses arising from patronage networks.

Legal recourse was sought in the Kawaala case by obtaining an injunction on the Kampala City Council, and justice was pursued by going to the police in the Kamuli case. Nevertheless, the main way in which accountability was sought was by the women withholding their votes and support from LC, Parliamentary and Constituent Assembly electoral candidates who they suspected had intervened in their struggle in a way they deemed inappropriate to gain political advantage. However, this electoral opposition was limited due to the peculiarities of the LC system, and in the Kiyembe case because the interests of the male electorate were diametrically opposed to those of the women. At the LC1 level, for example, in Kawaala, the residents were able to oust the LC1 committee because the councillors were elected directly by the residents themselves, but they were unable to affect the LC2 and LC3, councillors, who are elected by the electoral college. The same was true in Kitumba, where the women initially had the support of the LC1 councillors, but gradually came under the sway of the LC3 councillors. The women then sought and gained the support of LC1 councillors in neighboring villages but continued to face resistance from the LC2 and LC3 levels. This is a function of the fact that, while there is considerable accountability at the LC1 level because the councillors are elected directly by their constituents, the level of accountability diminishes as one goes further up the LC ladder because the councillors are elected from an increasingly smaller electoral college. The same is true for the Women's Secretaries. Above LC1, all women's secretary positions up to the District level are elected indirectly by an electoral college from a lower level.

The problems of accountability above the LC1 level in Kitumba and Kawaala follow patterns found more generally in the country. While there are many examples of councillors at the LC1, LC2, and LC3 levels who have been thrown out for corruption and forms of mismanagement, the instances become more infrequent after the LC1 level, often because of fear, sometimes even because of threats of violence, and at times out of a feeling of powerlessness and people's lack of knowledge of their rights (Burkey, 1991: 34).

Conclusions

Women's exclusions from political life in Uganda have meant that they have been forced to seek autonomous associations from which to mobilize around issues that are important to them. Somewhat paradoxically, this positioned them well in the context of a regime that wanted to give the impression that it was open to the advancement of women politically, economically and socially. Although major impediments to women's participation persisted, the women's movement in the 1980s and 1990s was able to make significant gains and to begin to assert itself.

Women's political activity is embedded in their other activities, often within multi-purpose organizations that do not have explicit political goals. Thus, women's political involvement needs to be understood in the context of interwoven public-private lives and spheres. Without an understanding of the connectedness of women's reproductive, domestic, cultural, economic, political and other activities and interests, women's political agendas are difficult to discern and appreciate. Women's interests in political involvement have proven to be different from those of other interest groups in that women do not simply want greater political representation or the passage of laws on issues that are of concern to them. They are also seeking a change in the terms and conditions under which politics is carried out. Their struggles and the way they mobilize themselves have challenged narrow political mobilization along ethnic and religious lines. In the same vein women have sought greater inclusiveness in politics along a number of lines; they have demanded greater accountability, and fought corruption and patronage practices; they have sought to protect their autonomy of association; and they have sought to validate the politics of self-help and voluntarism in providing community services for the most vulnerable sectors of society.

The women in the cases analyzed in this book found themselves not only involved in struggles over access to resources involving health facilities, market space, and community infrastructure, but also fighting for a redefinition of politics and how politics is conducted. This is because, in order to accomplish their goals, it was not sufficient simply to win access to these resources but rather a matter of ensuring that they as women had control over these resources. In each case they were forced to confront the limitations of various institutions, including the local council system, the church, the Kampala City Council, and many others who opposed their leadership because they were women. These struggles forced the women to analyze the gender dimensions of their problems and theorize about the broader implications of their conflicts for gender relations and women's oppression. Thus, women's interests in these struggles had practical everyday goals, while at the same time being an expression of their interest in broader more fundamental change.

Given all the constraints on women's access to political power, even under conditions in Uganda that are more propitious than those in other African countries, one might wonder why women's associational autonomy matters. The fact that at the turn of the millennium we see women struggling, both at the national and the local level, around issues that they have never before attempted to take on is significant in itself. That they are on the losing side of many of these battles should come as no surprise. They are dealing with a state which, although more responsive than most African states, has difficulties responding, given its own weaknesses and lack of commitment to women's concerns beyond what is politically expedient. Women are also dealing with a deeply embedded political culture that until the 1990s has not regarded women's claims to equality and political leadership as legitimate demands. We are tempted to insist on instantaneous change and yet we know that, in most societies, transformations in values, norms and cultures are always slow.

In fact, the pace of change in Uganda with respect to women appears to be relatively fast when placed in a broader historical and comparative perspective. Who would have thought in 1990 that a woman would be Vice-President by 1996 and that many women were seriously thinking of running for President in 2001? This is a country where as recently as 1980 only one woman held a parliamentary seat and where today 18 percent of the seats are held by women, a considerably larger percentage than we find in the United States or many other industrialized countries.

This book has documented the most important formal institutional changes that have affected the status of women in Uganda. But there are other elements to this social revolution that need to be appreciated. The case studies demonstrate that the most significant changes occur in the fabric of people's daily lives and take place in the context of interpersonal, community and collective struggles over resources and power. There are no short cuts here. These are painful struggles that have to be endured and worked through. In the process, there are often more losses than victories. But ultimately when change begins to occur in the daily lives of people, then we know it has truly begun to take hold. This book has described the beginnings of this process.

The temptation is so often to look for legislative and other institutional changes as the markers of reform. While they are absolutely essential, true social change does not take place until consciousness, behavior and political culture change. Change is not made up of absolute victories, but rather of a series of partial gains, transformations in consciousness and incremental steps backward and forward. That deep thorough-going transformations of power are a product of fierce struggle should come as no surprise. As one of the members of Ekikwenza Omubi in Kitumba put it, "You cannot claim to be a steady walker before you have stumbled on stones."

Notes

1   Interview in Kitumba, 17 March 1993.
2   *New Vision,* 11 August 1993 and 20 June 1990.
3   "Kamuli Women Chase CM," *New Vision,* 14 December 1993.
4   "Widow Strips Naked, Father-in-Law Faints," *Monitor,* 22–3 March 1996.
5   *New Vision,* 17 April 1989, translation, John Okidi.
6   *New Vision,* 5 August 1992.
7   *New Vision,* 5 August 1992.
8   Interview with Gertrude Kasozi, Kitumba, 2 April 1993.
9   Interview with Gertrude Kasozi, Kitumba, 7 July 1995.
10 The LC Committee includes a chairman, vice-chairman/secretary for children's welfare, general secretary, and secretaries for youth, women, information and mass mobilization, social services and education, security and finance.
11 Local Governments (Resistance Councils) Statute, 1993.
12 Interview with Wilberforce Sserwaniko, Kawaala, Kampala, 26 July 1995.
13 Interview with 3.1, Kawaala, Kampala, 18 June 1993.
14 Interview with Ruth Kijjambu, Kampala, 13 July 1993.
15 Interview with Salome Ssegawa, Kampala, 18 June 1993.
16 "Politician Hubby Snatchers Should Be Censored," *Monitor,* 8 May 1996.
17 Interview with Hon. Rebecca Kadaga, Kampala, 24 April 1993.
18 "Women Disadvantaged Even in CA Elections," *New Vision,* 18 January 1994, p. 17.
19 "The Task Ahead for a Woman Legislator," *Arise* No. 5, 1992, pp. 16–17.
20 Discussion with Miria Matembe, Washington, DC, July 1995; *New Vision,* 13 July 1994.
21 Apparently at that time the reserved seats for youth and workers were not filled but they existed on paper.
22 A woman candidate is first nominated by two registered voters. She then gets a list of names signed by a minimum of ten registered voters in her constituency and pays a nomination fee of Ush. 200,000.
23 "Who is a Politician?" and "Out of the House, but Still a Politician?", *Arise,* No. 19, October-December 1996, pp. 18 and 21.
24 "Politics is Not a Male Domain," *Arise,* No. 19, October-December 1996, p. 24.
25 "Who is a Politician?" *Arise,* No. 19, October-December 1996, pp. 18 and 21.
26 "Out of the House, but Still a Politician?", *Arise,* No. 19, October-December 1996, p. 21.
27 Focus group discussion with Kiyembe market women, Kampala, 27 June 1995.

Appendix A

Survey Methods

In 1993 I carried out a cluster stratified survey in Kampala, Luwero, Mbale and Kabale to learn more about the associational activities of men and women in these locations. Because no prior baseline survey was available, the survey was fairly comprehensive. It sought basic demographic information of the respondent; past and present organizational involvement; reasons for and extent of involvement; demographic information pertaining to the organization itself; the activities, finances, organization, goals, leadership, registration, successes, and problems of the major association in which the respondent was involved. It also surveyed the political activities of group members, the relationship of the organization to the local councils, district administration, ministries, and local and national women's organizations. The questionnaires also interrogated more general questions pertaining to the individual's political leanings, views on women's leadership, on how the years of conflict in Uganda had changed women's roles and perceptions of themselves, and on major problems women face.

The towns were divided into six sub-counties, which in turn were divided into parishes. The parishes were divided into local councils (LCs). Some parishes had as few as one local council, others as many as thirty. I had data on the number of households in each local council and parish. I also had detailed maps of all the local councils surveyed.

I listed the parishes and selected every fourth one to include in my sample in the case of Kampala (based on census data). I calculated the exact number of households for each parish and listed them. For each stratification according to gender, I calculated an interval to get the desired number of interviews, allowing for a 20 percent failure rate. I used this interval to figure out the exact parish and local council in which clusters of eight were to be located. In the case of Kabale alone I used clusters of ten. After getting letters of permission from the District Administrator in each district, I got lists of council households from the local council chairpersons and located eight to ten consecutive households from that list which we had selected. I used respondent-selection key charts to determine which particular adult individual in each household to interview. In other words, I identified randomly based on census data a particular set of eight housing units (ten in Kabale) in a parish, and then identified the local council number and name in which it was located. Two stratifications were made based on gender.

With the help of six enumerators we were able to interview 552 individuals in Kampala (92 percent success rate), 249 in Kabale (99 percent success rate), 135 in

Luwero (85 percent success rate), and 206 in Mbale (80 percent success rate), with a total of 1143 (20 percent men, 80 percent women). The interviews were conducted in Luganda and Lukiga. The demographic background of the respondents corresponded very closely to the census data in terms of religious, ethnic, age, and other key variables.

Appendix B

List
of Interviews

1992

Edith Natakunda, West Road Women's Association, ACFODE, Kampala, 2 June
1992.
Hope Mwesigye, FIDA, (became MP), Kampala, 19 June 1992
Maxine Ankrah, Sociology, Makerere University, Kampala, 19 June 1992
Harriet Birungi, Makerere Institute for Social Research, Kampala, 26 June 1992
Sylvia Tamale, Law Faculty, Makerere, Kampala, June 1992
Christine Guwatudde, Ministry of Women in Development, Kampala, 26 June 1992
Lucia Kiwale, Ministry of Women in Development, Kampala, 26 June 1992
Dr. Baryeku, Assistant District Medical Officer, Jinja, June 1992
Kyoyenda Women's Group, focus group, Mutai, Jinja, June 1992
Masese Housing Project, Jinja, focus group, June 1992
Ruth Kisubika, Women's Studies Program, Makerere University, Kampala, June
1992
Margaret Kikakihampo, ACFODE, Kampala, June 1992
Lucia Kiwale, Ministry of Women in Development, Kampala, 30 June 1992
Mangali, UWCFT, Kampala, 2 July 1992
Yeri Wakabi, FIDA, Kampala, 3 July 1992
Pumla Kisosonkole, former MP, Kampala, 14 October 1992, RK

1993

Sauda Kitangana Semakookiro, Uganda Teachers Association, Kampala, 22 January
1993, JK
Sempa, Mothers Union, Kampala, 21 January 1993, JK
Harriet Najjemba, RC II Namirembe Bakuli Women's Group, Kampala, 21 January
1993, JK
Mary Sepuya, Uganda Women Engineers and Technicians Association, Kampala, 21
January 1993, JK
Musisi Kiguli, UWCFT, 25 January 1993, JK

Olivia Sebunja, Namasuba Pinda Zone Women's Club, Kampala, 31 January 1993
Kabowa Women's Association, focus group, Kampala, 2 February 1993,
Kabowa Women's Association, focus group, Kampala, 5 February 1993
Olivia Kazibwe,Disabled Women's Association of Mukono, 8 February 1993, JK
Juliet Kakooza, Kiyembe Women's Credit Society, 10 February 1993, JK
Jenifer Kibanda, YWCA, 16 February, 1993, JK
Damalie Rumanda, AIDS Information Centre, Kampala, 20 February 1993, JK
Deborah Kasente, 14 February 1993, 21 February 1993
Milly Kanankulya, Mothers Union, 26 February 1993, JK
Idali Wanendeya, Uganda Women Entrepreneuers Association, 27 February 1993, JK
A. Kyaddondo, Uganda War Widows Foundation, Kampala, 7 March 1993, JK
Ruth Tumwesigye, Uganda War Widows Foundation, Kampala, 7 March 1993, JK
Dr. Baryeku, Assistant District Medical Officer, Jinja, 15 March 1993
DMO Jinja, 15 March 1993
Grace Asaba, Tusitukirewamu Handicraft and Co-operative Union, 20 March 1993, JK
Sarah Ntiro, Kampala, 21 March 1993
Joy Babuwe, Gayaza Old Girls Association, 24 March 1993, JK
Teo Kaggwa, Zibulatudde Women's Club, Kampala, 24 March 1993, PN
Tabitha Mulyampiti, Kampala, 26 March, 1993
Margaret Zziwa, MP, Kampala, 27 March 1993
Diane Matovu, Kampala, 28 March 1993
Lucia Kiwale, Kampala, 28 March 1993
Irene Wekiya, MP, Kampala, 29 March 1993
Norah Matovu, NAWOU, Kampala, 29 March 1993
Mary Mugyenyi, Women's Studies Department, Makerere University, 29 March 1993
Irene Wekiya, Kampala, 30 March 1993
Alice Ndidde, Kampala, 31 March 1993
Kitumba Health Committee, focus group, Kitumba, 2 April 1993
Dr. Balyeku, Deputy District Medical Officer, Jinja, 2 April 1993
RCIII Kitumba, focus group, Kitumba 3 April 1993
Jinja Gombolola chief, 3 April 1993
Gertrude Kisozi, Kitumba, 3 April 1993
Kitumba Women's Group, 4 April 1993
Kyebaja Kobona Women's Group, focus group, Iganga, 16 April 1993, RM
G.W.L., Medical assistant, Kitumba Health Center, 19 April 1993
David Kitimbo, District Medical Officer, Jinja, 19 April 1993
Gombolola chief, Mafubira, Jinja, 19 April 1993
Headmaster, Primary School, Kitumba, 19 April 1993
Biribawa Women's Club, Kitumba, 26 April, 1993, RM
Headmaster of Primary School, Kitumba, 26 April, 1993
Deputy Headmaster, Kitumba Primary School, 27 April, 1993
Twaha Bamutaze, Chairman RC I, Mauta, 27 April, 1993, RM
George Ngobi, Chairperson RC I, Buwekula, 27 April, 1993, RM
Rachel Katawera, Mafubira, 27 April 1993, RM
Headmaster, Primary School, Kitumba 28 April, 1993, RM
Buwekula Women's Club, focus group, RM
RCI, Kitumba, 29 April 1993, RM

Irene Mutesi, Kitumba, 29 April 1993, RM
Mrs. Lukalu's sister, Kitumba, 29 April 1993, RM
Florence Nekyon, NAWOU, Kampala, 4 May 1993, JK
Kiyembe focus group, Kampala, 8 May 1993
Ruth Wagage, Jinja, 8 May 1993
Juliet Baweera, Kitintale, Mutungo Parish, Kampala 11 May 1993
Margaret Gita, treasurer to RCI Council, Zone 2, Kampala, 11 May 1993
RC I secretary for women Nalongo Margaret of Namuli Zone Najjanakumbi,
Rubaga Division
Florence Nekyon, NAWOU, 21 May 1993
Kiyembe Market, focus group, 22 May 1993
Nora Matovu, NAWOU, 23 May 1993
Kiyembe Market, focus group, 27 May 1993
Professor J. B. Kwesiga, 30 May 1993
Kiyembe Market, focus group, 30 May 1993
Enid Rwakatungu, Kabale 20 May 1993
Sara Igoyola, Bugulete
Mrs. Wanyama, RCV Women's Secretary Bukooli County, 1 June 1993, RM
Florence Bironso, UWCFT, Iganga, 1 June 1993, RM
Sarah Nakendo, Bukooli Women's Association, 1 June 1993, RM
Alice Kigenyi, Bukooli Women's Association, 1 June 1993, RM
Mrs. Kyabukooli, Bukooli Women's Association, 2 June 1993, RM
Mrs. Nabweyo, Busowa, 2 June 1993, RM
Sarah Nakendo, Bukooli Women's Asociation, 3 June 1993
Monica Madooba, Safe Motherhood Project, Bugiri, 3 June 1993, RM
Mrs. Kirinde, Bukooli Women's Association, 4 June 1993, RM
Mwaidhuma Maganda, Mirembe Women's Association, Bukooli, 4 June 1993, RM
Bukooli Women's Oil Milling Project, focus group, 4 June 1993, RM
Buwanume Mukwaya Co-operative Group, focus group, Kamuli, June 1993
Mrs. Dhizaala, Bugulete Women's Group, June 1993
Sarah Igoyola, Bugulete Women's Group, June 1993
Mrs. Kabali, Bugulete Women's Group, June 1993
Nabirye Florence Kagona, Bugulete Women's Group, June 1993
Margaret Kazungu, Bugulete Women's Group, June 1993
Moses Kwewalyanga, Kamuli, June 1993
Edward Masiga, June 1993
Grace Nanangwe, Kamuli, June 1993
Joyce Muhire, Kampala, 18 June 1993
Focus group, Kawaala, 18 June 1993
RCI Treasurer, Kawaala, 18 June 1993
RC I Treasurer and women's secretary, 18 June 1993
Tugume Robbina, Kabale, June 1993
Twinobusigye, Kabale, 2 June 1993
Tulyahuhoro, Kabale, 3 June 1993
Evelyne Kasaza, Kabale, 3 June 1993
Caroline Nalongo, Kabale, 3 June 1993
Fede, DA's office, Kabale, 4 June 1993
Bernice Byobona, Kabale, 4 June 1993
Irene Mbaruka, Kabale, 4 June 1993
Mustafa, Kabale, 4 June 1993

Grace Tindikahwa, Kabale, 6 June 1993
Bernice Byobona, Kabale, 6 June 1993
Enid Rwakatungu, Kabale, 7 June 1993
Mary Kamerwa, Kabale, 7 June 1993
Grace Kayumba, Kabale, 7 June 1993
Wasta Munabi, Kabale, 8 June 1993
Kigogota Women's Group, 8 June 1993
Kuchwekana, Kabale, June 1993
Martha Bekita, Kabale, June 1993
Eddie Byaharugo, Kabale, 9 June 1993
Rebecca Kadaga, MP, FIDA, Kampala, 11 June 1993
Florence Nekyon, NAWOU, 15 June 1993
Nora Matovu, NAWOU, 15 June 1993
Deborah Ossiye, ACFODE, NAWOU, Kampala, 15 June 1993
Ruth Muguta, Community Development Officer, 15 June 1993
Kawala info officer, 16 June 1993
Joyce Muhire, Kampala, 17 June 1993
Joyce Muhire, Kampala, 18 June 1993
1.5 MS, interview by author, 18 June 1993
1.6 NK, interview by author, 18 June 1993
Irene Ereemye Balikuddembe, Kamuli, June 1993
Feibe Waigambulizi, Kamuli, July 1993
Ruth Kisubika re Kawaala, July 1993
WID, 2 July 1993
Irene Ereemye Balikuddembe, Kamuli, 1993
Rebecca Kadaga, MP, Kampala, 7 July 1993
Olivia Mutibwa, Uganda Association of University Women, 8 July 1993
A.J. Ratter, 8 July 1993
Joyce Muhire, Kampala, 8 July 1993
Evelyne Nyakojo, ACFODE, Kampala, 12 July 1993
Rebecca Nsimbi, UWCFT, Kampala, 13 July 1993
Barbara Shuey, Canadian Embassy, 13 July 1993
Rebecca Musoke, ACFODE, 13 July 1993
Ruth Kijjambu, Kampala, 13 July 1993
Godfrey Kibirige, Mayanja N. Kangi Co. Associates, 13 July 1993
George Kaddu, Kampala, 16 July 1993
Ahamed Kasolo, 16 July 1993
James Kapere, RC I Chairman, Kiyembe, Kampala, 16 July 1993
Charles Ssenfuka, Chairman Sub-RC, Kiyembe, Kampala 16 July 1993
Mrs. Namachwa, Community Development Assistant, Kampala Central, 16 July 1993
Miria Matembe, MP, ACFODE, 16 July 1993
Joy Kwesiga, 16 July 1993
Deborah Etoori, 16 July 1993
Corine Hoeben, UWCFT, 16 July 1993
James Kapere, 16 July 1993, RM
Kiyembe focus group, 16 July 1993
Wasswa Ziritwawula 18 July 1993
Professor J. B. Kwesiga 18 July 1993
1.4 GN, 18 July 1993

C. D. Rauxen Zedriga, DENIVA, Kampala, 19 July 1993
Eyoka, 19 July 1993
Ruth Kijjambu, 19 July 1993
Mpaji, 21 July 1993
Imelda Ndaba, Kangulunura Club, JK
Theresa Kayondo, Catholic Women's Guild, JK
Mary Kitamurike, Kampala, JK
Juliet Nakuyingi, Mountain Club of Uganda, Kampala, JK
Hadiya Nasolo, Nakawa Women's Unity Association, Kampala, JK

1995

Joyce Muhire, Kampala, 25 June 1995
Wilberforce Sserwaniko, Kampala, 25 June 1995
Hilda Tadria, ACFODE co-founder, Kampala, 26 June 1995
Kiyembe market, focus group, 27 June 1995
Hon. Joyce Mpanga, MP, former Minister of Women in Development, Kampala, 1
     July 1995
Rebecca Muliira, Kampala, 2 July 1995
Mary Okurut, 4 July 1995
Salome Bosa, former head of Uganda Law Society, head of NOCEM, 4 July 1995
Rebecca Muliira, Kampala, 5 July 1995
Musoke, ACFODE, Kampala, 5 July 1995
Gertrude Kasozi Kitumba, 7 July 1995
Mr. Kasozi, Kitumba, 7 July 1995
Irene Ereemye Balikuddembe, Kamuli, 7 July 1993
Sarah Igoyola, Kamuli, 7 July 1995
Winnie Byanyima, MP, head of FOWODE, Kampala, 8 July 1995
Rebecca Muliira, Kampala, 9 July 1995
Grace Bantyeba, Women's Studies Department, Makerere University, 10 July 1995
Pumla Kisosonkole, Kampala, 10 July 1995
Rebecca Muliira, Kampala, 11 July 1995
Hemi Bhatia, July 1995
Joy Kwesiga, July 1995
Aulikki Kuusela, Washington D.C., World Bank, August 1995

1996

Anne Tallantire, Cambridge, January 1996
Eileen West, Cambridge, January 1996
Louis Pirouet, Cambridge, January 1996
Gladys Essex, Birmingham (phone interview), January 1996
Ingrid Pasteur, Bromsgrove (phone interview), January 1996
Peggy Parry, Leicester, January 1996
Hemi Bhatia, Leicester, January 1996
Olive Burkitt, Bisley, Gloucestershire, January 1996
Nancy Kirwan, Cheltenham, Gloucestershire, January 1996
Sugra Visram, London, January 1996
Sarah Markandya, London, January 1996

Appendix C

Constitution
of Ekikwenza Omubi
Women's Project
1990

1. Name of the project is "Ekikwenza Omubi Women's Project"
2. a. Objects [objectives]: to provide education to needy children, i.e., orphans, semi-orphans, and to poor parents without employment or meaningful sources of income, physically handicapped, displaced refugee parents and to promote economic and social status of women.
   b. To co-ordinate, promote income-generating projects, social welfare of the children, their families and the community as a whole and build health-care centers.
   c. To aim at the improvement of women's health.
   d. To provide domiciliary service, immunization and food promotion, cura-tive service, children's health and mothercraft.
   e. To encourage income-generating activities and promote adult literacy.
   f. To collect and register or gather information or statistics concerning the carers of the children [those who tend children], expectant mothers, breast feedings, parents and community, and/or exchange the same with sister caring organizations for possible assistance.
   g. To establish and initiate small-scale industries and emphasize arts and crafts of whatever description, drama and games, poultry farming, brick-making, weaving and operating of any projects of whatever description for the pro-duction of article(s) and items for the purposes of income generating.
   h. To promote, maintain or benefit the interests of the community.
   i. To manage, improve, cultivate and maintain land, buildings, tenants and their properties and to deal with or dispossess the same either together or in portion for such consideration as the projects may make necessary.
   j. To cooperate with any other organization or person whose aims are similar.
   k. To promote and encourage the projects of nationals.
   l. To raise, borrow or give security for money or other value by mortgage or charge lien upon any or all the property of the project.
   m. To enter into any arrangements or contracts with the government or its foundations, companies, officials or all or any bodies thereunder, persons, firms or other established bodies as described.

n. To generally do all or anything which might be seen directly or indirectly conducive toward the attainment of the foregoing objects.

o. To lease, hire, rent or promote for hire, charge, or mortgage property of any description that may be conveniently used so as to implement any of the foregoing objects [objectives].

p. To implement and do all such other lawful things and acts as are incidental to any of them and for the purposes of avoiding any misunderstanding or misinterpretation as to the avoidance of doubt that the project is a non-profit oriented organization.

q. To employ and/or hire any persons on the terms and conditions of the project in whatever manner for the implementation of the project's objects [objectives] and to remunerate or pay such employed or hired persons in accordance with the terms and conditions stipulated by the project, which remuneration shall be reviewed from time to time in consideration of economic trends.

3. Officers
    There shall be a governing council or Executive Committee which shall comprise:
    a. chairperson
    b. vice-chairperson
    c. secretary/administrative (ex officio) who shall have no casting vote
    d. vice-secretary
    e. treasurer/book keeper
    f. five elected members from the parent body/council

4. Trustees: There shall be two trustees of the project, each of whom shall be a member of the project. Each trustee shall hold office for 3 years and they shall be elected by the Executive Committee. They may be removed for any good cause. They may be eligible for re-election.

5. Patrons:
    a. There shall be a patron or patrons of the project as may from time to time with their consent be elected by the Executive Committee.
    b. All patrons will be members of the project without compensatory payment.

6. Membership
    a. enrolled children
    b. their mothers
    c. interested persons

7. Membership shall be by invitation

8. Health Centres:
    a. Health Centres shall be established throughout Uganda.
    b. Each Health Centre shall have a governing committee comprising a chairman, secretary, treasurer, medical officer, all drawn from the concerned area.
    c. Executive Committee member shall be ex-officio member of the committee.

9. Founders: The founder member shall be a permanent member.

10. Government Co-ordinator: the project shall from time to time work with relevant government ministries or departments.

11. Property and Finance
    a.   All fixed assets of the project including any investments of funds shall be vested in the trustees on behalf of the project.
    b.   Subject to any general or special direction from the general council the Executive Committee shall have ultimate control and disposal of all property and funds of the project, provided that previous consent of the trustees shall be necessary for any investment and for any disposal or dealings with any fixed assets which are or should be vested in them.
    c.   The sources of funding shall be:
        i)   members' subscriptions
        ii)   admission fees/if any
        iii)   proceeds from sales of assets
        iv)   projects
        v)   donations
        vi)   other belongings of the project
        vii)   all monies received shall be put in Uganda Commercial Bank, Jinja Branch or any other Bank agreed upon by the committee
        viii)   the financial year of the project shall be from 1st January to 31st December
        ix)   the books shall be audited every year.

12. Minutes: It shall be the duty of the secretary to ensure that adequate minutes are kept at all meetings including branch meetings.

13. Committees: There shall be an Executive Committee of the project and the officers in article 3 shall form the same. The committee shall run the affairs of the project.
    a.   There shall be branch committees which shall be composed of
        i.   zone leader, project committee
        ii.   zone leader shall be chairperson
    b.   There shall be a general council/body which shall be the controlling authority.
    c.   Life-spans of the executive committee shall be three years.

14. Meetings
    a.   There shall be a general meeting once a year to deliberate on general matters of the project and more particularly
        i.   to receive reports of the project's activities
        ii.   to receive and pass [approve] the annual accounts
        iii.   to elect office bearers
        iv.   to do such other business as the meeting deems necessary.
    b.   The Executive Committee shall hold such regular meetings as are necessary provided that meetings shall be held at least once every month.
    c.   Any five members of the Executive Committee and in case of a general meeting a quarter of the members of the project may call a meeting by requisition in writing or petition the chairperson to convene the meeting.
    d.   An extraordinary meeting of the Executive Committee can be called without pre-notice or requirement in writing.

e. The annual or any general meeting of the project shall be called by the secretary in consultation with the Executive Committee; at least 7 days notice shall be required.

f. Voting at every meeting shall be by lining up or any manner agreed upon by members present and every member attending shall have one vote. There shall be no voting by proxy.

g. All decisions of the meeting shall be recorded in the form of a resolution signed by the chairman and secretary.

h. Unless otherwise decided by the meeting, the secretary shall be the returning officer and in case of absence the meeting shall elect a temporary chairperson.

Appendix D

Developing Kawaala through Self-Help Participation

"The Proposed
Kawaala Land Development Project"
drawn up by the Residents

Section 1: Project Design

The following project proposal presents a strategy for developing and thus transforming Kawaala village into a planned service area so that the Village can have all the basic services of a developed community. The proposal calls for the upliftment of both the social and physical status of Kawaala residential area, but at the same time attaching and recognizing the human right to have somewhere to live and own property. The project shall neither be a means nor a political strategy to displace the present families nor to destroy the existing structures but shall act as a vehicle to improve standards of the whole area. It (the project) is designed on popular participation development technique.

Section 2: Project Strategy

i. The Kawaala land development project, unlike other City Council projects, shall basically use the beneficiary full participation approach; whereby the beneficiaries, project programme designer, and financiers shall be involved at all stages and respect each and every other party.
ii. Like any other people-oriented development project, Kawaala Land Development Project will have neither a principal nor an inferior implementing partner. All the participating partners shall be on a par.
iii. The project will ensure the control of slums, and desist from the repetition of the past and current mistakes experienced in other similar project planning and implementation.
iv. The project shall not be a source enriching a few at the expense of the people of Kampala. In order to avoid resource wastage(s) and misappropriation, every effort/measure will be used to minimize uncalled-for compensation or by not encroaching on the right of ownership and existence of people in the area and destruction of existing structures.

v.   The overall objective of the project is to promote the social, cultural, political and cordial relationship between the plot/bibanja owners found at Kawaala and the KCC through self-help participation approach.

Section 3: Project Description

The Kawaala land development project is a joint undertaking between the plots/bibanja owners. who are the ultimate beneficiaries of the project and Kampala City Council, the custodian of the City Land and the initiator of the project.

Purpose

The project is intended to:
i.   Transform Kawaala into a planned serviced village.
ii.   Restore:
      a. The telephone services once existing in the village
      b. An adequate and regular piped water supply which broke down due to negligence by the Water Board
iii. Provide:
      a. An efficient and continuous sewage/refuse disposal system
      b. Improvement on the existing two Privately owned Schools found in Kawaala
iv.   Advise: On the implementation of proposed health/Dispensary centre whose land site is already available and on compensation paid to the former owners of the area. This centre has already been renovated and improved by the residents of the area through contributing funds
v.   Improve: The traditional road communication system within the village
vi.   Ensure: A secure ownership of plots and bibanja by the present owners
vii. Encourage: Present plots/bibanja owners to develop their areas
viii. Maintain: The social and cultural well-being of the beneficiaries.

Section 4: Means to Achieve Purpose(s)

For the project purpose(s) cited above to be achieved the following means shall be used:
i.   Lease offers will be granted to all plot/bibanja owners in the first instance without any difficulty or hindrances.
ii.   Physical planning and surveying of Kawaala to be carried out in consultation with and with full participation of the plot/bibanja owners.
iii. There shall be prompt and adequate compensation to all those who may be affected in any way by Kawaala land development project.

Section 5: Results Expected

As a result of the project
i.   The village will have an established, planned and serviced development
ii.   The plot/bibanja owners will have obtained security of tenure on their plots/bibanja as a basis of development
iii. The village will have been built by its present residents, thus deepening the sense of ownership and cementing the community spirit and belongingness

iv.   Kawaala will turn out a model planned serviced urban community in which the
      Africa village perspective will be portrayed
v.   There will be an established cemented trust between the City authorities and
      the residents, thus paving the way for future development projects within the
      City Council jurisdiction and elsewhere in Uganda
vi.   The village community therein shall enjoy and utilize both the social and phys-
      ical infrastructure services to the expectation of the residents and the initiators.

Section 6: Responsibilities of Participating Partners

The Kawaala land development project shall have three main participating partners
whose responsibilities shall be:

Kawaala Residents/Plot/Bibanja Owners

a.   The present and existing plot/bibanja owners as beneficiaries shall directly par-
      ticipate, and be consulted and involved in the project proposal, planning,
      implementation, monitoring and evaluation
b.   Shall pay for leases granted on their plots/bibanja by the Kampala City Council
c.   Shall co-operate with other participating partners
d.   Shall extend all the necessary social and physical infrastructure services to their
      homes
e.   Shall pay for the services to the City Council as and when they fall due.

Kampala City Council

The Kampala City Council shall participate in the project as the custodian of the
public land within the City Council jurisdiction within which the Kawaala land
development project falls and will be implemented. The Kampala City Council's
responsibilities, primarily through its supervisory role, will be to:

a.   Provide lease offers to all plot/bibanja owners as per the previously agreed
      upon dimensions and measurements, i.e., measurement ranging from 1/8 of an
      acre to 1/2 of an acre. Those with less than 1/8 of an acre will be catered for.
b.   Either install or improve on the required social and physical infrastructure out-
      lined in the project description
c.   Carry out and pay for the land planning, and surveying but in consultation and
      full participation of the present plot/bibanja owners
d.   The City Council and plot/bibanja owners shall be the principal implementing
      partners for the project.

The World Bank

The responsibility and role of the World Bank shall be limited to:

a.   Affording financial assistance/or loans to Kampala City Council for the pur-
      pose(s) of funding the improvement/or provision/or construction and installing
      the social and physical infrastructures as may be agreed upon and/or required
      by the residents of the community
b.   The World Bank shall not be involved in the structural planning of houses or
      the land physical planning
c.   The World Bank and the City Council shall neither import nor impose unac-
      ceptable structural and physical plans on the people of Kawaala

d.   The Bank shall not have any direct relationship with the plot/bibanja owners.
     Its working relationship shall end at or with Kampala City Council.

Section 7: Implementation and Evaluation of the Report

a.   Kampala City Council and current plot/bibanja owners shall undertake the
     implementation of activities listed above under project purpose(s) number(s) (i)
     to (viii).
b.   The Kawaala plot/bibanja owners shall participate and collaborate in the mon-
     itoring and evaluation process of the project with the Council authorities.

Section 8: Project Funding

The Kawaala land development project shall be funded by:

i.   The people themselves through self-help. Areas for self-financing will include:
     a. Pay leases
     b. Home development
ii. The KCC will fund the social and physical infrastructures, like roads, water, etc.

Sources of Funding

The World Bank will finance the KCC to implement the social and physical infrastructure services.

Section 9: Budget

Kampala City Council will enumerate the anticipated costs of planned inputs and
activities realistically, ensuring the participation and involvement of beneficiaries in
this exercise as regards this contribution.

Section 10: Cost Recovery

a.   Kampala City Council expects to recover costs through revenue collected from
     taxes and rates for services provided.
b.   Kawaala residents will co-operate in paying taxes, rates, etc. introduced by
     Kampala City Council for the services provided

Section 11: Logical Framework

a.   The project ensures that it belongs to the Kawaala residents
b.   Trust between Kampala City Council and plot/bibanja owners is established
c.   The project establishes specific, concrete and realistic designs and planning
d.   The project establishes an easy review of actual and intended effects.

References

Abdullah, Hussaina. 1995. 'Wifeism and Activism: The Nigerian Women's Movement,' in *Challenge of Local Feminisms*, edited by A. Basu. Boulder, CO: Westview Press.

ACFODE. 1988. *Women Breaking Through*. Kampala: Action for Development.

Achieng, Judith. 1998. 'Women Work for 16 hours, Men only 6,' *The Monitor*, 8 April.

Agrawal, Arun. 1997. *Community in Conservation: Beyond Enchantment and Disenchantment*. Gainesville, FL: University of Florida Press.

Akello, Grace. 1982. 'Self Twice-removed: Ugandan Women,' *Change (UK) International Reports: Women and Society* 8.

Allen, M. B. E. 1930. 'The Women and Girls of Uganda,' *Uganda Church Review* October–December (20): 115–17.

Alvarez, Sonia E. 1989a. 'Politicizing Gender and Engendering Democracy.' in *Democratizing Brazil*, edited by A. Stepan. New York: Oxford University Press.

Alvarez, Sonia E. 1989b. 'Women's Movements and Gender Politics in the Brazilian Transition', in *The Women's Movement in Latin America: Feminism and the Transition to Democracy*, edited by J. S. Jaquette. London: Unwin Hyman.

Alvarez, Sonia. 1990. *Engendering Democracy in Brazil: Women's Movements in Transition Politics*. Princeton, NJ: Princeton University Press.

Amadiume, Ifi. 1995. 'Gender, Political Systems and Social Movements: A West African Experience,' in *African Studies in Social Movements and Democracy*, edited by M. Mamdani and E. Wamba-dia-Wamba. Dakar: CODESRIA.

Amooti, Ndyakira. 1994. 'US Journalists Told to Leave,' *New Vision*, 26 September.

Ankrah, Maxine E. 1987. 'Conflict: The Experience of Ugandan Women in Revolution and Reconstruction.' Unpublished paper.

Ankrah, Maxine E. 1996. 'ACFODE: A Decade and Beyond,' *Arise* 17 (January–June): 21–2.

Apter, David. 1961. *The Political Kingdom in Uganda. A Study in Bureaucratic Nationalism*. London: Oxford University Press.

Apter, David E. 1991. 'Institutionalism Revisited,' *International Social Science Journal* (129): 463–81.

Asedri, Vivian. 1993. 'US Concerned by *Monitor* Ban,' *New Vision*, 11 October.

Atkinson, Ronald Raymond. 1978. 'A History of the Western Acholi of Uganda c. 1675–1900: A Study in the Utilization and Analysis of Oral Data.' Ph.D. thesis, Northwestern University, Evanston, IL.

Azarya, Victor. 1994. 'Civil Society and Disengagement in Africa,' in *Civil Society and the State in Africa*, edited by J. Harbeson, D. Rothchild and N. Chazan. Boulder, CO: Lynne Rienner Publishers.

Azarya, Victor, and Naomi Chazan. 1987. 'Disengagement from the State in Africa: Reflections on the Experience of Ghana and Guinea,' *Comparative Studies in Society and History* 19 (1): 106–31.

Baguma, Henry. 1994. 'Women, Youth Delegates Blast Statute,' *Kampala*, 7 April 1994.

Bagyendera, Hope. 1977. 'Women's Participation in Women's Clubs', BA dissertation, Social Administration Department, Makerere University, Kampala.

Baine, Alex. 1993. 'Bishop Challenges Women'. *New Vision*, 31 March.

Bakunzi, Didas. 1995a. 'Cheeye to Pay Mutebile 4.8m/-,' *New Vision*, 25 February.

Bakunzi, Didas. 1995b. 'New Press Bill Opposes Censorship'. *New Vision*, 13 January.

Bangura, Yusuf. 1996. 'The Concept of Policy Dialogue and Gendered Development: Understanding its Institutional and Ideological Constraints.' Paper read at UNRISD/CPD workshop 'Working Towards a More Gender Equitable Macro-Economic Agenda,' 26–8 November, at Rajendrapur, Bangladesh.

Barkan, Joel D., Michael L. McNulty and M. A. O. Ayeni. 1991. "Hometown" Voluntary Associations, Local Development, and the Emergence of Civil Society in Western Nigeria,' *Journal of Modern African Studies* 29 (3): 457–80.

Barrig, Maruja. 1989. 'The Difficult Equilibrium Between Bread and Roses: Women's Organizations and the Transition from Dictatorship to Democracy in Peru,' in *The Women's Movement in Latin America*, edited by J. S. Jaquette. London: Unwin Hyman.

Bates, Robert H. 1981. *Markets and States in Tropical Africa: The Political Basis of Agricultural Policies*. Berkeley, CA: University of California Press.

Bayart, Jean-François. 1986. 'Civil Society in Africa,' in *Political Domination in Africa*, edited by P. Chabal. Cambridge: Cambridge University Press.

Bayart, Jean-François. 1993. *The State in Africa: The Politics of the Belly*. London and New York: Longman.

Bell, Jane. 1960. 'Charity and Social Welfare in Uganda,' *Corona*, September/October.

Berkeley, Bill. 1994. 'An African Success Story?', *The Atlantic Monthly* (September): 22–30.

Bird, G. E. 1930. 'Women's Work in Uganda,' *Uganda Church Review* October–December (20): 113–14.

Birungi, Sarah. 1994. 'Breaking into Business,' *Daily Topic*, 8 March 1994.

Bitangaro, Barbara. 1993. 'FIDA Petitions AG,' *New Vision*, 14 July.

Bongyereirwe, Henry. 1993. 'Disabled Decry Marginalization,' *New Vision*, 5 May.

Boone, Catherine. 1994. 'States and Ruling Classes in Africa,' in *State Powers and Social Forces*, edited by J. S. Migdal, A. Kohli and V. Shue. Cambridge: Cambridge University Press.

Bouvard, Marguerite Guzman. 1994. *Revolutionizing Motherhood: The Mothers of Plaza de Mayo*. Wilmington, DE: Scholarly Resources Inc.

Boyd, Rosalind. 1989. 'Empowerment of Women in Contemporary Uganda: Real or Symbolic?', *Labour Capital and Society* 22 (1 April).

Bratton, Michael. 1989. 'The Politics of Government-NGO Relations in Africa,' *World Development* 17 (4): 569–87.

Bratton, Michael. 1994a. 'Civil Society and Political Transitions in Africa,' in *Civil Society and the State in Africa*, edited by J. W. Harbeson, D. Rothchild and N. Chazan. Boulder, CO: Lynne Rienner Publishers.

Bratton, Michael. 1994b. 'Micro-Democracy? The Merger of Farmer Unions in Zimbabwe,' *African Studies Review* 37 (1).

Bratton, Michael, and Nicolas van de Walle. 1997. *Democratic Experiments in Africa: Regime Transitions in Comparative Research*. Cambridge and New York: Cambridge University Press.

Brett, E. A. 1991. 'Rebuilding Survival Strategies for the Poor: Organizational Options for Reconstruction in the 1990s,' in *Changing Uganda*, edited by H. B. Hansen and M. Twaddle. London: James Currey.

Brett, E. A. 1992. *Providing for the Rural Poor: Institutional Decay and Transformation in Uganda*. Kampala: Fountain Publishers.

Brett, E. A. 1993. 'Voluntary Agencies as Development Organizations: Theorizing the Problem of Efficiency and Accountability,' *Development and Change* 24: 269–303.

Brett, E. A. 1994. 'Rebuilding Organisation Capacity in Uganda under the National Resistance Movement,' *Journal of Modern African Studies* 32 (1): 53–80.

Brett, E. A. 1995. 'Creating a Basis for Democratic Transition in Uganda,' in *Uganda: Landmarks in Rebuilding a Nation*, edited by P. Langseth, J. Katorobo, E. Brett and J. Munene. Kampala: Fountain Press.

Brown, Leslie. 1981. *Three Worlds: One World Account of a Mission*. London: Rex Collings.

Brown, Winifred. 1988. *Marriage, Divorce and Inheritance: The Uganda Council of Women's Movement for Legislative Reform*. Cambridge African Monographs, No. 10. Cambridge: African Studies Centre.

Bujra, Janet. 1979. 'Introduction: Female Solidarity and the Sexual Division of Labour,' in *Women United, Women Divided*, edited by P. Caplan and J. Bujra. Bloomington, IN: Indiana University Press.

Bunker, Stephen G. 1987. *Peasants Against the State: The Politics of Market Control in Bugisu, Uganda, 1900–1983*. Urbana, IL and Chicago: University of Illinois Press.

Burkey, Ingvild. 1991. 'People's Power in Theory and Practice: The Resistance Council System in Uganda.' BA thesis, Political Science, Yale University.

Busharizi, Paul, and Alice Emasu. 1995. 'Tilting the Balance,' *Women's Vision*, 15 August.

Businge, Betty. 1994. 'Women, Youth Councils Idle'. *New Vision*, 13 August.

Byanyima, Winnie. 1996. 'A Fresh Vision for Women MPs!,' *Monitor*, 26–9, 15 January.

Caleb, Opio Sam. 1996. 'Kadaga's Opponent Weeps, Flees Rally,' *Monitor*, 12 June.

Callaghy, Thomas M. 1984. *The State-Society Struggle: Zaire in Comparative Perspective*. New York: Columbia University Press.

Caplan, Robert D. 1997. 'Was Democracy Just a Moment?,' *The Atlantic Monthly* (December): 55–80.

Center for the Strategic Initiatives of Women. 1996. *The Outcry for Peace in the Sudan*. Washington, DC: Center for the Strategic Initiatives of Women.

Chambers, Robert. 1995. *Poverty and Livelihoods: Whose Reality Counts?*: Institute of Development Studies, Sussex University, Brighton.

Charlton, Sue Ellen M., Jana Everett, and Kathleen Staudt, eds. 1989. *Women, the State, and Development*. Albany, NY: State University of New York Press.

Chazan, Naomi. 1982. 'The New Politics of Participation in Tropical Africa,' *Comparative Politics* 14 (2): 169–89.

Chazan, Naomi. 1992. 'Africa's Democratic Challenge,' *World Policy Journal* 9 (2): 279–307.

Chazan, Naomi. 1994. 'Engaging the State: Associational Life in Sub-Saharan Africa,' in *State Power and Social Forces: Domination and Transformation in the Third World*, edited by J. Migdal, A. Kohli and V. Shue. Cambridge: Cambridge University Press.

Chazan, Naomi, Robert Mortimer, John Ravenhill, and Donald Rothchild. 1988. *Politics and Society in Contemporary Africa*. Boulder, CO: Lynne Rienner Publishers.

Chazan, Naomi, and Donald Rothchild. 1993. 'The Political Repercussions of Economic Malaise,' in *Hemmed In: Responses to Africa's Economic Decline*, edited by T. Callaghy and J. Ravenhill. New York: Columbia University Press.

Chibita, Monica Balya. 1996. 'On God's Call,' *Women's Vision*, 30 January.

Chinchilla, Norma Stoltz. 1992. 'Marxism, Feminism, and the Struggle for Democracy in Latin America,' in *The Making of Contemporary Social Movements in Latin America*, edited by A. Escobar and S. Alvarez. Boulder, CO: Westview Press.

Davis, Lance E., and Douglass C. North. 1971. *Institutional Change and American Economic Growth*. Cambridge: Cambridge University Press.

Ddungu, Expedit. 1989. *Popular Forms and the Question of Democracy: The Case of Resistance Councils in Uganda*. Kampala: Center for Basic Research.

Ddungu, Expedit, and Arnest Wabwire. 1991. *Electoral Mechanisms and the Democratic Process: The 1989 RC-NRC Elections*. Kampala: Center for Basic Research.

Dei, George J. Sefa. 1994. 'The Women of a Ghanaian Village: A Study of Social Change,' *African Studies Review* 37 (2): 121–45.

Department of Statistics. 1992a. *Final Results of the 1991 Population and Housing Census*. Entebbe: Ministry of Finance and Economic Planning.

Department of Statistics. 1992b. *Jinja District: The 1991 Population and Housing Census (District Summary Series)*. Entebbe: Ministry of Finance and Economic Planning.

Department of Statistics. 1992c. *Kamuli District: The 1991 Population and Housing Census (District Summary Series)*. Entebbe: Ministry of Finance and Economic Planning.

Diamond, Irene, and Nancy Harstock. 1981. 'Beyond Interests in Politics: A Comment on Virginia Sapiro's "When are Interests Interesting? The Problem of Political Representation of Women,"' *American Political Science Review* 75: 717–21.

Dicklitch, Susan. 1994. 'Defining Political Space: The Uses of Local Resistance Councils in Jinja, Uganda.' Paper read at African Studies Association, 2–5 November, at Toronto, Ontario.

Dicklitch, Susan. 1998. *Elusive Promise Of NGOs In Africa: Lessons From Uganda*. New York: St. Martin's Press.

Doornbos, Martin R. 1978. *Not all the King's Men: Inequality as a Political Instrument in Ankole, Uganda*. The Hague, Paris, New York: Mouton Publishers.

Drata, Lambert. 1994. 'NGO makes Kamuli Women Rich,' *New Vision*, 6 July.

Elkan, Walter. 1956. 'The Employment of Women in Uganda,' *African Women*.

Evans, Peter, Dietrich Rueschemeyer, and Theda Skocpol, eds. 1985. *Bringing the State Back In*. Cambridge: Cambridge University Press.

Fallers, Lloyd A. 1965. *Bantu Bureaucracy: A Century of Political Evolution among the Basoga of Uganda*. Chicago: University of Chicago Press.

Fatton, Robert. 1995. 'Africa in the Age of Democratization: The Civic Limitations of Civil Society,' *African Studies Review* 38 (2): 67–99.

Feeny, David. 1988. 'The Demand for and Supply of Institutional Arrangements,' in *Rethinking Institutional Analysis and Development: Issues, Alternatives, and Choices*, edited by V. Ostrom, D. Feeny and H. Picht. San Francisco: International Center for Economic Growth.

Feijoó, Maria del Carmen. 1989. 'The Challenge of Constructing Civilian Peace: Women and Democracy in Argentina,' in *The Women's Movement in Latin America*, edited by J. S. Jaquette. London: Unwin Hyman.

Feldman, Rayah. 1983. 'Women's Groups and Women's Subordination: An Analysis of Politics Towards Rural Women in Kenya,' *Review of African Political Economy* 27/28: 67–85.

Ferguson, Anne, Kimberly Ludwig, Beatrice Liatto Katundu, and Irene Manda. 1995. *Zambian Women in Politics: An Assessment of Changes Resulting from the 1991 Political Transition*. East Lansing, MI: Michigan State University.

Forrest, Joshua B. 1988. 'The Quest for State "Hardness" in Africa', *Comparative Politics* 20 (4): 423–42.

Friedrich Ebert Foundation. 1995. *Women's Landmarks in the Democratisation Process in Uganda*. Kampala: Friedrich Ebert Foundation.

Gargan, Edward. 1986. 'As Ugandans Lay to Rest Old Evils, New Fears about the Future Arise, *New York Times*, 14 August.

Gariyo, Zie. 1994. 'NGOs and Development in East Africa: The View from Below.' Paper presented to a Workshop on 'NGOs and Development: Performance and Accountability in the New World Order,' University of Manchester, 27–29 June.

Geiger, Susan. 1998. 'Exploring Feminist Epistemologies and Methodologies through the Life Histories of Tanzanian Women.' Paper read at International Gender Studies Circle Colloquium, University of Wisconsin-Madison, 17 April.

Geisler, Gisela. 1987. 'Sisters Under the Skin: Women and the Women's League in Zambia,' *Journal of Modern African Studies* 25 (1): 43–66.

Gipwola, Julie. 1995. 'Society Stifling Women's Potential,' *New Vision*, 14 January.

Githongo, John. 1998. 'What Happened to the Ngilu Campaign Wave?', *East African*, 5–11 January.

Goetz, Anne Marie. 1995. 'Institutionalizing Women's Interests and Accountability to Women in Development,' *IDS Bulletin* 26 (3): 1–10.

Gombay, Christie. 1993. *Eating Cities: Urban Management and Markets in Kampala, Uganda*, unpublished paper.

Gray, John Milner. 1934. 'Early History of Buganda,' *Uganda Journal* 2 (4): 259–70.

Gray, Sir John Milner. 1956. 'Kibuka,'. *Uganda Journal* 20 (1): 52–71.

Griffith, Owen G. 1952–4. Unpublished memoir of Sir Andrew Cohen as Governor of Uganda by his Private Secretary.

Gureme, Francis. 1994. 'Press Bill Needs Complete Overhaul,' *New Vision*, 12 October.

Guwatudde, Christine R. N. 1987. 'Church Affiliated NGOs Addressing Rural Women in Uganda: A Case of Two Development Projects.' MA thesis, Development Studies, Institute of Social Studies, The Hague.

Gyimah-Boadi, E. 1998. 'The Rebirth of African Liberalism,' *Journal of Democracy* 9 (2).

Hansen, Holger Bernt. 1977. *Ethnicity and Military Rule in Uganda*. Vol. 43, *Research Report*. Uppsala: Scandinavian Institute of African Studies.

Hanson, Holly. 1994. 'Reconfiguring the Social Order: The Moral Uses of Land in Buganda, 1900–1927.' Paper presented at the Thirty-Seventh Annual Meeting of the African Studies Association, Toronto, Ontario, 3–6 November.

Harbeson, John. 1994. 'Civil Society and Political Renaissance in Africa,' in *Civil Society and the State in Africa*, edited by J. Harbeson, D. Rothchild and N. Chazan. Boulder, CO: Lynne Rienner Publishers.

Hastie, Catherine. 1962. 'Training Courses for Women's Club Leaders in Uganda,' *African Women* 4 (4): 77–81.

Hirschmann, David. 1991. 'Women and Political Participation in Africa: Broadening the Scope of Research,' *World Development* 19 (12): 1679–94.

Hyden, Goran. 1980. *Beyond Ujamaa in Tanzania: Underdevelopment and an Uncaptured Peasantry*. London: Heinemann.

Hyden, Goran. 1986. 'Urban Growth and Rural Development,' in *African Independence: The First Twenty-Five Years*, edited by G. M. Carter and P. O'Meara. Bloomington, IN: Indiana University Press.

Hyden, Goran. 1992. 'Governance and the Study of Politics,' in *Governance and Poli-*

tics in Africa, edited by G. Hyden and M. Bratton. Boulder, CO & London: Lynne Rienner Publishers.

Isaacman, Allen. 1989. 'Peasants and Rural Social Protest in Africa,' Minneapolis, MN: Institute of International Studies, University of Minnesota.

Jamal, Vali. 1991. 'Inequalities and Adjustment in Uganda,' *Development and Change* 22: 321–37.

Jamwa, Tezira. 1993. 'Seminar Stresses Unity,' *New Vision*, 20 January.

Jaquette, Jane S. 1989. 'Conclusion: Women and the New Democratic Politics,' in *The Women's Movement in Latin America*, edited by J. S. Jaquette. London: Unwin Hyman.

Jenkins, Elizabeth. 1945. 'Girl Guiding in Uganda', *Uganda Church Review* 75: 55–9.

Jónasdóttir, Anna G. 1988. 'On the Concept of Interest, Women's Interests, and the Limitations of Interest Theory,' in *The Politics of Interests of Gender: Developing Theory and Research with a Feminist Face*, edited by K. B. Jones and A. G. Jónasdóttir. London, Newbury Park, New Delhi: Sage Publications.

Jones, Kathleen B. 1988. 'Introduction', in *The Politics of Interests of Gender: Developing Theory and Research with a Feminist Face*, edited by K. B. Jones and A. G. Jónasdóttir. London, Newbury Park, New Delhi: Sage Publications.

Joseph, Richard. 1987. *Democracy and Prebendal Politics in Nigeria*. New York: Cambridge University Press.

Joseph, Richard, ed. 1990. *African Governance in the 1990s*. Atlanta, GA: The Carter Center of Emory University.

Joseph, Richard. 1998. 'Class, State, and Prebendal Politics in Nigeria', in *Africa: Dilemmas of Development and Change*, edited by P. Lewis. Boulder, CO: Westview Press.

Kabira, Wanjiku Mukabi, and Elizabeth Akinyi Nzioki. 1993. *Celebrating Women's Resistance*. Nairobi: African Women's Perspective.

Kabuchu, Hope. 1990a. 'A Brick by Brick Progress,' *New Vision*, 7 February.

Kabuchu, Hope. 1990b. 'Plans to Phase out National Council of Women Underway,' *New Vision*, 12 September.

Kabukaire, Sarah Catherine. 1992. 'The Development of Women's Organisations in Kamuli District.' BA thesis, Sociology, Makerere University, Kampala.

Kagambirwe, Karyeija, Stephen Ilungole, and Angela Kamugasa. 1998. 'Women Retain Stand on Assets,' *New Vision*, 27 April.

Kaggwa, Apolo. 1971 [1904]. *The Kings of Buganda (Basekabaka be Buganda)*. Translated by M.S.M. Kiwanuka. Nairobi: East African Publishing House.

Kagoro, Barbara. 1989. 'Profiles of NRA Women Soldiers of Bombo Unit,' *New Vision*, 16 February.

Kahera, Hamisi. 1993a. 'In Rukungiri, Women are "Men",' *Monitor*, 17 September.

Kahera, Hamisi. 1993b. 'Kyeijanga Group Scores Success,' *New Vision*, 1 December.

Kakwenzire, Joan. 1989. 'Concessions Given to Uganda Women,' *New Vision*, 26 March.

Kakwenzire, Joan. 1990. 'Ugandan Women Suffer Discrimination,' *New Vision*, 26 September.

Kalebbo, Geoffrey Denye. 1996a. 'How to Make it to Parliament,' *Women's Vision*, 30 April, 16.

Kalebbo, Geoffrey Denye. 1996b. 'Women on the Frontline,' *Women's Vision*, 30 April.

Kalema, W. W. 1965. *Report of the Commission on Marriage, Divorce and the Status of Women, 1965*. Entebbe: Government Printer.

Kamya, Julius. 1996. 'No Apologies for Boosting Girls—Prof. Sebuwufu,' *Monitor*, 19–22 January: 9.

Kanyinga, Karuti. 1993. 'NGOs in Kenya,' in *Social Change and Economic Reform in Africa*, edited by P. Gibbon. Uppsala: Scandinavian Institute of African Studies.

Kasente, Deborah. 1994. 'Women in the Constituent Assembly in Uganda.' Paper presented in public forum at African Women and Governance Seminar and Training Workshop, Entebbe, 24–30 July.

Kasfir, Nelson. 1976. *The Shrinking Political Arena: Participation and Ethnicity in African Politics, with a Case Study of Uganda*. Berkeley, Los Angeles and London: University of California Press.

Kasfir, Nelson. 1994. 'Strategies of Accumulation and Civil Society in Bushenyi, Uganda: How Dairy Farmers Responded to a Weakened State,' in *Civil Society and the State in Africa*, edited by J. Harbeson, D. Rothchild and N. Chazan. Boulder, CO: Lynne Rienner Publishers.

Kasfir, Nelson. 1998. 'No-party Democracy in Uganda,' *Journal of Democracy* 9 (2): 49–63.

Katunzi, Pius Muteekani. 1998. 'Baganda to Submit Views on Land Bill,' *Saturday Monitor*, 9 May.

Kawamara, Sheila. 1993. 'Press Bill Unresolved,' *New Vision*, 25 November.

Kayizzi, Fred. 1994. 'Kibuga Woman Leader Booted,' *New Vision*, 23 February: 11.

Kiggundu, Patrick. 1992. 'Women: Resting on the NRM Platter,' *New Vision*, 5 August.

Kiggundu, Patrick. 1994. 'Honeymoon Over for Ugandan Journalists,' *New Vision*, 13 May.

Kigozi, James. 1993. 'Rate of Schoolgirl Dropouts High,' *New Vision*, 8 March.

Kiragga, Abdulgadikr. 1993. 'Cheeye Summoned,' *New Vision*, 20 November.

Kisubika, Ruth P. 1993. 'Contributions of Pre-Independence Women's Organisations to the Empowerment of Women in Uganda.' MA thesis, Women's Studies, Makerere University, Kampala.

Kuuya, Tsitsi. 1995. 'As I See It: Women and the Electoral Process,' *Zimbabwe Women's Resource Centre & Network News Bulletin* 7 (4): 7–8.

Kwesiga, Joy. 1994. 'The Women's Movement in Uganda: Future Prospects.' Paper presented to the Uganda Society, Kampala, 28 July.

Kwesiga, Joy C. 1996a. 'Charting Women's Path to their Full Realisation of their Full Potential as Human Beings,' *Arise* 17 (January–June): 3–7.

Kwesiga, Joy C. 1996b. 'Electoral Colleges for District Women Representatives to Parliament: A Test for Maturity or a Half-hearted Act', *Arise*, 26.

Kwesiga, J. B., and A. J. Ratter. 1993. *Realizing the Development Potential of NGOs and Community Groups in Uganda*. Kampala: Ministry of Finance and Economic Planning.

Kyambadde, Savio. 1996. 'Lady With a Spanner,' *Women's Vision*, 14 May.

Lachenmann, Gudrun. 1993. 'Civil Society and Social Movements in Africa: The Case of the Peasant Movement in Senegal,' *The European Journal of Development Research* 5 (2): 68–100.

Landell-Mills, Pierre. 1992. 'Governance, Cultural Change, and Empowerment,' *Journal of Modern African Studies* 30 (4).

Langseth, Petter. 1996. 'Civil Service Reform: A General View,' in *Democratic Decentralisation in Uganda: A New Approach to Local Governance*, edited by S. Villadsen and F. Lubanga. Kampala: Fountain Publishers.

Lawrence, J. C. D. 1957. *The Iteso*. London: Oxford University Press.

Lemarchand, Réne. 1992. 'Uncivil States and Civil Societies: How Illusion Became Reality,' *Journal of Modern African Studies* 30 (2): 177–91.

Leonard, David K. 1991. *African Successes: Four Public Managers of Kenyan Rural Development.* Berkeley, CA: University of California Press.

Lewis, Peter. 1992. 'Political Transition and the Dilemma of Civil Society in Africa,' *Journal of International Affairs* 46 (1): 31–54.

Lind, Amy Conger. 1992. 'Power, Gender, and Development: Popular Women's Organizations and the Politics of Needs in Ecuador,' in *The Making of Contemporary Social Movements in Latin America,* edited by A. Escobar and S. Alvarez. Boulder, CO: Westview Press.

Little, Kenneth. 1973. *African Women in Towns: An Aspect of Africa's Social Revolution.* Cambridge: Cambridge University Press.

Low, D. A. 1988. 'The Dislocated Polity,' in *Uganda Now: Between Decay and Development,* edited by H. B. Hansen and M. Twaddle. London, Athens, OH and Nairobi: James Currey, Ohio University Press, Heinemann Kenya.

Lubogo, Y. K. 1962. *A History of Busoga.* Jinja: East African Literature Bureau.

Lubwama, Eva. 1990. 'Abolish Anti-women Law, Urges Museveni,' *New Vision,* 31 March.

Lupa-Lasaga, Vukoni. 1996. 'Women Gave it to Kaguta,' *Crusader,* 14–16 May.

MacGaffey, Janet. 1986. 'Women and Class Formation in a Dependent Economy: Kisangani Entrepreneurs,' in *Women and Class in Africa,* edited by C. Robertson and I. Berger. New York: Africana Publishing Company.

Maddox, H. E. 1946 [1901]. 'The Women of Ankole: Extracts from "Mengo Notes"-I,' *Uganda Journal* 10 (1): 37–8.

Malaba, Tom. 1996. 'Wasswa Lule Pins Kityo on Kawaala Project', *Monitor,* 18 June.

Mama, Amina. 1995. 'Feminism or Femocracy? State Feminism and Democratisation in Nigeria,' *Africa Development* 20 (1): 37–58.

Mamdani, Mahmood. 1996. *Citizen and Subject: Contemporary Africa and the Legacy of Late Colonialism.* Princeton, NJ: Princeton University Press.

Mamdani Mahmood. 1994. 'Africa Was Highly Decentralised', *New Vision,* 20 December: 14–15.

Mamdani Mahmood. 1993. 'Movement or Parties: Which Way Uganda?', *New Vision,* 16 February: 10–11.

Mamdani, Mahmood. 1990. 'Uganda: Contradictions of the IMF Programme and Perspective', *Development and Change* 21: 427–67.

Mamdani, Mahmood. 1988. 'Democracy in Today's Uganda', *New Vision,* 16 March: 6–7.

March, Kathryn and Rachelle Taqqu. 1986. *Women's Informal Associations in Developing Countries: Catalysts for Change?* Boulder, CO: Westview Press

Marchand, Marianne H. 1995. 'Latin American Women Speak on Development,' in *Feminism/Postmodernism/Development,* edited by M.H. Marchand and J.L. Parpart. London and New York: Routledge.

Martin, Joan. 1990. 'Motherhood and Power: The Production of a Women's Culture of Politics in a Mexican Community', *American Ethnologist* 17 (August): 470–90.

Matembe, Miria R.K. 1991. 'How Far Have the Women of Uganda Gone in Realising Their Rights'. Unpublished paper.

Maxwell, Daniel G. 1993. 'Food, Land and Household Logic: Urban Farming in Kampala'. Paper presented at the IDRC/Canadian Association of African Studies Conference, Toronto, 12–15 May.

Maxwell, Daniel and Samuel Zziwa. 1992. Urban Farming in Africa: *The Case of Kampala, Uganda*. Nairobi: ACTS Press.

Mazrui, Ali A. 1975. *Soldiers and Kinsmen in Uganda: The Making of a Military Ethnocracy*. Beverly Hills, CA and London: Sage Publications.

McKinley, James C. 1998. 'A New Model for Africa: Good Leaders Above All,' New York Times, 25 March, A11.

McNeil, Leslie. 1979. 'Women of Mali: A Study in Sexual Stratification.' B.A. Thesis, Harvard University.

Meagher, Kate. 1990. 'The Hidden Economy: Informal and Parallel Trade in Northwestern Uganda,' *Review of African Political Economy* 47: 64–83.

Michaelson, Marc. 1994. 'Wangari Maathai and Kenya's Green Belt Movement: Exploring the Evolution and Potentialities of Consensus Movement Mobilization,' *Social Problems* 41 (November): 540–61.

Migdal, Joel S. 1988. *Strong Societies and Weak States*. Princeton, NJ: Princeton University Press.

Mikell, Gwendolyn. 1984. 'Filiation, Economic Crisis and the Status of Women in Rural Ghana,' *Canadian Journal of African Studies* 18 (1): 195–218.

Mirembe, Mercy. 1990. 'Dignified Sex Battle at Katimba,' *ACFODE Newsletter*, 5.

Mittleman, James. 1975. *Ideology and Politics in Uganda: From Obote to Amin*. Ithaca, NY and London: Cornell University Press.

Moghadam, Valentine M., ed. 1994. *Identity Politics and Women: Cultural Reassertions and Feminisms in International Perspective*. Boulder, CO: Westview Press.

Molyneux, Maxine. 1986. 'Mobilization without Emancipation? Women's Interests, State and Revolution,' in *Transition and Development: Problems of Third World Socialism*, edited by R. Fagen, C. D. Deere and J. J. Coraggio. New York: Monthly Review Press and Center for the Study of the Americas.

Monga, Célestin. 1996. *The Anthropology of Anger: Civil Society and Democracy in Africa*. Boulder, CO: Lynne Rienner Publishers.

Morna, Colleen Lowe. 1995. 'Plus ça Change'. *Africa Report* January–February: 55–60.

Morris, H. F. 1957. 'The Making of Ankole,' *Uganda Journal* 21 (1): 1–15.

Moser, Caroline O. 1991. 'Gender Planning in the Third World: Meeting Practical and Strategic Needs,' in *Gender and International Relations*, edited by R. Grant and K. Newland. Bloomington, IN: Indiana University Press.

Mugagga, Robert. 1998. '1998 A-level Results Out,' *The Monitor*, 30 June.

Mugambe, Beatrice. 1996. 'Are Women Afraid of Seeking Elective Office?,' *Arise*, 32–3.

Mugisa, Anne. 1993. 'FIDA Raps Legal System,' *New Vision*, 7 July.

Mugisa, Peter. 1994. 'And in the Economic Front . . .,' *New Vision*, 10 May.

Muhangi, Jossy. 1991. 'Women Demand Castration for Men over Sex Abuse,' *New Vision*, 18 December.

Mulyampiti, Tabitha. 1994. 'Political Empowerment of Women in the Contemporary Uganda: Impact of Resistance Councils and Committees.' MA thesis, Women's Studies, Makerere University, Kampala.

Museveni, Yoweri K. 1992. *What is Africa's Problem?* Kampala: NRM Publishers.

Musheshe, Jr., Mwalimu. 1990. 'Preface.' in *A Directory of Non-Governmental Organisations in Uganda*, edited by DENIVA. Kampala: DENIVA.

Musisi, Nakanyike. 1992. 'Colonial and Missionary Education: Women and Domesticity in Uganda, 1900–1945,' in *African Encounters with Domesticity*, edited by K. T. Hansen. New Brunswick, NJ: Rutgers University Press.

Musisi, Nakanyike B. 1991. 'Women, "Elite Polygyny", and Buganda State Formation,' *Signs* 16 (4).

Musoke, David. 1996. 'Women Petition Museveni,' *New Vision*, 18 May.

Mutazindwa, Francis. 1993. 'Arresting Police Must Have Warrant–FIDA,' *New Vision*, 16 December: 11.

Muteekani, Pius Katunzi, and Robert Mukasa. 1998. 'Land Bill Passed, Ganda MPs Happy,' *The Monitor*, 30 June.

Mutibwa, Phares. 1992. *Uganda Since Independence: A Story of Unfulfilled Hopes.* Trenton, NJ: Africa World Press.

Mutono, Allen. 1994. 'Potholes on the Road to Press Freedom,' *New Vision*, 7 March.

Mutumba, Richard. 1995. 'Government Warned Over Editor's Trial,' *New Vision*, 4 March.

Mwanasali, Musifiky. 1994. 'Accumulation, Regulation and Development: The Grass-roots Economy in the Upper Zaire Region (1975–1992)', PhD thesis, Political Science, Northwestern University, Evanston, IL.

Mwaniki, Nyaga. 1986. 'Against Many Odds: The Dilemmas of Women's Self-Help Groups in Mbeere, Kenya,' *Africa* 56 (2): 210–28.

Mwenda, Andrew M. 1998. 'Insight: Sebaggala Win Hatched at Ssemogerere's Home Last Dec. LCV Polls Shatter Movement Myths,' *The Sunday Monitor*, 26 April.

Mwesige, Peter, and Vukoni Lupa-Lasaga. 1996. 'I Like Museveni, but He Must Go—Mutagamba,' *The Crusader*, 9 February.

Mwesigwa, Catherine. 1994. 'From Pots to Politics,' *Daily Topic*, 15 March 1994.

National Council of Women (NCW). 1991. *Directory of Women's Groups in Uganda: Results of a Survey Conducted under the UNDP/NCW/NGO Project 'Partners in Development.* Kampala: NCW.

National Council of Women. n.d. *A Brief on the National Council of Women.* Kampala: NCW.

Ndawula, Kalema. 1996. 'Master of the Wheel.' *Women's Vision*, 19 March.

Ndegwa, Stephen N. 1996. *The Two Faces of Civil Society: NGOs and Politics in Africa.* West Hartford, CT: Kumarian Press.

Nelson, Barbara. 1993. 'Mobilizing Women as Women: Identities, Ideologies, and Opportunities,' Paper presented at the annual American Political Science Association meeting, 1–5 September, Washington, DC.

North, Douglass. 1989. 'Institutions and Economic Growth: An Historical Introduction,' *World Development* 17 (September): 1319–32.

Nsibambi, Apolo R. 1990. 'Resistance Councils and Committees: A Case Study from Makerere,' in *Changing Uganda*, edited by H. B. Hansen and M. Twaddle. London: James Currey.

Nviri, Elizabeth. 1994a. 'Anti-Rape Group Formed,' *New Vision*, 4 March.

Nviri, Elizabeth. 1994b. 'Define Role of Women's Councils,' *New Vision*, 12 April.

Nzegwu, Nkiru. 1993. 'Recovering Igbo Traditions: A Case for Indigenous Women's Organization in Development.' Unpublished paper.

Nzinjah, John. 1994. 'NOCEM Man Sacked,' *New Vision*, 24 February.

Nzomo, Maria. 1996. 'The Dynamics of Democratic Transition in Kenya: The Gender Dimension.' Paper read at Transitions in Africa, Niamey, Niger, 3–6 June.

Oakerson, Ronald. 1988. 'Reciprocity: A Bottom-up View of Political Development,' in *Rethinking Institutional Analysis and Development: Issues, Alternatives, and Choices*, edited by V. Ostrom, D. Feeny and H. Picht. San Francisco: International Center for Economic Growth.

Ofkansky, Thomas P. 1996. *Uganda: Tarnished Pearl of Africa*. Boulder, CO: Westview Press.

Ofwono-Opondo. 1994. 'Akabway Rejects NOCEM,' *New Vision*, 13 February.

Oguttu, Wafula. 1992. 'Topic Editor Sacked,' *New Vision*, 1 July.

Okonjo, Kamene. 1994. 'Reversing the Marginalization of the Invisible and Silent Majority: Women in Politics in Nigeria,' in *Women and Politics Worldwide*, edited by B. J. Nelson and N. Chowdhury. New Haven, CT and London: Yale University Press.

Okurut, Mary Karooro. 1995. 'Of "Sweet" Things at Women's Elections', *Monitor*, 6 June.

Onsando, Wilkista. 1996. 'Maendeleo ya Wanawake: What is Going On?' *Presence Magazine* March/April: 26–7.

Onyango-Ku-Odongo and J. B. Webster. 1976. *The Central Lwo During the Aconya*. Nairobi, Kampala, Dar es Salaam: East African Literature Bureau.

Onyango-Obbo, Charles. 1997. 'Ear to the Ground: Museveni & Co. are Living a Lie,' *Monitor*, 16 July.

Ostrom, Elinor. 1992. *Crafting Institutions for Self-governing Irrigation Systems*. San Francisco: Institute for Contemporary Studies.

Ostrom, Vincent, David Feeny, and Hartmut Picht. 1988. *Rethinking Institutional Analysis and Development: Issues, Alternatives, and Choices*. San Francisco: International Center for Economic Growth.

Ottemoeller, Dan. 1995. 'Political Institutionalization in Uganda: Why the Langi Don't Like "Resistance Councils".' Paper read at African Studies Association meeting, Orlando, FL.

Ottemoeller, Dan. 1998. 'Popular Perceptions of Democracy: Elections and Attitudes in Uganda,' *Comparative Political Studies* 31 (1): 98–124.

Patai, Daphne. 1991. 'U.S. Academics and Third World Women: Is Ethical Research Possible?' in *Women's Words: The Feminist Practice of Oral History*, edited by S. B. Gluck and D. Patai. New York and London: Routledge.

Pérez-Alemán, Paola. 1992. 'Economic Crisis and Women in Nicaragua,' in *Unequal Burden: Economic Crises, Persistent Poverty, and Women's Work*, edited by L. Beneria and S. Feldman. Boulder, CO: Westview Press.

Putnam, Robert D. with Robert Leonardi, and Raffaella Nonetti. 1993. *Making Democracy Work: Civic Traditions in Modern Italy*. Princeton, NJ: Princeton University Press.

Ray, Benjamin C. 1991. *Myth, Ritual, and Kingship in Buganda*. Oxford: Oxford University Press.

Roscoe, Rev. John. 1965. *The Baganda: An Account of their Native Customs and Beliefs*. First edn, London: Macmillan; 1911. London: Frank Cass,

Rueschemeyer, Dietrich, Evelyne Huber Stephens, and John D. Stephens. 1992. *Capitalist Development & Democracy*. Chicago: University of Chicago Press.

Sabiti, Makara. 1992. *The Role of Resistance Councils and Committees in Promoting Democracy in Uganda*. Department of Political Science and Public Administration, Makerere University, Kampala.

Sacks, Karen. 1979. *Sisters and Wives: The Past and Future of Sexual Equality*. Westport, CT and London: Greenwood Press.

Sandbrook, Richard. 1986. 'The State and Economic Stagnation in Tropical Africa,' *World Development* 14 (3): 319–32.

Schatzberg, Michael. 1988. *The Dialectics of Oppression in Zaire*. Bloomington, IN and Indianapolis: Indiana University Press.

Schiller, Laurence D. 1990. 'The Royal Women of Buganda,' *International Journal of African Historical Studies* 23 (3): 455–73.

Senkatuka, M. 1948. 'African Women's Clubs,' *Uganda Church Review* 79: 48–9.

Senkatuka, Mary E. 1955. 'Women's Clubs in Uganda,' *African Women* 1 (2).

Senteza-Kajubi, W. 1991. 'Educational Reform During Socio-Economic Crisis,' in *Changing Uganda: The Dilemmas of Structural Adjustment and Revolutionary Change*, edited by H. B. Hansen and M. Twaddle. London: James Currey.

Serwanga, Moses. 1993. 'Disabled Women Neglected,' *New Vision*, 27 November.

Sheldon, Kathleen. 1992. 'Women's Organizations in the 1990s,' *ACAS Bulletin* 36–37 (Fall): 3–6.

Simwogerere, Kyazze. 1994. 'NRM Deserves a Kiss from Women—Mrs. Ssebagereka'. *The Monitor*, 28 October.

Ssemirembe, Godfrey. 1993. 'Ugandan Women Change History,' *Weekly Topic*, 5 February, 22.

Ssemogerere, Karoli. 1998. 'Museveni Just Being Brave on LC-V Polls,' *The Monitor*, 29 April.

Stacey, Judith. 1991. 'Can There be a Feminist Ethnography?' in *Women's Words: The Feminist Practice of Oral History*, edited by S. B. Gluck and D. Patai. New York and London: Routledge.

Staudt, Kathleen. 1986. 'Stratification: Implications for Women's Politics,' in *Women and Class in Africa*, edited by C. Robertson and I. Berger. New York: Africana Publishing Company.

Steady, Filomena Chioma. 1976. 'Protestant Women's Associations in Freetown, Sierra Leone,' in *Women in Africa: Studies in Social and Economic Change*, edited by N. J. Hafkin and E. G. Bay. Stanford, CA: Stanford University Press.

Stephen, Lynn. 1992. 'Women in Mexico's Popular Movements: Survival Strategies Against Ecological and Economic Impoverishment,' *Latin American Perspectives* 19 (72, No. 1): 73–96.

Sternbach, Nancy Saporta, Marysa Marysa Navarro-Aranguren, Patricia Chuchryk, and Sonia E. Alvarez. 1992. 'Feminisms in Latin America: From Bogotá to San Bernardo,' *Signs: Journal of Women in Culture and Society* 17 (2).

Strobel, Margaret. 1979. *Muslim Women in Mombasa, 1890–1975*. New Haven, CT: Yale University Press.

Tadria, Hilda. 1987. 'Changes and Continuities in the Position of Women in Uganda,' in *Beyond Crisis: Development Issues in Uganda*, edited by P. D. Wiebe and C. P. Dodge. Kampala: Makerere Institute of Social Research.

Tamale, Sylvia. 1999. *When Hens Begin to Crow: Gender and Parliamentary Politics in Uganda*. Boulder, CO: Westview Press.

Tamale, Sylvia, and Jennifer Okumu-Wengi. 1992. 'The Legal Status of Women in Uganda.' Paper read at Workshop on Women and the Law in East Africa, at Nairobi, Kenya, 15–17 June.

Tanzarn, Nite Baza. 1996. 'Entrepreneurship: The Way Ahead for Women,' *Arise* July–September (18): 14–15.

Tideman, Per. 1994. 'New Local State Forms and "Popular Participation" in Buganda,' in *The New Local Level Politics in East Africa: Studies in Uganda, Tanzania and Kenya*, edited by P. Gibbon. Uppsala: Scandinavian Institute of African Studies.

Tinkasimire, Therese. 1996. 'Women in Decision-Making Within the Catholic Church in Uganda,' *Arise* July–September (18): 12–13.

Trager, Lillian. Forthcoming. 'Structural Adjustment, Hometowns, and Local Development in Nigeria,' in *Economic Analysis Beyond the Local System*, edited by R. B. Blanton, P. N. Peregrine, D. Winslow and T. D. Hall. Lanham, MD: University Press of America.

Tripp, Aili M. 1994. 'Gender, Political Participation and the Transformation of Associational Life in Uganda and Tanzania,' *African Studies Review* 37 (1).

Tripp, Aili Mari. 1996. 'Urban Women's Movements and Political Liberalization in East Africa,' in *Courtyards, Markets, City Streets: Women in Urban Africa*, edited by K. Sheldon. Boulder, CO: Westview Press.

Tripp, Aili Mari. 1997. *Changing the Rules: The Politics of Liberalization and the Urban Informal Economy in Tanzania*. Berkeley, CA: University of California Press.

Tsikata, Edzodzinam. 1989. 'Women's Political Organisations 1951–1987,' in *The State, Development and Politics in Ghana*, edited by E. Hanson and K. Ninsin. London: CODESRIA.

UNDP. 1995. *Human Development Report*. New York and Oxford: Oxford University Press.

UNICEF. 1989. *'The Women and Children of Uganda. A Situation Analysis*. New York: UNICEF.

United Nations. 1994. *Women in Politics and Decision Making in the Late Twentieth Century*. New York: UN Publications.

Vereecke, Catherine. 1993. 'Better Life for Women in Nigeria: Problems, Prospects, and Politics of a New National Women's Program,' *African Study Monographs* 14 (2): 79–95.

Villadsen, Sørensen. 1996. 'Decentralisation of Governance,' in *Democratic Decentralisation in Uganda: A New Approach to Local Governance*, edited by S. Villadsen and F. Lubanga. Kampala: Fountain Publishers.

Wakoko, Florence, and Linda Lobao. 1996. 'Reconceptualizing Gender and Reconstructing Social Life: Ugandan Women and the Path to National Development,' *Africa Today* 43 (3): 307–22.

Waliggo, Rev. John Mary. 1996a. 'Women Reps Should be Elected by All Voters'. *New Vision*, 23 January, 4.

Waliggo, Rev. John Mary 1996b. 'Did Women Get a Raw Deal?' *Arise* (17): 37–43.

Wamanga, Lawrence. 1994. 'Musoke Voted Sportsman of the Year,' *New Vision*, 4 January.

Ward, Kevin. 1995. 'The Church of Uganda amidst Conflict,' in *Religion & Politics in East Africa*, edited by H. B. Hansen and M. Twaddle. London, Nairobi, Kampala and Athens, OH: James Currey, EAEP, Fountain Publishers, Ohio University Press.

Wasike, Alfred. 1994a. 'Press Rejects Bill,' *New Vision*, 19 September.

Wasike, Alfred. 1994b. 'Scribes Protest Editor Arrest,' *New Vision*, 8 October.

Wasike, Alfred. 1995a. 'Editor Still Held,' *New Vision*, 19 April.

Wasike, Alfred. 1995b. 'Journalists Reject Bill,' *New Vision*, 16 April.

Watson, Catherine. 1988. 'Uganda's Women: A Ray of Hope,' *Africa Report* July–August.

Waylen, Georgina. 1996. *Gender in Third World Politics*. Boulder, CO: Lynne Rienner.

Webster, J. B., D. H. Okalany, C. P. Emudong, and N. Egimu-Okuda. 1973. *The Iteso During the Asonya*. Nairobi: East African Publishing House.

Weebe, Maxine, and Mark Ogola. 1992. 'Women Protest Tide of Sex Abuse,' *New Vision*, 9 January.

White, Carolyn Day. 1973. 'The Role of Women as an Interest Group in the Ugandan Political System.' M.A. thesis, Makerere University, Kampala.

Whyte, Susan Reynolds. 1991. 'Medicines and Self-help: the Privatization of Health Care in Eastern Uganda,' in *Changing Uganda*, edited by H. B. Hansen and M. Twaddle. London: James Currey.

Widner, Jennifer. 1997. 'Political Parties and Civil Societies in Sub-Saharan Africa,' in *Democracy in Africa: The Hard Road Ahead*, edited by M. Ottaway. Boulder, CO: Lynne Rienner Publishers.

Wolf, Diane L. 1996. 'Situating Feminist Dilemmas in Fieldwork,' in *Feminist Dilemmas in Fieldwork*, edited by D. L. Wolf. Boulder, CO: Westview Press.

Woods, Dwayne. 1992. 'Civil Society in Europe and Africa: Limiting State Power through a Public Sphere,' *African Studies Review* 35 (2): 77–100.

Wrigley, Christopher. 1988. 'Four Steps Toward Disaster,' in *Uganda Now: Between Decay and Development*, edited by H. B. Hansen and M. Twaddle. London: James Currey.

Wunsch, James S., and Dele Olowu. 1991. *The Failure of the Centralized State: Institutions and Self-Governance in Africa*. Boulder, CO: Westview Press.

Young, Crawford. 1976. *The Politics of Cultural Pluralism*. Madison, WI: University of Wisconsin Press.

Young, Crawford. 1994. *The African Colonial State in Comparative Perspective*. New Haven, CT and London: Yale University Press.

Yunus, Mugabe. 1996. 'Women Aspirants "Hijack" Party,' *Monitor*, 4 June.

Zziwa, Hassan Badru. 1996. 'Women's Soccer Should be Supported,' *Monitor*, 29 April–1 May, 15.

Index

Abdullah, Hussaina, 18
accountability, 2, 7, 8, 10, 66, 94, 133, 193, 198–200, 207, 214, 218, 235–8 *passim*
ACFODE, 62, 63, 68, 70, 73–5, 80–5 *passim*, 106, 117, 129, 130, 133–4, 139, 162–3, 174
Achieng, Judith, 142
Acholi, 33, 36, 49, 127, 128
ADF 57–8
advocacy, 120, 135
Africa, 2–16 *passim*, 19, 26, 27, 52, 83, 90, 94, 197, 199, 238; East, 7, 83; West, 94 *see also individual countries*
Africa Now, 60
Africom, 148–9
age, 99, 134
Agrawal, Arun, 218
Agreement, Uganda (1900), 32, 37, 126, 184
agriculture, 21, 22, 25, 92, 93, 95, 107, 111–13 *passim*, 142, 148, 182, 188, 199
aid, 61, 108, 171–20, 123 *see also* World Bank
AIDS, 75, 81, 107, 115, 153
Akabway, Steve, 136
Akello, Frances, 39
Akello, Grace, 35, 49
Akiika Embuga Self–help Association, 76, 105
Akina Mama wa Afrika, 76
Akongo, 33
Allen, M.B.E., 34
alliance building, 152–4, 207–8, 224, 225
Alvarez, Sonia E., 12, 165
Amadiume, Ifi, 7–8, 13
Amin, Idi, 8, 22–3 *passim*, 40, 42, 48–50, 52, 55–7 *passim*, 60, 68, 75, 83, 108, 109, 112, 124, 128, 129, 167, 233
Amina, Nakanyike, 111
Amooti, Ndyakira, 60
Ankole, 32–3, 126, 128
Ankrah, Maxine E., 50–2 *passim*, 70, 84, 110, 117

anti–colonialism, 36–7, 49
anti–Westernism, 49
apolon ka etale, 33
Apter, David E., 32, 220
Argentina, 176
Arise, 82, 134
armed forces, 55, 56 *see also* NRA
Asedri, Vivian, 60
Asia/Asians, 40–2, 49, 55, 112, 167
assembly, freedom of, 2, 67
associations, farmers', 6, 22; women's, 5–20 *passim*, 23, 25–7, 34–7, 59, 68–123, 129–40, 199–204 *passim*, 220, 224, 233, gender–specific, 91–3, 142–63, 167–8, 220, multi–purpose, 93–5, 101, 106, 107, 237 *see also individual entries*; reasons for joining, 107–9; youth, 6, 59, 90
Association of Women Medical Doctors, 106
Association of Women Teachers, 74
Atkinson, Ronald Raymond, 33
autonomy, 1–27, 197, 214, 219; associational, 5–20, 27, 47–8, 68–104, 163, 197, 214, 219, 223, 233–5, 238
Azarya, Victor, 4, 20, 21

Babangida, Maryam, 17–18; President, 9, 17
Bagaya, Princess Elizabeth, 49
Baguma, Henry, 89
Bagyendera, Hope, 35, 93, 106
Baine, Alex, 107
Bakunzi, Didas, 60
Balawa, Dan, 222
Bamwoze, Bishop, 135, 234
Banakazadde Begwanga, 36
Banda, Hastings, 15
Bangura, Yusuf, 19
Barkan, Joel D., 7
Barrig, Maruja, 164, 165
Bates, Robert H., 3, 216
Bayart, Jean–Francois, 2, 21